LUTHER'S WORKS

American Edition

VOLUME 35

Published by Concordia Publishing House

and Fortress Press in 55 volumes

General Editors are Jaroslav Pelikan (for vols. 1-30)

and Helmut T. Lehmann (for vols. 31-55)

LUTHER'S WORKS

VOLUME 35

Word and Sacrament

I

EDITED BY

F. THEODORE BACHMANN

GENERAL EDITOR

HELMUT T. LEHMANN

FORTRESS PRESS / PHILADELPHIA

5802 C 76

GENERAL EDITORS'
PREFACE

The first editions of Luther's collected works appeared in the sixteenth century, and so did the first efforts to make him "speak English." In America serious attempts in these directions were made for the first time in the nineteenth century. The Saint Louis edition of Luther was the first endeavor on American soil to publish a collected edition of his works, and the Henkel Press in Newmarket, Virginia, was the first to publish some of Luther's writings in an English translation. During the first decade of the twentieth century, J. N. Lenker produced translations of Luther's sermons and commentaries in thirteen volumes. A few years later the first of the six volumes in the Philadelphia (or Holman) edition of the *Works of Martin Luther* appeared. But a growing recognition of the need for more of Luther's works in English has resulted in this American edition of Luther's works.

The edition is intended primarily for the reader whose knowledge of late medieval Latin and sixteenth-century German is too small to permit him to work with Luther in the original languages. Those who can will continue to read Luther in his original words as these have been assembled in the monumental Weimar edition (*D. Martin Luthers Werke. Kritische Gesamtausgabe*; Weimar, 1883-   ). Its texts and helps have formed a basis for this edition, though in certain places we have felt constrained to depart from its readings and findings. We have tried throughout to translate Luther as he thought translating should be done. That is, we have striven for faithfulness on the basis of the best lexicographical materials available. But where literal accuracy and clarity have conflicted, it is clarity that we have preferred, so that sometimes paraphrase seemed more faithful than literal fidelity. We have proceeded in a similar way in the matter of Bible versions, translating Luther's translations. Where this could be done by the use of an existing English version—King James, Douay, or Revised Standard—we have done so. Where it could not, we have supplied our own. To indicate

v

this in each specific instance would have been pedantic; to adopt a uniform procedure would have been artificial—especially in view of Luther's own inconsistency in this regard. In each volume the translator will be responsible primarily for matters of text and language, while the responsibility of the editor will extend principally to the historical and theological matters reflected in the introductions and notes.

Although the edition as planned will include fifty-five volumes, Luther's writings are not being translated in their entirety. Nor should they be. As he was the first to insist, much of what he wrote and said was not that important. Thus the edition is a selection of works that have proved their importance for the faith, life, and history of the Christian church. The first thirty volumes contain Luther's expositions of various biblical books, while the remaining volumes include what are usually called his "Reformation writings" and other occasional pieces. The final volume of the set will be an index volume; in addition to an index of quotations, proper names, and topics, and a list of corrections and changes, it will contain a glossary of many of the technical terms that recur in Luther's works and that cannot be defined each time they appear. Obviously Luther cannot be forced into any neat set of rubrics. He can provide his reader with bits of autobiography or with political observations as he expounds a psalm, and he can speak tenderly about the meaning of the faith in the midst of polemics against his opponents. It is the hope of publishers, editors, and translators that through this edition the message of Luther's faith will speak more clearly to the modern church.

J.P.
H.T.L.

CONTENTS

BG — *Luthers Werke für das christliche Haus,* edited by Georg Buchwald *et al.* (Braunschweig, 1889-1892).

C. R. — *Corpus Reformatorum,* edited by C. G. Bretschneider and H. E. Bindseil (Halle, 1834-1860).

CL — *Luthers Werke in Auswahl,* edited by Otto Clemen *et al.* (Bonn, 1912-1933; Berlin, 1955-1956).

EA — D. *Martin Luthers sämmtliche Werke* (Frankfurt and Erlangen, 1826-1857).

LW — American edition of *Luther's Works* (Philadelphia and St. Louis, 1955-   ).

MA³ — *Martin Luther.* Ausgewählte Werke (München, 1948-   ).

MA³, Er — *Martin Luther.* Ergänzungsbände Werke (München, 1954-   ).

Migne — *Patrologiae, Series Latina,* 221 vols. in 222 (Paris, 1844-1904), J. P. Migne, editor.

PE — *Works of Martin Luther* (Philadelphia, 1915-1943).

St. L. — D. *Martin Luthers sämmtliche Schriften,* edited by Johann Georg Walch. Edited and published in modern German, 23 vols. in 25 (St. Louis, 1880-1910).

WA — D. *Martin Luthers Werke.* Kritische Gesamtausgabe (Weimar, 1883-   ).

WA, Br — D. *Martin Luthers Werke.* Briefwechsel (Weimar, 1930-1948).

WA, TR — D. *Martin Luthers Werke,* Tischreden (Weimar, 1912-1921).

WA, DB — D. *Martin Luthers Werke.* Deutsche Bibel (Weimar, 1906-   ).

INTRODUCTION TO
Word and Sacrament

For the individual believer as well as for the corporate church, Word and sacrament comprise the life-giving center, without which there would be no Christian faith. As Luther expressed it in his *Smalcald Articles* of 1537, "God will not deal with us except through his external Word and sacrament."[1]

In this American Edition of *Luther's Works*, Volumes 35-38 contain nearly thirty of Luther's writings which have special bearing on this subject. They span most of his reforming career, from 1519, the eventful year of the election of Charles V and of the Leipzig Debate, to 1544, less than two years before his death. About two-thirds of the material in these volumes is here being offered in English translation for the first time.

According to Luther's understanding, the Word of God is not simply to be equated with the written text of the Scriptures, for it goes much deeper than historical description or moral precept. Rather, it is a uniquely life-imparting power, a message communicated by men in whom the Scriptures had become alive. The church, therefore, is for Luther "not a pen-house but a mouth-house,"[2] in which the living Word is proclaimed.

Despite all outward diversity the Word of God is one. In his penetrating study of Luther and the Old Testament, Heinrich Bornkamm has this to say, "In all the christological prophecies of the Old Testament Christ is always present in a twofold manner, namely, as he who speaks, and as the one who is foretold."[3] For Luther "the pre-existent Christ of the Old Testament and the incarnate Christ of the New Testament would not be the same person if

---

[1] Theodore G. Tappert (ed.), *The Book of Concord* (Philadelphia: Muhlenberg Press, 1959), p. 313.

[2] WA 10ᴵ, 2, 48.

[3] *Luther und das Alte Testament* (Tübingen: Mohr, 1948), p. 171.

they did not perform the same work of God, namely, to judge through the law and to justify through the gospel."[4]

This interpretation of the Scriptures, so characteristically christo-logical, is suggested in some of Luther's prefaces to the biblical books here in Volume 35, but even more so in many of his expository writings and in his sermons. There his hermeneutics come to full expression, and his understanding of the Scriptures in their concrete historical sense is vivified by his grasp of the Word as the oral proclamation of the gospel, the *viva vox evangelii*.

Throughout his career Luther contended that Word and sacrament belong together. On the basis of scriptural authority he reduced the number of sacraments from seven to three and then to two (1520). While his recognition of the importance of genuine repentance found expression in his temporary retention of penance as a sacrament (1519), this he later included under confession, absolution, and church discipline, or the power of the keys.[5] His chief attention thus centered on baptism and the Lord's Supper which he recognized as the visible Word.

Luther sees the sacraments in the light of their Old Testament lineage. This is no mere correspondence of baptism with circumcision or of the Lord's Supper with the Passover, as has usually been the understanding of scholastic Lutheranism.[6] Instead of looking at outward correspondence, Luther looks more deeply into the nature of the Word and of God's promise. While in the Old Testament the promise of God is hidden under the law, Luther nevertheless sees an aspect of the pre-existent Christ in Moses. Luther contends that God "has helped man to find the hidden Word in the Old Testament and to understand its meaning by adding signs to his promise."[7]

While these signs, according to Luther, prefigure the churchly sacraments, they are not—as Zwingli contended—to be understood merely as marks of recognition among Christians. Nor do these signs

---

[4] Regin Prenter, "Luther on Word and Sacrament" in *More About Luther* ("Martin Luther Lectures," Vol. II [Decorah, Iowa: Luther College Press, 1958]), p. 79.

[5] See *The Sacrament of Penance,* in this volume, pp. 3-22. See also the *Smalcald Articles,* Part III, Art. VIII. Tappert (ed.), *The Book of Concord,* p. 312, and *The Babylonian Captivity of the Church. LW* 36, 18, 124.

[6] Bornkamm, *op. cit.,* p. 158.

[7] *Ibid.,* p. 152.

of themselves justify; they are not substitutes for the Word, instead they substantiate the Word and the intention of God. "The same God," said Luther, "who now saves us by baptism and the bread, saved Abel by his sacrifice, Noah by the rainbow, Abraham by circumcision, and all the others by their respective signs."[8] These signs, therefore, are not derived from Jewish ceremonial worship, as though from men, but from the mighty acts which are of God's own doing. For Luther everything depends on what God does.

Because baptism is God's action, and is inseparable from the death of Jesus Christ in history, it cannot be repeated. Contrary to the teaching of the Roman scholastics, baptism does not eradicate sin; rather, it forgives sin and gives Christ once and for all to the one baptized. Man being what he is, a baptized sinner, he must practice daily repentance as a return to that life given him in baptism.

Since baptism is a sign, a visible Word, its significance endures throughout the believer's life on earth. Yet, as Luther explains, its significance competes with the continuing natural life and impulses of the baptized person. That person, paradoxically, is at one and the same time righteous in Christ and sinful in his own flesh: *simul justus et peccator*.[9]

Luther sees the Christian as living by faith in his Redeemer through whom he has the hope of being ultimately released from his own contradictory estate. The righteousness which he has in Christ is the righteousness of Another. Yet because this Other is Christ and not himself, the believer has hope. Hence, as Prenter has put it, "God's Word and work in the unrepeatable act of baptism assume the character of a *promise*—a pledge."[10] That this promise is understood as binding on God's part becomes evident in Luther's treatise on baptism (1519). There he sets forth the concept of God's covenant, saying, "This blessed sacrament of baptism helps you because in it God allies himself with you and becomes one with you in a gracious covenant of comfort."[11] This action of God surely requires a response. And the response extends over the lifetime of the

---

[8] *The Babylonian Captivity of the Church. LW* 36, 65.
[9] Prenter, *op. cit.*, pp. 87-89.
[10] *Ibid.*, p. 91.
[11] *The Holy and Blessed Sacrament of Baptism,* in this volume, p. 33.

one baptized, expressing itself in a desire to die in order that he might live.[12] For the life that is ready to die is the kind that lives by faith in the forgiving and life-giving Word of God.

Because of its central place in the life of the church and of its vital function as visible Word, Luther had most of all to say on the Lord's Supper. Better even than his activity as a translator of the Scriptures, his engagement in discussion and controversy over the Lord's Supper spells out the successive stages of his career as a reformer. From his 1519 *The Blessed Sacrament of the Holy and True Body of Christ* to his 1544 *Brief Confession Concerning the Holy Sacrament*, a dozen works present us with an unfolding of Luther's thought on the Lord's Supper as well as with a gauge of his involvement over it with contemporaries through explication and controversy. Since the Introductions to these writings in the four volumes on Word and Sacrament will bring details, it is enough here simply to mention the broad trend of developments. Biographies like Roland Bainton's *Here I Stand* (Nashville, 1950), or Ernest G. Schwiebert's *Luther and His Times* (St. Louis, 1950) readily supply the historical context for these thirty-five years. In Bainton's work the chronology of events (pp. 18-20) is especially helpful.

From an initial scriptural reinterpretation of the Lord's Supper directed mainly against the Romanists (Vols. 35-36), Luther found it necessary, in 1525, to take an increasingly firm stand against sectarians, like Thomas Münzer, and sacramentarians, like Zwingli (Vols. 36-37),[13] which brought forth his classic expositions of the subject in the years 1527-1528. Against the double front of Romanists and sectarians Luther thereafter carried forward the defense of his understanding of the sacrament (Vol. 38). This defense ranged from the Marburg Colloquy (1529), through the lull of the Wittenberg Concord (1536), to his short-lived resumption (1544) of controversy against Bullinger in Zurich as well as against the roving Caspar Schwenkfeld.

Luther's view of the Lord's Supper may here be sketched on the basis of the excellent account given by Leipzig's knowledgeable theologian, Ernst Sommerlath, in the new and thoroughly revised

---

[12] *Ibid.*

[13] See also Part II of *Against the Heavenly Prophets.* LW 40, 144-223.

third edition of *Die Religion in Geschichte und Gegenwart*.[14] Luther's position rested squarely on the Words of Institution. This, however, did not mean that he championed a one-sided literalism, but that he took these words in the full context of God's redemption of man. Luther's interpretation is thus intimately bound up with the New Testament concept of faith in God, of the work of the Holy Spirit, and of salvation in Jesus Christ. As in Christ the divine and human natures are united, so also in the sacrament in a corresponding way the bread (and wine) and the body (and blood) of Christ are united. Thus the sacrament is placed into the heart of the New Testament revelation. Indeed, the basic fact of the Incarnation, the indwelling of God among men, makes Jesus Christ himself the primitive sacrament.

Thus Luther asserted the *real* presence of Christ with a simple and scriptural sense of reality. The medieval Roman dogma of transubstantiation held a different kind of real presence, while at the other end of the scale the enthusiasts spiritualized the real presence altogether.[15] For Luther this scriptural realism meant the bodily presence of Christ in the sacrament; he understood man's salvation as wrapped up in the living Word made visible in the Lord's Supper. Just as the incarnate Christ was on earth in the body, so he is received bodily in the Lord's Supper.

This means, moreover, that the sacrament not only points like a sign to man's salvation but also conveys it to him. In his treatises of 1519-1520[16] Luther countered the Romanists by emphasizing that the chief significance of the Lord's Supper lay in its being a seal that guarantees and a sign that points to the salvation God intends for man. Since it conveys the body and blood of Christ it also bestows the salvation which it signifies. The sacrament of the altar is a vehicle

---

[14] See Sommerlath, "Abendmahl," *Die Religion in Geschichte und Gegenwart* (3rd ed., 6 vols.; Tübingen: Mohr, 1957 ff.), I, 34-37. Cf. the similar article by the same author in the new *Evangelisches Kirchenlexikon* (4 vols.; Göttingen: Vandenhöck und Ruprecht, 1956-1960), I, 11-14.

[15] See the discussion by the former Erlangen and now Australian theologian, Hermann Sasse, *This Is My Body, Luther's Contention for the Real Presence in the Sacrament of the Altar* (Minneapolis: Augsburg, 1959), as well as Robert Fischer's Introduction to *LW* 37.

[16] See in this volume, *The Blessed Sacrament of the Holy and True Body of Christ,* pp. 45-73, and *A Treatise on the New Testament, That Is, the Holy Mass,* pp. 75-111, and *The Babylonian Captivity of the Church. LW* 36, 19 ff.

or bridge over which the gift itself comes to us. Thanks to the Words of Institution, the accent falls pointedly on the personal reception "for you," by means of which God makes personal faith possible. In short, the Word announces and then actually bestows the gift of God's grace.

The sacrament is therefore not simply subordinate to the Word but takes its place visibly on the same level as the preached Word, bringing its special gift of the bodily-spiritual communion with Christ. The communion available in the Lord's Supper is given nowhere else in this same vivified way. In exalted words Luther praised the inwardness of such communion, which is closer than any other humanly imaginable.

To sum up: that for which Luther contends in Word and sacrament he intends for the whole church. The Word—proclaimed and visible—is one. "Where the Word is, there is the church."[17] As Bornkamm reminds us, it is Luther's understanding of the Word that enables him to see one undivided church from paradise to Judgment Day. As God's signs in the Old Testament prefigure the sacraments in the New Testament, so the congregation of the faithful under the old covenant foreshadows the church of the new covenant. Sacrament and church are functions of the Word, its signs and its fruition.[18]

To say this, however, is to anticipate the next section, Volumes 39-41, on Church and Ministry. For this section on Word and Sacrament bibliographical helps in addition to those already mentioned will be found in Volume 31, pp. xi-xiii.

E. T. B.

---

[17] *Ubi est verbum, ibi est ecclesia* were Luther's words in the disputation held at Wittenberg February 3, 1542, at the promotion of Johannes Macchabaeus Scotus. *WA* 39[II], 176.

[18] Bornkamm, *op. cit.*, pp. 176, 184.

INTRODUCTION TO VOLUME 35

At first sight this volume may look like a miscellany of occasional writings and biblical prefaces. To a degree this is true, especially when compared to other volumes in this edition of Luther's works. Yet this apparent diffuseness is also an asset. For the selections here presented offer a good introduction not only to the subject of Word and Sacrament in the rise of the Reformation but also to the creativity of Luther in his on-going role as Reformer. His writings here reproduced, and for the most part chronologically ordered, are drawn from a fifteen-year span that begins in 1519, the year of the Leipzig Debate, and concludes—apart from certain later revisions of the biblical prefaces—in 1534, the year of Luther's German Bible.

The first four selections in the volume are significant for providing an understanding of Luther's early view of the sacraments. Three of the treatises stem from the same year, 1519, just prior to his excommunication. In the first, *The Sacrament of Penance,* Luther treats of confession and absolution. Here, less than a year before his total exclusion of penance from the number of sacraments, Luther is already distinguishing between penance on the one hand and the true sacrament of penance on the other. While the former—the sacrament as commonly practiced—may be said to include contrition, confession, and satisfaction as its three "parts," the latter— as Luther sees the matter scripturally delineated—actually consists rather of God's word in the absolution, the faith which trusts in that word, and the peace and forgiveness which flow from such faith. The second in this 1519 trilogy on the sacraments is Luther's treatise on *The Holy and Blessed Sacrament of Baptism.* In this sacrament too Luther finds three main things: the sign—immersion; the thing signified—death of the old man and resurrection of the new; and the third and "most necessary part"—the faith which needs to be exercised with respect to God's covenant promise. The third treatise, *The Blessed Sacrament of the Holy and True Body of Christ, and the Brotherhoods,* is Luther's first extended statement on the Lord's Supper. In it he does not yet speak of such controversial issues as the sacrifice of the mass or the mode of the Real Presence, and actually retains the terminology associated with transubstantiation. This sacrament too has three parts: outward sign, inward significance, and living faith. Regarding the sign, Luther thinks it would be well if the laity were permitted to receive both kinds in the sacrament. He describes the chief significance of the sacrament in terms of "*synaxis* or *communio,* that is, fellowship" with Christ and all the saints. And he makes everything to depend upon faith, in contrast to the current view of the sacrament as an *opus operatum.*

To this 1519 trilogy on the sacraments we have added Luther's 1520 *Treatise on The New Testament, that is, the Holy Mass,* which is significant as a transition to Luther's earliest definitive statement on the sacraments which followed in the latter part of the same year in *The Babylonian Captivity of the Church* (*LW* 36, 3-126). Here for the first time Luther examines the question of sacrifice in the mass, firmly discarding the view that the mass is basically a good work or sacrifice which men perform, in favor of the view that the mass is basically a testament or promise of God sealed by the death of his Son. In every promise of God there are two things to be considered, the word and the sign; and the former is mightier than the latter.

A second group of treatises within this volume deals primarily with the matter of the authority of God's Word and with the fundamental distinction to be made between law and gospel. Intended as an introduction to the Christmas and Advent sermons in his "Wartburg Postil," Luther's *Brief Instruction on What to Look for and Expect in the Gospels* (1521) points to the one gospel proclaimed in the four Gospels, namely, that Christ—before he can ever become for us an example to be followed—must be, and indeed is, first of all God's gift to be received in faith. The gospel is essentially proclamation, Christ coming to us through the sermon. The New Testament is itself our proper guide to Scripture, for it directs us to the Old Testament in which we find Christ wrapped as in swaddling cloths and laid in a manger. In the second treatise of this group, *Avoiding the Doctrines of Men* (1522), Luther expounds specific passages— and corrects the interpretation of other passages falsely cited to the contrary—to establish the sole authority of God's Word in matters of Christian life and conduct. His purpose is to assert the true nature of Christian liberty as a comfort to those whose consciences have been bound by the restrictive regulations of monasticism on food, drink, clothing, chastity, and other external matters, all of which go beyond the express word of Scripture. Out of the tumult of the Peasants' Rebellion (1525), fomented in large measure by religious fanatics endeavoring to establish theocratic government under Mosaic law, comes the third treatise in this group, *How Christians Should Regard Moses*. It is a classic statement of Luther's insistence upon the crucial distinction between law and gospel, of the relationship between the Old and New Testaments, and of the place of the law—specifically the Mosaic law of the Old Testament, including the Ten Commandments—in the life of the Christian and in the contemporary ordering of society. Essentially Moses provided the constitution for the temporal kingdom of the Jews, and is totally irrelevant for non-Jewish temporal government today, except insofar as Moses agrees with both the New Testament and the law implanted within all men by nature. Moses' chief significance for the Christian lies not in the sphere of legal requirements—where indeed some of the Old Testament prescriptions may yet be worthy of emulation—but in the area of those things which are not to be derived equally well from nature, namely, God's promises and pledges about Christ, and the numerous examples of the faith thus engendered by them. The key to interpreting Moses in a valid way is given in Luther's suggestion to determine clearly the audience intended by any given statement in the Old Testament, whether God's word at any given point is intended for a specifically delimited group, time, and situation, or is rather of universal significance, and hence still binding today.

Two treatises in this volume deal specifically with the problem of translating the Scriptures into the language of the people, a task which occupied Luther—and a whole company of consultants—for more than two decades, in fact, throughout his entire career as Reformer. His publication of the complete Bible in German in 1534 marked a milestone not simply in the life of the church but also in the history of German language and literature. The skill and care with which he proceeded become obvious in Luther's discussion of the task and principles of the translator, particularly as that discussion is punctuated with a case-by-case defense and explanation of specific renderings. His *On Translating: An Open Letter* (1530) deals with questions involved in rendering the New Testament from its original Greek into German; it is particularly illuminating—and not only to the specialist—with respect to such a verse as Rom. 3:28, where Luther had been extensively criticized for supplementing Paul's original affirmation, "a man is justified by faith," with the clarifying adverb "alone." *Defense of the Translation of the Psalms* (1531) points up corresponding problems with respect to the Old Testament, where Luther is insistent that the sense, rather than merely the words, of the Hebrew original must be expressed in the foreign tongue.

In the final portion of this volume we have collected Luther's biblical prefaces, written and rewritten in connection with the various books and groups of books to which they refer as these issued periodically from Luther's pen in translation and in revision, beginning as early as the 1522 New Testament and continuing until the last revision of the complete Bible which Luther was able to oversee shortly before his death. The prefaces were designed, in accordance with long-standing custom, to provide a brief summary and orientation for the reader of the respective Bible portions. In addition to such basic prefaces as those to the Pentateuch, Psalms, Prophets, and New Testament, including the classic preface to Romans, we have here included the less significant but still interesting prefaces to those eight apocryphal books which Luther placed between the Testaments in his 1534 edition of the whole Bible.

While most of this volume involved merely a careful revision of earlier English translations—sometimes, as in the case of certain biblical prefaces, on the basis of better critical editions of the original text than were available to the earlier translators—a number of the selections are here being offered for the first time in English: *The Sacrament of Penance* (1519); *A Brief Instruction on What to Look for and Expect in the Gospels* (1521); *How Christians Should Regard Moses* (1525); *Defense of the Translation of the Psalms* (1531); and the *Prefaces to the Apocrypha*.

In a sense the question of authority runs through all the writings here before us. From the first selection onward it becomes plain that Luther dares to undertake what he does not wilfully but humbly, and only on the authority of the Word of God in the Scriptures. As he sees the situation, the church as a whole is called upon not only to proclaim the Word in its purity but also to live by it in the obedience of faith. This, as Luther never wearies to point out, is not the obedience of a legalistic Romanism nor the enthusiasm of a misguided sectarianism, but the confidence of an informed evangelicalism that has come to know the creative power of God in his dual approach to his children through law and gospel.

E. T. B.

LUTHER'S WORKS

VOLUME 35

THE SACRAMENT OF PENANCE

1519

Translated by E. Theodore Bachmann

INTRODUCTION

This is the first of a group of three teaching sermons on the sacraments prepared by Luther in 1519 for the seeking Christian. The sacramental system, perfected during the later Middle Ages and administered by the priesthood, retained a powerful hold over the people. Behind the system stood a massive papal authority that operated much, if not most, of the time without reference to scriptural authority. While the number of sacraments was generally accepted as seven—including confirmation, ordination, marriage, and extreme unction—Luther could, at this time, find authority for retaining at most three: penance, baptism, and the Lord's Supper.

Amid the mounting theological debate after 1517 friends prodded Luther to clarify the confusion over the sacraments. In 1519 he produced the trilogy that is here presented, on penance, baptism, and the Lord's Supper. Published separately during the last quarter of the year, these sermons were dedicated by Luther to Margaret, duchess of Brunswick, a woman he had never seen but of whose "pious love of the Scripture" he had often been told.[1] On December 18 of that year Luther wrote to his friend, Georg Spalatin, secretary to Elector Frederick:

> There is no reason why you or any man should expect from me any sermon on the other sacraments, until I learn by what text I can prove that they are sacraments. I esteem none of the others a sacrament, for that is not a sacrament, save what is expressly given by a divine promise exercising our faith. We can have no intercourse with God save by the word of him promising and by the faith of man receiving the promise. At another time you will hear more about their fables of the seven sacraments. . . .[2]

---

[1] See the letter from Luther to Margaret, duchess of Brunswick, of mid-October, 1519, in Preserved Smith and Charles Jacobs (eds. and trans.), *Luther's Correspondence and Other Contemporary Letters* (2 vols.; Philadelphia: The Lutheran Publication Society, 1913-1918), I, 227, No. 184; see also p. 228, No. 185.

[2] *Ibid.*, pp. 263-264, No. 206.

As to penance itself, the situation was problematic. By 1520 Luther was to reduce the number of sacraments to two, and omit penance because it lacked a divinely instituted visible sign.[3] But this did not mean that he took penance more lightly than before. Rather he was trying to rescue it from some of the difficulties into which it had fallen. The double meaning of the Latin word obscured the vital content behind traditional forms; the Vulgate rendering of Matt. 3:2 *et al., poenitentiam agite,* could mean either to repent (penitence) or to do penance. In line with the latter meaning, the church in the later Middle Ages had refined the sacrament of penance, so that its material aspect consisted in *contrition* (genuine remorse for one's sins), *confession* (to the priest), and *satisfaction* (making good, on the priest's orders, what had been done wrong). Its formal aspect consisted in the *absolution* given by the priest, while the effective aspect consisted in receiving the *forgiveness* of sins.[4] In his definitive *Summa Theologica,* Thomas Aquinas too had distinguished between the external penance-as-a-sacrament and the internal penance-as-a-virtue,[5] or, in effect, between *doing* penance and *being* repentant. While he recognized satisfaction as a "fruit" of the virtue of being repentant, he nevertheless made it an integral "part" of the sacrament of penance, not a matter of the individual's being, but of the individual's doing.

What Luther thus saw was a church enmeshed in a type of activism that tortured rather than comforted the sensitive and distressed conscience and that found it more profitable to encourage endless doing rather than confident being. In actual practice this meant that the church was fostering salvation by works instead of justification by faith, a human situation contrary to Scripture and

---

[3] *The Babylonian Captivity of the Church* (1520). LW 36, 124; cf. pp. 18 and 81-91. In 1529 he wrote in his Large Catechism, Part IV, par. 74: "Baptism, both by its power and by its signification, comprehends also the third sacrament, formerly called Penance, which is really nothing else than Baptism." Theodore G. Tappert (ed.), *The Book of Concord* (Philadelphia: Muhlenberg Press, 1959), p. 445. Cf. also in this volume, pp. 14-16.
[4] *LW* 31, 19-21; *PE* 1, 17-20; and *The Catholic Encyclopedia* (16 vols.; New York, 1907-1914), XI, 622-629, "Penance."
[5] Fathers of the English Dominican Province (trans.), *The "Summa Theologica" of St. Thomas Aquinas* (London: Washbourne, 1917), Part III, ques. 84-85, pp. 1-40.

forced upon men not by divine authority but by papal, and therefore human, authority. It is Luther's respect for the Word of God and his concern for the faith of man that gives pastoral point to his sermon on the sacrament of penance. With great understanding he shows that the exercise of authority on the part of the church is intended to be a service to the people; the reverse is not true, that the needs of the people are to be exploited as a service to the church.

Personal experience had shown Luther the difference between the "torturers," who applied only what they called a "method of confession," and the counselors, like Staupitz, who disclosed that confession does not end but begins with "the love of justice and of God."[6] In 1518, while looking back upon his own struggles, Luther confided to Staupitz that almost no word in the Bible was "more bitter to me than 'penitence' (although I zealously simulated it before God and tried to express an assumed and forced love), now no word sounds sweeter. . . ."[7]

After 1517 the abuses allowed by the church in the realm of penance and indulgence drew Luther's continued burning indignation, expressed in his *Explanations of the Ninety-five Theses*[8] and his *Sermo de poenitentia*,[9] both of 1518, and elsewhere. The force of his attack was such that a friend like Wolfgang Capito, in a letter from Basel dated September 4 of the same year, cautioned him to move into battle not frontally but obliquely, and thus stand a better chance of reaching his objective.[10]

Whether Luther could actually heed such counsel is problematic, but the important thing is that *The Sacrament of Penance* became his clear and forthright statement on genuine repentance and assured forgiveness; all of it based on confident faith in the Word which, given in the Scriptures, God addresses to man through his servants—even through the humblest believer.

---

[6] Letter from Luther to Staupitz, May 30, 1518. Smith and Jacobs, *op. cit.*, I, 91, No. 65.

[7] *Ibid.*

[8] *LW* 31, 83-89.

[9] *WA* 1, (317) 319-324.

[10] Smith and Jacobs, *op. cit.*, I, 110.

The Sacrament of Penance, written originally in German, was first published by Johann Grünenberg in Wittenberg, under the title, *Eyn Sermon von dem Sacrament der pusz, D. M. L.* The first edition of this tract appeared about mid-October, 1519, not, as many have supposed, during the same year as Luther's *Sermo de poenitentia*.[11] Before the end of 1519 there were four editions, one of them appearing in Leipzig. Within two years ten more editions were out, coming from printers in Nürnberg, Augsburg, Erfurt, and Strassburg.

The original text is that of Grünenberg, a copy of which in the Ducal Library at Wolfenbüttel bears a notation in Luther's own hand.[12] The following translation—the first into English—is based on this text as it is reprinted in WA 2, (709) 714-723. We have omitted only the brief dedicatory letter to Duchess Margaret.

---

[11] See the discussion on date in WA 2, 709-710.
[12] WA 2, 712.

THE SACRAMENT OF PENANCE

By Doctor Martin L.A.W.[1]

1. Forgiveness in the sacrament of penance is of two kinds: forgiveness of the punishment and forgiveness of the guilt. Concerning the first, the forgiveness of the punishment, or satisfaction, enough has been said in the treatise on indulgences which appeared some time ago.[2] It is not very significant and is an immeasurably lesser thing than the forgiveness of guilt, which one might call a godly or heavenly indulgence, one that only God himself can grant from heaven.

2. The difference between these two types of forgiveness is this: the indulgence, or the forgiveness of punishment, does away with works and efforts of satisfaction[3] that have been imposed and thus reconciles a person outwardly with the Christian Church. But the forgiveness of guilt, the heavenly indulgence, does away with the heart's fear and timidity before God; it makes the conscience glad and joyful within and reconciles man with God. And this is what true forgiveness of sins really means, that a person's sins no longer bite him or make him uneasy, but rather that the joyful confidence overcomes him that God has forgiven him his sins forever.

3. However a person who does not find within himself such a [glad] conscience and rejoice in his heart over God's grace, cannot

---

[1] L.A.W., meaning Luther, Augustinian, Wittenberg, is one of various abbreviations frequently used to denote Luther's authorship. Cf. pp. 29, 79.

[2] *A Sermon on Indulgence and Grace* (1518). Bertram Lee Woolf, *The Basis of the Protestant Reformation* ("Reformation Writings of Martin Luther," Vol. I [2 vols.; New York: Philosophical Library, 1953-1956]), pp. 50-55; WA 1, 243-246.

[3] Following confession, the priest assigned certain good works to be done as "penances" by way of making satisfaction for sin. Cf. in the Introduction, pp. 6-7; cf. also pp. 35-36.

be helped by any indulgence[4] even though he were to buy all the letters of indulgence ever issued. For a person can be saved quite apart from any letters of indulgence, by death making satisfaction or paying for his sin. No one can be saved, however, without a joyful conscience and a glad heart toward God (that is, without the forgiveness of guilt). So it would be much better to buy no indulgences at all, than to forget this forgiveness of guilt or omit to practice it first and foremost every day.

4. For [attaining] such forgiveness of guilt and for calming the heart in the face of its sins, there are various ways and methods. Some think to accomplish this through letters of indulgence. They run to and fro, to Rome or to St. James,[5] buying indulgences here and there. But this is mistaken and all in vain. Things thereby get much worse, for God himself must forgive sins and grant peace to the heart. Some put themselves out with many good works, even too much fasting and straining. Some have ruined their bodies and gone out of their minds, thinking by virtue of their works to do away with their sins and soothe their heart. Both of these types are defective in that they want to do good works before their sins are forgiven, whereas on the contrary, sins must be forgiven before good works can be done. For works do not drive out sin, but the driving out of sin leads to good works. For good works must be done with joyful heart and good conscience toward God, that is, out of the forgiveness of guilt.

5. The true way and the right method, without which there is no other, is that most worthy, gracious, and holy sacrament of penance,[6] which God gave for the comfort of all sinners when he

---

[4] An indulgence was a commutation or relaxation of the satisfaction imposed on a contrite sinner. By the late Middle Ages it had been elaborated into an instrument whereby—usually for a fee—the temporal punishment for sin, due either on earth or in purgatory, could through the sacrament of penance be removed, for the dead as well as for the living. Cf. LW 31, 19-22 and PE 1, 17-22.

[5] Tradition supposes St. James the Apostle to have been buried at Compostela, a city in northwestern Spain whose full name is Santiago [St. James] de Compostela. Next to Jerusalem and Rome, this was the most famous place of pilgrimage.

[6] Within a year Luther had excluded penance from the list of sacraments. Cf. in the Introduction, p. 6.

gave the keys to St. Peter in behalf of the whole Christian Church and, in Matthew 16[:19], said, "Whatever you bind on earth shall be bound in heaven, and whatever you loose on earth shall be loosed in heaven." This holy, comforting, and gracious word of God must enter deeply into the heart of every Christian, where he may with great gratitude let it become part of him. For the sacrament of penance consists in this: forgiveness of sin, comfort and peace of conscience, besides joy and blessedness of heart over against all sins and terrors of conscience, as well as against all despair and assaults [anfechtung] by the gates of hell [Matt. 16:18].

6. Now there are three things in the holy sacrament of penance. The first is absolution. These are the words of the priest which show, tell, and proclaim to you that you are free and that your sins are forgiven you by God according to and by virtue of the above-quoted words of Christ to St. Peter. The second is grace, the forgiveness of sins, the peace and comfort of the conscience, as the words declare. This is why it is called a sacrament, a holy sign, because in it one hears the words externally that signify spiritual gifts within, gifts by which the heart is comforted and set at peace. The third is faith, which firmly believes that the absolution and words of the priest are true, by the power of Christ's words, "Whatever you loose . . . shall be loosed," etc.

Everything, then, depends on this faith, which alone makes the sacraments accomplish that which they signify, and everything that the priest says come true. For as you believe, so it is done for you.[7] Without this faith all absolution and all sacraments are in vain and indeed do more harm than good. There is a common saying among the teachers that goes like this: Not the sacrament, but the faith that believes the sacrament is what removes sin. St. Augustine says this: The sacrament removes sin, not because it takes place, but because it is believed.[8] For this reason in the sacrament one must studiously discern faith; and this we would now sketch out further.

---

[7] Cf. Matt. 8:13; 9:29.
[8] Cf. Tract 80, 3, *On the Gospel According to St. John,* "Whence does water have such great power that it cleanses the body and purifies the heart, except from the word—not because it is spoken but because it is believed?" Migne 35, 1840.

11

7. It follows, then, in the first place, that the forgiveness of guilt, the heavenly indulgence, is granted to no one on account of the worthiness of his contrition over his sins, nor on account of his works of satisfaction, but only on account of his faith in the promise of God, "Whatever you loose . . . shall be loosed," etc. Although contrition and good works are not to be neglected, one is nevertheless in no case to build upon them, but only upon the sure words of Christ, who pledges to you that when the priest looses you, you shall be loosed. Your contrition and works may deceive you, and the devil will very soon overturn them in [the hour of] death and of temptation [anfechtung]. But Christ, your God, will not lie to you, nor will he waver; neither will the devil overturn his words for him. If you build upon them with a firm faith, you will be standing on the rock against which the gates and all the powers of hell cannot prevail [Matt. 16:18].

8. It follows further that the forgiveness of guilt is not within the province of any human office or authority, be it pope, bishop, priest, or any other. Rather it depends exclusively upon the word of Christ and your own faith. For Christ did not intend to base our comfort, our salvation, our confidence on human words or deeds, but only upon himself, upon his words and deeds. Priests, bishops, and popes are only servants who hold before you the word of Christ, upon which you should depend and rely with firm faith as upon a solid rock. Then the word will sustain you, and so your sins will have to be forgiven. Moreover this is why the word is not to be honored for the sake of the priests, bishops, or pope; but priests, bishops, and pope are to be honored for the sake of the word, as those who bring to you the word and message of your God that you are loosed from sins.

9. It follows in addition that in the sacrament of penance and forgiveness of guilt a pope or bishop does nothing more than the lowliest priest. Indeed where there is no priest, each individual Christian—even a woman or child—does as much. For any Christian can say to you, "God forgives you your sins, in the name," etc., and if you can accept that word with a confident faith, as though God were saying it to you, then in that same faith you are surely absolved.

So completely does everything depend on faith in God's word. No pope, bishop, or priest can do anything to your faith. Neither can anyone give to another any better word of God than that common word he spoke to St. Peter, "Whatever you loose . . . shall be loosed." This word must be in every absolution; indeed every absolution depends upon it.

Even so one should observe, and not despise, the established orders of authority. Only, make no mistake about the sacrament and its effect, as if it counted for more when given by a bishop or a pope than when given by a priest or a layman. As the priest's mass and baptism and distribution of the holy body of Christ is just as valid as if the pope or bishop were doing it, so it is with absolution, that is, the sacrament of penance. The fact that they reserve certain cases for absolution[9] does not make their sacrament any greater or better. It is the same as if for some reason they withheld from anybody the mass, baptism, or the like. Nothing would thereby be either added to or taken away from baptism and the mass.

10. Therefore if you believe the word of the priest when he absolves you (that is, when he looses you in the name of Christ and in the power of his words, saying, "I absolve you from your sins"), then your sins are assuredly absolved also before God, before all angels and all creatures—not for your sake, or for the priest's sake, but for the sake of the very Word of Christ, who cannot be lying to you when he says, "Whatever you loose . . . shall be loosed." Should you, however, not believe that your sins are truly forgiven and removed, then you are a heathen, acting toward your Lord Christ like one who is an unbeliever and not a Christian; and this is the most serious sin of all against God. Besides you had better not go to the priest if you will not believe his absolution; you will be doing yourself great harm by your disbelief. By such disbelief you make your God to be a liar when, through his priest, he says to you, "You are loosed from your sins," and you

---

[9] In "reserved cases," specified sins—even those not of public or flagrant character—could be absolved only by the pope or bishop, or one appointed by them. Cf. *LW* 36, 86-88 and *PE* 2, 105-106.

13

retort, "I don't believe it," or, "I doubt it." As if you were more certain in your opinion than God is in his words, whereas you should be letting personal opinions go, and with unshakeable faith giving place to the word of God spoken through the priest. For if you doubt whether your absolution is approved of God and whether you are rid of your sins, that is the same as saying, "Christ has not spoken the truth, and I do not know whether he approves his own words, when he says to Peter, 'Whatever you loose . . . shall be loosed.'" O God, spare everybody from such diabolical disbelief.

11. When you are absolved from your sins, indeed when amid your awareness of sin some devout Christian—man or woman, young or old—comforts you, then receive this absolution in such faith that you would readily let yourself be torn apart or killed over and over again, or readily renounce everything else, rather than doubt that you have been truly absolved before God. Since by God's grace it is commanded of us to believe and to hope that our sins are forgiven us, how much more then ought you to believe it when God gives you a sign of it through another person! There is no greater sin than not to believe this article of "the forgiveness of sins" which we pray daily in the Creed. And this sin is called the sin against the Holy Spirit. It strengthens all other sins and makes them forever unforgivable. Consider, therefore, what a gracious God and Father we have. He not only promises us forgiveness of sins, but also commands us, on pain of committing the most grievous sin of all, to believe that they are forgiven. With this same command he constrains us to have a joyful conscience while he uses the terrible sin [against the Holy Spirit] as a means of driving us away from sins and from a bad conscience.

12. A number of people have been teaching us that we should, and must necessarily, be uncertain about absolution, and doubt whether we have been restored to [the state of] grace[10] and our sins forgiven—on the grounds that we do not know whether our contrition has been adequate or whether sufficient satisfaction has

---

[10] The grace of justification, bestowed originally in baptism and lost through mortal (but not venial) sin, could be regained through the sacrament of penance. See Roy J. Deferrari (trans.), Henry Denzinger's *The Sources of Catholic Dogma* (St. Louis: Herder, 1957), Nos. 796, 807, 894.

been made for our sins.[11] And because this is not known, the priest cannot at once assign appropriate penance.[12] Be on guard against these misleading and un-Christian gossips. The priest is necessarily uncertain as to your contrition and faith, but this is not what matters. To him it is enough that you make confession and seek an absolution. He is supposed to give it to you and is obligated to do so. What will come of it, however, he should leave to God and to your faith. You should not be debating in the first place whether or not your contrition is sufficient. Rather you should be assured of this, that after all your efforts your contrition is not sufficient. This is why you must cast yourself upon the grace of God, hear his sufficiently sure word in the sacrament, accept it in free and joyful faith, and never doubt that you have come to grace—not by your own merits or contrition but by his gracious and divine mercy, which promises, offers, and grants you full and free forgiveness of sins in order that in the face of all the assaults [anfechtung] of sin, conscience, and the devil, you thus learn to glory and trust not in yourself or your own actions, but in the grace and mercy of your dear Father in heaven. After that be contrite all the more and render satisfaction as well as you can. Only, let this simple faith in the unmerited forgiveness promised in the words of Christ go before and remain in command of the situation.

13. Those, however, who do not desire peace think then that they have produced adequate contrition and works—beyond that, they make Christ a liar and flirt with the sin against the Holy Spirit, in addition to treating the most worthy sacrament of penance unworthily. So they receive their deserved reward: they build on sand [Matt. 7:26], trusting themselves more than God. The result must necessarily be an ever greater uneasiness of conscience, a vain striving after impossible things, a quest for assurance and comfort that they never find. Such a perversion issues finally in despair and eternal damnation. For what else are they seeking but

---

[11] Cf. Luther's clever dialogue on the matter of uncertain absolution in *The Keys* (1530). LW 40, 338-345.

[12] Penance is not only the name of the sacrament, but also the term commonly used to designate a work of satisfaction enjoined upon the recipient of the sacrament. *The Catholic Encyclopedia*, XI, 618. Cf. p. 9, n. 3.

15

a certainty achieved by their own efforts? As though they wanted by their own works to reinforce God's word, through which they are supposed to be strengthened in faith—and begin to buttress heaven, to which they should be clinging for their own support. That is, they will not let God be merciful. They want him only for judge, as if he should not forgive anything freely unless it were first recompensed to him. Yet in the entire gospel we read of no one of whom God required anything but faith; out of grace he bestowed all his benefits full and free upon the unworthy, bidding them afterward to live aright and to go in peace, etc.

14. Do not worry about whether a priest in his absolution errs, is himself bound [Matt. 16:19],[13] or is merely jesting. If you just receive the words sincerely and believe them, as long as you neither know nor despise his error or bond, you are nevertheless absolved and have the full sacrament. For as already indicated, this sacrament does not depend on the priest, nor on your own actions, but entirely on your faith; you have as much as you believe.[14] Without this faith you could have all the contrition in the world, but it would still be only the remorse of Judas that angers rather than reconciles God. For nothing reconciles God better than when one does him the honor [of acknowledging that] he is truthful and gracious; and no one does this except the one who believes his words. Thus David praises him, "Lord, thou art slow to anger, merciful, and truthful."[15] And this same truth saves us from all sins, if we cling to it by faith.

15. It follows that the keys or the authority of St. Peter is not an authority at all but a service; and the keys have not been given to St. Peter but to you and me. The keys are yours and mine. For St. Peter, insofar as he is a pope or a bishop, does not need them; to him they are neither necessary nor helpful. Their entire virtue lies rather in this, that they help sinners by comforting and strengthen-

---

[13] The Council of Trent later defined the matter in similar terms but with a basic difference, "Even priests who are bound by mortal sin exercise as ministers of Christ the office of forgiving sins by virtue of the Holy Spirit conferred in ordination." Denzinger, *op. cit.*, No. 902.

[14] Cf. p. 11, especially n. 8.

[15] Luther's rendering of Ps. 86:15 is based on the Vulgate (85:15).

ing their conscience. Thus Christ ordered that [the exercise of] authority in the church should be a rendering of service; and that by means of the keys the clergy should be serving not themselves but only us. For this reason, as one sees, the priest does no more than to speak a word, and the sacrament is already there. And this word is God's word, even as God has promised. The priest, moreover, has sufficient evidence and reason to grant absolution when he sees that one desires it from him. Beyond that, he is not obligated to know anything. I say this in order that the most gracious virtue of the keys should be cherished and honored, and not despised because of abuses by some who do little more than threaten, annoy, and pronounce the ban.[16] They create nothing but tyranny out of this lovely and comforting authority, as if Christ were thinking only of the will and dominion of the priests when he instituted the keys and did not even know to what use they should be put.

16. Just so no one accuses me again of forbidding good works, let me say that one should with all seriousness be contrite and remorseful, confess and do good works. This I maintain, however, as best I can: that in the sacrament we let faith be the chief thing, the legacy through which one may attain the grace of God. After that we can do a lot of good [works]—to the glory of God alone and to the benefit of our fellow men, and not in order that we might depend upon that as sufficient to pay for our sin. For God gives us his grace freely and without cost; so we should also serve him freely and without cost.

Besides, everything that I have said about this sacrament is said to them whose conscience is troubled, uneasy, erring, and terrified, who would gladly be loosed from their sin and be righteous, but who do not know where to begin. For these are the ones who likewise have true contrition, indeed they are too contrite and fainthearted. God comforts people like these through the prophet Isaiah,

---

[16] Derived from the civil law of the Holy Roman Empire where it meant to outlaw or banish, the term became increasingly current in the church after the twelfth century as the common name for a declaration of excommunication. Samuel Macauley Jackson (ed.), *The New Schaff-Herzog Encyclopedia of Religious Knowledge* (12 vols.; Grand Rapids, Michigan: Baker Book House, 1949-1954), I, 434.

chapter 40, "Cry to the fainthearted and say to them, *consolamini,* be comforted, you faint of heart; behold your God."[17] And in Matthew 11[:28], Christ says, "Come to me, you who are burdened and troubled, I will comfort you," etc. The hardhearted, however, who do not as yet seek comfort for their conscience, have likewise not yet experienced this tormenting anxiety. To them this sacrament is of no use. One must first soften them up with the terrible judgment of God and cause them to quail, so that they too may learn to sigh, and seek for the comfort of this sacrament.

17. In confession, if a priest wishes to inquire, or if you want to examine yourself, as to whether or not you are truly contrite, I have no objections. Just so no one becomes so bold in the sight of God that he claims to have sufficient contrition. Such an attitude is presumptuous and fabricated, for no one has sufficient contrition for his sin.[18] [I would allow] even that the inquiry be greatly expanded as to whether a person firmly believes the sacrament, that his sins are forgiven him as Christ said to the paralytic, "My son, have faith and your sins are forgiven you" [Matt. 9:2]; and to the woman, "Have faith, my daughter, your faith has made you well" [Matt. 9:22]. Such inquiry has become quite rare in this sacrament; we operate only with contrition, sin, satisfaction, and indulgence. And so one blind man keeps leading the other [Matt. 15:14]. Actually in this sacrament the priest, in his word, brings God's message about sin and the forgiveness of guilt. Hence he should indeed be the one who inquires and discerns most of all whether a person is receptive to the message. Such receptivity can never consist in anything other than faith and the desire to receive this message. Sin, contrition, and good works should be treated in sermons before the sacrament and confession.

18. It may happen that God does not cause a person to find the forgiveness of guilt, and the turbulence and uneasiness of conscience persist after the sacrament as before. Here one must deal

---

[17] Cf. Isa. 40:1, 9 (Vulgate).

[18] This does not contradict what was said in the preceding paragraph about a person being too contrite to believe the absolution. What Luther says here *(Niemant hatt gnugsam rew)* is that no one is ever contrite enough to deserve the absolution. Cf. pp. 14-16.

wisely, for the fault is in the faith. It is just as impossible that the heart should not be joyful when it believes its sins are forgiven, as that it should not be troubled and uneasy when it believes its sins are unforgiven. Now if God allows faith to remain weak, one should not despair on that account, but rather recognize it as a trial and temptation [*anfechtung*] by means of which God tests, prods, and drives a person to cry out all the more and plead for such faith, saying with the father of the possessed boy in the gospel, "O Lord, help my unbelief" [Mark 9:24], and with the apostles, "O Lord, increase our faith" [Luke 17:5]. Thus does a person come to learn that everything depends on the grace of God: the sacrament, the forgiveness, and the faith. Giving up all other hope, despairing of himself, he comes to hope exclusively in the grace of God and cling to it without ceasing.

19. Now penance and the sacrament of penance are two different matters.[19] As said above[20] the sacrament consists in three things: in the word of God, that is, the absolution; in the faith [which trusts] in this absolution; and in the peace, that is, the forgiveness of sins which surely follows faith. But penance has also been divided into three "parts": contrition, confession, and satisfaction.[21]

Now just as in contrition there is many an abuse, as has already been noted,[22] so it is also in the case of confession and satisfaction. There are a host of books on these subjects,[23] but unfortunately

---

[19] Cf. the Thomistic distinction referred to in the Introduction on p. 6 and there documented in note 5.

[20] See p. 11.

[21] Thomas so listed the three (*Summa Theologica*. Fathers of the English Dominican Province [trans.], *op. cit.*, Part III, ques. 90, pp. 90-97), holding that while satisfaction is a "fruit" of penance-as-a-virtue it is nonetheless a "part" of penance-as-a-sacrament (*ibid.*, p. 93).

[22] See pp. 12-18.

[23] The discipline of theological casuistry, which developed out of the momentously elaborated ecclesiastical institution of penance and gave rise to such manuals of penance for the guidance of confessors as those compiled by Archbishop Theodore of Canterbury (d. 690) and the Venerable Bede (d. 735), received a tremendous impetus from the Fourth Lateran Council (1215), which made auricular confession universally obligatory. A list of the more renowned writings—"*summae* of cases of conscience"—from that of the thirteenth century Raymond of Penaforte to that of Luther's contemporary, Sylvester Prierias, is given in *Schaff-Herzog*, II, 438.

very few on the sacrament of penance. Where, however, the sacrament proceeds correctly in faith, there penance—confession, contrition, and satisfaction—is a less weighty matter, and there is no danger of there being too little or too much. For the faith of the sacrament makes all the crooked straight and fills up all the uneven ground. So no one who has this sacramental faith can err, whether in contrition, confession, or satisfaction; and even if he does err, it does him no harm. Where there is no faith, however, there neither contrition, nor confession, nor satisfaction is adequate. For this reason so many books and teachings appear on contrition, confession, and satisfaction. These serve only to frighten hearts into confessing often; whether the sins they confess are venial or mortal,[24] they do not know. Yet this time we desire to say a little more about the subject.

20. Venial sins one need not confess to the priest, but only to God. Now, however, another question arises: What are mortal and venial sins? There has never yet been a teacher, nor will there ever be one, learned enough to give us a dependable rule for distinguishing venial from mortal sins, except in such obvious offenses against God's commandments as adultery, murder, theft, falsehood, slander, betrayal, hatred, and the like. It is, moreover, entirely up to God to judge which other sins he regards as mortal. Nor is it possible for man to recognize this, as Psalm 19[:12][25] says, "O God, who can discern all his sins? Cleanse me from secret sins." Therefore private confession is no place for [reciting] sins other than those which one openly recognizes as deadly, those which at the time are oppressing and frightening the conscience. For if one

---

[24] *Teglich adder todtlich*, literally, "daily or deadly," but cf. *WA* 1, 322 with *WA* 6, 626 for Luther's equation of *peccata venialia* with *teglich sund*. Mortal sin is a transgression committed deliberately and with full knowledge of its gravity; it deprives the soul of grace and consigns to eternal punishment unless properly confessed and absolved. Sin is venial when the matter is less serious or its true gravity is not known or when there is no wilful consent; usually more frequent, it does not deprive of grace, can be omitted in confession without guilt, and expiated by prayer or other good works. Cf. Denzinger, *op. cit.*, No. 899; Donald Attwater (ed.), *A Catholic Dictionary* (New York: Macmillan, 1958), p. 464; *LW* 31, 20.

[25] Where Luther gives correct Psalm references to the Vulgate version, in which Psalms 10–146 are numbered differently than in the RSV, we have given the corresponding RSV reference.

were to confess all his sins, he would have to be confessing every moment, since in this life we are never without sin. Even our good works are not pure and without sin. Yet it is not fruitless to confess the slighter sins, particularly if one is not aware of any mortal sins. For as has been said, in this sacrament God's word is heard, and [through it] faith is strengthened more and more. And even if one should have nothing to confess, it would still be profitable for the sake of that very faith to hear often the absolution, God's word. Thus one would grow accustomed to believing in the forgiveness of sins. This is why I said that the faith of the sacrament does everything, even though the confession be too much or too little. Everything is profitable to him who believes God's sacrament and word.

Concerning satisfaction let this now suffice: the best kind of satisfaction is to sin no more and to do all possible good toward your fellow-man, be he enemy or friend. This kind of satisfaction is rarely mentioned; we think to pay for everything simply through assigned prayers.

21. This is the authority of which Christ speaks, in Matthew 9[:6-8], to the unbelieving scribes, "That you may know that the son of man has authority on earth to forgive sins—he said to the paralytic—'Arise, take up your bed and go home.' And he rose and went home. When the crowds saw it, they were afraid, and they glorified God, who had given such authority to men." Now this authority to forgive sins is nothing other than what a priest, indeed, if need be, any Christian, may say to another when he sees him afflicted or affrighted in his sins. He can joyously speak this verdict, "Take heart, your sins are forgiven" [Matt. 9:2]. And whoever accepts this and believes it as a word of God, his sins are surely forgiven.

Where, however, there is no such faith, it would do no good even if Christ or God himself spoke the verdict. For God cannot give a person something he does not want to have. And that person does not want to have it, who does not believe that it is being given to him; he does the word of God a great dishonor, as was said above.[26] You see, then, that the whole church is full of the forgiveness of sins.

---

[26] Cf. pp. 14-16.

But few there are who really accept and receive it. For they do not believe it and would rather rely upon their own works.

So it is true that a priest genuinely forgives sin and guilt, although he is in no position to give to the sinner that faith which receives and accepts the forgiveness. For this faith God must give. Nevertheless the forgiveness is genuine, as true as if God had spoken it, whether it is grasped by faith or not. Such authority to forgive sins, and thus to render a verdict in God's place, no one possessed in the Old Testament, neither high priest nor ordinary priests, neither kings nor prophets, nor anyone else among the people. The only exceptions occurred at God's express order, as when Nathan confronted King David [II Sam. 12:1-15]. But in the New Testament every Christian has this authority to forgive sins, where a priest is not at hand. And he has it through the promise of Christ, where he said to Peter, "Whatever you loose on earth shall be loosed in heaven" [Matt. 16:19]. Had this been said to Peter alone, then in Matthew 18[:18] Christ would not have said to all in general, "Whatever you loose on earth shall be loosed in heaven." There he is speaking to all Christendom, and to each [Christian] in particular. The great thing about the Christian is that God cannot be fully loved and praised if we are no longer given to hear more than one man speaking to us in such a word. Now the world is full of Christians, yet no one pays any attention to this or gives God thanks.

To sum it all up:

Whoever believes, to him— { everything is helpful, nothing is harmful.

Whoever does not believe, to him— { everything is harmful, nothing is helpful.

THE HOLY AND BLESSED SACRAMENT OF BAPTISM

1519

Translated by Charles M. Jacobs

Revised by E. Theodore Bachmann

INTRODUCTION

The Holy and Blessed Sacrament of Baptism captures and conveys the elemental dynamic of this rite of entrance into the communion of saints. It deals illuminatingly with a subject that seems as much in need of thoughtful restudy in our day as it was in the sixteenth century. Coming off Johann Grünenberg's press in Wittenberg on November 9, 1519, this treatise was the second in Luther's 1519 trilogy on the sacraments, dedicated to the Duchess Margaret of Brunswick.[1]

The unfolding of Luther's thoughts on baptism in these twenty paragraphs follows a logical progression. He speaks first of the "sign," and defines the meaning of the word "baptism" in terms of immersion (1-2). Next he tells what the putting in and the drawing out "signify," namely, the death of the old man and the resurrection of the new—an operation which begins at baptism and continues through all of life until the sinner dies, in which God affords constant comfort through his covenant of grace (3-11). Finally Luther treats of "faith" as the "third thing" in the sacrament, the "most necessary part"; it needs to be exercised daily with respect to God's covenant promise, to the exclusion of all reliance upon works and supplementary man-made vows, and precisely in the suffering attendant upon a life lived in the estate in which God has placed us (12-20).

This treatise is notably free from polemics. Indeed when Luther came to revising congregational worship in 1523, he took over with only minor modifications the customary Roman order of baptism then being used at Wittenberg.[2] In 1526, however, he revised this order by abbreviating it drastically; yet he added nothing new. This new order proved popular and was later appended to the Small

---

[1] See p. 5.
[2] *PE* 6, (193) 197-206; *WA* 12, (38) 42-48.

Catechism and included in many of the contemporary church orders.[3]

Before long a polemical note entered the discussion of baptism when, in the early 1520's, the Anabaptists came on the scene. Therefore Luther's treatise here before us should be followed by a reading of his letter, in 1528, to two pastors *Concerning Rebaptism*.[4] Moreover this was only the beginning of a new explication and defense of the sacrament of baptism. In 1529 came his teaching on baptism in the Small and Large Catechisms.[5] After 1528 Luther preached at least twenty-three sermons on baptism. The first four, delivered in 1528, laid the basis of his exposition of the subject in the catechisms.[6] In 1532 came a series of three;[7] in February, 1534, a series of six[8] plus a longer sermon in three parts later the same year;[9] in 1538 another series of six;[10] and in 1539 a series of three.[11]

All of this is evidence of the earnestness with which Luther regarded baptism throughout his career as a reformer of the church. The keynote of his emphasis affirms that baptism is not the work of man but of God. Therefore the actions of men can neither make nor nullify this sacrament. Baptism is a command of God given us through the Scriptures, notably but not only in such passages as Mark 16:16 or Matt. 28:18-19. Above all, baptism is exalted for us by Jesus Christ; God honors our baptism in that of his son.[12]

The following translation, made originally by Charles M. Jacobs[13] and here revised, is from the original publication by Grünenberg, *Eyn Sermon von dem heyligen hochwirdigen Sacrament der Tauffe*, as reprinted with the subsequent variations noted

---

[3] *PE* 6, (193) 207-209; *WA* 19, (531) 537-541; 30[I], 339-342.

[4] *LW* 40, (227) 229-262.

[5] Tappert (ed.), *The Book of Concord*, pp. 348-349, 436-446.

[6] *Katechismuspredigten. WA*, 30[I], 18-23, 50-52, 109-116.

[7] *WA* 36, 96-117.

[8] *WA* 37, 258-267, 270-275, 278-284, 288-293, 299-304.

[9] *WA* 37, 627-672.

[10] *WA* 46, 145-155, 167-185, 194-201.

[11] *WA* 47, 640-659.

[12] Cf. Luther's sermon of March 10, 1532, on Matt. 3:16-17. *WA* 36, 126-134.

[13] *PE* 1, (51) 56-71.

in *WA* 2, (724) 727-737. Between 1519 and 1523 a total of sixteen different editions appeared in Wittenberg, Leipzig, Nürnberg, and other cities. In 1543 came also a Latin translation. At once recognized as a work of fundamental importance, this treatise has found a place in all major collections of Luther's works.

THE HOLY AND BLESSED
SACRAMENT OF BAPTISM

D.M.A.[1]

1. Baptism [*Die Taufe*] is *baptismos* in Greek, and *mersio* in Latin, and means to plunge something completely into the water, so that the water covers it. Although in many places it is no longer customary to thrust and dip infants into the font, but only with the hand to pour the baptismal water upon them out of the font,[2] nevertheless the former is what should be done. It would be proper, according to the meaning of the word *Taufe,* that the infant, or whoever is to be baptized, should be put in and sunk completely into the water and then drawn out again. For even in the German tongue the word *Taufe* comes undoubtedly from the word *tief* [deep] and means that what is baptized is sunk deeply into the water. This usage is also demanded by the significance of baptism itself. For baptism, as we shall hear, signifies that the old man and the sinful birth of flesh and blood are to be wholly drowned by the grace of God. We should therefore do justice to its meaning and make baptism a true and complete sign of the thing it signifies.

2. Baptism is an external sign or token, which so separates us from all men not baptized that we are thereby known as a people of Christ, our Leader, under whose banner of the holy cross we continually fight against sin. In this holy sacrament we must there-

---

[1] Doctor Martin, Augustinian. See p. 9, n. 1; cf. p. 79.

[2] While various forms of ablution have apparently been practiced in all periods, immersion was probably the most ancient; in the Latin Church it prevailed until the twelfth century, and in some places until the sixteenth century. (*The Catholic Encyclopedia,* II, 261-262.) The oldest baptismal order of the Münster bishopric (*ca.* 1400-1414) prescribes triple immersion. The 1521 order of the Schwerin diocese, however, allows a choice between immersion and washing [*abwaschen*]. While Luther's preference was for immersion—his 1523 order of baptism prescribed dipping the child into the font (*PE* 6, 201)—Bucer and Zwingli both favored pouring. (*CL* 1, 185, n. 12).

29

fore pay attention to three things: the sign, the significance of it, and the faith.

The sign consists in this, that we are thrust into the water in the name of the Father and of the Son and of the Holy Spirit; however, we are not left there but are drawn out again. This accounts for the expression: *aus der Taufe gehoben*.[3] The sign must thus have both its parts, the putting in and the drawing out.

3. The significance of baptism is a blessed dying unto sin and a resurrection in the grace of God, so that the old man, conceived and born in sin, is there drowned, and a new man, born in grace, comes forth and rises. Thus St. Paul, in Titus 3[:5], calls baptism a "washing of regeneration," since in this washing a person is born again and made new. As Christ also says, in John 3[:3, 5], "Unless you are born again of water and the Spirit (of grace), you may not enter into the kingdom of heaven." For just as a child is drawn out of his mother's womb and is born, and through this fleshly birth is a sinful person and a child of wrath [Eph. 2:3], so one is drawn out of baptism and is born spiritually. Through this spiritual birth he is a child of grace and a justified person. Therefore sins are drowned in baptism, and in place of sin, righteousness comes forth.

4. This significance of baptism—the dying or drowning of sin —is not fulfilled completely in this life. Indeed this does not happen until man passes through bodily death and completely decays to dust. As we can plainly see, the sacrament or sign of baptism is quickly over. But the spiritual baptism, the drowning of sin, which it signifies, lasts as long as we live and is completed only in death. Then it is that a person is completely sunk in baptism, and that which baptism signifies comes to pass.

Therefore this whole life is nothing else than a spiritual baptism which does not cease till death, and he who is baptized is condemned to die. It is as if the priest, when he baptizes, were to say, "Lo, you are sinful flesh. Therefore I drown you in God's name and in his name condemn you to death, so that with you all your sins

---

[3] Literally, "lifted up out of the baptismal water," the expression was commonly used in the past tense to mean "be baptized," in the present tense to mean "stand sponsor." Cf. *PE* 1, 57, n. 1.

may die and be destroyed." Wherefore St. Paul, in Romans 6[:4], says, "We were buried with Christ by baptism into death." The sooner a person dies after baptism, the sooner is his baptism completed. For sin never ceases entirely while the body lives, which is so wholly conceived in sin that sin is its very nature, as the prophet says [Ps. 51:5], "Behold I was conceived in sin, and in iniquity did my mother bear me." There is no help for the sinful nature unless it dies and is destroyed with all its sin. Therefore the life of a Christian, from baptism to the grave, is nothing else than the beginning of a blessed death. For at the Last Day God will make him altogether new.

5. Similarly the lifting up out of the baptismal water is quickly done, but the thing it signifies—the spiritual birth and the increase of grace and righteousness—even though it begins in baptism, lasts until death, indeed, until the Last Day. Only then will that be finished which the lifting up out of baptism signifies. Then shall we arise from death, from sins, and from all evil, pure in body and soul, and then shall we live eternally. Then shall we be truly lifted up out of baptism and be completely born, and we shall put on the true baptismal garment of immortal life in heaven. It is as if the sponsors, when they lift the child up out of baptism, were to say, "Lo, your sins are now drowned, and we receive you in God's name into an eternal life of innocence." For in this way will the angels at the Last Day raise up all Christians—all the devout baptized—and will there fulfill what baptism and the sponsors signify, as Christ declares in Matthew 24[:31], "He will send out his angels, and they will gather unto him his elect from the four places of the winds, from the rising to the setting of the sun."

6. Baptism was foreshown of old in Noah's flood, when the whole world was drowned, except for Noah with his three sons and their wives, eight souls, who were saved in the ark. That the people of the world were drowned signifies that in baptism sins are drowned. But that the eight in the ark, with animals of every sort, were preserved, signifies—as St. Peter explains in his second epistle[4]

---

[4] II Pet. 2:5; cf. I Pet. 3:20-21.

—that through baptism man is saved. Now baptism is by far a greater flood than was that of Noah. For that flood drowned men during no more than one year, but baptism drowns all sorts of men throughout the world, from the birth of Christ even till the day of judgment. Moreover while that was a flood of wrath, this is a flood of grace, as is declared in Psalm 29[:10],[5] "God will make a continual new flood." For without doubt many more people have been baptized than were drowned in the flood.

7. From this it follows, to be sure, that when someone comes forth out of baptism, he is truly pure, without sin, and wholly guiltless. Still, there are many who do not properly understand this. They think that sin is no longer present, and so they become remiss and negligent in the killing of their sinful nature, even as some do when they have gone to confession. For this reason, as I have said above, it should be properly understood and known that our flesh, so long as it lives here, is by nature wicked and sinful.

To correct this wickedness God has devised the plan of making our flesh altogether new, even as Jeremiah [18:4-6] shows. For the potter, when the vessel "was spoiled in his hand," thrust it again into the lump of clay and kneaded it, and afterward made another vessel, as seemed good to him. "So," says God, "are you in my hands." In the first birth we are spoiled; therefore he thrusts us into the earth again by death, and makes us over at the Last Day, that we may be perfect and without sin.

This plan, as has been said, begins in baptism, which signifies death and the resurrection at the Last Day. Therefore so far as the sign of the sacrament and its significance are concerned, sins and the man are both already dead, and he has risen again; and so the sacrament has taken place. But the work of the sacrament has not yet been fully done, which is to say that death and the resurrection at the Last Day are still before us.

8. A baptized person is therefore sacramentally altogether pure and guiltless. This means nothing else than that he has the sign of

---

[5] Quoting the Vulgate version from memory, Luther inevitably presents many variations from the familiar text of Scripture. Cf. p. 20, n. 25.

God; that is to say, he has the baptism by which it is shown that his sins are all to be dead, and that he too is to die in grace and at the Last Day is to rise again to everlasting life, pure, sinless, and guiltless. With respect to the sacrament, then, it is true that he is without sin and guilt. Yet because all is not yet completed and he still lives in sinful flesh, he is not without sin. But although not pure in all things, he has begun to grow into purity and innocence.

Therefore when a person comes to mature age, the natural and sinful appetites—wrath, impurity, lust, greed, pride, and the like —begin to stir; whereas there would be none of these if all sins were drowned in the sacrament and were dead. But the sacrament only signifies that they are to be drowned through death and the resurrection at the Last Day. So St. Paul, in Romans 7[:17-20], and the saints with him, lament that they are sinners and have sin in their nature, even though they were baptized and were holy. They lament in this way because the natural and sinful appetites are always active so long as we live.

9. You ask, "How does baptism help me, if it does not altogether blot out and remove sin?" This is the place for a right understanding of the sacrament of baptism. This blessed sacrament of baptism helps you because in it God allies himself with you and becomes one with you in a gracious covenant of comfort.

In the first place you give yourself up to the sacrament of baptism and to what it signifies. That is, you desire to die, together with your sins, and to be made new at the Last Day. This is what the sacrament declares, as has been said. God accepts this desire at your hands and grants you baptism. From that hour he begins to make you a new person. He pours into you his grace and Holy Spirit, who begins to slay nature and sin, and to prepare you for death and the resurrection at the Last Day.

In the second place you pledge yourself to continue in this desire, and to slay your sin more and more as long as you live, even until your dying day. This too God accepts. He trains and tests you all your life long, with many good works and with all kinds of sufferings. Thereby he accomplishes what you in baptism have desired,

33

namely, that you may become free from sin, die, and rise again at the Last Day, and so fulfill your baptism. Therefore we read and see how bitterly he has let his saints be tortured, and how much he has let them suffer, in order that, almost slain, they might fulfill the sacrament of baptism, die, and be made new. For when this does not happen, when we do not suffer and are not tested, then the evil nature gains the upper hand so that a person invalidates his baptism, falls into sin, and remains the same old man he was before.

10. So long as you keep your pledge to God, he in turn gives you his grace. He pledges himself not to impute to you the sins which remain in your nature after baptism, neither to take them into account nor to condemn you because of them. He is satisfied and well pleased if you are constantly striving and desiring to conquer these sins and at your death to be rid of them. For this reason, although evil thoughts and appetites may be at work, indeed even though at times you may sin and fall, these sins are already broken by the power of the sacrament and covenant. The one condition is that you rise again and enter again into the covenant, as St. Paul says in Romans 8[:1]. No one who believes in Christ is condemned by the evil, sinful inclination of his nature, if only he does not follow it and give in to it. St. John the Evangelist writes in his epistle [I John 2:1-2], "If any one does sin, we have an advocate with God, even Jesus Christ, who has become the forgiveness of our sins." All this takes place in baptism, where Christ is given us, as we shall hear in the treatise which follows.[6]

11. Now if this covenant did not exist, and God were not so merciful as to wink at our sins, there could be no sin so small but it would condemn us. For the judgment of God can endure no sin. Therefore there is no greater comfort on earth than baptism. For it is through baptism that we come under the judgment of grace and mercy, which does not condemn our sins but drives them out by many trials. There is a fine sentence of St. Augustine which says, "Sin is altogether forgiven in baptism; not in such a manner that it is

---

[6] *The Blessed Sacrament of the Holy and True Body of Christ, and the Brotherhoods* (1519), in this volume, pp. 45-73, was the third in a group of three treatises, of which this was the second.

34

no longer present, but in such a manner that it is not imputed."[7] It is as if he were to say, "Sin remains in our flesh even until death and works without ceasing. But so long as we do not give our consent to it or desire to remain in it, sin is so overruled by our baptism that it does not condemn us and is not harmful to us. Rather it is daily being more and more destroyed in us until our death."

For this reason no one should be terrified if he feels evil lust or love, nor should he despair even if he falls. Rather he should remember his baptism, and comfort himself joyfully with the fact that God has there pledged himself to slay his sin for him and not to count it a cause for condemnation, if only he does not say Yes to sin or remain in it. Moreover these wild thoughts and appetites, and even a fall into sin, should not be regarded as an occasion for despair. Regard them rather as an admonition from God that we should remember our baptism and what was there spoken, that we should call upon God's mercy and exercise ourselves in striving against sin, that we should even welcome death in order that we may be rid of sin.

12. Here, then, is the place to discuss the third thing in the sacrament: faith. Faith means that one firmly believes all this: that this sacrament not only signifies death and the resurrection at the Last Day, by which a person is made new to live without sin eternally, but also that it assuredly begins and achieves this; that it establishes a covenant between us and God to the effect that we will fight against sin and slay it, even to our dying breath, while he for his part will be merciful to us, deal graciously with us, and— because we are not sinless in this life until purified by death—not judge us with severity.

So you understand how in baptism a person becomes guiltless, pure, and sinless, while at the same time continuing full of evil inclinations. He can be called pure only in the sense that he has started to become pure and has a sign and covenant of this purity

---

[7] Augustine (354-430), bishop of Hippo, wrote in his *De Nuptiis et concupiscentia* I, 25, 28: *Si autem quaeritur, quomodo ista concupiscentia carnis maneat in regenerato, in quo universorum facta est remissio peccatorum . . . ad haec responditur, dimitti concupiscentiam carnis in Baptismo, non ut non sit, sed ut in peccatum non imputetur.* Migne 44, 429-430.

and is ever to become more pure. Because of this God will not count against him his former[8] impurity. A person is thus pure by the gracious imputation of God, rather than by virtue of his own nature. As the prophet says in Psalm 32[:1-2], "Blessed is he whose transgression is forgiven; blessed is the man to whom the Lord imputes no iniquity."

This faith is of all things the most necessary, for it is the ground of all comfort. He who does not possess such faith must despair of his sins. For the sin which remains after baptism makes it impossible for any good works to be pure before God. For this reason we must boldly and without fear hold fast to our baptism, and set it high against all sins and terrors of conscience. We must humbly admit, "I know full well that I cannot do a single thing that is pure. But I am baptized, and through my baptism God, who cannot lie, has bound himself in a covenant with me. He will not count my sin against me, but will slay it and blot it out."

13. So, then, we understand that the innocence which is ours by baptism is so called simply and solely because of the mercy of God. For he has begun this work in us, he bears patiently with our sin, and he regards us as if we were sinless. This also explains why Christians are called in the Scriptures the children of mercy, a people of grace, and men of God's good will.[9] It is because through baptism they have begun to become pure; by God's mercy with respect to the sins that still remain they are not condemned; until, finally, through death and at the Last Day, they become wholly pure, just as the sign of baptism shows.

Therefore those people err greatly who think that through baptism they have become wholly pure. They go about in their ignorance and do not slay their sin. Indeed they do not admit that it is sin. They simply persist in it, and so make their baptism of no effect. They continue to depend only on a few external works. Meanwhile pride, hatred, and other evils in their nature, which they disregard, grow worse and worse.

How contrary this is! Sin, evil inclination, must be recognized

---

[8] *Nachstelligen.* CL 1, 190, n. 22, suggests the meaning, *rückständige, frühere.*
[9] The reference may perhaps be to I Pet. 2:10, Luke 2:14, Eph. 5:1.

as truly sin.[10] That it does not harm us, however, is to be ascribed to the grace of God. He will not count sin against us if only we keep striving against it with many trials, tasks, and sufferings, and at last slay it at death. To them who do this not, God will not forgive their sins. For they do not live according to their baptism and covenant, and they hinder the work of God and of their baptism which has been begun.

14. Those who presume to blot out and put away their sin by "satisfaction"[11] are the same sort of people. They go so far as to disregard their baptism, as if they had no more need of it beyond the fact of having once been baptized. They do not know that baptism is in force all through life, even until death, yes—as said above— even to the Last Day. For this reason they presume to find some other way of blotting out sin, namely, by works. So for themselves and for all others, they create evil, terrified, and uncertain consciences, and despair at the hour of death. They do not know how they stand with God, thinking that by sin they have now lost their baptism and that it profits them no more.

Guard yourself, by all means, against this error. For as has been said, if anyone has fallen into sin, he should all the more remember his baptism, how God has here made a covenant with him to forgive all his sins, if only he will fight against them even until death. Upon this truth, upon this alliance with God, a man must joyfully dare to rely. Then baptism again goes into force and operation. Then his heart again becomes peaceful and glad, not in his own works or "satisfaction," but in the mercy of God promised to him in baptism, a mercy which God will keep forever. This faith a person must hold so firmly that he would cling to it even though everything and all sins attacked him. For he who lets himself be forced away from this faith makes God a liar in his promise in the sacrament of baptism.

---

[10] Luther is combating the view that man's innate concupiscence is not really sin, a teaching which was finally promulgated as dogma in a decree of the Council of Trent, 1546, "This concupiscence, which at times the Apostle calls *sin* [Rom. 6:12ff.], the holy Synod declares that the Catholic Church has never understood to be called sin." Denzinger, *The Sources of Catholic Dogma*, p. 248.
[11] Cf. p. 9, n. 3 and pp. 14-15.

15. It is faith like this that the devil attacks most of all. If he can overthrow it, he has won the battle. For the sacrament of penance (of which we have already spoken)[12] also has its foundation in this sacrament, inasmuch as sins are forgiven only to those who are baptized, to those whose sins God has promised to forgive. The sacrament of penance thus renews and points out again the sacrament of baptism. It is as if the priest, in the absolution, were saying, "Lo, God has now forgiven you your sin, as he long since promised you in baptism; and now he has commanded me, by the power of the keys,[13] to assure you of this forgiveness. Therefore you now come again into that which baptism is and does. Believe, and you have it. Doubt, and you are lost. So we find that through sin baptism is indeed hindered in its work, in the forgiveness and the slaying of sin. Yet only by lack of faith in its operation is baptism canceled out. Faith, in turn, removes the hindrance to the operation of baptism. Thus everything depends on faith.

To speak quite plainly, it is one thing to forgive sins, and another thing to put them away or drive them out. The forgiveness of sins is obtained by faith, even though they are not entirely driven out. But to drive out sins is to exercise ourselves against them, and at last it is to die, for in death sin perishes completely. But both the forgiveness and the driving out of sins are the work of baptism. Thus the Apostle writes to the Hebrews [12:1], who were baptized and whose sins were forgiven, that they should lay aside the sin which clings to them. For so long as I believe that God will not count my sins against me, my baptism is in force and my sins are forgiven, even though they may still in a great measure be present. After that follows their driving out through sufferings, death, and the like. This is what we confess in the article [of the Creed], "I believe in the Holy Ghost, the forgiveness of sins," and so forth. Here there is special reference to baptism, in which the forgiveness takes place

---

[12] *The Sacrament of Penance* (1519), in this volume, pp. 3-22, was published just before the present treatise on baptism.

[13] According to Roman teaching, this power to forgive and to retain sin (Matt. 16:19) belonged to the priest and was normally exercised in the sacrament of penance.

through God's covenant with us; therefore we must not doubt this forgiveness.

16. It follows, then, that baptism makes all sufferings, and especially death, profitable and helpful, so that they simply have to serve baptism in the doing of its work, that is, in the slaying of sin. It cannot be otherwise. For he who would fulfil the work and purpose of his baptism and be rid of sin, must die. Sin, however, does not like to die, and for this reason it makes death so bitter and so horrible. Such is the grace and power of God that sin, which has brought death, is driven out again by its very own work, namely, by death itself.

You find many people who wish to live in order that they may become righteous and who say that they would like to be righteous. Now there is no shorter way or manner than through baptism and the work of baptism, which is suffering and death. Yet so long as they are not willing to take this way, it is a sign that they do not properly intend or know how to become righteous. Therefore God has instituted many estates in life in which men are to learn to exercise themselves and to suffer. To some he has commanded the estate of matrimony, to others the estate of the clergy, to others the estate of temporal rule, and to all he has commanded that they shall toil and labor to kill the flesh and accustom it to death. Because for all who are baptized, their baptism has made the repose, ease, and prosperity of this life a very poison and a hindrance to its work. For in the easy life no one learns to suffer, to die with gladness, to get rid of sin, and to live in harmony with baptism. Instead there grows only love of this life and horror of eternal life, fear of death and unwillingness to blot out sin.

17. Consider now the lives of men. Many there are who fast, pray, go on pilgrimage, and exercise themselves in such things, thinking thereby only to heap up merit and to sit down in the high places of heaven; they no longer learn[14] to slay their evil vices. But fasting and all such exercises should be aimed at holding down the old Adam, the sinful nature, and at accustoming it to do without all that

---

[14] *Leren.* Many of the earliest editions read *lernen* instead (*WA* 10^{II}, 487) and, along with *CL* 1, 193, n. 4, we have so construed it.

is pleasing for this life, and thus preparing it more and more each day for death, so that the work and purpose of baptism may be fulfilled. And all these exercises and toils are to be measured not by their number or their greatness, but by the demands of baptism. That is to say, everyone is to take upon himself so much of these works as is good and profitable for the suppressing of his sinful nature and for the preparation of it for death. He is to increase or diminish these works according as he sees sin increasing or diminishing. As it is, people go their way and take upon themselves this, that, and the other task, doing now this, now that, according to the appearance or reputation of the work. Afterward they let it drop just as quickly and thus become altogether inconstant, till in the end they amount to nothing. Indeed some of them so rack their brains over the whole business, and so abuse nature, that they are useless both to themselves and to others.

All this is the fruit of that doctrine with which we have been so infatuated as to think that after repentance or baptism we are without sin and that our good works are to be heaped up for their own sake or as a "satisfaction" for sins already done, but not for the blotting out of sin as such. This is encouraged by those preachers who preach unwisely the legends and deeds of the blessed saints and hold them up as examples for all. The ignorant easily fall for these things, and effect their own destruction out of the examples of the saints. God has given every saint a special way and a special grace for living according to his baptism. But baptism and its significance God has set as a common standard for everyone. Each of us is to examine himself according to his station in life and is to find what is the best way for him to fulfil the work and purpose of his baptism, namely, to slay sin and to die in order that Christ's burden may thus grow light and easy [Matt. 11:30] and not be carried with worry and care. Solomon has this to say of it, "The toil of a fool only wearies him, because he does not know the way to the city" [Eccles. 10:15]. For even as they are worried who wish to go to the city and cannot find their way, so it is with these men also; all their life and labor is a burden to them, and yet accomplishes nothing.

18. In this place, then, belongs the common question whether baptism, and the vow which we there make to God, is something

more or greater than the vows of chastity, of the priesthood, or of the clergy. Since baptism is common to all Christians, it is supposed that the clergy have taken a special and a higher vow.

I answer: From what has been said, this is an easy question to answer. For in baptism we all make one and the same vow: to slay sin and to become holy through the work and grace of God, to whom we yield and offer ourselves, as clay to the potter [Jer. 18:4-6]. In this no one is any better than another. But for a life in accordance with baptism, for the slaying of sin, there can be no one method and no special estate in life. This is why I said that each man must test himself that he may know in what estate he may best slay sin and put a check upon his nature. It is true, then, that there is no vow higher, better, or greater than the vow of baptism. What more can we promise than to drive out sin, to die, to hate this life, and to become holy?

Over and above this vow, a person may indeed bind himself to an estate which will be suitable to him and helpful for the completion of his baptism. It is just as though two men went to the same city, and the one went by the footpath, the other by the highway, just as each thought best. So he who binds himself to the estate of matrimony, walks in the toils and sufferings which belong to that estate and lays upon himself its burdens, in order that he may grow used to pleasure and sorrow, avoid sin, and prepare himself for death better than he could do outside of that estate.

But he who seeks more suffering, and by much exercise would speedily prepare himself for death and soon attain the goal of his baptism, let him bind himself to chastity or to the spiritual order. For the spiritual estate, if it is as it ought to be, should be full of torment and suffering in order that he who belongs to it may have more exercise in the work of his baptism than the man who is in the estate of matrimony, and through such torment quickly grow used to welcoming death with joy, and so attain the purpose of his baptism.

Now above this estate there is yet a higher one, that which rules in the spiritual order: the estate of bishop, priest, and so forth. These men should be well practiced in sufferings and works, and at every hour be ready for death—to die not only for their own sake, but also for the sake of those who are their subjects.

Yet in all these estates the standard, of which we spoke above, should never be forgotten, namely, that a man should so exercise himself only to the end that sin may be driven out. He should not be guided by the number or the greatness of the works. But, alas! how we have forgotten our baptism and what it means, what vows we made there, and that we are supposed to walk in its works and to attain its purpose! So, too, we have forgotten about the ways to that goal and about the estates. We hardly know to what end these estates were instituted, or how we are to act in them for the fulfilling of our baptism. They have been made a sparkling show, and little more remains of them than a worldly display. As Isaiah [1:22] says, "Your silver has become dross, your wine mixed with water." On this may God have mercy! Amen.

19. If, then, the holy sacrament of baptism is a matter so great, gracious, and full of comfort, we should diligently see to it that we ceaselessly, joyfully, and from the heart thank, praise, and honor God for it. For I fear that by our thanklessness we have deserved our blindness and become unworthy of recognizing such grace. The whole world was, and still is, full of baptism and the grace of God. But we have been led astray into our own anxious works, and then into indulgences and other similar false comforts. We have thought that we are not to trust God until we are righteous and have made satisfaction for our sin, as though we would buy God's grace from him or pay him for it.

In truth, he who does not see in God's grace how it bears with him as a sinner and will make him blessed, he who looks forward only to God's judgment, will never be joyful in God, and can neither love nor praise him. But if we hear and firmly believe that in the covenant of baptism God receives us sinners, spares us, and makes us pure from day to day, then our heart must be joyful, and love and praise God. Thus God says through the prophet, "I will spare them as a man spares his son" [Mal. 3:17]. Wherefore it is needful that we give thanks to the Blessed Majesty, who shows himself so gracious and merciful toward us poor condemned worms. And the work itself we must magnify and acknowledge.

20. At the same time, however, we must also beware lest a false security creep in and say to itself, "If baptism is so gracious and

great a thing that God will not count our sins against us, and as soon as we turn again from sin everything is right by virtue of baptism, then for the present I will live and do my own will. Afterward, or when about to die, I will remember my baptism and remind God of his covenant, and then fulfil the work and purpose of my baptism."

Baptism is indeed that great a thing, that if you turn again from sins and appeal to the covenant of baptism, your sins are forgiven. But watch out, if you thus wickedly and wantonly sin [and go presuming] on God's grace, that the judgment does not lay hold upon you and anticipate your turning back. Beware lest, even if you then desired to believe or trust in your baptism, your trial [*anfechtung*] be, by God's decree, so great that your faith is not able to stand. If they scarcely remain who do not sin or who only fall because of sheer weakness, where shall your wickedness remain, which has tempted and mocked God's grace?[15]

Let us therefore walk with fear, that with a firm faith we may hold fast to the riches of God's grace and joyfully give thanks to his mercy forever and ever. Amen.

---

[15] Cf. I Pet. 4:18.

THE BLESSED SACRAMENT OF THE HOLY AND TRUE BODY OF CHRIST, AND THE BROTHERHOODS

1519

Translated by Jeremiah J. Schindel
Revised by E. Theodore Bachmann

INTRODUCTION

This last treatise in Luther's trilogy of 1519 on the sacraments[1] is his first extended statement on the Lord's Supper. He addressed it specifically to laymen[2] and dedicated it to Margaret, duchess of Brunswick. He also made it double-pronged in that he contrasted the spiritual reality of the communion with the corrupt practices of certain fraternal groups; this accounts for the bifocal title.

Luther structures this treatise according to the three parts of the sacrament: the outward sign (paragraphs 1-3, but cf. 14-16), the inward significance (4-16), and the living faith (17-22). He then appends his critique of the brotherhoods.

His proposal that the laity should receive both of the elements was promptly attacked by Duke George of Saxony when he read one of the first copies just before Christmas, 1519. By December 27 he was complaining to the Elector Frederick of Saxony and soon forwarded his protests also to the Saxon bishops of Meissen and Merseburg. Later Pope Leo X echoed this protest in the bull of June 15, 1520, which condemned forty-one of Luther's alleged errors.

Here, as yet, Luther raised no such controversial issues as the sacrifice of the mass or the mode of the Real Presence. In fact there is a strong suggestion that he probably still accepted the doctrine of transubstantiation. The main thing is that here he offered a practical interpretation of what the body of Christ means in the life of those who would seek to die as well as to live like Christians.

Ecclesiastically, Luther admitted, a person can be excommunicated and thus deprived of the formal ministrations of the papal hierarchy. But what Luther is here talking about is a fellowship that goes deeper and rises higher than human designs. Therefore Luther could later show uncommon confidence in burning the bull

---

[1] See pp. 5, 25.
[2] The subtitle read, *"Fur die Leyen."* WA 2, 739.

of Leo X; no such device, he believed, could ever separate him from the communion of saints.[3]

The third part was theologically the crux of the treatise. The nature of faith, Luther points out, is all too often misunderstood, particularly because of the confusing terminology employed by the scholastic theologians. In trying to guarantee the objective reality of the sacrament the scholastics had called its celebration an *opus operatum*, a faithless work. Luther, on the contrary, contended for the sacrament as an *opus operantis*, a working faith.

This led him to the practical problems of Christian living. Between the sacraments on the one hand, and an upright moral and ethical life on the other, Luther saw a profound connection. The brotherhoods or fraternal associations provided a kind of case study for Luther's sacramentally sensitive theological ethics. Societies or sodalities of laymen organized for charitable and devotional purposes, they also filled a social need among the workers in the various trades and occupations from which they drew their membership. Luther looked upon them as centers of group selfishness, spiritual pride, and immoral conduct, far removed from the opposite pole of the communion of saints.

The following translation, based on one made originally by Jeremiah J. Schindel,[4] is from the original printing by Johann Grünenberg, *Eyn Sermon von dem Hochwirdigen Sacrament, des heyligen waren Leychnams Christi. Und von den Bruderschafften*, that appeared in Wittenberg some time before December 24, 1519, and has been reproduced with annotations from later texts in WA 2, (738) 742-758. By 1525 a total of fourteen editions had come out in German, and in 1524 a translation in Latin.

---

[3] Cf. *A Treatise Concerning the Ban* (1520). PE 2, (35) 37-54.
[4] *PE* 2, (7) 9-31.

THE BLESSED SACRAMENT OF
THE HOLY AND TRUE BODY
OF CHRIST, AND THE
BROTHERHOODS

1. The holy sacrament of the altar, or of the holy and true body[1] of Christ, also has three parts[2] which it is necessary for us to know. The first is the sacrament, or sign. The second is the significance of this sacrament. The third is the faith required with each of the first two. These three parts must be found in every sacrament. The sacrament must be external and visible, having some material form or appearance. The significance must be internal and spiritual, within the spirit of the person. Faith must make both of them together operative and useful.

2. The sacrament, or external *sign*, consists in the form or appearance of bread and wine, just as baptism has water as its sign; only the bread and wine must be used in eating and drinking, just as the water of baptism is used by immersion or pouring. For the sacrament, or sign, must be received, or at least desired, if it is to work a blessing. Of course at present both kinds are not given to the people daily, as in former times.[3] But this is not necessary since the priesthood partakes of it daily in sight of the people. It is enough

---

[1] *Waren Leychnams* is the actual body which was given into death. *MA*[8], Er 2, 540, n. 382, 2.

[2] Cf. *The Sacrament of Penance*, in this volume, p. 11, and *The Holy and Blessed Sacrament of Baptism*, in this volume, pp. 29-30.

[3] The custom of giving only the bread but not the wine to the laity was enacted into canon law by the Council of Constance which burned an earlier advocate of both kinds, John Huss, as a heretic, even though the council itself admitted the custom's divergence from the institution of Jesus and the practice of the early church. Denzinger, *The Sources of Catholic Dogma*, No. 626.

that the people desire it daily and at present receive one kind, as the Christian Church ordains and provides.[4]

3. For my part, however, I would consider it a good thing if the church should again decree[5] in a general council that all persons be given both kinds, like the priests. Not because one kind is insufficient, since indeed the desire of faith is alone sufficient, as St. Augustine says, "Why do you prepare stomach and teeth? Only believe, and you have already partaken of the sacrament."[6] But it would be fitting and fine that the form, or sign, of the sacrament be given not in part only, but in its entirety, just as I said of baptism: it would be more fitting to immerse in the water than to pour with it, for the sake of the completeness and perfection of the sign.[7] For this sacrament [of the Body of Christ], as we shall see, signifies the complete union and the undivided fellowship of the saints; and this is poorly and unfittingly indicated by [distributing] only one part of the sacrament. Nor is there as great a danger in the use of the cup as is supposed,[8] since the people seldom go to this sacrament. Besides Christ was well aware of all future dangers, and yet he saw fit to institute both kinds for the use of all his Christians.

4. The *significance* or effect of this sacrament is fellowship of all the saints. From this it derives its common name *synaxis* [Greek] or *communio* [Latin], that is, fellowship. And the Latin *communicare* [commune or communicate], or as we say in German, *zum sacrament*

---

[4] Later Luther continued to allow for the voluntary use of one kind, but he soon expressed himself more forthrightly on the propriety of both kinds and the wickedness of forbidding both kinds. Cf. *A Treatise on the New Testament, that is, the Holy Mass*, in this volume, pp. 106-107. *LW* 36, 19-28.

[5] The Council of Basel had concluded the *Compactata* of Prague (November 30, 1433), which reversed the decision of Constance to the extent of allowing the followers of Huss to administer the sacrament in both kinds. Cf. *LW* 36, 27 and 13.

[6] *Sermo* 112, cap. 5. Migne 38, 645.

[7] Cf. p. 29.

[8] The danger, readily conceded by pious laity who trembled at the thought of it, was that a drop of the consecrated wine might fall to the floor. Since the bread was regarded as the more important anyway—and could be placed in the mouth of the communicant without his even having to touch it—it seemed possible, by expending with reception of the wine, to avoid the danger of desecrating the sacrament. Cf. Albert Hauck (ed.), *Realencyklopädie für protestantische Theologie und Kirche* (3rd ed., 24 vols.; Leipzig: Hinrichs, 1896-1913), XII, 721.

gehen [go to the sacrament], means to take part in this fellowship. Hence it is that Christ and all saints are one spiritual body,[9] just as the inhabitants of a city are one community and body, each citizen being a member of the other and of the entire city. All the saints, therefore, are members of Christ and of the church, which is a spiritual and eternal city of God.[10] And whoever is taken into this city is said to be received into the community of saints and to be incorporated into Christ's spiritual body and made a member of him. On the other hand *excommunicare* [excommunicate] means to put out of the community and to sever a member from this body; and that is called in our language "putting one under the ban"—though a distinction [is to be made in this regard] as I shall show in the following treatise, concerning the ban.[11]

To receive this sacrament in bread and wine, then, is nothing else than to receive a sure sign of this fellowship and incorporation with Christ and all saints. It is as if a citizen were given a sign, a document, or some other token to assure him that he is a citizen of the city, a member of that particular community. St. Paul says this very thing in I Corinthians 10[:17], "We are all one bread and one body, for we all partake of one bread and of one cup."

5. This fellowship consists in this, that all the spiritual possessions of Christ and his saints[12] are shared with and become the common property of him who receives this sacrament. Again all sufferings and sins also become common property; and thus love engenders love in return and [mutual love] unites. To carry out our homely figure, it is like a city where every citizen shares with all the others the city's name, honor, freedom, trade, customs, usages, help,

---

[9] Cf. Rom. 12:5; I Cor. 12:5.

[10] Cf. Isa. 60:14; Heb. 12:22; Rev. 3:12.

[11] See *A Treatise Concerning the Ban* (1520) (*PE* 2, 35-54), where Luther distinguishes between the external ban (excommunication) which excludes from the church's sacramental fellowship and the internal ban (sin and unbelief) which excludes from the fellowship with Christ. Cf. in this volume, p. 144.

[12] As early as 1515-1516 in his lectures on Romans [12:13] Luther distinguished between the contemporary understanding of "saints" as those who "are blessed and participating in glory" and the biblical understanding of "saints" as "all those who believe in Christ." *WA* 56, 469; *MA*³, Er 2, 398. This second sense is implicit in his use of the term here and throughout this treatise.

support, protection, and the like, while at the same time he shares all the dangers of fire and flood, enemies and death, losses, taxes, and the like. For he who would share in the profits must also share in the costs,[13] and ever recompense love with love.[14] Here we see that whoever injures one citizen injures an entire city and all its citizens; whoever benefits one [citizen] deserves favor and thanks from all the others. So also in our natural body, as St. Paul says in I Corinthians 12[:25-26], where he gives this sacrament a spiritual explanation, "The members have [the same] care for one another; if one member suffers, all suffer together; if one member is honored, all rejoice together." This is obvious: if anyone's foot hurts him, yes, even the little toe, the eye at once looks at it, the fingers grasp it, the face puckers, the whole body bends over to it, and all are concerned with this small member; again, once it is cared for all the other members are benefited. This comparison must be noted well if one wishes to understand this sacrament, for Scripture uses it for the sake of the unlearned.

6. In this sacrament, therefore, man is given through the priest a sure sign from God himself that he is thus united with Christ and his saints and has all things in common [with them], that Christ's sufferings and life are his own, together with the lives and sufferings of all the saints. Therefore whoever does injury to [the believer], does injury to Christ and all the saints, as he says through the prophet [Zech. 2:8], "He who touches you touches the apple of my eye." On the other hand whoever does him a kindness does it to Christ and all his saints; as he says in Matthew 25[:40], "As you did it to one of the least of these my brethren, you did it to me." Again, man must be willing to share all the burdens and misfortunes of Christ and

---

[13] Cf. the English aphorism, "What's none of my profit shall be none of my peril" (Vincent Stuckey Lean, *Lean's Collectanea* [Bristol: Arrowsmith, 1904], IV, 178) with its German equivalents in Karl F. Wander (ed.), *Deutsches Sprichwörter-Lexikon* (5 vols.; Leipzig: Brockhaus, 1867-1880), I, 1557, "*Geniessen*," Nos. 3, 4, 10, 14.

[14] Cf. the English aphorism, "Love is love's reward" (*Lean's Collectanea*, IV, 39), with its German equivalents in Wander (ed.), *Sprichwörter-Lexikon*, III, 136ff., "*Liebe*," Nos. 146, 386, 388, 635, 661, and especially No. 410 which also cites the English, "Love can neither be bought nor sold, its only price is love."

his saints, the cost as well as the profit. Let us consider more fully these two [sides of the fellowship].

7. Now adversity assails us in more than one form. There is, in the first place, the sin that remains in our flesh after baptism: the inclination to anger, hatred, pride, unchastity, and so forth. This sin assails us as long as we live.[15] Here we not only need the help of the community [of saints] and of Christ, in order that they might with us fight this sin, but it is also necessary that Christ and his saints intercede for us before God, so that this sin may not be charged to our account by God's strict judgment. Therefore in order to strengthen and encourage us against this same sin, God gives us this sacrament, as much as to say, "Look, many kinds of sin are assailing you; take this sign by which I give you my pledge that this sin is assailing not only you but also my Son, Christ, and all his saints in heaven and on earth. Therefore take heart and be bold. You are not fighting alone. Great help and support are all around you." King David speaks thus of this bread, "The bread strengthens a man's heart" [Ps. 104:15]. And the Scriptures in numerous places ascribe to this sacrament the property of strengthening, as in Acts 9[:18-19] [where it is written] of St. Paul, "He was baptized, and when he had received the food, he was strengthened."

In the second place the evil spirit assails us unceasingly with many sins and afflictions. In the third place the world, full of wickedness, entices and persecutes us and is altogether bad. Finally our own guilty conscience assails us with our past sins; and there is the fear of death and the pains of hell. All of these afflictions make us weary and weak, unless we seek strength in this fellowship, where strength is to be found.

8. Whoever is in despair, distressed by a sin-stricken conscience or terrified by death or carrying some other burden upon his heart, if he would be rid of them all, let him go joyfully to the sacrament of the altar and lay down his woe in the midst of the community [of saints] and seek help from the entire company of the spiritual body— just as a citizen whose property has suffered damage or misfortune at the hands of his enemies makes complaint to his town council and

---

[15] Cf. pp. 30-34.

fellow citizens and asks them for help. The immeasurable grace and mercy of God are given us in this sacrament to the end that we might put from us all misery and tribulation [*anfechtung*] and lay it upon the community [of saints], and especially on Christ. Then we may with joy find strength and comfort, and say, "Though I am a sinner and have fallen, though this or that misfortune has befallen me, nevertheless I will go to the sacrament to receive a sign from God that I have on my side Christ's righteousness, life, and sufferings, with all holy angels and the blessed in heaven and all pious men on earth. If I die, I am not alone in death; if I suffer, they suffer with me. [I know that] all my misfortune is shared with Christ and the saints, because I have a sure sign of their love toward me." See, this is the benefit to be derived from this sacrament; this is the use we should make of it. Then the heart cannot but rejoice and be strengthened.

9. When you have partaken of this sacrament, therefore, or desire to partake of it, you must in turn share the misfortunes of the fellowship, as has been said. But what are these? Christ in heaven and the angels, together with the saints, have no misfortunes, except when injury is done to the truth and to the Word of God. Indeed, as we have said, every bane and blessing of all the saints on earth affects them. Here your heart must go out in love and learn that this is a sacrament of love. As love and support are given you, you in turn must render love and support to Christ in his needy ones. You must feel with sorrow all the dishonor done to Christ in his holy Word, all the misery of Christendom, all the unjust suffering of the innocent, with which the world is everywhere filled to over-flowing. You must fight, work, pray, and—if you cannot do more—have heartfelt sympathy. See, this is what it means to bear in your turn the misfortune and adversity of Christ and his saints. Here the saying of Paul is fulfilled, "Bear one another's burdens, and so fulfil the law of Christ" [Gal. 6:2]. See, as you uphold all of them, so they all in turn uphold you; and all things are in common, both good and evil. Then all things become easy, and the evil spirit cannot stand up against this fellowship.

When Christ instituted the sacrament, he said, "This is my body which is given for you, this is my blood which is poured out for you. As often as you do this, remember me."[16] It is as if he were saying, "I am the Head, I will be the first to give himself for you. I will make your suffering and misfortune my own and will bear it for you, so that you in your turn may do the same for me and for one another, allowing all things to be common property, in me, and with me. And I leave you this sacrament as a sure token of all this, in order that you may not forget me, but daily call to mind and admonish one another by means of what I did and am still doing for you, in order that you may be strengthened, and also bear one another in the same way."

10. This is also a reason, indeed the chief reason, why this sacrament is received many times, while baptism is received but once. Baptism is the taking up or entering upon a new life,[17] in the course of which boundless adversities assail us, with sins and sufferings, both our own and those of others. There is the devil, the world, and our own flesh and conscience, as I have said. They never cease to hound us and oppress us. Therefore we need the strength, support, and help of Christ and of his saints. These are pledged to us here, as in a sure sign, by which we are made one with them—incorporated into them—and all our woe is laid down in the midst of the community [of saints].

For this reason it even happens that this holy sacrament is of little or no benefit to those who have no misfortune or anxiety, or who do not sense their adversity. For it is given only to those who need strength and comfort, who have timid hearts and terrified consciences, and who are assailed by sin, or have even fallen into sin. How could it do anything for untroubled and secure spirits, who neither need nor desire it? For the Mother of God[18] says, "He fills only the hungry [Luke 1:53], and comforts them that are distressed."

11. In order that the disciples, therefore, might by all means be worthy and well prepared for this sacrament, Christ first made them

---

[16] Cf. p. 82, n. 5.

[17] Cf. p. 30.

[18] Luther often called the Virgin Mary by this term of veneration which was common in Western Christendom. Cf. his discussion of the name in *The Magnificat* (1521). LW 21, 326-327.

sorrowful, held before them his departure and death, by which they became exceedingly troubled. And then he greatly terrified them when he said that one of them would betray him. When they were thus full of sorrow and anxiety, disturbed by sorrow and the sin of betrayal, then they were worthy, and he gave them his holy body[19] to strengthen them.[20] By which he teaches us that this sacrament is strength and comfort for those who are troubled and distressed by sin and evil. St. Augustine says the same thing, "This food demands only hungry souls, and is shunned by none so greatly as by a sated soul which does not need it."[21] Thus the Jews were required to eat the Passover with bitter herbs, standing and in haste [Exod. 12:8, 11]; this too signifies that this sacrament demands souls that are desirous, needy, and sorrowful. Now if one will make the afflictions of Christ and of all Christians his own, defend the truth, oppose unrighteousness, and help bear the needs of the innocent and the sufferings of all Christians, then he will find affliction and adversity enough, over and above that which his evil nature, the world, the devil, and sin daily inflict upon him. And it is even God's will and purpose to set so many hounds upon us and oppress us, and everywhere to prepare bitter herbs for us, so that we may long for this strength and take delight in the holy sacrament, and thus be worthy (that is, desirous) of it.

12. It is Christ's will, then, that we partake of it frequently, in order that we may remember him and exercise ourselves in this fellowship according to his example. For if his example were no longer kept before us, the fellowship also would soon be forgotten. So we at present see to our sorrow that many masses are held and yet the Christian fellowship which should be preached, practiced, and kept before us by Christ's example has virtually perished. So much so that we hardly know any more what purpose this sacrament serves or how it should be used. Indeed with our masses we frequently destroy this fellowship and pervert everything. This is the fault of the preachers who do not preach the gospel or the sacra-

---

[19] *Leychnam;* cf. p. 49, n. 1.
[20] Following Matt. 26:20-25 and Mark 14:17-21, Luther places the announcement of the betrayal prior to the institution of the Lord's Supper.
[21] Cf. Augustine's commentary on Ps. 22:26 (Vulgate 21:27) in Migne 36, 178.

ments, but their humanly devised fables about the many works [of satisfaction][22] to be done and the ways to live aright.

But in times past this sacrament was so properly used, and the people were taught to understand this fellowship so well, that they even gathered food and material goods in the church, and there—as St. Paul writes in I Corinthians 11[23]—distributed among those who were in need. We have a vestige of this [practice] in the little word "collect" in the mass,[24] which means a general collection, just as a common fund is gathered to be given to the poor. Those were the days too when so many became martyrs and saints. There were fewer masses, but much strength and blessing resulted from the masses; Christians cared for one another, supported one another, sympathized with one another, bore one another's burdens and affliction. This has all disappeared, and now there remain only the many masses and the many who receive this sacrament without in the least understanding or practicing what it signifies.

13. There are those, indeed, who would gladly share in the profits but not in the costs. That is, they like to hear that in this sacrament the help, fellowship, and support of all the saints are promised and given to them. But they are unwilling in their turn to belong also to this fellowship. They will not help the poor, put up with sinners, care for the sorrowing, suffer with the suffering, intercede for others, defend the truth, and at the risk of [their own] life, property, and honor seek the betterment of the church and of all Christians. They are unwilling because they fear the world. They do not want to have to suffer disfavor, harm, shame, or death, although it is God's will that they be thus driven—for the sake of the truth and of their neighbors—to desire the great grace and strength of this sacrament. They are self-seeking persons, whom this sacrament does not benefit. Just as we could not put up with a citizen who wanted to be helped, protected, and made free by the community, and yet in his turn would do nothing for it nor serve it. No, we on our part must make the evil of others our own, if we desire Christ and his

---

[22] Cf. pp. 12-18.
[23] I Cor. 11:21, 33; cf. Acts 2:44-46.
[24] Cf. p. 95.

saints to make our evil their own. Then will the fellowship be complete, and justice be done to the sacrament. For the sacrament has no blessing and significance unless love grows daily and so changes a person that he is made one with all others.

14. To signify this fellowship, God has appointed such signs of this sacrament as in every way serve this purpose and by their very form stimulate and motivate us to this fellowship. For just as the bread is made out of many grains ground and mixed together, and out of the bodies of many grains there comes the body of one bread,[25] in which each grain loses its form and body and takes upon itself the common body of the bread; and just as the drops of wine, in losing their own form, become the body of one common wine and drink—so it is and should be with us, if we use this sacrament properly. Christ with all saints, by his love, takes upon himself our form [Phil. 2:7], fights with us against sin, death, and all evil. This enkindles in us such love that we take on his form, rely upon his righteousness, life, and blessedness. And through the interchange of his blessings and our misfortunes, we become one loaf, one bread, one body, one drink, and have all things in common. O this is a great sacrament,[26] says St. Paul, that Christ and the church are one flesh and bone. Again through this same love, we are to be changed and to make the infirmities of all other Christians our own; we are to take upon ourselves their form and their necessity, and all the good that is within our power we are to make theirs, that they may profit from it. That is real fellowship, and that is the true significance of this sacrament. In this way we are changed into one another and are made into a community by love. Without love there can be no such change.

---

[25] The figure is very ancient, going back at least into the second century as attested by a document unknown to Luther, *The Didache* 9:4, "As this piece [of bread] was scattered over the hills [the reference is likely to the sowing of wheat on the hillsides of Judea] and then was brought together and made one, so let your church be brought together from the ends of the earth into your kingdom." Cyril C. Richardson (trans., ed.), *Early Christian Fathers* ("The Library of Christian Classics," Vol. I [Philadelphia: Westminster Press, 1953]), p. 175.

[26] In the Vulgate of St. Jerome, the Greek word *mysterion* (mystery) in Eph. 5:32 is translated *sacramentum*. Cf. Luther's later discussion of the term in *LW* 36, 93-95.

15. Christ appointed these two forms of bread and wine, rather than any other, as a further indication of the very union and fellowship which is in this sacrament. For there is no more intimate, deep, and indivisible union than the union of the food with him who is fed. For the food enters into and is assimilated by his very nature, and becomes one substance with the person who is fed. Other unions, achieved by such things as nails, glue, cords, and the like, do not make one indivisible substance of the objects joined together. Thus in the sacrament we too become united with Christ, and are made one body with all the saints, so that Christ cares for us and acts in our behalf. As if he were what we are, he makes whatever concerns us to concern him as well, and even more than it does us. In turn we so care for Christ, as if we were what he is, which indeed we shall finally be—we shall be conformed to his likeness. As St. John says, "We know that when he shall be revealed we shall be like him" [I John 3:2]. So deep and complete is the fellowship of Christ and all the saints with us. Thus our sins assail him, while his righteousness protects us. For the union makes all things common, until at last Christ completely destroys sin in us and makes us like himself, at the Last Day. Likewise by the same love we are to be united with our neighbors, we in them and they in us.

16. Besides all this, Christ did not institute these two forms solitary and alone, but he gave his true natural flesh in the bread, and his natural true blood in the wine, that he might give a really perfect sacrament or sign. For just as the bread is changed[27] into his true natural body[28] and the wine into his natural true blood, so truly are we also drawn and changed into the spiritual body, that is, into the fellowship of Christ and all saints and by this sacrament put into possession of all the virtues and mercies of Christ and his saints,

---

[27] *Vorwandelt.* While this term and the imagery involving change are associated with the doctrine of transubstantiation, it is clear that, through rejecting all scholastic speculation concerning substance (see p. 63), Luther is already beginning to call into question that very doctrine which within a year he was to condemn as "the second captivity of the sacrament" (*LW* 36, 28-35). Cf. Charles E. Hay (trans.) Reinhold Seeberg's *History of Doctrines* (Grand Rapids: Baker, 1952), II, 286, n. 1, "Literally, transubstantiation is here retained, but really Luther is only concerned to hold fast the idea that the body is 'in' the bread."

[28] *Leychnam;* cf. p. 49, n. 1.

as was said above[29] of a citizen who is taken and incorporated into the protection and freedom of the city and the entire community. For this reason he instituted not simply the one form, but two separate forms—his flesh under the bread, his blood under the wine—to indicate that not only his life and good works, which are indicated by his flesh and which he accomplished in his flesh, but also his passion and martyrdom, which are indicated by his blood and in which he poured out his blood, are all our own. And we, being drawn into them, may use and profit from them.

17. So it is clear from all this that this holy sacrament is nothing else than a divine sign, in which are pledged, granted, and imparted Christ and all saints together with all their works, sufferings, merits, mercies, and possessions, for the comfort and strengthening of all who are in anxiety and sorrow, persecuted by the devil, sins, the world, the flesh, and every evil. And to receive the sacrament is nothing else than to desire all this and firmly to believe that it is done.

Here, now, follows the third part of the sacrament,[30] that is, the *faith* on which everything depends. For it is not enough to know what the sacrament is and signifies. It is not enough that you know it is a fellowship and a gracious exchange or blending of our sin and suffering with the righteousness of Christ and his saints. You must also desire it and firmly believe that you have received it. Here the devil and our own nature wage their fiercest fight, so that faith may by no means stand firm. There are those who practice their arts and subtleties by trying [to fathom] what becomes of the bread when it is changed into Christ's flesh and of the wine when it is changed into his blood and how the whole Christ, his flesh and blood, can be encompassed in so small a portion of bread and wine. It does not matter if you do not see[31] it. It is enough to know that

---

[29] See pp. 50-55.

[30] The three parts are listed on p. 49.

[31] *Suchist,* literally "seek." *WA* 2, 750, n. 1 and *MA*³ 1, 390, 17 both suggest that *siehest* may have been intended. There need not have been a typographical error here, however. The Indogermanic antecedent of *suchen* in meaning was close to the Latin *sagio,* to perceive. Luther may have been using the term with its early connotations, in the sense of tracing a thing down or ferreting it out until you fathom or grasp it. Cf. Jacob Grimm and Wilhelm Grimm (eds.), *Deutsches Wörterbuch* (16 vols.; Leipzig: Hirzel, 1854-1954), X, 835.

it is a divine sign in which Christ's flesh and blood are truly present. The how and the where, we leave to him.[32]

18. See to it that here you exercise and strengthen your faith, so that when you are sorrowful or when your sins press you and you go to the sacrament or hear mass, you do so with a hearty desire for this sacrament and for what it signifies. Then do not doubt that you have what the sacrament signifies, that is, be certain that Christ and all his saints are coming to you with all their virtues, sufferings, and mercies, to live, work, suffer, and die with you, and that they desire to be wholly yours, having all things in common with you. If you will exercise and strengthen this faith, then you will experience what a rich, joyous, and bountiful wedding feast your God has prepared for you upon the altar. Then you will understand what the great feast of King Ahasuerus signifies [Esther 1:5]; and you will see what that wedding feast is for which God slew his oxen and fat calves, as it is written in the gospel [Matt. 22:2-4]. Then your heart will become truly free and confident, strong and courageous against all enemies [Ps. 23:5]. For who will fear any calamity if he is sure that Christ and all his saints are with him and have all things, evil or good, in common with him? So we read in Acts 2[:46] that the disciples of Christ broke this bread and ate with great gladness of heart. Since, then, this work is so great that the smallness of our souls would not dare to desire it, to say nothing of hoping for it or expecting it, therefore it is necessary and profitable to go often to the sacrament, or at least in the daily mass to exercise and strengthen this faith on which the whole thing depends and for the sake of which it was instituted. For if you doubt, you do God the greatest dishonor and make him out to be a faithless liar; if you cannot believe, then pray for faith, as was said earlier in the other treatise.[38]

19. See to it also that you give yourself to everyone in fellowship and by no means exclude anyone in hatred or anger. For this sacrament of fellowship, love, and unity cannot tolerate discord and disunity. You must take to heart the infirmities and needs of others, as if they were your own. Then offer to others your strength, as if

---

[32] See *The Babylonian Captivity of the Church*. LW 36, 32-35.
[38] Cf. *The Sacrament of Penance* (1519), pp. 3-22.

it were their own, just as Christ does for you in the sacrament. This is what it means to be changed into one another through love, out of many particles to become one bread and drink, to lose one's own form and take on that which is common to all.[34]

For this reason slanderers and those who wickedly judge and despise others cannot but receive death in the sacrament, as St. Paul writes in I Corinthians 11[:29]. For they do not do unto their neighbor what they seek from Christ, and what the sacrament indicates. They begrudge others anything good; they have no sympathy for them; they do not care for others as they themselves desire to be cared for by Christ. And then they fall into such blindness that they do not know what else to do in this sacrament except to fear and honor Christ there present[35] with their own prayers and devotion. When they have done this, they think they have done their whole duty. But Christ has given his holy body for this purpose, that the thing signified by the sacrament—the fellowship, the change wrought by love—may be put into practice. And Christ values his spiritual body, which is the fellowship of his saints, more than his own natural body. To him it is more important, especially in this sacrament, that faith in the fellowship with him and with his saints may be properly exercised and become strong in us; and that we, in keeping with it, may properly exercise our fellowship with one another. This purpose of Christ the blind worshipers do not perceive. In their devoutness they go on daily saying and hearing mass, but they remain every day the same; indeed every day they become worse but do not perceive it.

Therefore take heed. It is more needful that you discern the spiritual than the natural body of Christ; and faith in the spiritual body is more necessary than faith in the natural body. For the natural without the spiritual profits us nothing in this sacrament; a change must occur [in the communicant] and be exercised through love.

20. There are many who regardless of this change of love and faith rely upon the fact that the mass or the sacrament is, as they

---

[34] See pp. 59-60.

[35] *Kegenwertig*, i.e., present in the consecrated host.

say, *opus gratum opere operato*,[36] that is, a work which of itself
pleases God, even though they who perform it do not please him.
From this they conclude that however unworthily masses are said,
it is nonetheless a good thing to have many masses, since harm
comes [only] to those who say or use them unworthily. I grant everyone [the right to] his opinion, but such fables do not please me. For,
[if you desire] to speak in these terms, there is no creature or work
that does not of itself please God, as is written in Genesis 1[:31],
"God saw all his works and they pleased him." What is the result if
bread, wine, gold, and all good things are misused, even though of
themselves they are pleasing to God? Why, the consequence of that
is condemnation. So also here: the more precious the sacrament, the
greater the harm which comes upon the whole community [of saints]
from its misuse. For it was not instituted for its own sake, that it
might please God, but for our sake, that we might use it right,
exercise our faith by it, and through it become pleasing to God.
If it is merely an *opus operatum*,[37] it works only harm everywhere;
it must become an *opus operantis*.[38] Just as bread and wine, no
matter how much they may please God in and of themselves, work
only harm if they are not used, so it is not enough that the sacrament be merely completed (that is, *opus operatum*); it must also be
used in faith (that is, *opus operantis*). And we must take care lest
with such dangerous interpretations the sacrament's power and virtue be lost on us, and faith perish utterly through the false security
of the [outwardly] completed sacrament.

All this comes from the fact that they pay more attention in this
sacrament to Christ's natural body than to the fellowship, the spiritual body. Christ on the cross was also a completed work which was
well pleasing to God. But to this day the Jews have found it a stumbling block because they did not construe it as a work that is made
use of in faith. See to it, then, that for you the sacrament is an *opus*

---

[36] Literally, a work (that is) acceptable by (virtue of) the work (having been)
performed.

[37] *Opus operatum* is an action that is done, completed, finished, considered as
such without reference to the doer of it.

[38] *Opus operantis* is an action considered with reference to the doer of it, the
action of the one acting.

operantis, that is, a work that is made use of, that is well pleasing to God not because of what it is in itself but because of your faith and your good use of it. The Word of God too is of itself pleasing to God, but it is harmful to me unless in me it also pleases God. In short, such expressions as *opus operatum* and *opus operantis* are vain words of men,[39] more of a hindrance than a help. And who could

---

[39] *Opus operatum* and *opus operantis* were terms used generally in discussion of the difference between the sacraments of the old law and those of the new. The latter, according to Alexander of Hales (d. 1245), are in their own right signs *and* causes of invisible grace, and hence superior to the former which were merely signs but *not* causes. "Otherwise," added Thomas Aquinas (d. 1274), "they would have obviated the necessity of Christ's passion (Gal. 2:21)." Thus the sacraments of the Old Testament *signified* the passion of Christ and its effects; but they had no *power* to justify—their effect depended rather on the faith they were able to stimulate in the believer. The sacraments of the New Testament, on the other hand, in and of themselves effectively impart grace *ex opere operato,* i.e., simply through the use of them, apart from any act of the soul. Thomas, however, still presupposed faith; not as the *cause* of the sacrament's effect to be sure, but as the *receptivity* for the sacrament's effect. Bonaventura (d. 1274) also included faith as a factor in the justification of the New Testament sacraments, only he regarded it as something supplementary to the *opus operatum,* the external action in and of itself, to which the justifying grace and its effect were inseparably attached.

From this reduction of faith to something *supplementary,* it was only a step to the elimination of it as something altogether *expendable.* The step was taken by Duns Scotus (d. 1308) and Gabriel Biel (d. 1495) when they defined the subjective condition for the sacrament's effecting a blessing no longer in terms of a positive disposition, but in terms of the negative absence of any impediment. Reception of the sacrament in and of itself invariably imparts grace so long as man does not "interpose an obstacle," such as positive disbelief or mortal sin. Thus the scholastics all agreed that the sacraments impart grace *ex opere operato.* They differed as to whether faith was necessary for the *reception* of that grace. According to Duns Scotus and Gabriel Biel the necessity of faith is expressly denied and a purely passive receptivity is held to be sufficient. Intended originally to affirm that the power and effect of the sacrament are caused not by any disposition on man's part but solely by God and the sufferings of Christ, the concept *ex opere operato* thus came ultimately to mean that the proper disposition on the part of the recipient need not be one of positive faith but of merely negative passivity. It was this latest, fullest, and perhaps logical development of the scholastic view that Luther is attacking. F. Kattenbusch in Hauck (ed.), *Realencyklopädie,* XVII, 363-365.

The concept of the *opus operatum* also proved useful for guaranteeing the validity of the sacrament irrespective of the personal worthiness of the celebrating priest (see p. 102 and *LW* 36, 47, 55). Ultimately Luther's solution lay not in the preference for *operantis* over *operatum* but in the rejection of the *opus* altogether. The sacrament is not a good work or sacrifice on the part of man, but a testament or promise on the part of God, to be received by man in faith—not an *officium* but a *beneficium* (see p. 93 and *LW* 36, 35-57).

tell of all the abominable abuses and misbeliefs which daily multiply about this blessed sacrament, some of which are so spiritual and holy that they might almost lead an angel astray?

Briefly, whoever would understand the abuses need only keep before him the aforesaid use and faith of this sacrament; namely, that there must be a sorrowing, hungry soul, who desires heartily the love, help, and support of the entire community—of Christ and of all Christendom—and who does not doubt that in faith [all these desires] are obtained, and who thereupon makes himself one with everyone. Whoever does not take this as his point of departure for arranging and ordering his hearing or reading of masses and his receiving of the sacrament is in error and does not use this sacrament to his salvation. It is for this reason also that the world is overrun with pestilences, wars, and other horrible plagues,[40] because with our many masses we only bring down upon us greater disfavor.

21. We see now how necessary this sacrament is for those who must face death, or other dangers of body and soul, that they not be left in them alone but be strengthened in the fellowship of Christ and all saints. This is why Christ instituted it and gave it to his disciples in the hour of their extreme need and peril. Since we then are all daily surrounded by all kinds of danger, and must at last die, we should humbly and heartily give thanks with all our powers to the God of all mercy for giving us such a gracious sign, by which— if we hold fast to it in faith—he leads and draws us through death and every danger unto himself, unto Christ and all saints.

Therefore it is also profitable and necessary that the love and fellowship of Christ and all saints be hidden, invisible, and spiritual, and that only a bodily, visible, and outward sign of it be given to us. For if this love, fellowship, and support were apparent to all, like the transient fellowship of men, we would not be strengthened or trained by it to desire or put our trust in the things that are unseen and eternal [II Cor. 4:18]. Instead we would be trained to put our trust only in things that are transient and seen, and would become so accustomed to them as to be unwilling to let them go; we would not

---

[40] Cf. I Cor. 11:30.

follow God, except so far as visible and tangible things led us. We would thereby be prevented from ever coming to God. For everything that is bound to time and sense must fall away, and we must learn to do without them, if we are to come to God.

For this reason the mass and this sacrament are a sign by which we train and accustom ourselves to let go of all visible love, help, and comfort, and to trust in the invisible love, help, and support of Christ and his saints. For death takes away all the things that are seen and separates us from men and transient things. To meet it, we must, therefore, have the help of the things that are unseen and eternal. And these are indicated to us in the sacrament and sign, to which we cling by faith until we finally attain to them also with sight and senses.

Thus the sacrament is for us a ford, a bridge, a door, a ship, and a stretcher, by which and in which we pass from this world into eternal life. Therefore everything depends on faith. He who does not believe is like the man who is supposed to cross the sea, but who is so timid that he does not trust the ship; and so he must remain and never be saved, because he will not embark and cross over. This is the fruit of our dependence on the senses and of our untrained faith, which shrinks from the passage across the Jordan of death; and the devil too has a gruesome hand in it.

22. This was signified long ago in Joshua 3[:14-17]. After the children of Israel had gone dry-shod through the Red Sea [Exod. 14:21-22]—in which [event] baptism was typified—they went through the Jordan also in like manner. But the priests stood with the ark in the Jordan, and the water below them was cut off, while the water above them rose up like a mountain—in which [event] this sacrament is typified. The priests hold and carry the ark in the Jordan when, in the hour of our death or peril, they preach and administer to us this sacrament, the fellowship of Christ and all saints. If we then believe, the waters below us depart; that is, the things that are seen and transient do nothing but flee from us. The waters above us, however, well up high; that is, the horrible torments of the other world, which we envision at the hour of death, terrify us as if they would overwhelm us. If, however, we pay no attention to them,

and walk over with a firm faith, then we shall enter dry-shod and unharmed into eternal life.

We have, therefore, two principal sacraments in the church, baptism and the bread. Baptism leads us into a new life on earth; the bread guides us through death into eternal life. And the two are signified by the Red Sea and the Jordan, and by the two lands, one beyond and one on this side of the Jordan. This is why our Lord said at the Last Supper, "I shall not drink again of this wine until I drink it new with you in my Father's kingdom" [Matt. 26:29]. So entirely is this sacrament intended and instituted for a strengthening against death and an entrance into eternal life.

In conclusion, the blessing of this sacrament is fellowship and love, by which we are strengthened against death and all evil. This fellowship is twofold: on the one hand we partake of Christ and all saints; on the other hand we permit all Christians to be partakers of us, in whatever way they and we are able. Thus by means of this sacrament, all self-seeking love is rooted out and gives place to that which seeks the common good of all; and through the change wrought by love there is one bread, one drink, one body, one community. This is the true unity of Christian brethren. Let us see, therefore, how the neat-looking brotherhoods, of which there are now so many, compare and square with this.

The Brotherhoods[41]

1. First let us consider the evil practices of the brotherhoods.

---

[41] Originally made up of monks and monasteries, later primarily of laymen, these sodalities ("fraternities," "confraternities") were associations for devotional purposes. Members were obligated to the recitation of certain prayers and the attendance upon certain masses at stipulated times. Each member was believed to participate—and, most important of all, even after death—in the benefits accruing from these "good works" of all the other members. In the case of most of the sodalities, membership (for which the fees ranged from one to twenty gulden) entitled the member to the enjoyment of certain indulgences. In 1520 little Wittenberg boasted of twenty such fraternities; Hamburg had more than one hundred. In 1519 Degenhard Peffinger, of Wittenberg, was a member of eight such fraternities in his home city and through their cartel relationships derived benefits from twenty-seven more in other places. The brotherhood of St. Peter in Salzburg was united in fellowship with eighty other fraternities. Hauck (ed.), *Realencyklopädie*, III, 434-437; Karl Benrath (ed.), *An den christlichen Adel deutscher Nation, von D. Martin Luther* (Halle: Verein für Reformationsgeschichte, 1884), pp. 106-107.

One of these is their gluttony and drunkenness. After one or more masses are held,[42] the rest of the day and night, and other days besides, are given over to the devil; they do only what displeases God. Such mad reveling has been introduced by the evil spirit, and he calls it a brotherhood, whereas, it is more a debauch and an altogether pagan, yes, a swinish way of life. It would be far better to have no brotherhoods in the world at all than to countenance such misconduct. Temporal lords and cities should unite with the clergy in abolishing it. For by it God, the saints, and all Christians are greatly dishonored; and the divine services and feast days are made into a laughingstock for the devil. Saints' days are supposed to be kept and hallowed by good works. And the brotherhood is also supposed to be a special convocation of good works; instead it has become a collecting of money for beer. What have the names of Our Lady,[43] St. Anne,[44] St. Sebastian,[45] or other saints to do with your brotherhoods, in which you have nothing but gluttony, drunkenness, useless squandering of money, howling, yelling, chattering, dancing, and wasting of time? If a sow were made the patron saint of such a brotherhood she would not consent. Why then do they afflict the dear saints so miserably by taking their names in vain in such shameful practices and sins, and by dishonoring and blaspheming with such evil practices the brotherhoods named after these saints? Woe unto them who do this, and [unto them who] permit it!

2. If men desire to maintain a brotherhood, they should gather provisions and feed and serve a tableful or two of poor people, for

---

[42] A brotherhood usually came together monthly—often weekly—as well as on the day of its particular saint and on festival days of its related monastic order, ostensibly for pious exercises but in reality for feasting and debauchery which had long been a source of concern to the civil and ecclesiastical authorities as well as to the Reformers. Henry C. Lea, *A History of Auricular Confession and Indulgences* (Philadelphia: Lea, 1896), III, 474-476.

[43] The Carmelites were possibly the first to form sodalities with the specific purpose of devotion to the Virgin Mary, having organized in the fourteenth century the "Confraternity of Our Lady of Mount Carmel." Jackson (ed.), *The New Schaff-Herzog Encyclopedia of Religious Knowledge*, III, 226.

[44] According to tradition, St. Anne was the mother of the Holy Virgin; sodalities to her honor and bearing her name spread, as Kolde says, "like an epidemic" after the fourteenth century. Hauck (ed.), *Realencyklopädie*, III, 437.

[45] St. Sebastian was martyred on January 20 (year unknown) in Rome under Diocletian, who was emperor in 284-305. *Schaff-Herzog*, X, 320.

the sake of God. The day before they should fast,[46] and on the feast day remain sober, passing the time in prayer and other good works. Then God and his saints would be truly honored; there would be improvement too, and a good example would be given to others. Or they should gather the money which they intend to squander for drink, and collect it into a common treasury, each craft for itself. Then in cases of hardship, needy fellow workmen might be helped to get started, and be lent money, or a young couple of the same craft might be fitted out respectably from this common treasury. These would be works of true brotherhood; they would make God and his saints look with favor upon the brotherhoods, of which they would then gladly be the patrons. But where men are unwilling to do this, where they insist on following the old ways of simulated brotherhood, I admonish that they not do it on the saints' days, nor in the name of the saints or of the brotherhood. Let them take some other weekday and leave the names of the saints and of their brotherhoods alone, lest the saints one day punish it. Although there is no day which is not dishonored by such doings, at least the festivals and the names of the saints should be spared. For such brotherhoods call themselves brotherhoods of the saints while they do the work of the devil.

3. There is another evil feature of the brotherhoods, and it is of a spiritual nature. That is the false opinion they have that their brotherhood is to be a benefit to no one but themselves, those who are members on the roll or who contribute. This damnably wicked opinion is an even worse evil than the first, and it is one of the reasons why God has brought it about that with their gluttony, drunkenness, and the like the brotherhoods are becoming such a mockery and blasphemy of God. For in them men learn to seek their own good, to love themselves, to be faithful only to one another, to despise others, to think themselves better than others, and to presume to stand higher before God than others. And so perishes the communion of saints, Christian love, and the true brotherhood which is established in the holy sacrament, while selfish love grows in them. That is, by means of these many external brotherhoods devoted to

---

[46] Cf. pp. 39-40.

works they oppose and destroy the one, inner, spiritual, essential brotherhood common to all saints.

When God sees this perverted state of affairs, he perverts it still more, as is written in Psalm 18[:26], "With the perverse thou wilt be perverted."[47] So God brings it to pass that they make themselves and their brotherhoods a mockery and a disgrace. And he casts them out of the common brotherhood of saints—which they have opposed and with which they do not make common cause—and into their own brotherhood of gluttony, drunkenness, and unchastity; so that they, who have neither sought nor thought of anything more than their own, may find their own. Then, too, God blinds them so that they do not recognize it as an abomination and disgrace, but adorn their misconduct with the names of saints, as though they were doing the right thing. Beyond this, God lets some fall into so deep an abyss that they boast publicly and say that whoever is in their brotherhood cannot be condemned; just as if baptism and the sacrament, instituted by God himself, were of less value and more uncertain than that which they have concocted out of their blinded heads. Thus will God dishonor and blind those who, with their crazed conduct and the swinish practices of their brotherhoods, mock and blaspheme his feasts, his name, and his saints, to the detriment of that common Christian brotherhood which flowed from the wounds of Christ.

4. Therefore for the correct understanding and use of the brotherhoods, one must learn to distinguish correctly between brotherhoods. The first is the divine, the heavenly, the noblest, which surpasses all others as gold surpasses copper or lead—this being the fellowship of all saints, of which we spoke above.[48] In this we are all brothers and sisters, so closely united that a closer relationship cannot be conceived. For here we have one baptism, one Christ, one sacrament, one food, one gospel, one faith, one Spirit, one spiritual body [Eph. 4:4-5], and each person is a member of the other [Rom. 12:5]. No other brotherhood is so close and strong.

---

[47] This rendering is according to the Douay Version, which is based on the Vulgate from which Luther is quoting.
[48] See pp. 50-67.

For natural brothers are, to be sure, of one flesh and blood, one heritage and home; yet they must separate and join themselves to the blood and heritage of others [in marriage]. The organized brotherhoods have one roll, one mass, one kind of good works, one festival day, one fee; and, as things are now, their common beer, common gluttony, and common drunkenness. But none of these penetrates so deeply as to produce one spirit, for that is done by Christ's brotherhood alone. For this reason, too, the greater, broader, and more comprehensive it is, the better it is.

Now all other brotherhoods should be so conducted as to keep this first and noblest brotherhood constantly before their eyes and regard it alone as great. With all their works they should be seeking nothing for themselves; they should rather do them for God's sake, entreating God that he keep and prosper this Christian fellowship and brotherhood from day to day. Thus when a brotherhood is formed, they should let it be seen that the members are a jump ahead of others in rendering Christendom some special service with their prayers, fastings, alms, and good works, and [that they do this] not in order to seek selfish profit or reward, or to exclude others, but to serve as the free servants of the whole community of Christians.

If men had such a correct conception, God would in return also restore good order, so that the brotherhoods might not be brought to shame by debauchery. Then blessing would follow: a general fund could be gathered, whereby material aid too could be given to other persons. Then the spiritual and material works[49] of the brotherhoods would be done in their proper order. And whoever does not want to follow this [proper] order in his brotherhood, I advise him to let the brotherhood go, and get out of it; it will [only] do him harm in body and soul.

But suppose you say, "If I do not get something special out of the brotherhood, of what use is it to me?" I answer: True, if you are seeking something special [for yourself], of what use indeed is the brotherhood, or the sisterhood either? But if by it you serve the community and other men, as is customarily the nature of love [to

---

[49] *Merck* (in WA 2, 757, l. 7) in all likelihood was intended to be *werck;* cf. WA 21, 161, l. 8.

do], you will have your reward for this love without any desire or search on your part. If, however, you consider the service and reward of love too small, this is evidence that yours is a perverted brotherhood. Love serves freely and without charge, which is why God in return also gives to it every blessing, freely and without charge. Since, then, everything must be done in love, if it is to please God at all, the brotherhood too must be a brotherhood in love. It is the nature of that which is done in love, however, not to seek its own,[50] or its own profit, but to seek that of others, and above all that of the community [of saints].

5. To return once more to the sacrament, since the Christian fellowship is at present in a bad way, such as it has never been before, and is daily growing worse, especially among those in high places, and since all places are full of sin and shame, you should be concerned not about how many masses are said, or how often the sacrament is celebrated—for this will make things worse rather than better—but about how much you and others increase in that which the sacrament signifies[51] and in the faith[52] which it demands. For therein alone lies improvement. And the more you find yourself being incorporated into the fellowship of Christ and his saints, the better it is with you. [It is good] if you find that you are becoming strong in the confidence of Christ and his dear saints, so that you are certain that they love you and stand by you in all the trials of life and of death; and that you, in turn, take to heart the short-comings and lapses of all Christians and of the entire community [of saints] [as these occur] in any individual Christian, so that your love goes out to each one and you desire to help everyone, hate no one, suffer with all, and pray for all. See, as the work of the sacrament proceeds aright, you will come many times to weep, lament, and mourn over the wretched condition of Christendom today. If, however, you find no such confidence in Christ and his saints, and the needs of Christendom and of every single neighbor do not trouble or move you, then beware of all other good works, by which you

---

[50] I Cor. 13:5 (KJV); cf. I Cor. 10:24.
[51] Cf. p. 49 and pp. 50-62.
[52] Cf. p. 49 and pp. 62-67.

72

think you are godly and will be saved. They are surely nothing but hypocrisy, sham, and deceit, for they are without love and fellowship; and without these nothing is good. To sum it all up: *Plenitudo legis est dilectio,* "Love is the fulfilling of the law" [Rom. 13:10]. Amen.

[*Postscript*][53]

There are some who have unnecessarily rejected this treatise because I said in the third paragraph:[54] I should consider it a good thing if a Christian council were to decree that both kinds be given to everyone. They have opened their mouth so wide that they are saying, "This is an error and it is offensive." God in heaven have mercy! That we should live to see the day when Christ—the noble Lord and God—is publicly insulted and blasphemed by his own people, who rebuke his order as an error! It would have been enough had they allowed it to remain a permissive order and not turned it into a command. Then, at least, it would not be forbidden or regarded as an error. Yet I beg them to look carefully at the second and third paragraphs,[55] in which I have stated clearly that one kind is sufficient. I have experienced too that my writings are being rejected only by those who have not read them and who do not intend to do so. To such men I send my greetings and inform them that I am paying no attention to their blind and frivolous criticism; as long as God grants me life, I do not intend to tolerate it, that they so brazenly condemn and blaspheme my Lord Christ as an erring, offensive, and revolutionary teacher—they can act accordingly.

---

[53] This paragraph is found only in two of the Wittenberg printings, the so-called Editions C (*WA* 2, 739) and N (*WA* 9, 791), the only two which profess to having been corrected by Luther himself.

[54] See p. 50.

[55] See pp. 49-50.

A TREATISE ON THE NEW TESTAMENT, THAT IS, THE HOLY MASS

1520

Translated by Jeremiah J. Schindel

Revised by E. Theodore Bachmann

INTRODUCTION

This *Treatise on the New Testament, that is, the Holy Mass*, penetrates to the heart of Christian worship and boldly replaces the traditional notion of the mass as a sacrifice with the scriptural teaching of the Lord's Supper as a testament. Therein lies the far-reaching importance of this primarily devotional but theologically constructive treatise. Published in July of 1520 by Johann Grünenberg at Wittenberg, the treatise was written sometime between the two more famous works, *An Open Letter to the Christian Nobility* in June, in which Luther merely touched on the sacrament,[1] and *The Babylonian Captivity of the Church* in September, in which he dealt with the matter at great length.[2]

The treatise falls logically into two main parts. Sections 1-15 deal constructively with the basic meaning of this sacrament, section 12 offering a kind of preliminary recapitulation. The remaining sections contain Luther's rejection of the Roman teaching on the mass as a sacrifice and good work (16-28), and of the consequent abuses, such as masses for the dead, suppression of the testamental Words of Institution, withholding of the cup, and the differentiation and multiplication of masses (29-39).

In his work on *The Blessed Sacrament of the Holy and True Body of Christ, and the Brotherhoods,* Luther still spoke of the presence of Christ's body and blood in terms of the Roman doctrine of transubstantiation.[3] Less than a year later, in *The Babylonian Captivity of the Church,* he was publicly to reject transubstantiation as a merely human opinion which one is free to accept or not to accept.[4] Here in *A Treatise on the New Testament,* Luther's position on the Real Presence is stated with forceful simplicity,[5] yet in terms no longer reminiscent of transubstantiation.

---

[1] *PE* 2, 136-137.
[2] *LW* 36, 19-57.
[3] Cf. p. 59, n. 27.
[4] *LW* 36, 28-35.
[5] See pp. 86-87.

As to sacrifice, the treatise is significant in that it represents Luther's first clear and public attack on the Roman doctrine of the mass as a bloodless repetition of the sacrifice once made on Calvary—a theory which forgets that the mass is really a testament and sacrament in which God promises and gives something to us, not we to him.[6] However while rejecting the Roman sacrificial theory, Luther does not remove the fact of sacrifice from the mass. Christ in heaven is our Mediator, bringing our sacrifice of prayer and thanksgiving, indeed, of our very selves, to the Father. We do not offer Christ; he offers us. We lay ourselves upon him through faith; he in turn offers himself for us—continually—in heaven. The fact that each one does this for himself—each one by his own faith offers Christ to God—furnishes the basis on which Luther builds the evangelical doctrine of the priesthood of all believers, "All Christian men are priests, all women priestesses."[7]

Because it accentuated the Words of Institution in place of the sacrifice of the mass, the treatise set off a Romanist reaction led by Johann Dobneck Cochlaeus (d. 1552). His vitriolic rebuttal of 1521 claimed to find in the treatise one hundred fifty-four statements whose total effect was to align Luther with heretics, Hussites, and radicals.[8]

The following translation, a revision of that originally made by Jeremiah J. Schindel,[9] is based on the first printing of this treatise, *Eyn Sermon von dem newen Testament. das ist von der heyligē Messe,* as it has been reproduced, with annotations, in WA 6, 353-378. By 1524, fourteen editions had appeared in various cities. Because of its fundamental importance this treatise has found a place in all major collections of Luther's works.

---

[6] Cf. pp. 93-94.
[7] Cf. pp. 99-103.
[8] *WA* 6, 351.
[9] *PE* 1, 294-326.

A TREATISE ON THE NEW TESTAMENT, THAT IS, THE HOLY MASS

D.M.L.A.[1]

Jesus[2]

1. Experience, all chronicles, and the Holy Scriptures as well, teach us this truth: the less law, the more justice; the fewer commandments, the more good works. No well-regulated community ever existed long, if at all, where there were many laws. Therefore, before the ancient law of Moses, the patriarchs of old had no prescribed law and order for the service of God other than the sacrifices, as we read of Adam, Abel, Noah, and others. Afterward circumcision was enjoined upon Abraham and his household, until the time of Moses, through whom God gave the people of Israel a variety of laws, forms, and practices, for the sole purpose of teaching human nature how utterly useless many laws are to make people righteous. For although the law leads and drives away from evil to good works, it is impossible for man to do them willingly and gladly, for he has always an aversion to the law and would rather be free. Now where there is unwillingness, there can never be a good work. For what is not done willingly is not good, but only seems to be good. Consequently all the laws cannot make one really righteous without the grace of God. Instead they inevitably produce only Pharisees, hypo-

---

[1] Doctor Martin Luther, Augustinian. Cf. p. 9, n. 1; p. 29, n. 1.
[2] The word "Jesus" often appeared at the head of Luther's published works, apparently in keeping with St. Paul's admonition in Col. 3:17, "Whatever you do, in word or deed, do everything in the name of the Lord Jesus." *PE* 1, 25, n. 1.

crites, pretenders, and haughty saints, such as have their reward here [Matt. 6:2] and never please God. Thus God says to the Jews in Malachi 1[:10], "I have no pleasure in you; for who is there among you that would even as much as shut a door for me, willingly and out of love?"

2. Another result of many laws is that many sects and divisions in the congregations[3] arise from them. One adopts this way, another that, and there grows up in each man a false, secret love for his own sect, and a hatred, or at least a contempt for and a disregard of the other sects. Thus brotherly, free, and mutual love perishes and selfish love prevails. So Jeremiah [2:28] and Hosea [8:11], indeed, all the prophets, lament that the people of Israel divided themselves into as many sects as there were cities in the land, each desiring to outdo the others. Out of this [spirit] there arose also the Sadducees and Pharisees in the gospel.

So we observe today that through the spiritual law[4] very little justice and righteousness have arisen in Christendom. The world has been filled with fakes and hypocrites and with so many sects, orders, and divisions of the one people of Christ that almost every city is divided into ten parties or even more. And they daily devise new ways and methods (as they think) of serving God, until it has come to this, that priests, monks, and laity have become more hostile toward each other than Turks and Christians. Yes, there are deadly enemies among the priests and among the monks. They wrangle about their self-contrived ways and methods like fools and madmen, not only to the hindrance, but also to the very destruction of Christian love and unity. Each one clings to his sect and despises the others; and they regard the laymen as though they were no Christians at all. This lamentable condition is only a result of the laws.

3. Christ, in order to prepare for himself an acceptable and beloved people, which should be bound together in unity through love, abolished the whole law of Moses. And that he might not give further occasion for divisions and sects, he appointed in return but

---

[3] *Gemeinden,* i.e., parishes.
[4] *Geystliche gesetz* is Luther's customary term for the law of the church or "canon law."

one law or order for his entire people, and that was the holy mass. (For although baptism is also an external ordinance, yet it takes place but once, and is not a practice of the entire life, like the mass.) Henceforth, therefore, there is to be no other external order for the service of God except the mass. And where the mass is used, there is true worship; even though there be no other form, with singing, organ playing, bell ringing, vestments, ornaments, and gestures. For everything of this sort is an addition invented by men. When Christ himself first instituted this sacrament and held the first mass, there was no tonsure, no chasuble, no singing, no pageantry, but only thanksgiving to God and the use of the sacrament. According to this same simplicity the apostles and all Christians for a long time held mass, until there arose the various forms and additions, by which the Romans held mass one way, the Greeks another. And now it has finally come to this: the chief thing in the mass has been forgotten, and nothing is remembered except the additions of men!

4. Now the nearer our masses are to the first mass of Christ, the better they undoubtedly are; and the further from Christ's mass, the more dangerous. For that reason we may not boast of ourselves, over against the Russians or the Greeks, that we alone celebrate mass properly, any more than a priest who wears a red chasuble may boast over against him who wears one of white or black. For such external additions or differences may by their dissimilarity produce sects and dissension, but they can never make the mass better. Although I neither wish nor am able to displace or discard such additions, still, because such pompous forms are perilous, we must never permit ourselves to be led away by them from the simple institution of Christ and from the right use of the mass. And, indeed, the greatest and most useful art is to know what really and essentially belongs to the mass, and what is added and foreign to it. For where there is no clear distinction, the eyes and the heart are easily misled by such sham into a false impression and delusion. Then what men have contrived is considered the mass; and what the mass [really] is, is never experienced, to say nothing of deriving benefit from it. Thus alas! it is happening in our times. For I fear every day more than a thousand masses are said, of which perhaps not

81

one is a real mass. O dear Christians, to have many masses is not to have *the* mass. There is more to it than that.

5. If we desire to observe mass properly and to understand it, then we must surrender everything that the eyes behold and that the senses suggest—be it vestments, bells, songs, ornaments, prayers, processions, elevations, prostrations, or whatever happens in the mass—until we first grasp and thoroughly ponder the words of Christ, by which he performed and instituted the mass and commanded us to perform it. For therein lies the whole mass, its nature, work, profit, and benefit. Without the words nothing is derived from the mass.

Now the words are these: *Take and eat, this is my body, which is given for you. Take and drink of it, all of you, this is the cup of the new and eternal testament in my blood, which is poured out for you and for many for the forgiveness of sins.*[5] These words every Christian must have before him in the mass. He must hold fast to them as the chief part of the mass, in which even the right, basic, and good preparation for the mass and sacrament is taught, as we shall see.

6. If man is to deal with God and receive anything from him, it must happen in this manner, not that man begins and lays the first stone, but that God alone—without any entreaty or desire of man—must first come and give him a promise. This word of God is the beginning, the foundation, the rock, upon which afterward all works, words, and thoughts of man must build. This word man must gratefully accept. He must faithfully believe the divine promise and by no means doubt that it is and comes to pass just as God promises. This trust and faith is the beginning, middle, and end of all works and righteousness. For because man does God the honor of regarding and confessing him as true, he becomes to man a gracious God, who in turn honors man and regards and confesses him as true. Thus it is not possible that a man, of his own reason and strength, should by works ascend to heaven, anticipating God and moving

---

[5] Luther renders the Words of Institution generally after the manner of the canon of the mass (see the text in *LW* 36, 319), thus incorporating features from the several scriptural accounts: Matt. 26:26-28; Mark 14:22-24; Luke 22:19-20; and I Cor. 11:24-25. Cf. *LW* 36, 37, n. 84.

him to be gracious. On the contrary God must anticipate all [of man's] works and thoughts, and make a promise clearly expressed in words, which man then takes and keeps in a good, firm faith. Then there follows the Holy Spirit, who is given to man for the sake of this same faith.[6]

7. Such a promise was given to Adam after his fall, when God spoke to the serpent [Gen. 3:15], "I will put enmity between you and the woman, and between your seed and her seed; he shall bruise your head, and you shall bruise his heel." In these words, however obscurely, God promises help to human nature, namely, that by a woman the devil shall again be overcome. This promise of God sustained Adam and Eve and all their children until the time of Noah. They believed in it, and by this faith they were saved; otherwise they would have despaired.

Similarly, after the flood, God made a promise to Noah and his children [Gen. 9:9-11], until the time of Abraham [Gen. 12:1-3]. God summoned Abraham out of his fatherland and promised him that by his descendants all nations should be blessed [Gen. 22:18]. This promise Abraham believed and obeyed and thereby was justified and became a friend of God [Gen. 15:6]. In the same book this promise to Abraham is cited significantly and repeatedly, enlarged, and clarified, until Isaac is promised to him [Gen. 18:10-14], who was to be the seed from which Christ and every blessing should come. Abraham's children were kept in this faith in God's promise until the time of Christ, although in the meantime the promise was continually renewed and made more definite through David and many prophets. In the gospel [Luke 16:22] the Lord calls this promise "Abraham's bosom." For in it were kept all who, with a right faith, clung to this promise and, with Abraham, waited for Christ.

Then came Moses, who declared the same promise under many forms [figuren] in the law. Through him God promised the people of Israel the land of Canaan, while they were still in Egypt [Exod.

---

[6] Cf. Luther's recognition of the activity of the Holy Spirit in the believer even prior to faith, in his explanation to the third article of the Apostles' Creed in the Small Catechism.

3:6-8]. They believed this promise and by it they were sustained and led into that land.

8. In the New Testament, likewise, Christ made a promise or solemn vow, which we are to believe and thereby come to righteousness and salvation. This promise is the words just cited, where Christ says, "This is the cup of the New Testament."[7] These we shall now examine.

Not every vow is called a testament, but only a last irrevocable will of one who is about to die, whereby he bequeaths his goods, allotted and assigned to be distributed to whom he will. Just as St. Paul says to the Hebrews [9:16-17] that a testament must be made operative by death, and is not in effect while the one still lives who made the testament. For other vows, made as long as one lives, may be altered or recalled and hence are not called testaments. Therefore wherever in Scripture God's testament is referred to by the prophets, in that very word the prophets are taught that God would become man and die and rise again, in order that his word, in which he promises such a testament, might be fulfilled and confirmed. For if God is to make a testament, as he promises, then he must die; and if he is to die, then he must be a man. And so that little word "testament" is a short summary of all God's wonders and grace, fulfilled in Christ.

9. Christ also distinguishes this testament from others and says that it is a new and everlasting testament, in his own blood, for the forgiveness of sins; whereby he disannuls the old testament. For the little word "new" makes the testament of Moses obsolete and worthless, one that is no longer in effect. The old testament was a promise made through Moses to the people of Israel, to whom was promised the land of Canaan. For this testament God did not die, but the paschal lamb had to die instead of Christ and as a type of Christ. And so this was a temporal testament in the blood of the paschal lamb, which was shed for the obtaining and possessing of the land of Canaan. And as the paschal lamb, which died in the old testament for the land of Canaan, was a temporal and transitory thing, so too the old testament—together with that very possession

---

[7] Cf. Luke 22:20, I Cor. 11:25, and p. 82, n. 5.

or land of Canaan allotted and promised therein—was temporal and transitory.

But Christ, the true paschal lamb [I Cor. 5:7], is an eternal divine Person, who dies to ratify the new testament. Therefore the testament and the possessions therein bequeathed are eternal and abiding. And that is what he means when he contrasts this testament with the other. "A new testament," he says, so that the other may become obsolete [Heb. 8:13] and no longer be in effect. "An eternal[8] testament," he says, not temporal like that other one; not to dispose of temporal lands and possessions, but of eternal blessings. "In my blood," he says, not in the blood of a lamb [Heb. 9:12]. The purpose of all this is that the old should be altogether annulled and should give place to the new alone.

10. What then is this testament, or what is bequeathed to us in it by Christ? Truly a great, eternal, and unspeakable treasure, namely, the forgiveness of all sins, as the words plainly state, "This is the cup of a new eternal testament in my blood, which is poured out for you and for many for the forgiveness of sins."[9] It is as if Christ were saying, "See here, man, in these words I promise and bequeath to you forgiveness of all your sins and the life eternal. In order that you may be certain and know that such a promise remains irrevocably yours, I will die for it, and will give my body and blood for it, and will leave them both to you as a sign and seal, that by them you may remember me." As Christ says, "As often as you do this, remember me" [I Cor. 11:25]. Even as a man who bequeaths something stipulates also [in his will] what shall be done for him afterward—as is the custom at present in the requiems and masses for the dead—so also Christ has made a requiem for himself in this testament. Not that he needs it, but because it is necessary and profitable for us to remember him; we are thereby strengthened in faith, confirmed in hope, and made ardent in love. For as long as we live on earth our lot is such that the evil spirit and all the world assail us

---

[8] This nonscriptural adjective is from the text of the canon of the mass. Cf. p. 82, n. 5; and LW 36, 164 n. 35.
[9] Cf. p. 82, n. 5.

with joys and sorrows in order to extinguish our love for Christ, blot out our faith, and weaken our hope. Wherefore we urgently need this sacrament, in which we may gain new strength when we have grown weak and may daily exercise ourselves unto the strengthening and uplifting of the spirit.

11. In all his promises, moreover, in addition to the word, God has usually given a sign, for the greater assurance and strengthening of our faith. Thus he gave Noah the sign of the rainbow [Gen. 9:12-17]. To Abraham he gave circumcision as a sign [Gen. 17:11]. To Gideon he gave the rain on the ground and on the fleece [Judg. 6:36-40]. So we constantly find in the Scriptures many of these signs, given along with the promises. For in this way also worldly testaments are made; not only are the words written down, but seals and the marks of notaries are affixed, so that it may always be binding and authentic.

This is what Christ has done in this testament. He has affixed to the words a powerful and most precious seal and sign: his own true flesh and blood under the bread and wine. For we poor men, living as we do in our five senses, must always have along with the words at least one outward sign to which we may cling and around which we may gather—in such a way, however, that this sign may be a sacrament, that is, that it may be external and yet contain and signify something spiritual; in order that through the external we may be drawn into the spiritual, comprehending the external with the eyes of the body and the spiritual or inward with the eyes of the heart.

12. Now we see how many parts there are in this testament, or mass. There is, first, the testator who makes the testament, Christ. Second, the heirs to whom the testament is bequeathed, we Christians. Third, the testament itself, the words of Christ—when he says, "This is my body which is given for you. This is my blood which is poured out for you, a new eternal testament," etc.

Fourth, the seal or token is the sacrament, the bread and wine, under which are his true body and blood. For everything that is in this sacrament must be living. Therefore Christ did not put it in dead writing and seals, but in living words and signs which we use from day to day. And this is what is meant when the priest elevates the host, by which he addresses us rather than God. It is as if he were saying to us, "Behold, this is the seal and sign of the testament in which Christ has bequeathed to us the remission of all sins and eternal life." In agreement with this is also that which is sung by the choir, "Blessed be he who comes to us in the name of God,"[10] whereby we testify how [in the sacrament] we receive blessings from God, and do not sacrifice or give to God.

Fifth, there is the bequeathed blessing which the words signify, namely, remission of sins and eternal life. Sixth, the duty, remembrance, or requiem, which we are to do for Christ; that is, that we should preach his love and grace, hear and meditate upon it, and by it be incited and preserved unto love and hope in him. As St. Paul explains it in I Corinthians 11[:26], "As often as you eat this bread and drink this cup you proclaim the death of Christ." And this is what an earthly testator does, who bequeaths something to his heirs, that he may leave behind him a good name, the good will of men, and a blessed memory, that he should not be forgotten.

13. From all this it is now easily seen what the mass is, how one should prepare himself for it, how observe and how use it, and how many are the abuses of it. For just as one would act if ten thousand guldens were bequeathed to him by a good friend, so, and in even greater measure, we ought to conduct ourselves toward the mass. It is nothing else than an exceedingly rich and everlasting and good testament bequeathed to us by Christ himself, bequeathed in such a way that Christ would have no other reason to die except that he desired to make such a testament. So fervently desirous was he to pour out his eternal treasures, as he says, "With great desire I have desired to eat this passover with you before I die" [Luke 22:15]. This is also why it happens that in spite of so many masses we remain so blind and cold. For we do not know what the mass is, what we do in it, or what we get from it.

Since, then, the mass is nothing else than a testament, the first

---

[10] This line is from the Sanctus in the mass. Cf. Matt. 21:9.

and by far the best preparation for it is truly a hungry soul and a firm and joyful faith of the heart which accepts such a testament. Who would not go with great and joyful desire, hope, and comfort, and demand a thousand gulden, if he knew that at a certain place these had been bequeathed to him; especially if there were no other condition than that he remember, laud, and praise the testator? So in this matter, you must above all else take heed to your heart, that you believe the words of Christ, and admit their truth, when he says to you and to all, "This is my blood, a new testament, by which I bequeath you forgiveness of all sins and eternal life." How could you do him greater dishonor and show greater disrespect to the holy mass than by not believing, or by doubting? For he desired this to be so certain that he himself even died for it. Surely such doubt would be nothing else than denying and blaspheming Christ's sufferings and death, and every blessing which he has thereby obtained.

14. Everything depends, therefore, as I have said, upon the words of this sacrament. These are the words of Christ. Truly we should set them in pure gold and precious stones, keeping nothing more diligently before the eyes of our heart, so that faith may thereby be exercised. Let someone else pray, fast, go to confession, prepare himself for mass and the sacrament as he chooses. You do the same, but remember that this is all pure foolishness and self-deception, if you do not set before you the words of the testament and arouse yourself to believe and desire them. You would have to spend a long time polishing your shoes, preening[11] and primping to attain an inheritance, if you had no letter and seal with which you could prove your right to it. But if you have a letter and seal, and believe, desire, and seek it, it must be given to you, even though you were scaly, scabby, stinking, and most filthy.

So if you would receive this sacrament and testament worthily, see to it that you give emphasis to these living words of Christ, rely

---

[11] *Fedder ab leszen,* literally, "plucking feathers." In its proverbial usage the phrase implied fawning, adulation, currying favor; see Wander (ed.), *Sprichwörter-Lexikon,* I, 955, *"Federlesen."* Such usage is attested in Luther; see Grimm, *Deutsches Wörterbuch,* III, 1394.

on them with a strong faith, and desire what Christ has promised you in them; then it will be yours, then you will be worthy and well prepared. This faith and confidence must and will make you joyful and awaken a bold love for Christ, by means of which you will gladly begin to lead a really good life and with all your heart to flee from sin. For he who loves Christ will surely do what pleases him and will leave undone what does not please him. But who will love Christ unless he tastes the riches of this testament of Christ, bequeathed to poor sinners out of pure mercy and without cost? This taste comes by the faith which believes and trusts the testament and promise. If Abraham had not believed the promise of God, he would never have amounted to anything. Just as certainly, then, as Abraham, Noah, and David accepted and believed God's promises to them, so certainly must we also accept and believe this testament and promise.

15. Now there are two temptations which never cease to assail you. The first is that you are entirely unworthy of so rich a testament. The second is that, even if you were worthy, the blessing is so great that human nature is terrified by the very greatness; for what do not the forgiveness of all sins and eternal life bring with them? If either of these temptations comes to you, you must, as I have said,[12] value the words of Christ more than [your own] thoughts. He will not lie to you; but your own thoughts will deceive you.

Just as if a poor beggar, yes, even a scoundrel, were bequeathed a thousand gulden, he would not demand them because of his merit or worthiness or fail to claim them because of the size of the sum. Indeed if anyone should reproach him for his unworthiness or for the size of the sum, he would surely not let that sort of talk frighten him. He would simply say, "What is that to you? I know very well that I am unworthy of this inheritance. I am not demanding possession on my own merits, as though it had been due me, but on the favor and grace of the testator. If he has not thought it too much to bequeath it to me, why should I so run myself down as not to claim or take it?" So also with respect to the sacrament,

---

[12] Cf. pp. 12-18.

a timid and fainthearted conscience must rely, against its own thoughts, upon the testament of Christ and be daring in firm faith despite personal unworthiness and the greatness of the blessing. For this is precisely what makes it a divine testament, that it brings blessings so great to people so unworthy; God desires thereby to awaken love for him above all things. So Christ comforted those dejected ones who thought the blessing too great, and said, "Fainthearted little flock, fear not; it has pleased your Father to give you the eternal kingdom" [Luke 12:32].

16. But see what they have made of the mass! In the first place they have hidden these words of the testament and have taught that they are not to be spoken to the laity, that these are secret words to be spoken in the mass only by the priest. Has not the devil here in a masterly way stolen from us the chief thing in the mass and put it to silence? For who has ever heard it preached that one should give heed in the mass to these words of the testament and rely upon them with a firm faith? And yet this should have been the chief thing. Thus they have been afraid, and have taught us to be afraid, where there is no cause for fear,[13] indeed, where all our comfort and safety lie.

How many miserable consciences, which perished from fear and sorrow, could have been comforted and rescued by these words! What devil has told them that the words which should be the most familiar, the most openly spoken among all Christians—among priests and laity, men and women, young and old—are to be hidden in greatest secrecy? How should it be possible for us to know what the mass is, or how to use and observe it, if we are not to know the words in which the very mass consists.[14]

But would to God that we Germans could say mass in German and sing these "most secret" words loudest of all! Why should not we Germans say mass in our own language, when the Latins, Greeks and many others observe mass in their language? Why should we not also keep secret the words of baptism, "I baptize you in the name

---

[13] Luther's rendering of Ps. 14:5 is based on the Vulgate (13:5).
[14] *Steht und geht.*

of the Father and of the Son and of the Holy Spirit. Amen"? [Matt. 28:19]. If everyone may speak in German, and aloud, these words, which are no less the holy word and promise of God, why should not everyone also be permitted to hear and speak aloud and in German those words of the mass?

17. Let us learn, then, that in every promise[15] of God there are two things which one must consider: the word and the sign. As in baptism there are the words of the baptizer and the dipping in water,[16] so in the mass there are the words and the bread and wine. The words are the divine vow, promise, and testament. The signs are the sacraments, that is, sacred signs. Now as the testament is much more important than the sacrament, so the words are much more important than the signs. For the signs might well be lacking, if only one has the words; and thus without sacrament, yet not without testament, one might be saved. For I can enjoy the sacrament in the mass every day if only I keep before my eyes the testament, that is, the words and promise of Christ, and feed and strengthen my faith on them.

We see, then, that the best and greatest part of all sacraments and of the mass is the words and promise of God, without which the sacraments are dead and are nothing at all, like a body without a soul, a cask without wine, a purse without money, a type without a fulfilment, a letter without the spirit, a sheath without a knife, and the like. Wherefore it is true that when we use, hear, or see the mass without the words or testament, and pay attention only to the sacrament and sign, we are not observing the mass even halfway. For sacrament without testament is a keeping of the case without the jewel, a quite one-sided separation and division.

18. I fear, therefore, that there is at present more idolatry in Christendom through the mass than ever occurred among the Jews. For we hear nowhere that the mass is directed toward the feeding and strengthening of faith, for which alone it was established by Christ. Instead it is observed only as a sacrament without testament.

---

[15] *Gelübde*, literally, "vow."
[16] On the mode of baptism, see p. 29.

Many have written of the fruits of the mass,[17] and indeed have greatly exalted them; nor do I question the value of these fruits. But see to it that you regard them all, compared to this one thing, as the body compared to the soul. God has here prepared for our faith a pasture, a table, and a feast; but faith is not fed except on the word of God alone. Therefore you must pay attention above all else to the words, exalt them, highly treasure them, and hold fast to them. Then you will have not simply the little drops of blessing[18] that drip from the mass, but the very fountainhead of faith, from which springs and flows every blessing. It is as the Lord says in John 4, "He who believes in me, out of his heart shall flow rivers of living water"; and, "Whoever drinks of the water that I shall give him will never thirst; it will become in him a spring of living water welling up to eternal life."[19] So we see that the first abuse of the mass is this, that we have lost the chief blessing, namely, the testament and faith. We shall also see what consequences this has now had.

19. It must necessarily follow where faith and the word or promise of God decline or are neglected, that in their place there arise works and a false, presumptuous trust in them. For where there is no promise of God there is no faith. Where there is no faith, there everyone presumptuously undertakes to better himself and make himself well pleasing to God by means of works. Where this happens, false security and presumption arise, as though man were pleasing to God because of his own works. Where it does not hap-

---

[17] The term "fruits of the mass" had reference not to that which the priest created and the communicant received, but simply to those blessings—both spiritual and material, for the dead as well as the living—which came simply through a devotional hearing of the mass. Numerous fixed catalogues, listing anywhere from six to twelve distinct "fruits" were known in Latin as far back as the thirteenth century. German catalogues based on them and dating from the fourteenth century introduced a poetic form and were frequently incorporated directly into the mass books and dealt with in sermons. The text of many of these formularies—in which faith is occasionally mentioned, far down in the list—together with a critique of their excessive claims and unjustified citing of authorities is given in Adolph Franz, *Die Messe im deutschen Mittelalter* (Freiburg im Breisgau: Herder, 1902), pp. 36-72.

[18] *Tropffrüchtlein.*

[19] Luther's double citation is from John 7:38 and 4:14.

pen, the conscience has no rest and knows not what to do in order to become well pleasing to God.

So too, I fear that many have made the mass into a good work, whereby they have thought to do a great service to Almighty God. Now if we have properly understood what has been said above, namely, that the mass is nothing else than a testament and sacrament in which God makes a pledge to us and gives us grace and mercy, I think it is not fitting that we should make a good work or merit out of it. For a testament is not *beneficium acceptum, sed datum;*[20] it does not take benefit from us, but brings benefit to us. Who has ever heard that he who receives an inheritance has done a good work? He simply takes for himself a benefit. Likewise in the mass we give nothing to Christ, but only receive from him; unless they are willing to call this a good work, that a person sits still and permits himself to be benefited, given food and drink, clothed and healed, helped and redeemed. Just as in baptism, in which there is also a divine testament and sacrament, no one gives God anything or does him a service, but instead takes something, so it is in all other sacraments[21] and in the sermon as well. For if one sacrament cannot be a meritorious good work, then no other can be a work either, since the sacraments are all of one kind, and it is the nature of a sacrament or testament that it is not a work but only an exercise of faith.

20. It is true, indeed, that when we come together to the mass to receive the testament and sacrament, and to nourish and strengthen faith, we there offer our prayer with one accord. (This prayer for the increase of faith, arising out of that very faith, is truly a good work.) We also distribute alms to the poor, as was done long ago when the Christians gathered food and other necessities which, after the mass, were distributed to the needy, as we learn from St.

---

[20] Not "a benefit received but a benefit conferred."

[21] The system of seven sacraments had been made official doctrine by the Council of Florence, 1439. In a letter to Spalatin of December 18, 1519, Luther wrote: "I esteem none of the others [besides baptism, Lord's Supper, and penance] as a sacrament." Ten months later only two of the three were still retained. Cf. *LW* 36, 7, 109, 124. Cf. also Luther's designation of baptism and the bread as "the two principal sacraments" as early as December, 1519, in this volume, p. 67.

Paul in I Corinthians 11.[22] But this work and prayer are quite another thing from the testament and sacrament, which no one can
offer or give either to God or to men. Rather every one takes and
receives of it for himself only, in proportion as he believes and
trusts. Now just as I cannot give or receive the sacrament of baptism, of penance, of extreme unction in any one's stead or for his
benefit, but I accept for myself alone the blessing therein offered
by God—and here there is no *officium* but *beneficium,* no work or
service but reception and benefit alone—so also no one can observe
or hear mass for another, but each one for himself alone. For there
is nothing there but a taking and receiving.

This is all easily understood, if one only considers what the
mass really is, namely, a testament and a sacrament. It is God's
word or promise, together with a sacred sign, the bread and the
wine under which Christ's flesh and blood are truly present. For by
what process of reasoning could a man be said to do a good work
for another when, like the others, he [himself] comes as one in need
and takes to himself the words and sign of God, in which God
promises and grants him grace and help? Surely, to receive God's
word, sign, and grace is not to give away something good or do a
good work, but simply to take for oneself.

21. Now since almost everyone has made out of the mass a sacrifice which they offer to God—which, without doubt, is the third and
very worst abuse—we must clearly distinguish here between what we
offer and what we do not offer in the mass.

The word "offering" has undoubtedly come into the mass and
remained until now because in the times of the apostles—when some
of the practices of the Old Testament were still observed—the Christians gathered food, money, and necessities which, as I have already
said, were distributed to the needy in connection with the mass. For
so we read in Acts 4[:34-35], that the Christians sold all they had
and brought it to the feet of the apostles, who then had it distributed,
out of the common possessions giving to each what he needed. Even
so the Apostle Paul teaches that all food and whatever we use should
be blessed with prayer and the word of God, and thanks for these

---

[22] I Cor. 11:21, 33; cf. Acts 2:44-46.

things be given to God [I Tim. 4:4-5]. Hence we say the *Benedicite* and the *Gratias*[23] at table. Such was the custom of the Old Testament, that when men thanked God for gifts received they lifted them up in their hands to God, as is written in the law of Moses.[24] This is why the apostles also lifted up [the offerings] in this way, thanked God, and blessed with the word of God the food and whatever else the Christians had gathered. And Christ himself, as St. Luke[25] writes, lifted up the cup, gave thanks to God, drank of it, and gave to the others, before he instituted the sacrament and testament.

22. Three traces of this usage have survived. First, the opening and closing prayers of the mass are called "collects," that is, "collections." This indicates that these prayers were spoken as a "blessing" and "thanksgiving" over the food which had been gathered, to bless it and to give thanks to God according to the teaching of St. Paul [I Tim. 4:4-5]. Second, after the Gospel the people still proceed to the offering, from which the chant that is sung at the time is called "offertory," that is, an offering. Third, the priest elevates in the paten and offers to God the unconsecrated host at the same time that the offertory is being sung and the people are making their offering. This shows that what is being offered to God by us is not the sacrament, but only these "collects" and offerings of food and goods that have been gathered, that God is being thanked for them, and they are being blessed for distribution to all the needy.

Then when the priest afterward in the secret mass[26] elevates

---

[23] Cf. "Blessing and Thanksgiving at Table" in Appendix II of the Small Catechism.

[24] Cf. Num. 18:30, 32 (KJV). Luther is referring to the root meaning of the common Old Testament word for "heave-offering": *rum* means in Hebrew "to lift." Scholars doubt, though, that the *terumah* or "heave-offering" implied a rite of "elevation"; it did involve the lifting out or taking away from a larger quantity for a special purpose. James Hastings (ed.), *A Dictionary of the Bible* (New York: Scribner's, 1900), III, 588.

[25] Cf. Luke 22:17.

[26] Cf. pp. 90-91, 106. The canon of the mass, the invariable part of the liturgy of the mass in which the elements were consecrated, was read in a whisper by the priest. Luther translated and criticized it in *The Abomination of the Secret Mass* (1525). *LW* 36, 307-328.

the consecrated host and cup, he does not say a word about the sacrifice, although at this point above all he should make mention of the sacrifice, if the mass were a sacrifice. But, as I have said above,[27] he elevates it not toward God but toward us, to remind us of the testament and to incite us to faith in that testament. In the same way, when he receives or administers the sacrament, he does not mention the sacrifice by a single word, which must and should be done if the sacrament were a sacrifice. Therefore the mass dare not and cannot be or be called a sacrifice because of the sacrament, but only because of the food which is gathered and the prayer in which God is thanked and the food is blessed.

23. Today the custom of gathering food and money at the mass has fallen into disuse, and not more than a trace of it remains in the offering of a pfennig at the high festivals, and especially at Easter, when cakes, meat, eggs, and so forth are still brought to the church to be blessed.[28] In place of such offerings and collections, endowed churches, monastic houses, and charitable institutions have now been erected. These were supposed to be maintained for just one purpose, that the needy in every city would be given all they require, so that there would be no beggars or poverty-stricken persons among the Christians, but that each and all would have from the mass enough for body and soul.

But [today] all this is reversed. Just as the mass is not properly explained to men, but is understood as a sacrifice and not as a testament, so, correspondingly, that which is and ought to be the offering —namely, the possessions of the churches and monastic houses—is never offered; neither are they given, with thanksgiving to God and with his blessing, to the needy who ought to be receiving them. This is also why God is provoked to anger and permits the possessions of the churches and monastic houses to become the occasion of war, of worldly pomp, and of such abuse that no other blessing is

---

[27] See p. 87.
[28] Easter was a time of particular joy since it meant the end of the strict Lenten fast. The prohibited foods were brought to the church for special blessing to insure that their renewed consumption after so long an abstinence would work for good rather than ill in both body and soul. Cf. p. 131, n. 2; cf. also Adolph Franz, *Die kirchlichen Benediktionen im Mittelalter* (Freiburg im Breisgau: Herder, 1902), I, 575-576.

so shamefully and blasphemously treated and destroyed. And since it does not serve the poor, for whom it was intended, it is indeed fitting and proper that it should remain unworthy to serve any other purpose but that of sin and shame.

24. Now if you ask what is left in the mass to give it the name of a sacrifice, since so much is said in the office about the sacrifice, I answer: Nothing is left. For, to be brief and to the point, we must let the mass be a sacrament and testament; it is not and cannot be a sacrifice any more than the other sacraments—baptism, confirmation, penance, extreme unction, etc.[29]—are sacrifices. Otherwise we should lose the gospel, Christ, the comfort [of the sacrament], and every grace of God. Therefore we must separate the mass clearly and distinctly from the prayers and ceremonies which have been added to it by the holy fathers. We must keep these two as far apart as heaven and earth, so that the mass may remain nothing else than the testament and sacrament comprehended in the words of Christ.

What there is over and beyond these words, we are to regard—in comparison with the words of Christ—in the same way that we regard the monstrance[30] and the corporal[31] in comparison with the host and the sacrament itself. Such furnishings we simply consider as additions for the reverent and fitting administration of the sacrament. Now just as we regard the monstrance, corporal, and altar cloths as compared with the sacrament, so we are to look upon all added words, works, and ceremonies of the mass in comparison with the words of Christ in which he gives and institutes this testament. For if the mass or sacrament were a sacrifice, we would have to say that it is a mass and sacrifice when the sacrament is brought to the sick in their home, or when those in health receive it in the church; and we would have to say that there are as many masses and sacrifices as the number of those who partake of the sacrament. If in this case it is not a sacrifice, how then is it a sacrifice in the hand of the priest? For it is still one and the same sacrament, one and

---

[29] See p. 93, n. 21.

[30] In this receptacle the consecrated host is shown to the people.

[31] The corporal is the linen cloth spread over the altar during the communion service, on which are set the communion vessels.

the same use, one and the same benefit. And in all respects it is the same sacrament and testament with all of us.

25. We should, therefore, give careful heed to this word "sacrifice," so that we do not presume to give God something in the sacrament, when it is he who in it gives us all things. We should bring spiritual sacrifices, since the external sacrifices have ceased and have been changed into the gifts to churches, monastic houses, and charitable institutions. What sacrifices, then, are we to offer? Ourselves, and all that we have, with constant prayer, as we say, "Thy will be done, on earth as it is in heaven" [Matt. 6:10]. With this we are to yield ourselves to the will of God, that he may make of us what he will, according to his own pleasure. In addition we are to offer him praise and thanksgiving with our whole heart, for his unspeakable, sweet grace and mercy, which he has promised and given us in this sacrament. And although such a sacrifice occurs apart from the mass, and should so occur—for it does not necessarily and essentially belong to the mass, as has been said[32]—yet it is more precious, more appropriate, more mighty, and also more acceptable when it takes place with the multitude and in the assembly, where men encourage, move, and inflame one another to press close to God and thereby attain without any doubt what they desire.

For Christ has so promised: where two are gathered in his name, there he is in the midst of them; and where two agree on earth about anything they ask, everything that they ask shall be done [Matt. 18:20, 19]. How much more shall they obtain what they ask when a whole city comes together to praise God and to pray with one accord! We would not need many indulgence letters if we proceeded properly in this matter. Souls would also be easily redeemed from purgatory[33] and innumerable blessings would follow. But,

---

[32] Cf. p. 91.

[33] Coupled with Luther's earlier affirmation of 1518, "I am positive that there is a purgatory" (*LW* 31, 126), was his insistence—already at that time—that "every matter concerning the souls in purgatory is most obscure" (*LW* 31, 141), and that therefore—by 1521—"those who do not believe in purgatory are not to be called heretics" (*LW* 32, 96). His first specific treatise on the subject, *Widerruf vom Fegefeuer* (1530) (*WA* 30[II], 367-390), was a refutation of the traditional arguments in support of the doctrine.

alas! that is not the way things are going. Everything is reversed. What the mass is intended to do, we take upon ourselves to do; and what we ought to be doing, we turn over to the mass to do. All this is the work of unlearned and false preachers.

26. To be sure this sacrifice of prayer, praise, and thanksgiving, and of ourselves as well, we are not to present before God in our own person. But we are to lay· it upon Christ and let him present it for us, as St. Paul teaches in Hebrews 13[:15], "Let us continually offer up a sacrifice of praise to God, that is, the fruit of lips that confess him and praise him"; and all this "through Christ." For this is why he is also a priest—as Psalm 110[:4] says, "You are a priest for ever after the order of Melchizedek"—because he intercedes for us in heaven. He receives our prayer and sacrifice, and through himself, as a godly priest, makes them pleasing to God. Again St. Paul says in Hebrews 9[:24], "He has ascended into heaven to be a mediator in the presence of God on our behalf"; and in Romans 8[:34], "It is Christ Jesus, who died, yes, who was raised from the dead, who sits on the right hand of God, who also makes intercession for us."

From these words we learn that we do not offer Christ as a sacrifice, but that Christ offers us. And in this way it is permissible, yes, profitable, to call the mass a sacrifice; not on its own account, but because we offer ourselves as a sacrifice along with Christ. That is, we lay ourselves on Christ by a firm faith in his testament and do not otherwise appear before God with our prayer, praise, and sacrifice except through Christ and his mediation. Nor do we doubt that Christ is our priest or minister in heaven before God. Such faith, truly, brings it to pass that Christ takes up our cause, presents us and our prayer and praise, and also offers himself for us in heaven. If the mass were so understood and for this reason called a sacrifice, it would be well. Not that we offer the sacrament, but that by our praise, prayer, and sacrifice we move him and give him occasion to offer himself for us in heaven and ourselves with him. It is as if I were to say, I had brought a king's son to his father as an offering, when actually I had done no more than induce that son to present my need and petition to the king and made the son my mediator.

27. Few, however, understand the mass in this way. For they suppose that only the priest offers the mass as a sacrifice before God. Actually this is done and should be done by everyone who receives the sacrament—yes, also by those who are present at the mass but do not receive the sacrament. Furthermore such an offering of sacrifice every Christian may make, wherever he is and at all times, as St. Paul says [Heb. 13:15], "Let us continually offer up a sacrifice of praise through him," and Psalm 110[:4], "You are a priest for ever." If he is a priest for ever, then he is at all times a priest and is offering sacrifices without ceasing before God. But we cannot be continually the same; therefore the mass has been instituted that we may there come together and offer such sacrifice in common.

Now whoever understands the mass otherwise or would use it otherwise than as a testament and sacrifice of this kind, let him take heed how he understands it. I understand it, as has been said, to be really nothing else than this: we receive the testament and at the same time we admonish ourselves to be intent upon strengthening our faith and not to doubt that Christ in heaven is our priest, that he offers himself for us without ceasing, and presents us and our prayer and praise, making all these acceptable. It is just as if I wished to offer the physical, earthly priest as a sacrifice in the mass and to appoint him to present my need and my praise of God, and he were to give me a token[34] that he would do it. Just as in this case I would be offering the priest as a sacrifice, so it is that I also offer Christ, in that I desire and believe that he accepts me and my prayer and praise and presents it to God in his own person. And in order to strengthen this faith of mine he gives me a token that he will do it. This token is the sacrament of bread and wine. Thus it becomes clear that it is not the priest alone who offers the sacrifice of the mass; it is this faith which each one has for himself. This is the true priestly office, through which Christ is offered as a sacrifice to God, an office which the priest, with the outward ceremonies of

---

[34] *Zeichen*, literally, "sign."

the mass, simply represents. Each and all are, therefore, equally spiritual priests before God.[35]

28. From this you can see for yourself that there are many who observe the mass and make this sacrifice properly, yet themselves know nothing about it. Indeed they do not realize that they are priests and can hold mass. Again there are many who take great pains and who apply themselves with all diligence, thinking that they are observing the mass quite well and making sacrifice properly; and yet there is nothing right about it. For all those who have the faith that Christ is a priest for them in heaven before God, and who lay on him their prayers and praise, their need and their whole selves, presenting them through him, not doubting that he does this very thing, and offers himself for them—these people take the sacrament and testament, outwardly or spiritually, as a token of all this, and do not doubt that all sin is there forgiven, that God has become their gracious Father, and that everlasting life is prepared for them.

All such, then, wherever they may be, are true priests. They truly observe the mass aright and also obtain by it what they desire. For faith must do everything. Faith alone is the true priestly office. It permits no one else to take its place. Therefore all Christian men are priests, all women priestesses, be they young or old, master or servant, mistress or maid, learned or unlearned. Here there is no difference, unless faith be unequal. On the other hand all who do not have such faith but who presume to make much of the mass as a sacrifice, and perform this office before God, are anointed idols. They simply observe the mass outwardly and do not themselves know what they are doing. They cannot be well pleasing to God, for without true faith it is impossible to please him at all, as St. Paul says in Hebrews 11[:6]. Now there are many who, hidden in their hearts, have such true faith and do not themselves know about it. And there are many who do not have such true faith; and of this, too, they are unaware.

29. Now we may ask: In view of the fact that it has become a widespread custom to institute masses for the dead—indeed many

---

[35] Cf. Rev. 1:6; 5:10. I Pet. 2:9.

101

books have been written about it—of what benefit are the masses celebrated for the souls in purgatory? The answer is: Be the custom what it may, God's word must take priority and stand firm, namely, that the mass is nothing else than a testament and sacrament of God and cannot be a good work or a sacrifice, although it may be received in connection with the sacrifice and good works, as was said above.

There is no doubt, therefore, that whoever observes mass the best he knows how, without this faith we have just described, benefits neither himself nor anyone else. For the sacrament in itself, without faith, does nothing. Yes, God himself, who indeed does all things, does and can do good to no one who does not firmly believe in him; how much less can the sacrament. It is easy to say that a mass is effective whether it be performed by a pious or a wicked priest, that it is acceptable *opere operati*, not *opere operantis*.[36] But to produce no other argument except that many people say this, and that this has become the custom, is poor proof of its correctness. Many have praised·pleasures and riches and have grown accustomed to them, yet this does not make them right. We should adduce arguments from Scripture or reason as well. Therefore let us be careful not to take the matter lightly. I cannot conceive that the institution of so many masses and requiems can be without abuse, especially since all this is done as good works and sacrifices by which to recompense God, whereas in the mass there is nothing else than the reception and enjoyment of divine grace, promised and given us in his testament and sacrament.

30. I will gladly agree that the faith which I have called the true priestly office is truly able to do all things in heaven, earth, hell, and purgatory; and to this faith no one can ascribe too much. It is this faith, I say, which makes us all priests and priestesses. Through it, in connection with the sacrament, we offer ourselves, our need, prayer, praise, and thanksgiving in Christ and through Christ; and thereby we offer Christ to God, that is, we move Christ and give him occasion to offer himself for us and to offer us with himself.

---

[36] Cf. p. 63, nn. 37, 38; and p. 64, n. 39.

And as I have said above,[37] if Christ promises to two persons [Matt. 18:19] the answers to all their prayers, how much more may so many obtain from him [in the mass] what they desire!

I know very well that some will be frivolous and call me a heretic in this matter. But, my dear fellow, you should also consider whether you can prove as easily as you can slander. I have read all that, and I know the books on which you rely. So you need not think that I do not know your art. But I say that your art has no foundation and that you cannot defend it. You will never make out of a sacrament or testament of God a sacrifice or work of satisfaction; indeed satisfaction itself is more of a human than a divine law.[38]

Therefore my advice is, let us hold fast to that which is sure and let the uncertain go.[39] That is, if we would help these poor [departed] souls[40] or anyone else, let us not take the risk of relying upon the mass as a sufficient work. Rather let us come together in the mass and with priestly faith[41] present every urgent need, in Christ and with Christ, praying for the souls [of the departed], and not doubting that we will be heard. Thus we may be sure that the soul is redeemed. For the faith which rests on the promise of Christ never deceives or fails.

31. So we read that St. Monica, the mother of St. Augustine,

---

[37] Cf. p. 98.

[38] See the Introduction to *The Sacrament of Penance*, in this volume, pp. 5-8. Cf. C. M. Jacobs' "Introduction to the Ninety-five Theses," *PE* 1, 18-20. In the letter to Johannes Staupitz which accompanied the theses, Luther insists that on the part of the papists "the doctrine of true penitence was passed by, and they presumed to praise not even that poorest part of penitence which is called 'satisfaction.'" *PE* 1, 41.

[39] *Lasst uns des gewissen spielen und das ungewisse farenn.* Luther used this German equivalent of Augustine's *Tene certum, dimitte incertum* in a sense analogous to that in which he often cited a favorite fable from Aesop about the dog who dropped the meat from his mouth for the sake of a mere reflection upon the water. Ernst Thiele, *Luthers Sprichwörtersammlung* (Weimar: Böhlaus, 1900), No. 33.

[40] In his translation, J. J. Schindel here inserted the words, "in purgatory." *PE* 1, 318.

[41] Cf. p. 101.

desired on her deathbed to be remembered in the mass.[42] If the mass were sufficient of itself to help everyone, what need would there be for faith and prayer? But you might say: If this is true, then anyone might observe mass and offer such a sacrifice, even in the open fields; for anyone may indeed have such a faith in Christ in the open fields, and offer and commit to him his prayer, praise, need, and cause, to bring it before God in heaven; besides he may also think of the sacrament and testament and may heartily desire it, and in this way receive it spiritually (for he who desires it and believes, receives it spiritually, as St. Augustine teaches)[43]—what need is there then to observe mass in the church?

I answer: It is true, such faith is enough and truly accomplishes everything. But how could you think of this faith, sacrifice, sacrament, and testament if it were not visibly administered in certain designated places and churches? The same is true in the case of baptism and absolution: although faith is sufficient without them, where nothing more can be done, still, if they never existed anywhere, who could think of them and believe in them or who could know or say anything about them? Moreover since God has instituted this sacrament, we must not despise it, but receive it with great reverence, praise, and gratitude. For if there were no other reason why we should observe mass outwardly and not be satisfied with inward faith alone, then this is reason enough, that God so instituted and wills it. And his will ought to please us above all things and should be sufficient reason to do or to omit anything.

There is also this advantage: since we are still living in the flesh and are not all so perfect as to govern ourselves in spirit, we need actually to come together, by example, prayer, praise, and thanksgiving to enkindle in one another such a faith, as I have said

---

[42] Born of Christian parents, *ca.* 332, Monica was privileged shortly before her death (387) to see her apostate son converted and baptized. Augustine, who became the greatest of all the Latin Church fathers, in his *Confessions,* IX, 11, records her last words, "Bury this body anywhere. Let its care give you no concern. One thing only do I ask of you, that you remember me at the altar of the Lord, wherever you may be." Vernon J. Bourke (trans.), Roy J. Deferrari's (ed.) *Saint Augustine: Confessions* ("The Fathers of the Church Series," Vol. XXI [New York: Fathers of the Church, Inc., 1953]), p. 254.

[43] *Sermo* 112, cap. 5. Migne 38, 645.

above,[44] and through the outward seeing and receiving of the sacrament and testament to move each other to the increase of this faith. There are many saints who, like St. Paul the Hermit,[45] remained for years in the desert without the mass and yet were never without it. But such a high spiritual example cannot be imitated by everyone or by the whole church.

32. But the chief reason for holding mass outwardly is the word of God, which no one can do without. It must be used and inculcated daily, not only because Christians are born, baptized, and trained every day, but because we live in the midst of the world, the flesh, and the devil, who do not cease to assail [anfechten] us and drive us into sin. Against these the most powerful weapon is the holy word of God, which even St. Paul calls "a spiritual sword" [Eph. 6:17], which is powerful against all sin. This is shown by the fact that the Lord, when he instituted the mass, said, "Do this in remembrance of me" [I Cor. 11:24-25], as if he were saying, "As often as you use this sacrament and testament you shall be preaching of me." As St. Paul also says in I Corinthians 11[:26], "As often as you eat this bread and drink this cup you preach and proclaim the Lord's death until he comes"; and Psalm 102[:21-22], "They shall declare in Zion the glory of the Lord, and in Jerusalem his praise, as often as the kings (that is, the bishops and rulers) and the people gather together to worship the Lord"; and Psalm 111[:4-5], "He has caused his wonderful works to be remembered in that he has provided food for all those who fear him."

In these passages you see how the mass was instituted to preach and praise Christ, to glorify his sufferings and all his grace and goodness, so that we may be moved to love him, to hope and believe in him, and thus, in addition to this word or sermon, to receive an outward sign, that is, the sacrament; to the end that our faith, provided with and confirmed by divine words and signs, may thereby become strong against all sin, suffering, death, and hell, and every-

---

[44] Cf. p. 98.
[45] Paul of Thebes, an Egyptian hermit of the third century, was long regarded as the first of the Christian hermits on the basis of a biography written ca. 376 by Jerome: Vita S. Pauli primi eremitae. Migne, 23, 17-28.

thing that is against us. And had there been no preaching, Christ would never have instituted the mass. He is more concerned about the word than about the sign. For the preaching ought to be nothing but an explanation of the words of Christ, when he instituted the mass and said, "This is my body, this is my blood," etc.[46] What is the whole gospel but an explanation of this testament? Christ has gathered up the whole gospel in a short summary with the words of this testament or sacrament. For the gospel is nothing but a proclamation of God's grace and of the forgiveness of all sins, granted us through the sufferings of Christ, as St. Paul proves in Romans 10 and as Christ says in Luke 24[:46-47]. And this same thing, as we have seen, is contained in the words of this testament.

33. From this we can see what a pity and perversion it is that so many masses are said and yet nothing at all is said of the gospel. They stand up and preach and give the poor souls chaff instead of grain, yes, death instead of life, intending afterward to make up for it with the number of masses. What sort of baptism would that be, if the baptizer simply poured water on the child and said not a word? I fear that the holy words of the testament are read so secretly, and kept so hidden from the laity,[47] because God in his wrath is thereby indicating that the whole gospel is no longer publicly preached to the people, that even as the summary of the gospel is hidden, so also has its public explanation ceased.

Next they took entirely from us one element, the wine,[48] though this does not matter much, since the word is more important than the sign; still I should like to know who gave them the power to do such a thing. In the same way they might take from us the other element and give us the empty monstrance to kiss as a relic and at last abolish everything that Christ has instituted. I fear it is a figure and a type that signifies nothing good in these perilous and perverted latter days. It is said that the pope has the power to do it. I say that is all fiction. The pope does not have a hair's breadth of power to change what Christ has made; and whatever of these things he

---

[46] Cf. p. 82, n. 5.
[47] Cf. p. 95, n. 26.
[48] Cf. p. 49, n. 3.

changes, that he does as a tyrant and Antichrist. I should like to hear how they will defend themselves.

Not that I should like to cause turmoil over this issue, for I regard the word as mightier than the sign; still I cannot stand for such an outrage. They not only do us wrong, but in addition insist that it is right. They force us not only to permit such a wrong, but also to praise it as right and good. Let them do what they will, so long as we are not obliged to acknowledge wrong as right. It is enough that we permit ourselves, with Christ, to be struck on the cheek [John 18:22-23]; but we do not have to praise it as though in striking us they had done well and earned God's reward.

34. But what about those poor priests and laymen who have departed so far from the true meaning of the mass and faith that they have even made it into a kind of magic? Some have masses said in order to become rich and prosperous in business; some, because they think that if they hear mass in the morning they will be safe during the day from all danger and want; some on account of sickness; others for still more foolish, yes, even sinful reasons.[49] Yet they all find priests perverted enough to take their money and do their bidding.

Furthermore they have now made one mass better than another. One is valued as useful for this, another for that. Thus they have made seven "golden masses."[50] The "mass of the holy cross" has

---

[49] Exaggerations and falsehoods concerning the "fruits of the mass" contributed to the wild excesses in popular faith and expectation. The mass was reduced to a mere rescue operation for use in case of sickness or need and a means of warding off all kinds of trouble. See p. 92, n. 17; see also the satirical poem cited in Franz, *Die Messe*, p. 72.

[50] The masses held for the Blessed Virgin in Hildesheim (modern territory of Lower Saxony) in connection with a week-long celebration beginning on the second Sunday after St. Michael's Day were, "on account of its magnificence," called "golden." Du Cange, *Glossarium mediae et infimae latinitatis* (Paris, 1844), IV, 435 (article *"Missa Aurea"*). This particular mass for time of special need was peculiar in having among other things seven distinct alternatives for its variable component parts, such as the collect. The power of the golden mass resided in the frequent mention of the mystery of the incarnation —the repetition of the phrase, "and the word became flesh"—and was believed to be so great that if such a thing were possible the very incarnation of Christ could by it be prayed into existence. See the text in Franz, *Die Messe*, pp. 282-286.

come to have a different virtue from the "mass of Our Lady."[51] In this matter they all keep silent and permit the people to go on for the sake of the cursed, filthy pfennigs which, through these various titles and virtues of the mass, keep piling up. So must faith, like Christ, be sold by its Judas [Matt. 26:14-16], that is, by covetousness and the thirst for money.

Some are also to be found who have mass said privately[52] for this and for that. In short the mass must do all kinds of things, except its own distinctive work, namely, faith—to which no one pays any attention. Those now are the best people on earth who have many masses said, as though they thought thereby to lay up many good works. All of this is the work of that arrogance which does nqt separate the hymns and prayers which have been added, from the true and original mass. For one mass is like another, and there is no difference except in faith. For the mass is best to him who believes most, and it serves only to increase faith, and for nothing else. True, indeed, the added prayers do serve one purpose or another, according to the meaning of their words. But they are not mass or sacrament.

35. I would advise then that where the masses are not directed toward such faith they be abolished and that there be fewer masses endowed for the souls of the dead. Truly we provoke God to anger more than we conciliate him with such masses. To what purpose are the priests in the chapter houses and cloisters so strictly bound to observe the annual masses?[53] They must not only be lacking in such faith but also be often personally unfit. Christ himself did not desire to bind anyone to such a practice. He left us wholly free when he said, "Do this, as often as you do it, in remembrance of me" [I Cor.

---

[51] In an article tracing the development of Mariology, Herbert Thurston notes in the later middle ages "the almost universal custom of leaving legacies to have a Mary-Mass, or Mass of Our Lady, celebrated daily at a particular altar." *The Catholic Encyclopedia*, XV, 464. The various Passion masses were distinguished from those devoted to the joys and sorrows of Mary. "The mass of the five wounds of Christ," e.g., was supposed to impart forty days indulgence for mortal sins and a full year's indulgence for venial sins. Franz, *Die Messe*, pp. 155-168.

[52] *Unter dem altertuch*, literally, "under the altar cloth."

[53] Annual masses were those said daily for a year. Du Cange, *op. cit.*, IV, 435 (article *"Missa Annualis"*).

11:25]. And we men bind ourselves so tightly and drive ourselves against our own conscience. I see too that such an endowed mass often has no valid basis, but that a secret greed underlies the obligation. So we burden ourselves with many masses in order that we may have sufficient income in temporal things. Afterward we say that we do it for God's sake. I fear that few would be found who would thus, gratuitously and for God's sake, burden themselves. If it should happen that all the masses are observed in the faith as already described, which I would scarcely expect, they are to be tolerated. But if they are not, then it would be best to have only one mass a day in a city, and that this mass be held in a proper manner in the presence of the assembled people. If at any time, however, we should desire to have more, then the people should be divided into as many groups as there are to be masses, and each group should be made to attend its own mass, there to exercise faith and to offer prayer, praise, and need in Christ, as was said above.[54]

36. If, then, the mass is a testament and sacrament in which the forgiveness of sins and every grace of God are promised and sealed with a sign, it follows self-evidently what is the best preparation for it. Without doubt the mass is given to them that need it and desire it. But who needs forgiveness of sins and God's grace more than just these poor miserable consciences who are driven and tormented by their sins, are afraid of God's wrath, judgment, death, and hell, and would be eager to have a gracious God, desiring nothing more greatly than this? These are truly they who are well prepared for the mass. For with them these words have found force and meaning, when Christ says, "Take and drink, this is my blood, which is poured out for you for the forgiveness of sins."[55] Where such a soul believes these words, as it ought, it receives from the mass all the fruits of the mass, that is, peace and joy, and thus is thereby well and richly fed in spirit.

But where there is no faith, there no prayer helps, nor the hearing of many masses. Things can only become worse. As Psalm 23 [:5] says, "Before my eyes thou hast prepared a table for me against

---

[54] Cf. pp. 98-101.
[55] Cf. p. 82, n. 5.

109

all my affliction [*anfechtung*]." Is this not a clear verse? What greater affliction [*anfechtung*] is there than sin and the evil conscience which is always afraid of God's anger and never has rest. Again, Psalm 111[:4-5] says, "He has caused his wonderful works to be remembered, and has provided food for those who fear him." It is certain, then, that for bold and satisfied spirits, whose sin does not prick them, the mass is of no value. For they have as yet no hunger for this food, since they are still too full. The mass demands and must have a hungry soul, which longs for the forgiveness of sins and divine favor.

37. But because this despair and unrest of conscience are nothing but an infirmity of faith, the severest malady which man can have in body and soul, and which cannot at once be speedily cured, it is useful and necessary that the more restless a person's conscience, the more should he go to the sacrament or hear mass. He should do this in such a way as to picture to himself therein the word of God and feed and strengthen his faith by it; never to make a work or sacrifice of it, but let it remain a testament and a sacrament, out of which he shall take and enjoy a benefit freely and of grace. Thereby his heart may become sweet toward God and obtain a comforting confidence toward him. For so sings the Psalter, Psalm 104[:15], "The bread strengthens man's heart, and the wine gladdens the heart of man."

38. Some have asked whether the sacrament is to be offered also to the deaf and dumb. Some think it a kindness to practice a pious fraud on them and think they should be given unblessed wafers. This mockery is not good; it will not please God, who has made them Christians as well as us. They deserve the same things that we do. Therefore if they are rational and can show by indubitable signs that they desire it in true Christian devotion, as I have often seen, we should leave to the Holy Spirit what is his work and not refuse him what he demands. It may be that inwardly they have a better understanding and faith than we; and this no one should maliciously oppose. Do we not read of St. Cyprian,[56] the holy martyr, that in Carthage where he was bishop he even had both

---

[56] Cyprian, famous bishop of Carthage, was beheaded as a martyr in A.D. 258.

elements given to the children,[57] although—for reasons of its own—that has now ceased? Christ had the children come to him and would not allow anyone to hinder them [Mark 10:14]. In like manner he withheld his blessings neither from the dumb nor the blind nor the lame. Why, then, should not his sacrament also be for those who heartily and in a Christian spirit desire it?

39. So we see with how very few laws and works Christ has weighed down his holy church and with how many promises he has lifted it up to faith. Yet now, alas! everything is completely turned around. We are driven by many long and burdensome laws and works to become righteous; yet nothing comes of it. But Christ's burden is light [Matt. 11:30] and soon produces an abundant righteousness, which consists in faith and trust and fulfils what Isaiah 10 [:22] says, "A little perfection will bring a flood full of righteousness."[58] That [burden] is faith. It is a little thing, to which belong neither laws nor works; indeed it cuts off all laws and works, and fulfils all laws and works. Therefore there flows forth from it nothing but righteousness. For so perfect is faith that, without any other labor and law, it makes everything that man does acceptable and well pleasing to God. I have said more about this in my little book, *On Good Works*.[59]

Therefore let us beware of sins, but much more of laws and good works, giving heed only to the divine promise and to faith. Then all good works will come of themselves. To this may God help us. Amen.

---

[57] Maurice Bévenot, S. J. (trans.), St. Cyprian's *The Lapsed* ("Ancient Christian Writers," Vol. XXV [Westminster, Maryland: Newman Press, 1957]), pp. 32-33. Cf. *LW* 36, 25-26.

[58] Vulgate.

[59] *A Treatise on Good Works* (1520). *PE* 1, (173) 184-285.

A BRIEF INSTRUCTION ON WHAT TO LOOK FOR AND EXPECT IN THE GOSPELS

1521

Translated by E. Theodore Bachmann

INTRODUCTION

Fresh from his epoch-making encounter with the emperor and the imperial diet at Worms, Luther was brought to the Wartburg, at Eisenach, on May 4, 1521. Without his library, and disinclined to be satisfied with the life of a country squire, he soon busied himself with writing a series of sermons based on the epistles and gospels for the church year, which ultimately became the so-called "Wartburg Postil."

In a letter of November 19, 1521, Luther dedicated the sermons to his own territorial ruler, Albert, count of Mansfeld.[1] He had at that time finished but twelve of the sermons, those on the Christmas cycle from Christmas Day through the Festival of the Epiphany, and was still planning to prepare four more for the Sundays in Advent. The dedicatory letter, however, was intended to cover both parts, as was the introduction to the Wartburg Postil, *A Brief Instruction on What to Look for and Expect in the Gospels*,[2] which had already been completed at least by the time of the letter.

Sent off secretly, this manuscript, including the *Brief Instruction*, was published at Wittenberg by Johann Grünenberg in March, 1522.[3] It appeared in time to go on sale at the Easter fair at Frankfurt-am-Main and soon found eager readers in many parts of Germany and also in Switzerland.

By April 25, 1522, the second part, the Advent sermons, was also off the press. Only in 1525 were the two parts finally published together, and then not in the chronological order of their original publication but in the order of the church year. Thus the *Brief Instruction* at last introduced the Advent as well as the Christmas sermons, as Luther originally intended it to do.

In this clear and simple preface Luther points out that despite the variations in the gospels and epistles, there is in the books of the

---

[1] *WA* 10^I, ^{1}, 1-8.
[2] *WA* 10^I, ^{2}, lii and lix.
[3] The text of this Christmas Postil is in *WA* 10^I, ^{1}, 8-728.

New Testament but one Christ and one gospel. This gospel is a discourse about Christ, the Son of God who became man for us, who died and was raised, and who is Lord over all things. Unlike Moses, Christ is not law but example; yet example only after he has first been received by faith as a gift of God to us. That gift is bestowed through the preaching of the gospel, which "is nothing else than Christ coming to us, or we being brought to him."

The tragedy of the times, according to Luther, is that such preaching has almost vanished, and a vast ignorance of the gospel pervades the church. Yet Scripture is its own powerful interpreter; and the Old Testament, so often ignored, opens the way to the New and to a renewal of the church. Abandon Scripture, warns Luther, and God abandons us to the lies of men. Prayerfully he hoped for a speedy return to the gospel, whereby his *Brief Instruction* and all other expositions might become superfluous, for the gospel itself is our proper guide and instructor in the Scriptures.

The following translation has been made from the original German, *Eyn kleyn unterricht, was man ynn den Evangelijs suchen und gewartten soll* as that has been reprinted, with annotations, in WA 10^{I}, ^{1}, 8-18.

A BRIEF INSTRUCTION ON WHAT TO LOOK FOR AND EXPECT IN THE GOSPELS

It is a common practice to number the gospels and to name them by books and say that there are four gospels. From this practice stems the fact that no one knows what St. Paul and St. Peter are saying in their epistles, and their teaching is regarded as an addition to the teaching of the gospels, in a vein similar to that of Jerome's[1] introduction.[2] There is, besides, the still worse practice of regarding the gospels and epistles as law books in which is supposed to be taught what we are to do and in which the works of Christ are pictured to us as nothing but examples. Now where these two erroneous notions remain in the heart, there neither the gospels nor the epistles may be read in a profitable or Christian manner, and [people] remain as pagan as ever.

One should thus realize that there is only one gospel, but that it is described by many apostles. Every single epistle of Paul and of Peter, as well as the Acts of the Apostles by Luke, is a gospel, even though they do not record all the works and words of Christ, but one is shorter and includes less than another. There is not one of the four major gospels anyway that includes all the words and works of Christ; nor is this necessary. Gospel is and should be nothing else than a discourse or story about Christ, just as happens among men when one writes a book about a king or a prince, telling what he did, said, and suffered in his day. Such a story can be told in various ways; one spins it out, and the other is brief. Thus the gospel is and

---

[1] Jerome (ca. 342-420), Eusebius Hieronymus, was the foremost biblical scholar of the ancient church and a friend of St. Augustine. He translated the entire Bible from the original Hebrew and Greek into popular Latin (Vulgate).

[2] In the prologue to his commentary on the Gospel of Matthew, Jerome writes, "It has been clearly demonstrated [on the basis of Ezek. 1:5, 10, and Rev. 4:7-8] that only four gospels ought to be acknowledged." Migne 7, 20.

should be nothing else than a chronicle, a story, a narrative about Christ, telling who he is, what he did, said, and suffered—a subject which one describes briefly, another more fully, one this way, another that way.

For at its briefest, the gospel is a discourse about Christ, that he is the Son of God and became man for us, that he died and was raised, that he has been established as a Lord over all things. This much St. Paul takes in hand and spins out in his epistles. He bypasses all the miracles and incidents[3] [in Christ's ministry] which are set forth in the four gospels, yet he includes the whole gospel adequately and abundantly. This may be seen clearly and well in his greeting to the Romans [1:1-4], where he says what the gospel is, and declares, "Paul, a servant of Jesus Christ, called to be an apostle, set apart for the gospel of God which he promised beforehand through his prophets in the holy scriptures, the gospel concerning his Son, who was descended from David according to the flesh and designated Son of God in power according to the Spirit of holiness by his resurrection from the dead, Jesus Christ our Lord," etc.

There you have it. The gospel is a story about Christ, God's and David's Son, who died and was raised and is established as Lord. This is the gospel in a nutshell. Just as there is no more than one Christ, so there is and may be no more than one gospel. Since Paul and Peter too teach nothing but Christ, in the way we have just described, so their epistles can be nothing but the gospel.

Yes even the teaching of the prophets, in those places where they speak of Christ, is nothing but the true, pure, and proper gospel—just as if Luke or Matthew had described it. For the prophets have proclaimed the gospel and spoken of Christ, as St. Paul here [Rom. 1:2] reports and as everyone indeed knows. Thus when Isaiah in chapter fifty-three says how Christ should die for us and bear our sins, he has written the pure gospel. And I assure you, if a person fails to grasp this understanding[4] of the gospel, he will never

---

[3] *Wunder und wandel* may be the equivalent of *die Wunder und das Leben Jesu* according to WA 10^{I}, ^{1}, 729, nn. 9, 22.

[4] *Wahn* is the equivalent of *Meinung* and the Latin *opinio*. WA 10^{I}, ^{1}, 10, n. 1.

be able to be illuminated in the Scripture nor will he receive the right foundation.

Be sure, moreover, that you do not make Christ into a Moses, as if Christ did nothing more than teach and provide examples as the other saints do, as if the gospel were simply a textbook of teachings or laws. Therefore you should grasp Christ, his words, works, and sufferings, in a twofold manner. First as an example that is presented to you, which you should follow and imitate. As St. Peter says in I Peter 4,[5] "Christ suffered for us, thereby leaving us an example." Thus when you see how he prays, fasts, helps people, and shows them love, so also you should do, both for yourself and for your neighbor. However this is the smallest part of the gospel, on the basis of which it cannot yet even be called gospel. For on this level Christ is of no more help to you than some other saint. His life remains his own and does not as yet contribute anything to you. In short this mode [of understanding Christ as simply an example] does not make Christians but only hypocrites. You must grasp Christ at a much higher level. Even though this higher level has for a long time been the very best, the preaching of it has been something rare. The chief article and foundation of the gospel is that before you take Christ as an example, you accept and recognize him as a gift, as a present that God has given you and that is your own. This means that when you see or hear of Christ doing or suffering something, you do not doubt that Christ himself, with his deeds and suffering, belongs to you. On this you may depend as surely as if you had done it yourself; indeed as if you were Christ himself. See, this is what it means to have a proper grasp of the gospel, that is, of the overwhelming goodness of God, which neither prophet, nor apostle, nor angel was ever able fully to express, and which no heart could adequately fathom or marvel at. This is the great fire of the love of God for us, whereby the heart and conscience become happy, secure, and content. This is what preaching the Christian faith means. This is why such preaching is called gospel, which in German means a

---

[5] I Pet. 2:21; cf. 4:1.

joyful, good, and comforting "message"; and this is why the apostles are called the "twelve messengers."[6]

Concerning this Isaiah 9[:6] says, "To us a child is born, to us a son is given." If he is given to us, then he must be ours; and so we must also receive him as belonging to us. And Romans 8[:32], "How should [God] not give us all things with his Son?" See, when you lay hold of Christ as a gift which is given you for your very own and have no doubt about it, you are a Christian. Faith redeems you from sin, death, and hell and enables you to overcome all things. O no one can speak enough about this. It is a pity that this kind of preaching has been silenced in the world, and yet boast is made daily of the gospel.

Now when you have Christ as the foundation and chief blessing of your salvation, then the other part follows: that you take him as your example, giving yourself in service to your neighbor just as you see that Christ has given himself for you. See, there faith and love move forward, God's commandment is fulfilled, and a person is happy and fearless to do and to suffer all things. Therefore make note of this, that Christ as a gift nourishes your faith and makes you a Christian. But Christ as an example exercises your works. These do not make you a Christian. Actually they come forth from you because you have already been made a Christian. As widely as a gift differs from an example, so widely does faith differ from works, for faith possesses nothing of its own, only the deeds and life of Christ. Works have something of your own in them, yet they should not belong to you but to your neighbor.

So you see that the gospel is really not a book of laws and commandments which requires deeds of us, but a book of divine promises in which God promises, offers, and gives us all his possessions and benefits in Christ. The fact that Christ and the apostles provide much good teaching and explain the law is to be counted a benefit just like any other work of Christ. For to teach aright is not

---

[6] *Tzwellff botten.* In Middle High German the singular form of the composite word was used to designate a single apostle. Luther derives the term for "messenger" *(Bote)* from the term for "message" *(Botschaft).* Cf. Grimm, *Deutsches Wörterbuch,* XVI, 1437.

the least sort of benefit. We see too that unlike Moses in his book, and contrary to the nature of a commandment, Christ does not horribly force and drive us. Rather he teaches us in a loving and friendly way. He simply tells us what we are to do and what to avoid, what will happen to those who do evil and to those who do well. Christ drives and compels no one. Indeed he teaches so gently that he entices rather than commands. He begins by saying, "Blessed are the poor,[7] Blessed are the meek," and so on [Matt. 5:3, 5]. And the apostles commonly use the expression, "I admonish, I request, I beseech," and so on. But Moses says, "I command, I forbid," threatening and frightening everyone with horrible punishments and penalties. With this sort of instruction you can now read and hear the gospels profitably.

When you open the book containing the gospels and read or hear how Christ comes here or there, or how someone is brought to him, you should therein perceive the sermon or the gospel through which he is coming to you, or you are being brought to him. For the preaching of the gospel is nothing else than Christ coming to us, or we being brought to him. When you see how he works, however, and how he helps everyone to whom he comes or who is brought to him, then rest assured that faith is accomplishing this in you and that he is offering your soul exactly the same sort of help and favor through the gospel. If you pause here and let him do you good, that is, if you believe that he benefits and helps you, then you really have it. Then Christ is yours, presented to you as a gift.

After that it is necessary that you turn this into an example and deal with your neighbor in the very same way, be given also to him as a gift and an example. Isaiah 40[:1, 2] speaks of that, "Be comforted, be comforted my dear people, says your Lord God. Say to the heart of Jerusalem, and cry to her, that her sin is forgiven, that her iniquity is ended, that she has received from the hand of God a double kindness for all her sin," and so forth. This double kindness is the twofold aspect of Christ: gift and example. These two are also signified by the double portion of the inheritance which the law of

---

[7] Martin Bucer's Latin translation of 1525 adds, "in spirit." WA 10^I, 1, 13, n. 2.

Moses [Deut. 21:17] assigns to the eldest son and by many other figures.

What a sin and shame it is that we Christians have come to be so neglectful of the gospel that we not only fail to understand it, but even have to be shown by other books and commentaries what to look for and what to expect in it. Now the gospels and epistles of the apostles were written for this very purpose. They want themselves to be our guides, to direct us to the writings of the prophets and of Moses in the Old Testament so that we might there read and see for ourselves how Christ is wrapped in swaddling cloths and laid in the manger [Luke 2:7], that is, how he is comprehended [Vorfassett] in the writings of the prophets. It is there that people like us should read and study, drill ourselves, and see what Christ is, for what purpose he has been given, how he was promised, and how all Scripture tends toward him. For he himself says in John 5 [:46], "If you believed Moses, you would also believe me, for he wrote of me." Again [John 5:39], "Search and look up the Scriptures, for it is they that bear witness to me."

This is what St. Paul means in Romans 1[:1, 2], where in the beginning he says in his greeting, "The gospel was promised by God through the prophets in the Holy Scriptures." This is why the evangelists and apostles always direct us to the Scriptures and say, "Thus it is written," and again, "This has taken place in order that the writing of the prophets might be fulfilled," and so forth. In Acts 17 [:11], when the Thessalonians heard the gospel with all eagerness, Luke says that they studied and examined the Scriptures day and night in order to see if these things were so. Thus when St. Peter wrote his epistle, right at the beginning [I Pet. 1:10-12] he says, "The prophets who prophesied of the grace that was to be yours searched and inquired about this salvation; they inquired what person or time was indicated by the Spirit of Christ within them; and he bore witness through them to the sufferings that were to come upon Christ and the ensuing glory. It was revealed to them that they were serving not themselves but us, in the things which have now been preached among you through the Holy Spirit sent from heaven, things which also the angels long to behold." What else does St. Peter here desire than to lead us into the Scriptures? It is as if he should be saying, "We preach and open the Scriptures to you through the Holy Spirit, so that you yourselves may read and see what is in them and know of the time about which the prophets were writing." For he says as much in Acts 4[3:24], "All the prophets who ever prophesied, from Samuel on, have spoken concerning these days."

Therefore also Luke, in his last chapter [24:45], says that Christ opened the minds of the apostles to understand the Scriptures. And Christ, in John 10 [:9, 3], declares that he is the door by which one must enter, and whoever enters by him, to him the gatekeeper (the Holy Spirit) opens in order that he might find pasture and blessedness. Thus it is ultimately true that the gospel itself is our guide and instructor in the Scriptures, just as with this foreword I would gladly give instruction and point you to the gospel.

But what a fine lot of tender and pious children we are! In order that we might not have to study in the Scriptures and learn Christ there, we simply regard the entire Old Testament as of no account, as done for and no longer valid. Yet it alone bears the name of Holy Scripture. And the gospel should really not be something written, but a spoken word which brought forth the Scriptures, as Christ and the apostles have done. This is why Christ himself did not write anything but only spoke. He called his teaching not Scripture but gospel, meaning good news or a proclamation that is spread not by pen but by word of mouth. So we go on and make the gospel into a law book, a teaching of commandments, changing Christ into a Moses, the One who would help us into simply an instructor.

What punishment ought God to inflict upon such stupid and perverse people! Since we abandoned his Scriptures, it is not surprising that he has abandoned us to the teaching of the pope and to the lies of men. Instead of Holy Scripture we have had to learn the *Decretales*[8] of a deceitful fool and an evil rogue. O would to God

---

[8] Papal and conciliar decisions, decrees, and pronouncements had been assembled and supplemented through the centuries until they constituted a very sizeable "body of canon law." Luther had consigned the entire collection to the flames on December 10, 1520, along with the papal bull which called for the burning of his books. Cf. *LW* 31, 381-395; and E. G. Schwiebert, *Luther and His Times* (St. Louis: Concordia, 1950), pp. 19-20.

that among Christians the pure gospel were known and that most speedily there would be neither use nor need for this work of mine. Then there would surely be hope that the Holy Scriptures too would come forth again in their worthiness. Let this suffice as a very brief foreword and instruction. In the exposition[9] we will say more about this matter. Amen.

---

[9] The reference is to Luther's commentary on the various texts of the Wartburg Postil to which this *Brief Instruction* was intended as a foreword. See the Introduction, pp. 115-116.

AVOIDING THE DOCTRINES OF MEN

and

A REPLY TO THE TEXTS CITED IN DEFENSE OF THE DOCTRINES OF MEN

1522

Translated by William A. Lambert
Revised by E. Theodore Bachmann

INTRODUCTION

After his return to Wittenberg, Luther wrote to Georg Spalatin on March 24, 1522,[1] that he had decided to dedicate a little book *de traditionibus hominum* to his kind host at the Wartburg, Hans von Berlepsch, with whom Luther had had many a searching conversation on the subject. Such a gesture would have been a mark of genuine gratitude for the months of hospitality. But because he was not sure of the wisdom of thus giving away the location of his recent "captivity," Luther declared himself ready, should Spalatin counsel anonymity, to dedicate the book to someone else. At the time Luther had not yet begun the actual writing. Later, in May, he reported being busily at work on his promised statement.[2] By May 29 it was off the press of Nickel Schirlentz in Wittenberg and was being forwarded to Spalatin for him to send it on as planned.[3] In place of a dedication to Berlepsch, *Avoiding the Doctrines of Men* was addressed to the general reader, in the hope that God would "grant grace and understanding" to all who read it.

Under ten headings Luther proceeded to interpret selected biblical texts, from Deuteronomy and Isaiah and Proverbs, from Christ and Paul and Peter, in order to bring comfort and courage to consciences troubled by the prolific monastic regulations concerning food, drink, garb, days, places, chastity, etc. Doctrines of men, declared Luther, can command only in external matters; but for the basic decisions of life, the Christian is to count on the Word of God alone.

The treatise, though finished, presently received a ringing supplement that bore international implications. For what he had previously said about the sacramental system in his *Babylonian Captivity of the Church* (1520),[4] Luther had received a stinging rebuttal from

---

[1] See the letter in Wilhelm M. L. de Wette, *Dr. Martin Luthers Briefe* (Berlin: Reimer, 1826), II, 158-159.

[2] Letter to Spalatin, May 20, 1522. *Ibid.*, p. 198.

[3] Letter to Spalatin. *Ibid.*, p. 172. On the date of this letter cf. *WA* 10^{II}, 61.

[4] *LW* 36, 3-126.

England's King Henry VIII in which he defended the seven sacraments. Bearing the title, *Assertio Septem Sacramentorum,* this work came either directly from Henry, who had once studied for the priesthood, or was ghosted under his name by John Fisher, bishop of Rochester.[5] At any rate after its festive presentation to Leo X at Rome, the pope in a bull of October 11, 1521, bestowed on Henry the title, "Defender of the Faith." Less than a year later Luther's blunt reply to "Henry the liar"[6] was published both in Latin and in German.[7] In the latter, Luther referred to his essay on *Doctrines of Men,* declaring, "God does not lie to me. All men are liars. And all the holy fathers, when they speak apart from the Scriptures, are as fallible as anyone else. But how the doctrines of men are to be avoided I have already forcefully demonstrated in a special booklet."[8]

This was not the end of the affair. Luther's sermon for the Eighth Sunday after Trinity (August 10, 1522) on the text Matt. 7:15, "Beware of false prophets!"[9] echoed some of his main contentions in *Doctrines of Men.* In that sermon Luther referred to a quotation from Augustine which had been one of Henry's main thrusts in the *Assertio.* Augustine had claimed, according to Luther's free citation, "I should not have believed the gospel, had I not been moved by the great authority of Christendom."[10] Sensing that an interpretation of this statement required more than a homiletical comment—he had already dealt with it in his Latin reply to Henry, which was not yet published—Luther then prepared a special treatise in German which dealt with the matter at length.[11] It bore the heading, *A Reply to the Texts Cited in Defense of the Doctrines of*

---

[5] *WA* 6, 494-495.

[6] *WA* 10[II], 262, l. 3.

[7] *Contra Henricum Regem Angliae,* though put into revised form about the middle of July, was not published until about the end of September, 1522. *WA* 10[II], (175) 180-222. *Antwort deutsch auf König Heinrichs Buch,* though started after the Latin version, was completed before it and published about August 1, 1522. *WA* 10[II], 227-262.

[8] *WA* 10[II], 239.

[9] *WA* 10[III], 257-258.

[10] *WA* 10[II], 260.

[11] See pp. 147-153

Men, and discussed Christ's words in Luke 10:16 and Matt. 23:2-3 in addition to the quotation from Augustine.

The exact date of publication is not known, but the *Reply* was printed by Johann Grünenberg at Wittenberg. Copies of it were first attached by Schirlentz to the original printing of *Doctrines of Men.* Already in 1522, however, Grünenberg brought out a complete edition of the two parts, bearing the double title.[12]

The following translation, a revision of the one done originally by William A. Lambert,[13] includes both treatises and is based on the original text as reprinted, with annotations, in *WA* 10^{II}, 72-92: *Von Menschenlehre zu meiden, und Antwort auf Sprüche, so man führet, Menschenlehre zu stärken* (1522).

---

[12] *WA* 10^{II}, 62-64.
[13] *PE* 2, 431-455.

AVOIDING THE
DOCTRINES OF MEN

Jesus[1]

To all who hear or read this little book may God grant grace and understanding. Amen.

I, Martin Luther, have published this little book for the comfort and saving of those poor consciences who are held captive in monasteries and convents by man-made laws, so that they may be able to arm and strengthen themselves through the Word of God and thus be steadfast amid the pains of death and other trials. At the same time, however, I here give notice to the insolent and undisciplined, whose only evidence of being Christian is that they can eat eggs, meat, and milk,[2] stay away from confession, break images, and so forth, that it is not my purpose here to have served them. For I regard them like those disgraceful people who fouled up the camp of Israel [Deut. 23:12-13], despite the fact that such discipline was enjoined upon everybody that whoever had to go was supposed to go outside the camp and cover his excrement with earth. So we must put up with these messy hoopoes[3] in our nest, until God sometime teaches them manners.

I want to have preached this Christian liberty only to the poor, humble, and captive consciences, so that wherever there are poor children, nuns, or monks, who would like to escape from their bondage, they may inform their consciences as to how it is possible to do this with God's approval and without danger, and how they may

---

[1] Cf. p. 79, n. 2.

[2] Pope Gregory I (590-604) laid down the rule on Lenten fasting, "We abstain from flesh-meat and from all things which come from flesh, as milk, cheese, and eggs." Herbert Thurston, *Lent and Holy Week* (London: Longmans, Green, 1914), p. 44.

[3] These handsome birds with filthy eating habits were declared unclean and not to be eaten in Lev. 11:19 and Deut. 14:18.

use such freedom in a disciplined and Christian way. To this end, may God grant his grace. Amen.

Reasons from Scripture for Avoiding the Doctrines of Men

I

Moses says in Deuteronomy 4[:2], "You shall not add anything to the word which I speak to you, nor take anything from it."

Now some will say that Moses here speaks only of his own word, for many books of the prophets as well as the entire New Testament have been added beyond the books of Moses. I reply: Nevertheless nothing new has been added, for the same thing that is found in the books of Moses is found also in the others. These other books, while using different words and narratives, do nothing more than illustrate how the word of Moses has been kept or not kept. Throughout them all there is one and the same teaching and thought. And here we can challenge them to show us one word in all the books outside those of Moses that is not already found in the books of Moses. For this much is beyond question, that all the Scriptures point to Christ alone. Indeed in John 5[:46] Christ says, "Moses wrote of me." Therefore everything in the other books is already in the books of Moses, as in a basic source.

II

Isaiah 29[:13], which our Lord quotes in Matthew 15[:8], says, "This people honors me with their lips, but their heart is far from me. They worship me in vain, however, in that they teach the doctrines and precepts of men."

Note this word of Christ; he calls it vain worship to worship God according to the doctrines of men. Christ is neither drunk nor a fool. And we are to build entirely on his word rather than on all angels and creatures.

III

The same Christ, in the same chapter, Matthew 15[:11], declares, "Not what goes into the mouth defiles a man, but what comes out of the mouth, this defiles a man."

This declaration and judgment must be firmly grasped, for it is powerful and overthrows with forcefulness all teaching, custom, and mode of life that distinguishes between foods. It liberates all consciences from all laws concerning food and drink. So it is allowable to eat milk, butter, eggs, cheese, and meat any day, be it Sunday or Friday, Lent or Advent; and no one needs to pay butter money or buy letters for that purpose.[4] For this word stands firm and does not deceive, "What goes into the mouth does not defile a man."

From this it follows, first, that it is a lie to claim that St. Peter instituted the fast days and that it is a commandment of the church, on pain of mortal sin, to forego eggs, butter, milk, and meat on fast days. For neither St. Peter nor the church prescribes or teaches anything contrary to Christ. And if they did, we should not obey them. Not that it would be wicked to practice such abstinence. But it is wicked to make a requirement or rule out of something essentially free and to pretend that something does defile and is sin of which Christ himself says that it is not sin and does not defile.

Second, it follows that for the pope to sell letters and grant permission to eat butter, meat, and so forth, is sheer knavery of the devil. For in this verse Christ has already permitted it and made it a matter of liberty.

Third, it is an error and a lie to say that gold-fasts,[5] ban-fasts,[6]

---

[4] Indulgences could be purchased permitting the off-season use of butter, etc. Such dispensations (Butterbriefe) "granted upon condition of a trifling alms to a specified object, were a favorite means of raising money. . . . One of the steeples of Rouen Cathedral . . . was commonly known as the 'butter tower' (tour de beurre) because it was built out of the contributions offered in exchange for leave to eat butter during Lent. Pope Innocent VIII in 1489 granted special faculties for this purpose to the then archbishop of Rouen." Thurston, op. cit., p. 45.

[5] Gold-fasts are the Ember fasts, on the three ember days of each of the four seasons of the year, possibly called "gold-fasts" because on these days rents were collected. PE 2, 433, n. 1. St. L. 19, 601, n. 4.

[6] Banfasten were fasts proclaimed by councils or bishops through public edict, or ban (bannum=edict poenale), in connection with special occasions or purposes. Joseph Hergenröther and Franz Kaulen (eds.), Kirchenlexikon (Freiburg im Breisgau: Herder, 1886), IV, 1273 (article "Fastenzeiten"). Cf. the description of the origin and method of the fast held at Mainz every year on the Second Sunday after Easter and the Nineteenth Sunday after Trinity right up until the eighteenth century, in Du Cange, Glossarium mediae et infimae latinitatis, III, 755 (article "Jejunium Bannitum").

and the fasts on the eve of apostles' and saints' days must be observed, on penalty of sin, as a commandment of the church. Against everything of the kind there stands this word of Christ, "What goes into the mouth does not defile a man." Rather fasting should forever be free and voluntary, both as to the day and as to the food.

Fourth, the orders of St. Benedict,[7] St. Bernard,[8] the Carthusians,[9] and all others, oppose Christ when they abstain from meat and the like as a matter of necessity and command, as if it would be a sin not to abstain. For their regulations flatly contradict what Christ says when they assert: What goes into the mouth defiles. To them, then, Christ must be a liar when he says, "What goes into the mouth does not defile a man."

So you see that this one saying of Christ mightily condemns all the [monastic] orders and their "religious regulations." For if what goes into the mouth does not defile, how much less will that defile which is put on the body, whether cowl, coat, shirt, pants, shoes, or cloak, whether green, yellow, blue, red, white, motley, or whatever? The same is true also of places, whether churches, cells, houses, or the rooms within them.

It follows that whoever regards it a sin for a monk to go without the garb of his order, whoever would not leave it a matter of freedom, also makes Christ a liar. For he makes that a sin which Christ freed from sin. He says Yes! where Christ says No! What are such monks, then, but people who say to Christ's very face, "You lie; there is sin, in what you say is not sin."

---

[7] Benedict of Nursia (ca. 480-ca. 550), the "Patriarch of Western Monasticism," withdrew from a morally loose contemporary society (at the close of a century that had seen the fall of Rome) and became a leader in the rising monastic movement. His permanent achievement was the community at Monte Cassino, halfway between Rome and Naples, which became the center of the Benedictine Order. Chapters 39-41 of his famous *Rule* set forth the dietary restrictions.

[8] Bernard of Clairvaux (1090-1153) was the best known leader of the rigorist Cistercian Order founded by Robert of Molesme in 1098, which followed the strictest application of the Benedictine Rule.

[9] The Carthusian Order was founded by St. Bruno of Cologne in 1084; in 1133 it devised its own Rule, a combination of strict Benedictinism and hermit-like asceticism.

It will not help them to quote St. Bernard, St. Gregory,[10] St. Francis[11] and other saints.[12] We must listen to what Christ says. Him alone did the Father make to be our teacher, when on Mount Tabor he said, Matthew 17[:5], "This is my beloved Son, with whom I am well pleased; listen to him." He did not say, "Listen to Bernard, Gregory," etc., but, listen to him, him, him, my beloved Son. Who knows how far the saints sinned or did right in this matter? What they did, they did not do as a matter of necessity and command. But if they did it as a matter of necessity and command, they erred; and we are not to forsake Christ in order to follow them.

All this is confirmed in the same passage in Matthew 15[:11, 18-20] where Christ continues, "What comes out of the mouth, this defiles a man. For out of the mouth, from the heart, come evil thoughts, fornication, adultery, theft, false witness, slander, and so forth. These are what defile a man."

Here we must ask: If that alone is sinful and unclean which proceeds from the heart, as Christ so powerfully contends and concludes, how then can butter, milk, eggs, or cheese defile? For these come not from the mouth or the heart, but from the bellies of cows and hens. Who has ever seen meat, tonsures, cowls, monasteries, or hair shirts coming out of men's mouths? Then it must have been the cows that sinned in giving milk and butter and bearing calves!

Therefore all the regulations of monks and men concerning food, clothing, places, and all things external are not only blasphemy against God and falsehood and deception, but sheer foolishness and monkey business as well. To be sure, a man may have an inordinate desire to eat excessively and dress extravagantly. But that comes from the heart and can happen just as well with fish and gray homespun as with meat and red velvet. In short Christ does not lie

---

[10] Gregory I, bishop of Rome (590-604), the first monk to become pope, did much to promote the introduction of the Benedictine Rule into monastic life.
[11] Francis of Assisi (1181 [82?]-1226), mystic and spiritual genius of the High Middle Ages, founded the Order of the Friars Minor, or Minorites.
[12] The usual defense as stated in the *Rule,* chap. 5, was that the order of a superior is to be received and obeyed as a divine command, "for the obedience given to superiors is given to God." Leonard J. Doyle (trans.), *St. Benedict's Rule for Monasteries* (Collegeville, Minnesota: St. John's Abbey Press, 1948), pp. 17-19.

when he declares, "Not what goes into the mouth defiles, but what comes out of the mouth, this defiles."

If, now, it is true that the failure to do what men command is not sinful or unclean, then the keeping and doing of it in turn is not necessarily clean or meritorious, since only that is clean and meritorious which is diametrically opposed to what is sinful and unclean. In monastic life as a whole, therefore, there is nothing either clean or meritorious. This is what the Lord Christ means when, in Matthew 15[:9], he says, "In vain do they worship me with the precepts of men." Why "in vain"? Because a neglect of these precepts is no sin, and the keeping of them is no merit; for both are free. They are deceiving themselves therefore when they ascribe merit where there is no merit and are afraid of sinning where there is no sin; as Psalm 14[:5] says, "They are frightened where there is no fear."[13]

IV

In I Timothy 4[:1-7] St. Paul says: "Now the Spirit expressly says that in later times some will depart from faith by giving heed to erring spirits and to doctrines of devils, through those who speak lies in hypocrisy, whose conscience is seared, who forbid marriage and enjoin abstinence from foods which God has created to be received with thanksgiving by those who believe and know the truth. For everything created by God is good, and nothing is to be rejected if it is received with thanksgiving; for then it is sanctified by the word of God and prayer. If you put these instructions before the brethren, you will be a good preacher of Christ, nourished on the words of faith and good doctrine to which you have attained. But have nothing to do with profane and old wives' fables."

O how this thunders and storms against all the works, doctrines, and orders of men! First if they boast that their regulations come from the pope and from the holy fathers, what will Christ's judgment be? Will he not say: Paul, my Apostle, is my chosen instrument, as Luke writes in Acts 9[:15]; why then have you not ascribed greater authority to his word than to that of the pope and of the

---

[13] Vulgate.

fathers, for you do not know whose instruments they are? How will they stand up to that?

Next we ask them whether butter, eggs, meat, milk, and all the food which they avoid on fast days and in their [monastic] orders have not been created by God and are not God's good creatures? Therefore it is certain that these are the men of whom Paul here says that they forbid the food which God has created and given to believers to use, and they forbid the married estate besides. Thus they cannot escape, for this passage fits and means them. So let us see what Paul thinks of them and how he reproves them.

1. They have departed from faith. For they could not possibly have introduced such doctrines and works if they had not thought thereby to become righteous and be saved. But such a notion is of itself a sure sign that they have fallen away from faith. As has frequently been said, it is faith alone that can do what they expect works to do.

2. They give heed to erring spirits. He does not say, "to erring persons," but "to erring spirits." These are they who profess spirituality, call themselves spiritual, and claim to be of the Spirit and in the Spirit. But since they are without faith, it is impossible for them not to err in spiritual matters. Hence this is a fitting succession: they depart from faith and follow after error in the spirit.

3. Their doctrines he calls "doctrines of devils." This also must follow where faith and the true Spirit are lacking. There the devil gives them the spirit of error and leads them on with brightly colored doctrines and works, so that they imagine themselves to be altogether spiritual. Since the doctrine does not originate in the Scriptures, however, it can be the doctrine of no one but the devil.

4. They are liars. For they quote the Holy Scriptures and the sayings of the fathers and at times also force them into agreement with their doctrines, as we see them doing every day. But this is deceitful and untrue, since the Scriptures are diametrically opposed to them.

5. Theirs is outright hypocrisy. This is true and requires no comment. For their entire existence is only sham and show in the external matters of food and clothing.

137

6. They have a seared conscience. That is, their conscience is unnatural. For as said above, where there is neither sin nor matter of conscience, they make things out to be sin and a matter of conscience. This is as unnatural as the scar of a burn is on the body.

7. They forbid marriage. They do this by creating an estate in which there shall be no marriage, as we see in the case of both priests and monks. Wherefore behold the judgment of God upon such doctrines and estates: they are the devil's doctrines, erroneous doctrines, false doctrines, faithless doctrines, hypocritical doctrines. God help us! Who would want to continue in them when God himself passes such judgment? What good does it do you to have made a thousand vows and oaths on the basis of such doctrines? Indeed the stricter the vow, the more fragile it is, because it was made against God according to the devil's doctrines.

Nevertheless see how cleverly they worm their way out and turn this text away from themselves. They say it applies not to them but to the Tatianists,[14] to those heretics who condemned marriage altogether. Yet Paul does not speak here of those who condemn marriage but of those who forbid it for the sake of hypocrisy, because they want to be spiritual. Suppose we grant, however, that Paul here speaks against the Tatianists. But if the pope does what the Tatianists did, why do Paul's words not apply to him as well? Be they Tatianists or the pope, this text speaks of those who forbid marriage. The words of Paul condemn the deed regardless of who does it. He who forbids marriage is the devil's disciple and apostle, as the words say clearly. And because the pope does it, he must be the devil's

---

[14] The Tatianists were the followers of Tatian, who lived in Syria in the middle of the second century. A noted Christian apologist and pupil of Justin Martyr, in later life he turned to heretical extremes of asceticism. Apparently basing his view of marriage upon I Cor. 7:5, Tatian ascribed the institution of marriage and the whole Old Testament law to the devil. Eusebius, the church historian, held that Tatian was the founder of a sect known as the Encratites, or Abstainers. *Eusebius: The Ecclesiastical History*, IV, 28-29. Modern historians see in Encratism an ascetic movement within the early church which rejected the use of wine and flesh-meat, and condemned marriage as being fornication. Thus Adolph Harnack can write that Tatian "connected himself with the Encratites." Neil Buchanan (trans.), Adolph Harnack's *History of Dogma* (Boston: Little, Brown, 1902), I, 238, n. 3. See Hauck (ed.), *Realencyklopädie für protestantische Theologie und Kirche*, XIX, 386-394, on Tatian; and V, 392-393, on the Encratites.

disciple, and so must all the pope's followers. Or else St. Paul is lying.

8. They forbid foods which God has created. Here once again you see that God himself through the mouth of St. Paul ascribes to the devil the doctrines of men. What greater and more terrible thing would you wish to hear concerning the doctrines of men than that they are a departure from faith, erroneous, false, devilish, hypocritical? Whoever is not satisfied with this text, what indeed will satisfy him? But if the doctrine that forbids certain kinds of food is devilish and un-Christian, those doctrines which concern clothes, tonsures, places, and all things external will be equally devilish and un-Christian.

Yet here again they worm their way out and claim that St. Paul is speaking of the Manicheans.[15] This is not what we are inquiring about. St. Paul speaks of those who forbid foods; and the pope and his followers do that, be they Manicheans or Tatianists. Paul is speaking of the deed which we see the pope doing. Therefore we cannot save the pope from this text. If somebody else arose today or tomorrow and forbade certain foods, would this text not apply to him because he is no Manichean? In that way one could make allowable that which Paul here forbids and claim that it does not apply to us but to the old Manicheans. Not so. Whether or not the pope is a Manichean, and all his monks and priests with him, I do not care. Yet I do say that in his teaching and works he contradicts the teaching of St. Paul as much as any Manichean.

9. They are ungrateful. For God has created foods, as St. Paul here says, to be received with thanksgiving. But this they cover up, so that they will surely not have to be grateful for God's goodness. The reason for this is that they do not believe and do not know the

---

[15] The Manicheans, strictly speaking not a Christian sect but a rival religious community, made inroads upon the Christian Church. Founded by the Babylonian Mani, who was born in the third century, they taught that all matter is inherently evil. Consequently the Manicheans had many fasts, averaging seven days in each month. A special class of adherents, the "elect" or perfect among them, abstained from meat, wine, and marriage. See Hauck (ed.), *Realencyklopädie*, XII, 193-228; see also Bertram Lee Woolf (trans.), Hans Lietzmann's *The Founding of the Church Universal* (New York: Scribner's, 1950), pp. 269-274.

truth. For Paul says, "To those who believe and to those who know the truth, these are given to be used with thanksgiving." But if they are unbelieving and do not know the truth, as St. Paul here accuses them, then they are surely heathen, un-Christian, blind, and foolish. And this, I maintain, is to praise the pope, the priests, and the monks!

10. They are wicked and harmful preachers. St. Paul rebukes them as such. For he says here that Timothy is a good preacher, nourished on the words of faith and good doctrine, whenever he puts these instructions before the brethren. It follows that they who teach the contrary must in turn be wicked preachers, nourished on the words of unbelief and wicked doctrine.

11. Such teaching is profane, and like old wives' tales. Paul calls it that. Is this not foolish talk? Paul implies that the great teachers have busied themselves with the kind of tales that old wives prattle about behind the stove, that it is profane, unspiritual, unholy chatter, though the teachers themselves construe it as pure holiness! Now who has ever heard the doctrines of men so terribly castigated in every way? They are apostate, unbelieving, un-Christian, pagan, erroneous, devilish, false, hypocritical, conscience-searing, ungrateful, dishonoring God and his creation, being harmful fables and old wives' chatter. Let him who can, flee from beneath this judgment of God.

V

St. Paul says again in Colossians 2[:16-23]: "Let no one burden your conscience in matters of food or drink, or with regard to a festival or a new moon or a sabbath. These are only a shadow of what is to come, but the body is in Christ. Let no one turn you aside from the goal who goes about by his own choice in the humility and spirituality of the angels, of whom he has never seen even one, being himself puffed up in vain by his sensuous mind. Nor does he hold fast to the Head, from whom the whole body, nourished and knit together through its joints and ligaments, grows with a growth that is from God. If then you are dead with Christ to the elemental spirits of the universe, why do you burden your conscience with regulations as if you were alive? For these say: This you shall not touch, this

140

you shall not eat or drink, this you shall not put on (referring to things which all perish as they are used), according to the commandments and doctrines of men, who have an appearance of wisdom because of their self-chosen spirituality and humility and because they do not spare the body and the needs of the flesh."

Is St. Paul speaking here too of the Manicheans or Tatianists? Or can we on this account excuse the papists? He speaks actually against those who take consciences captive. With doctrines of men they make matters of conscience out of food, drink, clothes, days, and everything that is external. And it cannot be denied that the pope, the chapters, and the monasteries with their rules and statutes do this very thing when they forbid the eating of meat, eggs, and butter, and the wearing of ordinary clothes such as other people wear. Now here stands Paul, saying:

1. Let no one burden your conscience, or judge or condemn you in matters of food, drink, clothing, or days. What, then, does this mean? Be not priests or monks; do not in any way keep the pope's precepts, or believe him when he says that a certain thing is sin or a matter of conscience. See, here God through Paul commands us to despise the laws of the pope and of the monasteries, and to keep them free, so that they do not take consciences captive. This is as much as saying, "Do not become monks or priests, and let him who has become a monk or a priest turn back, or else regard his position as a matter of freedom without constraint of conscience."

Although Paul wrote this of the Jews, who did such things according to the law of Moses (for he says that they are the shadow and type of things to come, but the body itself is in Christ), yet it holds much more against the ordinances of the pope and of the monks. For if what God has instituted comes to an end and shall no longer bind the consciences of men, how much less shall men either decree or keep anything that would bind the conscience? Beyond this, more is still to be said about these purely human laws.

2. Paul says, "Let no one turn you aside from the goal or set up bypaths toward the prize." What does this mean but to lead men toward works and away from faith, which alone is the one right road by which to gain the prize of salvation, and to strive toward

141

heaven over devious ways and claim that this is the way to gain the prize? Yet this is what the doctrines of the pope and the orders are doing. And what are the ways they propose? Listen to this:

3. "In the self-chosen humility and spirituality of angels," says Paul. What words could better fit the orders? Is it not true that the pope and all of them chatter much about their obedience? Obedience is supposed to be the noblest virtue. This is the precious spiritual humility of the papists. Yet who has commanded this humility? They themselves have invented it and chosen it, in order to seduce themselves. For with it they have exempted themselves from the common humility and obedience which God has commanded, namely, that everyone shall humble himself before, and be subject to, his fellow-man. Instead they are subject to no man on earth, but have withdrawn themselves entirely. They have fashioned an obedience and a humility of their own according to their own statutes. Still they claim that their own obedience is superhuman, perfect, and, as it were, angelic; even though there are no people on earth less humble and obedient than they.

In like manner they have also taken vows of chastity and poverty. They do not hold jobs like other people but, like the angels in heaven, they praise and worship God day and night. In short their life is heavenly, although nowhere on earth can you find more disgusting unchastity, greater wealth, less devout hearts, or more hardened people than in the spiritual estate, as everyone sees. Yet they seduce all the world from the true way to the bypath by means of their self-chosen, beautiful, spiritual, angelic life. I maintain that all this is not spoken of the Jews or of the Manicheans, but of the papists—whose deeds prove it.

4. He goes about in such spirituality and in ways that he has never seen, says Paul. This is the very worst feature about the doctrines of men and the life built upon them, that they are without foundation and warrant in the Scriptures. Men cannot know whether what they are doing is good or wicked, for their whole life is an uncertain venture. If you ask them whether they are certain that what they are and do is pleasing to God, they admit that they do not know, they must take the chance. "If it succeeds, it succeeds."[16]

---

[16] Cf. Wander (ed.), *Sprichwörter-Lexikon*, I, 1561, No. 17.

And this is all they can say, for they have no faith. Faith alone makes us certain that all that we are is pleasing to God, not because of our merit but because of his mercy. Thus all their humility and obedience, and all of their spirituality, is, at its very best, uncertain and in vain.

5. They puff themselves up in vain; that is, they have no reason for doing so. Although their practices are uncertain, unbelieving, and completely damnable, yet they dare to puff themselves up and claim that they have the best and only true way, that in comparison with theirs every other manner of living stinks and is nothing at all. Yet they neither see nor feel this puffed up sensuous mind of theirs, so great is their angelic humility and obedience! O the fruit of these doctrines of men!

6. They do not hold fast to the Head, who is Christ. For Christ and the doctrines of men cannot possibly agree. One must cancel the other. If the conscience finds comfort in Christ, the comfort derived from works and doctrines must fall; if it finds comfort in works, then Christ must fall. The heart cannot build upon a dual foundation. One of them must be abandoned. Now we see that all the comfort of the papists rests upon their practices. For if it did not rest there, they would pay no attention to them and would give them up; or else they would use them as matters of freedom, how and when they pleased.

If there were no other misfortune connected with the doctrines of men, this of itself would be all too great: that for the sake of such doctrines Christ must be abandoned, the Head lost, and the heart must build on such an abomination. For this reason, St. Peter calls the orders abominable—damnable sects which deny Christ. In II Peter 2[:1], he says, "There shall arise among you false teachers who will secretly bring in damnable heresies, even denying the Lord who bought them."

7. It is clear enough that with these words Paul means our spiritual estate, when he says, "If you are dead with Christ, why do you burden your consciences with regulations, such as, this you shall not touch, this you shall not eat, this you shall not wear?" etc. Who can here deny that God through St. Paul forbids us to teach and to hear all doctrines of men insofar as they constrain the con-

science? Who then can with a good conscience be a monk or a priest or be subject to the pope? They must indeed confess that their consciences are taken captive by such laws. Thus you see what a mighty saying this is against all the doctrines of men. It is dreadful to hear that they abandon Christ the Head, deny faith, and so must necessarily become heathen. And yet they think that their holiness sustains the world.

VI

Paul, in Galatians 1[:8-9], says, "Even if we ourselves, or an angel from heaven, should preach to you a gospel beyond that which we have preached to you, let him be accursed.[17] As we have said before, so now I say again: If anyone is preaching to you a gospel beyond that which you have received, let him be accursed."

In these words you hear the judgment of God against the pope and all the doctrines of men, that they are under the ban. Now this ban is not like the pope's ban. Rather it is eternal; it separates man from God, from Christ, from all salvation, and from everything that is good, and it makes him the companion of the devil. O what a terrible judgment is this!

Now see whether the pope, priests, and monks do not preach and teach a gospel beyond and different from that taught by Christ and his apostles. We said above that Christ teaches, "What goes into the mouth does not defile a man." Contrary to this and beyond it the pope, priests, and monks say, "Christ, what you say is a lie; for the eating of meat defiles a Carthusian and condemns him; and the same is true of the other orders." Is not this slapping Christ on the mouth, calling him a liar, blaspheming him, and teaching differently from what he taught? Therefore it is a just judgment that they, in their great holiness, are condemned as blasphemers of God with an everlasting ban.

VII

In Titus 1[:14] Paul says again, "Teach them not to pay attention to Jewish fables and commandments of men that turn them from the truth."

---

[17] *Das say eyn bann* is Luther's translation of the Vulgate *anathema sit*. This explains the reference to the "ban" which follows.

See what a straightforward command this is for us not to pay attention to the commandments of men. Is not this clear enough? And Paul states the reason, saying: they turn men from the truth, for as was also said above, the heart cannot trust in Christ and at the same time in the doctrines or works of men. Therefore as soon as a person turns to the doctrines of men he turns away from the truth and pays no [further] attention to it. On the contrary he who finds his comfort in Christ cannot pay attention to the commandments and works of men.

Note, therefore, whose ban you should fear most. The pope and his followers cast you far beyond hell if you do not heed their commandments. And Christ commands you not to heed them on pain of his ban. Consider then whom you desire to follow.

VIII

II Peter 2[:1-3] declares, "There shall arise among you false teachers, who secretly bring in damnable heresies, even denying the Lord who bought them. Because of them the way of truth will be blasphemed. And in their greed they will exploit you with false words."

See then, the orders and chapters are damnable sects. Why? Because they deny Christ and blaspheme the way of faith. How? Because Christ says that there is neither sin nor righteousness in eating, drinking, clothing, places, and the works of men; yet this they condemn. They teach and practice that sin and righteousness are involved in these things. Hence Christ must be a liar. He must be denied and blasphemed together with his doctrine and faith.

They also make use of false words, exaggerating their obedience, chastity, and worship of God. Yet they do this only through greed, in order that they might exploit us until they have brought all the wealth of the whole world into their possession—as those who, by their own worship of God, would help every man to heaven. For this reason they are and remain damnable and blasphemous sects.

IX

Christ says again in Matthew 24[:23-26], "Then if any one says to you 'Lo, here is Christ,' or 'There!' do not believe it. For false

Christs and false prophets will arise and show great signs and wonders, so as to deceive, if possible, even the elect. Lo, I have told you beforehand. So, if they say to you, 'Lo, he is in the wilderness,' do not go out; if they say 'Lo, he is in the cellar,' do not believe it."

Tell me, how can a monk be saved? He binds his salvation to a place and says, "Here I find Christ; were I not to remain here, I should be lost." But Christ says, "No, I am not here." Who will reconcile these two? Therefore it is clear from this word of Christ that all doctrines which bind the conscience to places are contrary to Christ. But if he does not allow the conscience to be bound to places, neither does he allow it to be bound to food, clothes, appearance, or anything else external. There is no doubt then that this passage speaks of the pope and his clergy. Christ himself here releases and sets free all priests and monks, in that he condemns all orders and monasteries. For he says, "Do not believe it; do not go out," etc.

He says the same thing also in Luke 17[:20-21], "The kingdom of God is not coming with external appearances, nor will they say, 'Lo, here it is!' 'Lo, there it is!' for behold, the kingdom of God is within you."[18]

Is this not clear enough? Surely the doctrines of men can regulate nothing but external things. But since the kingdom of God is not external, those teachers and their disciples must necessarily miss the kingdom and go astray.

Nor will it help them to say that the holy fathers instituted the orders. Christ has already destroyed this argument by saying that the very elect may be misled; that is, they will err, but not remain in their error. How else would it be a particularly enormous error, if it were not the elect who erred? Let the doctrines and practice of the saints be what it will, the words of Christ are certain and clear. Him we must follow, and not the saints whose doctrines and works are uncertain. What he says stands firm, "The kingdom of God is within you,"[19] and not outside of you, here or there.

X

Solomon, in Proverbs 30[:5-6], says, "Every word of God proves

---

[18] *Ist ynwendig ynn euch.*
[19] *Stehet bynnen euch.*

true: and is a shield to all who put their trust in it. Do not add to his words, lest he rebuke you, and you be found a liar."

With this I will end for the present. For there is much more in the prophets, especially in Jeremiah, of which I have written in the treatise on confession.[20] Here then Solomon concludes that he is a liar who adds anything to the words of God. For the word of God alone is to teach us, as Christ says in Matthew 23[:10], "Do not let yourselves be called masters. One Master is in you, even Christ." Amen. Let this suffice.

A REPLY TO THE TEXTS CITED IN DEFENSE OF THE DOCTRINES OF MEN

The first such text is Luke 10[:16], where Christ says, "He who hears you, hears me; and he who rejects you, rejects me." He says the same thing in Matthew 10[:40] and in Mark 6[:11]. Here, they claim, Christ demands of us that we accept their man-made laws.

I reply: That is not true. For immediately before speaking these words, Christ says, "Go your way and say, the kingdom of God is at hand."[21] With these words Christ stops the mouths of all the teachers of the doctrines of men and instructs the apostles what they are to teach. He himself puts the word into their mouth, saying that they shall preach of the kingdom of God. Now he who does not preach of the kingdom of God is not sent by Christ, and to him these words do not apply. Rather do these words demand of us that we should not listen to the doctrines of men.

Now to preach of the kingdom of God is nothing else than to preach the gospel, in which is taught the faith of Christ by which alone God dwells and rules in us. But the doctrines of men do not preach about faith, but about eating, clothing, times, places, persons,

---

[20] *Von der Beicht, ob die der Bapst macht habe zu gebieten* (1521). See WA 8, 138-185, especially pp. 143-144 where Luther discusses Jer. 23:16-32.
[21] Cf. Matt. 10:7 and Luke 10:3, 9.

and about purely external matters which are of no profit to the soul.

Now look at the pious shepherds and faithful teachers, how honestly they have dealt with the poor common people. This text, "Who hears you, hears me," they have in a masterful fashion torn out of its context and have terrified us with it, until they have subjugated us unto themselves. But what precedes, "Preach about the kingdom of God," they have taken good care not to mention. Bravely have they leaped over it, so that by no means should they be compelled to preach only the gospel. These noble and most excellent teachers! And we are even supposed to thank them in addition!

Again, in Mark, the last chapter [16:15], where Christ was sending out the disciples to preach, let us hear how he gives them commandment, sets a limit to their teaching, and bridles their tongues when he says, "Go into all the world and preach the gospel to every creature. He who believes will be saved," etc. He does not say, "Go and preach what you like, or what you think to be right." But he puts his own word into their mouth and bids them preach the gospel.

He says the same thing again in the last chapter of Matthew [28:19], "Go and teach all nations, baptizing them in the name of the Father and of the Son and of the Holy Spirit, teaching them to observe all that I have commanded you." See, here again he does not say, "Teach them to observe what you invent," but what I have commanded you. Therefore it cannot be otherwise: the pope and his bishops and teachers must be wolves and apostles of the devil, for they teach not the commands of Christ, but their own words.

So also in Matthew 25[:14-15], in the parable of the three servants, the Lord points out that the householder instructed the servants to trade not with their own property but with his, and gave the first five talents, the next two, and the third one.

The second text is Matthew 23[:2-3], where the Lord says, "The scribes and Pharisees sit in Moses' seat; so practice and observe whatever they tell you."

"Here, here," they say, "we have authority to teach what we think to be right."

I reply: If that is what Christ means, then we are in a sorry plight. Then every pope might create more new laws, until the world could no longer contain them all. But they treat this text just like the previous one. What does it mean to sit in Moses' seat? Let us ask, what did Moses teach? And if he were still sitting in his seat today, what would he be teaching? Beyond a doubt, nothing but what he taught of old, namely, the commandments and word of God. He has never yet uttered any doctrine of men. Rather as almost every chapter shows, he spoke what God commanded him to speak.

It follows, then, that he who teaches something different from Moses does not sit in Moses' seat. For the Lord calls it Moses' seat, because from it the doctrine of Moses should be spoken and taught. The same meaning is contained in the words which follow, where the Lord says, "But do not do what they do; for they preach, but do not practice. For they bind heavy burdens, hard to bear, and lay them on men's shoulders; but they themselves will not move them with their finger" [Matt. 23:3-4].

See, here he takes their works to task, because they lay many laws beyond the doctrines of Moses on men's shoulders, laws which they themselves will not touch. And afterward he says, "Woe to you, scribes and Pharisees, hypocrites! who say, 'If anyone swears by the temple, it is nothing; but if anyone swears by the gold of the temple, he is bound by his oath.' You blind fools. For which is greater, the gold or the temple that has made the gold sacred?" [Matt. 23:16-17]. Is it not clear enough here that Christ condemns their man-made doctrines? He can, therefore, not have sanctioned them by speaking of sitting in Moses' seat; else he would have contradicted himself. Therefore Moses' seat must mean no more than the law of Moses, and the sitting in it no more than the preaching of the law of Moses.

This is what Moses himself said of his seat and doctrine, in Deuteronomy 3[4:2], "You shall not add to the word which I command you, nor take from it"; and in Deuteronomy 13[12:32], "Do only that which I command you; and do not add to it or take from it." In Moses' seat they would have had to teach these doctrines too. Therefore Moses' seat cannot put up with the doctrines of men.

149

The third text is St. Augustine's word in his book *Against the Fundamental Letter of the Manicheans,* which goes like this, "I should not believe the gospel if I did not believe the church [*Kirche*]."[22]

"Look," they say, "the church is to be believed more than the gospel."

I answer: Even if Augustine had said so, who gave him the authority that we must believe what he says? What Scriptures does he quote to prove this statement? What if he erred here, as we know that he frequently did, just as did all the fathers? Should one single sentence of Augustine be so mighty as to refute all the texts quoted above? God would not have that; St. Augustine must yield to them.

Besides if that were St. Augustine's opinion, he would be contradicting himself. For in very many places he exalts the Holy Scriptures above the statements of all teachers, above the decrees of all councils and churches, and will have men judge him and the teachings of everyone else according to the Scriptures.[23] Why then do the faithful shepherds pass by such sayings of St. Augustine, plain and clear as they are, and land on this single statement, which sounds so obscure and so unlike the Augustine we know from all his writings? It can only be because they want to bolster up their tyranny with rotten and silly twaddle.

Moreover they operate like deceivers in that they not only ascribe to Augustine an opinion he did not hold, but they also falsify and pervert his words. For St. Augustine's words are actually these, "I should not believe the gospel, if the authority of all Christendom [*Ansehen der gantzen Christenheyt*] did not move me." Augustine speaks of the whole of Christendom and says that throughout the world it preaches with one accord the gospel, and not the *Fundamental Letter of the Manicheans.* It is this unanimous

---

[22] This free paraphrase is from Augustine's *Contra Epistolam Manichaei,* vi: "*Ego vero Evangelio non crederem, nisi me catholicae Ecclesiae commoveret auctoritas.*" Migne 42, 176. On the preceding page Augustine had written, "If the claim of truth be shown to be so evident that it cannot be called into question, it is to be preferred before all those things by which I am held in the Catholic faith."

[23] Cf., for example, *Contra Faustum Manichaeum* xi, 5. Migne 42, 248-249.

authority of all Christians that moves him to consider it the true gospel. But our tyrants say that they are themselves this Christendom, as if the common laymen were not also Christians. And what they teach is supposed to be called the doctrine of the Christian Church, though they are a minority, and we—who are universal Christendom—should also first be consulted about what is to be taught in the name of universal Christendom. See, so well do they treat this statement of St. Augustine that what he says of Christendom throughout the world is supposed to be understood of the Roman See.

Now how does it also follow from this saying that the doctrines of men are to be observed? What doctrine of men has ever been devised that has been accepted and preached by all of universal Christendom throughout the world? Not one; for the gospel alone is accepted by all Christians throughout the world.

Moreover we must not understand St. Augustine to say that he would not believe the gospel unless he were moved to do so by the authority of the whole of Christendom. For that would be false and un-Christian. Everyone must believe only because it is the word of God, and because he is convinced in his heart that it is true; even though an angel from heaven [Gal. 1:8] and all the world preached to the contrary. Augustine's meaning is rather, as he himself says, that he finds the gospel nowhere except in Christendom, and that this external proof can be given to heretics; that it is not their doctrine which is right, but this doctrine which all the world has with one accord accepted. For the eunuch believed in the gospel preached by Philip [Acts 8:35-37], even though he did not know whether many or few believed in it. So also Abraham believed the promise of God all by himself [Gen. 15:6], when no man yet knew of it. And Mary believed the message of Gabriel by herself too [Luke 1:38], and there was no one on earth who believed with her. In this way Augustine also had to believe, and all the saints, and we too; every one for himself alone.

For this reason St. Augustine's words cannot bear the interpretation the papists put on them, but they must be understood in terms of the external proof of faith, by which heretics are refuted and the weak are strengthened in faith, when they see that all the world preaches and regards as gospel that which they believe. And if this meaning cannot be found in St. Augustine's statement, then it is better to reject the statement; for it is contrary to the Scriptures, the Spirit, and all experience, if it has that other meaning.

Finally when they are refuted with Scripture so that they cannot escape, they begin to blaspheme God and say, "But St. Matthew, Paul, and Peter were also men; therefore their teachings are also the doctrines of men. If their doctrine is to be observed, then let the pope's doctrine be observed as well!" Such blasphemy is now being uttered even by some princes and bishops who nonetheless count themselves wise. When you hear such completely hardened and blinded blasphemers, turn away from them and stop your ears; they are not worthy that anyone should talk to them. For if that argument were to hold, then Moses also was a man, and all the prophets were men. Then we had best go our way, following our own fancy and really believing nothing at all, but simply regarding everything as the doctrine of men.

If, nevertheless, you desire to talk with them, then do it this way, and say: Very well, let St. Paul or Matthew be the doctrine of men. Then we must ask, whence comes their authority? How will they prove that they have authority to teach and to be bishops? Or how shall we know where the church is? If the papists say that St. Matthew in chapter 16[:19] or St. Paul in some place or other has so asserted, then answer: That does not hold; these are the doctrines of men, as you say; you must have God's Word to support you. And then you will find that these hardened blasphemers put themselves to shame and confusion with their own folly. They cannot even distinguish between a man who speaks for himself and one through whom God speaks. The words of the apostles were committed to them by God and confirmed and proved by great miracles, such as were never done for the doctrines of men. And if the papists are certain in themselves, and will prove it to us, that God has commanded them to teach as they do, we will believe them too as we believe the apostles. If it is uncertain whether the words of the apostles are from God, who will give us certainty that the papists' doctrines of men are from God? O the fury and madness, worthy of this age![24]

We do not condemn the doctrines of men just because they are the doctrines of men, for we would gladly put up with them. But we condemn them because they are contrary to the gospel and the Scriptures. While the Scriptures liberate consciences and forbid that they be taken captive by the doctrines of men, these doctrines of men captivate the conscience anyhow. This conflict between the Scriptures and the doctrines of men we cannot reconcile. Therefore because these two forms of doctrine contradict one another we allow even young children to judge here whether we are to give up the Scriptures, in which the one Word of God is taught from the beginning of the world, or whether we are to give up the doctrines of men, which were newly devised yesterday and which change daily?

We hope that everyone will agree with the decision that the doctrines of men must be forsaken and the Scriptures retained. For they will neither desire nor be able to keep both, since the two cannot be reconciled and are by nature necessarily opposed to one another, like fire and water, like heaven and earth. As Isaiah 55[:9] puts it, "As the heavens are higher than the earth, so are my ways higher than your ways." Now he who walks on the earth cannot at the same time walk in heaven, and he who walks in heaven cannot walk on the earth.

Therefore we request the papists that they first reconcile their doctrine with the Scriptures. If they accomplish that, we will observe their doctrines. But that they will not do until the Holy Spirit first becomes a liar. Therefore we say again: We censure the doctrines of men not because men have spoken them, but because they are lies and blasphemies against the Scriptures. And the Scriptures, although they too are written by men, are neither of men nor from men but from God. Now since Scriptures and the doctrines of men are contrary one to the other, the one must lie and the other be true. Now let us see to which of the two the papists themselves will ascribe the lie.

Let this be enough.

---

[24] *O furor et amentia his seculis digna.*

HOW CHRISTIANS SHOULD REGARD MOSES

1525

Translated by E. Theodore Bachmann

INTRODUCTION

The year of this sermon, 1525, was fraught with high tension and tragic turmoil. For Luther it had begun with the publication of *Against the Heavenly Prophets*,[1] his sharp attack against his former colleague, Andreas Karlstadt, and the Sacramentarians. Between January and August the explosive peasant uprising took place, and Luther's succession of well-intended but ill-timed and infelicitous pamphlets[2] alienated many. On May 27, Thomas Münzer, the religious radical and fomenter of peasant unrest, was put to death.[3]

Luther's opposition to both Karlstadt and Münzer derived from his theological convictions—stated in this treatise—concerning the relationship between law and gospel and the related problem of the relationship between the Old Testament and the New. Law and gospel are chosen ways through which God addresses his word to men. In the law God says No to man, the sinner; in the gospel he says Yes to man, the righteous—that man who has repented and believes his promise in Jesus Christ. Law and gospel are both present in both of the Testaments. They must always be distinguished but never identified or confused.[4]

For several years too the problem of usury and unfair interest rates had also occupied Luther's attention,[5] particularly since certain earnest evangelical Christians like Pastor Jacob Strauss at

---

[1] *LW* 40, (75) 79-223.

[2] *Admonition to Peace: A Reply to the Twelve Articles of the Peasants in Swabia* (late April [?], 1525). *PE* 4, (205) 219-244. *Against the Robbing and Murdering Hordes of Peasants* (early May, 1525). *PE* 4, (247) 248-254. *An Open Letter Concerning the Hard Book Against the Peasants* (early July, 1525). *PE* 4, (257) 259-281.

[3] See p. 403, n. 74.

[4] For a fuller understanding of Luther's thought on this vital matter one should, of course, look beyond this single writing to other treatises of divergent emphasis such as his 1539 polemic, *Against the Antinomians*. *WA* 50, (461) 468-477; and his 1543 discussion of *The Last Words of David*. *WA* 54, (16) 28-100.

[5] Luther had written on this subject at various times between 1519 and 1524. *PE* 4, (9) 12-69. *WA* 15, (279) 293-322. *WA*, Br 3, 176-177, 305-308. Smith and Jacobs, *Luther's Correspondence*, II, 236-238.

Eisenach and the court preacher Wolfgang Stein at Weimar had brought their considerable influence to bear on the Saxon princes in favor of substituting the more humane laws of the Old Testament for the then current imperial and canon laws. Luther opposed the notion that the Scriptures would be properly exalted if Mosaic precepts were suddenly, as law, to replace laws of the German state and church. He warned that while seemingly honoring the Scriptures, one can actually distort the meaning and intention of the Word of God. This entire discussion too stands in the background of this 1525 discourse on Moses.[6]

In the course of his career as an expositor of the Scriptures, Luther had developed a distinctive understanding of the Word of God. It is the Word of God, our Lord. We can receive *it* only by submitting to *him*. Such submission includes the recognition that he is the Lord who does and bestows all and whose lordship consists in his saving activity. But, contends Luther, if I now imagined that God's lordship expresses itself in certain legal statements or precepts which I had the possibility of ascertaining and expounding, then I should precisely *not* have understood what God's lordship really is. Instead I should then—despite all my own outward protest against Roman papism—have substituted a biblicistic for a papal police. Therefore I am not to make the Word of God function simply as a part of human law. "Moses" is not the Word of God in the sense that "Moses" could be substituted for a piece of human legislation.

How, then, is "Moses" Word of God, and how is "Moses" law? How do Word of God and law relate to each other?

Here Luther makes sometimes the most contrary statements. On the one hand "Moses" is completely abolished: "Moses does not pertain to us." On the other hand we hear Luther expressing the wish "that [today's] lords ruled according to the example of Moses."

Anyone who, like the enthusiasts, erects Mosaic law as a biblical-divine requirement does injury to the preaching of Christ. Just as the Judaizers of old, who would have required circumcision as an initial requirement, so also the enthusiasts and radicals of this later era do not see that Christ is the end of the Mosaic law. For

---

[6] Most of what follows in this introduction is based on an introduction to this same treatise provided by Georg Merz in MA³ 4, 398-401.

all the stipulations of that law, insofar as they go beyond the natural law, have been abolished by Christ. The Ten Commandments are binding upon all men only so far as they are implanted in everyone by nature. In this sense Luther declares that "Moses is dead."

Besides, the Jewish assembly of Sinai and of the decalogue has been replaced by the Christian congregation of Pentecost and of the new covenant. The era of Mosaic law extends from Sinai to Pentecost. In this era the Jewish people served its particular purpose, for this people, alone among all the peoples, was during that time span both state and church. It was just one national ethnic group among others on earth, but at the same time it was a peculiar people set apart for God as an instrument of his plan for all peoples.

So far as "Moses" is simply the *Sachsenspiegel* or law code of the Jewish people as a national ethnic group, it can be listed as just one code of laws among many, features of which may or may not be considered desirable in another age or nation. But so far as the Mosaic law is the law of the Old Testament congregation of God, it has a prophetic and promissory significance comparable to nothing in the laws of other peoples; and it has a continuing relevance not to any people simply as people but only to the post-Pentecost church of God spread among all peoples.

Delivered on August 27, 1525, *How Christians Should Regard Moses* was Number 29 in Luther's long series of seventy-seven sermons on Exodus preached from October 2, 1524, to February 2, 1527. It was reworked for separate publication and issued as a pamphlet from the press of Hans Weisz at Wittenberg on May 1, 1526. With slight later additions it was inserted by an editor as a fitting introduction to the 1527 printed volume of Luther's sermons on Genesis, a series that had been preached March 22, 1523—September 18, 1524. In that form, almost without modification, it was included in a 1528 exposition of the Ten Commandments, which was simply a reproduction of sermons 29-37 in the series on Exodus,[7] and again in the festival portion of certain editions of the church postils. Our translation, the first in English, is based on the first separate printing of 1526: *Eyn Unterrichtung wie sich die Christen ynn Mosen sollen schicken,* as it is given in WA 16, 363-393, text "U."

---

[7] *WA* 16, (xv) 363-393, text "A."

HOW CHRISTIANS SHOULD
REGARD MOSES

Dear friends, you have often heard that there has never been a public sermon from heaven except twice. Apart from them God has spoken many times through and with men on earth, as in the case of the holy patriarchs Adam, Noah, Abraham, Isaac, Jacob, and others, down to Moses. But in none of these cases did he speak with such glorious splendor, visible reality, or public cry and exclamation as he did on those two occasions. Rather God illuminated their heart within and spoke through their mouth, as Luke indicates in the first chapter of his gospel where he says, "As he spoke by the mouth of his holy prophets from of old" [Luke 1:70].

Now the first sermon is in Exodus[1] 19 and 20; by it God caused himself to be heard from heaven with great splendor and might. For the people of Israel heard the trumpets and the voice of God himself.

In the second place God delivered a public sermon through the Holy Spirit on Pentecost [Acts 2:2-4]. On that occasion the Holy Spirit came with great splendor and visible impressiveness, such that there came from heaven the sudden rushing of a mighty wind, and it filled the entire house where the apostles were sitting. And there appeared to them tongues as of fire, distributed and resting on each of them. And they were all filled with the Holy Spirit and began to preach and speak in other tongues. This happened with great spendor and glorious might, so that thereafter the apostles preached so powerfully that the sermons which we hear in the world today are hardly a shadow compared to theirs, so far as the visible splendor and substance of their sermons is concerned. For the apostles spoke in all sorts of languages, performed great miracles, etc. Yet through our preachers today the Holy Spirit does not cause

---

[1] Where Luther refers to a specific book of the Pentateuch by number (e.g., "The Second Book of Moses") we have given the corresponding English title.

himself to be either heard or seen; nothing is coming down openly from heaven. This is why I have said that there are only two such special and public sermons which have been seen and heard from heaven. To be sure, God spoke also to Christ from heaven, when he was baptized in the Jordan [Matt. 3:17], and [at the Transfiguration] on Mount Tabor [Matt. 17:5]. However none of this took place in the presence of the general public.

God wanted to send that second sermon into the world, for it had earlier been announced by the mouth and in the books of the holy prophets. He will no longer speak that way publicly through sermons. Instead, in the third place, he will come in person with divine glory, so that all creatures will tremble and quake before him [Luke 21:25-27]; and then he will no longer preach to them, but they will see and handle him himself [Luke 24:39].

Now the first sermon, and doctrine, is the law of God. The second is the gospel. These two sermons are not the same. Therefore we must have a good grasp of the matter in order to know how to differentiate between them. We must know what the law is, and what the gospel is. The law commands and requires us to do certain things. The law is thus directed solely to our behavior and consists in making requirements. For God speaks through the law, saying, "Do this, avoid that, this is what I expect of you." The gospel, however, does not preach what we are to do or to avoid. It sets up no requirements but reverses the approach of the law, does the very opposite, and says, "This is what God has done for you; he has let his Son be made flesh for you, has let him be put to death for your sake." So, then, there are two kinds of doctrine and two kinds of works, those of God and those of men. Just as we and God are separated from one another, so also these two doctrines are widely separated from one another. For the gospel teaches exclusively what has been given us by God, and not—as in the case of the law—what we are to do and give to God.

We now want to see how this first sermon sounded forth and with what splendor God gave the law on Mount Sinai. He selected the place where he wanted to be seen and heard. Not that God actually spoke, for he has no mouth, tongue, teeth, or lips as we do. But he who created and formed the mouth of all men [Exod. 4:11] can also make speech and the voice. For no one would be able to speak a single word unless God first gave it, as the prophet says, "It would be impossible to speak except God first put it in our mouth."[2] Language, speech, and voice are thus gifts of God like any other gifts, such as the fruit on the trees. Now he who fashioned the mouth and put speech in it can also make and use speech even though there is no mouth present. Now the words which are here written were spoken through an angel. This is not to say that only one angel was there, for there was a great multitude there serving God and preaching to the people of Israel at Mount Sinai. The angel, however, who spoke here and did the talking, spoke just as if God himself were speaking and saying, "I am your God, who brought you out of the land of Egypt," etc. [Exod. 20:1], as if Peter or Paul were speaking in God's stead and saying, "I am your God," etc. In his letter to the Galatians [3:19], Paul says that the law was ordained by angels. That is, angels were assigned, in God's behalf, to give the law of God; and Moses, as an intermediary, received it from the angels. I say this so that you might know who gave the law. He did this to them, however, because he wanted thereby to compel, burden, and press the Jews.

What kind of a voice that was, you may well imagine. It was a voice like the voice of a man, such that it was actually heard. The syllables and letters thus made sounds which the physical ear was able to pick up. But it was a bold, glorious, and great voice. As told in Deuteronomy 4[:12], the people heard the voice, but saw no one. They heard a powerful voice, for he spoke in a powerful voice, as if in the dark we should hear a voice from a high tower or roof top, and could see no one but only hear the strong voice of a man. And this is why it is called the voice of God, because it was above a human voice.

Now you will hear how God used this voice in order to arouse his people and make them brave. For he intended to institute the tangible [eusserliche] and spiritual government. It was previously stated how, on the advice of Jethro, his father-in-law, Moses had

---

[2] Cf. Num. 22:38.

established the temporal government and appointed rulers and judges [Exod. 18:13-26]. Beyond that there is yet a spiritual kingdom in which Christ rules in the hearts of men; this kingdom we cannot see, because it consists only in faith and will continue until the Last Day.

These are two kingdoms:[3] the temporal, which governs with the sword and is visible; and the spiritual, which governs solely with grace and with the forgiveness of sins. Between these two kingdoms still another has been placed in the middle, half spiritual and half temporal. It is constituted by the Jews, with commandments and outward ceremonies which prescribe their conduct toward God and men.

The law of Moses binds only the Jews and not the Gentiles

Here the law of Moses has its place. It is no longer binding on us because it was given only to the people of Israel. And Israel accepted this law for itself and its descendants, while the Gentiles were excluded. To be sure, the Gentiles have certain laws in common with the Jews, such as these: there is one God, no one is to do wrong to another, no one is to commit adultery or murder or steal, and others like them. This is written by nature into their hearts; they did not hear it straight from heaven as the Jews did. This is why this entire text does not pertain to the Gentiles. I say this on account of the enthusiasts. For you see and hear how they read Moses, extol him, and bring up the way he ruled the people with commandments. They try to be clever, and think they know something more than is presented in the gospel; so they minimize faith, contrive something new, and boastfully claim that it comes from the Old Testament. They desire to govern people according to the letter of the law of Moses, as if no one had ever read it before.

But we will not have this sort of thing. We would rather not preach again for the rest of our life than to let Moses return and to let Christ be torn out of our hearts. We will not have Moses as ruler or lawgiver any longer. Indeed God himself will not have it either. Moses was an intermediary solely for the Jewish people. It was to

---

[3] On the two kingdoms cf. pp. 289-290.

them that he gave the law. We must therefore silence the mouths of those factious spirits who say, "Thus says Moses," etc. Here you simply reply: Moses has nothing to do with us. If I were to accept Moses in one commandment, I would have to accept the entire Moses. Thus the consequence would be that if I accept Moses as master, then I must have myself circumcised,[4] wash my clothes in the Jewish way, eat and drink and dress thus and so, and observe all that stuff. So, then, we will neither observe nor accept Moses. Moses is dead. His rule ended when Christ came. He is of no further service.

That Moses does not bind the Gentiles can be proved[5] from Exodus 20[:1], where God himself speaks, "I am the Lord your God, who brought you out of the land of Egypt, out of the house of bondage." This text makes it clear that even the Ten Commandments do not pertain to us. For God never led us out of Egypt, but only the Jews. The sectarian spirits want to saddle us with Moses and all the commandments. We will just skip that. We will regard Moses as a teacher, but we will not regard him as our lawgiver—unless he agrees with both the New Testament and the natural law. There fore it is clear enough that Moses is the lawgiver of the Jews and not of the Gentiles. He has given the Jews a sign whereby they should lay hold of God, when they call upon him as the God who brought them out of Egypt. The Christians have a different sign, whereby they conceive of God as the One who gave his Son, etc.

Again one can prove it from the third commandment that Moses does not pertain to Gentiles and Christians. For Paul [Col. 2:16] and the New Testament [Matt. 12:1-12; John 5:16; 7:22-23; 9:14-16] abolish the sabbath, to show us that the sabbath was given to the Jews alone, for whom it is a stern commandment. The prophets referred to it too, that the sabbath of the Jews would be abolished. For Isaiah says in the last chapter, "When the Savior comes, then such will be the time, one sabbath after the other, one month after

---

[4] In a letter to Chancellor Brück of Saxony dated January 13, 1524, Luther wrote that the people of Orlamünde, Karlstadt's parish, would probably circumcise themselves and be wholly Mosaic. MA³ 4, 402, n. 182.

[5] *Zwingen* probably means *zwingend beweisen* as MA³ 4, 402, n. 183, 4 suggests.

the other," etc.[6] This is as though he were trying to say, "It will be the sabbath every day, and the people will be such that they make no distinction between days. For in the New Testament the sabbath is annihilated as regards the crude external observance, for every day is a holy day," etc.

Now if anyone confronts you with Moses and his commandments, and wants to compel you to keep them, simply answer, "Go to the Jews with your Moses; I am no Jew. Do not entangle me with Moses. If I accept Moses in one respect (Paul tells the Galatians in chapter 5[:3]), then I am obligated to keep the entire law." For not one little period in Moses pertains to us.

Question:

Why then do you preach about Moses if he does not pertain to us?

Answer to the Question:

Three things are to be noted in Moses.

I want to keep Moses and not sweep him under the rug,[7] because I find three things in Moses.

In the first place I dismiss the commandments given to the people of Israel. They neither urge nor compel me. They are dead and gone, except insofar as I gladly and willingly accept something from Moses, as if I said, "This is how Moses ruled, and it seems fine to me, so I will follow him in this or that particular."

I would even be glad if [today's] lords ruled according to the example of Moses. If I were emperor, I would take from Moses a model for [my] statutes; not that Moses should be binding on me, but that I should be free to follow him in ruling as he ruled. For example, tithing is a very fine rule, because with the giving of the tenth all other taxes would be eliminated. For the ordinary man

---

[6] Our rendering of Isa. 66:23 is here based on the Douay version, as Luther's was on the Vulgate.

[7] *Unter den banck stecken* (literally, "put under the bench") is a proverbial expression meaning to put aside, hide, or forget some despicable thing. WA 51, 661 and 724, No. 468. Wander (ed.), *Sprichwörter-Lexikon* I, 229, "Bank," No. 40. Cf. p. 253, n. 53.

it would also be easier to give a tenth than to pay rents and fees. Suppose I had ten cows; I would then give one. If I had only five, I would give nothing. If my fields were yielding only a little, I would give proportionately little; if much, I would give much. All of this would be in God's providence. But as things are now, I must pay the Gentile tax even if the hail should ruin my entire crop. If I owe a hundred gulden in taxes, I must pay it even though there may be nothing growing in the field. This is also the way the pope decrees and governs. But it would be better if things were so arranged that when I raise much, I give much; and when little, I give little.

Again in Moses it is also stipulated that no man should sell his field into a perpetual estate, but only up to the jubilee year.[8] When that year came, every man returned to the field or possessions which he had sold. In this way the possessions remained in the family relationship. There are also other extraordinarily fine rules in Moses which one should like to accept, use, and put into effect. Not that one should bind or be bound by them, but (as I said earlier) the emperor could here take an example for setting up a good government on the basis of Moses, just as the Romans conducted a good government, and just like the *Sachsenspiegel*[9] by which affairs are ordered in this land of ours. The Gentiles are not obligated to obey Moses. Moses is the *Sachsenspiegel* for the Jews. But if an example of good government were to be taken from Moses, one could adhere to it without obligation as long as one pleased, etc.

Again Moses says, "If a man dies without children, then his brother or closest relative should take the widow into his home and have her to wife, and thus raise up offspring for the deceased brother or relative. The first child thus born was credited to the deceased brother or relative" [Deut. 25:5-6]. So it came about that one man had many wives. Now this is also a very good rule.

When these factious spirits come, however, and say, "Moses has

---

[8] *Laut jar.* Cf. Lev. 25:8-55.
[9] This "Saxon code of law" was a thirteenth century compilation of the economic and social laws obtaining in and around Magdeburg and Halberstadt; it was influential in the codification of German law until the nineteenth century. The radical Reformers sometimes sought to replace it with the law of Moses or the Sermon on the Mount. Cf. *LW* 21, 90, n. 37 and *LW* 40, 98, n. 20.

commanded it," then simply drop Moses and reply, "I am not concerned about what Moses commands." "Yes," they say, "he has commanded that we should have one God, that we should trust and believe in him, that we should not swear by his name; that we should honor father and mother; not kill, steal, commit adultery; not bear false witness, and not covet [Exod. 20:3-17]; should we not keep these commandments?" You reply: Nature also has these laws. Nature provides that we should call upon God. The Gentiles attest to this fact. For there never was a Gentile who did not call upon his idols, even though these were not the true God. This also happened among the Jews, for they had their idols as did the Gentiles; only the Jews have received the law. The Gentiles have it written in their heart, and there is no distinction [Rom. 3:22]. As St. Paul also shows in Romans 2[:14-15], the Gentiles, who have no law, have the law written in their heart.

But just as the Jews fail, so also do the Gentiles. Therefore it is natural to honor God, not steal, not commit adultery, not bear false witness, not murder; and what Moses commands is nothing new. For what God has given the Jews from heaven, he has also written in the hearts of all men. Thus I keep the commandments which Moses has given, not because Moses gave commandment, but because they have been implanted in me by nature, and Moses agrees exactly with nature, etc.

But the other commandments of Moses, which are not [implanted in all men] by nature, the Gentiles do not hold. Nor do these pertain to the Gentiles, such as the tithe and others equally fine which I wish we had too. Now this is the first thing that I ought to see in Moses, namely, the commandments to which I am not bound except insofar as they are [implanted in everyone] by nature [and written in everyone's heart].[10]

The second thing to notice in Moses

In the second place I find something in Moses that I do not have from nature: the promises and pledges of God about Christ.

---

[10] The bracketed phrases in this paragraph are from the version given in the 1528 *Exposition of the Ten Commandments*. WA 16, 380, ll. 26, 31. See the Introduction, p. 159.

This is the best thing. It is something that is not written naturally into the heart, but comes from heaven. God has promised, for example, that his Son should be born in the flesh. This is what the gospel proclaims. It is not commandments. And it is the most important thing in Moses which pertains to us. The first thing, namely, the commandments, does not pertain to us. I read Moses because such excellent and comforting promises are there recorded, by which I can find strength for my weak faith. For things take place in the kingdom of Christ just as I read in Moses that they will; therein I find also my sure foundation.

In this manner, therefore, I should accept Moses, and not sweep him under the rug: first because he provides fine examples of laws, from which excerpts may be taken. Second, in Moses there are the promises of God which sustain faith. As it is written of Eve in Genesis 3[:15], "I will put enmity between you and the woman, and between your seed and her seed; he shall bruise your head," etc. Again Abraham was given this promise by God, speaking thus in Genesis [22:18], "In your descendants shall all the nations be blessed"; that is, through Christ the gospel is to arise.

Again in Deuteronomy 18[:15-16] Moses says, "The Lord your God will raise up for you a prophet like me from among you, from your brethren—him you shall heed; just as you desired of the Lord your God at Horeb on the day of the assembly," etc. Many are these texts in the Old Testament, which the holy apostles quoted and drew upon.

But our factious spirits go ahead and say of everything they find in Moses, "Here God is speaking, no one can deny it; therefore we must keep it." So then the rabble go to it. Whew! If God has said it, who then will say anything against it? Then they are really pressed hard like pigs at a trough. Our dear prophets have chattered thus into the minds of the people, "Dear people, God has ordered his people to beat Amalek to death" [Exod. 17:8-16; Deut. 25:17-19].[11] Misery and tribulation have come out of this sort of thing. The

---

[11] Thomas Münzer in a sermon of July, 1524, at Allstedt demanded that the princes wipe out all the godless, including godless rulers, priests, and monks. MA⁸ 4, 402, n. 187, 9. Cf. LW 40, 47.

peasants have arisen,[12] not knowing the difference, and have been led into this error by those insane factious spirits.

Had there been educated preachers around, they could have stood up to the false prophets and stopped them, and said this to them, "Dear factious spirits, it is true that God commanded this of Moses and spoke thus to the people; but we are not this people. Land, God spoke also to Adam; but that does not make me Adam. God commanded Abraham to put his son to death [Gen. 22:2]; but that does not make me Abraham and obligate me to put my son to death. God spoke also with David. It is all God's word. But let God's word be what it may, I must pay attention and know to whom God's word is addressed. You are still a long way from being the people with whom God spoke." The false prophets say, "You are that people, God is speaking to you." You must prove that to me. With talk like that these factious spirits could have been refuted. But they wanted to be beaten, and so the rabble went to the devil.

One must deal cleanly with the Scriptures. From the very beginning the word has come to us in various ways. It is not enough simply to look and see whether this is God's word, whether God has said it; rather we must look and see to whom it has been spoken, whether it fits us. That makes all the difference between night and day.[13] God said to David, "Out of you shall come the king," etc. [II Sam. 7:13]. But this does not pertain to me, nor has it been spoken to me. He can indeed speak to me if he chooses to do so. You must keep your eye on the word that applies to you, that is spoken to you.

The word in Scripture is of two kinds: the first does not pertain or apply to me, the other kind does. And upon that word which does pertain to me I can boldly trust and rely, as upon a strong rock. But if it does not pertain to me, then I should stand still. The false prophets pitch in and say, "Dear people, this is the word of God." That is true; we cannot deny it. But we are not the people. God has not given us the directive. The factious spirits came in and wanted to stir up something new, saying, "We must keep the Old Testa-

---

[12] On the Peasants' War see the Introduction, p. 157.
[13] *Da scheidet denn sich sommer und winter.*

170

ment also." So they led the peasants into a sweat and ruined them in wife and child. These insane people imagined that it had been withheld from them, that no one had told them they are supposed to murder. It serves them right. They would not follow or listen to anybody. I have seen and experienced it myself, how mad, raving, and senseless they were.[14]

Therefore tell this to Moses: Leave Moses and his people together; they have had their day and do not pertain to me. I listen to that word which applies to me. We have the gospel. Christ says, "Go and preach the gospel," not only to the Jews as Moses did, but to "all nations," to "all creatures" [Mark 16:15]. To me it is said, "He who believes and is baptized will be saved" [Mark 16:16]. Again, "Go and do to your neighbor as has been done to you."[15] These words strike me too, for I am one of the "all creatures." If Christ had not added, "preach to all creatures," then I would not listen, would not be baptized, just as I now will not listen to Moses because he is given not to me but only to the Jews. However because Christ says: not to one people, nor in this or in that place in the world, but to "all creatures," therefore no one is exempt. Rather, all are thereby included; no one should doubt that to him too the gospel is to be preached. And so I believe that word; it does pertain also to me. I too belong under the gospel, in the new covenant. Therefore I put my trust in that word, even if it should cost a hundred thousand lives.

This distinction should be noticed, grasped, and taken to heart by those preachers who would teach others; indeed by all Christians, for everything depends entirely upon it. If the peasants had understood it this way, they would have salvaged much and would not have been so pitifully misled and ruined. And where we understand it differently, there we make sects and factions, slavering among the rabble and into the raving and uncomprehending people without any distinction, saying, "God's word, God's word." But my dear fellow, the question is whether it was said to you. God

---

[14] In April and May, 1525, Luther had preached personally against the insurrection, both in Mansfeld and in Thuringia. *MA³* 4, 402, n. 188, 11.
[15] Cf. Matt. 7:12.

indeed speaks also to angels, wood, fish, birds, animals, and all creatures, but this does not make it pertain to me. I should pay attention to that which applies to me, that which is said to me, in which God admonishes, drives, and requires something of me.

Here is an illustration. Suppose a housefather had a wife, a daughter, a son, a maid, and a hired man. Now he speaks to the hired man and orders him to hitch up the horses and bring in a load of wood, or drive over to the field, or do some other job. And suppose he tells the maid to milk the cows, churn some butter, and so on. And suppose he tells his wife to take care of the kitchen and his daughter to do some spinning and make the beds. All this would be the words of one master, one housefather. Suppose now the maid decided she wanted to drive the horses and fetch the wood, the hired man sat down and began milking the cows, the daughter wanted to drive the wagon or plow the field, the wife took a notion to make the beds or spin and so forgot all about the kitchen; and then they all said, "The master has commanded this, these are the housefather's orders!" Then what? Then the housefather would grab a club and knock them all in a heap, and say, "Although it is my command, yet I have not commanded it of you; I gave each of you your instructions, you should have stuck to them."

It is like this with the word of God. Suppose I take up something that God ordered someone else to do, and then I declare, "But you said to do it." God would answer, "Let the devil thank you; I did not tell you to do it." One must distinguish well whether the word pertains to only one or to everybody. If, now, the housefather should say, "On Friday we are going to eat meat," this would be a word common to everybody in the house. Thus what God said to Moses by way of commandment is for the Jews only. But the gospel goes through the whole world in its entirety; it is offered to all creatures without exception. Therefore all the world should accept it, and accept it as if it had been offered to each person individually. The word, "We should love one another" [John 15:12], pertains to me, for it pertains to all who belong to the gospel. Thus we read Moses not because he applies to us, that we must obey him, but because he agrees with the natural law and is conceived better than the Gentiles would ever have been able to do. Thus the Ten Commandments are a mirror of our life, in which we can see wherein we are lacking, etc. The sectarian spirits have misunderstood also with respect to the images;[16] for that too pertains only to the Jews.

Summing up this second part, we read Moses for the sake of the promises about Christ, who belongs not only to the Jews but also to the Gentiles; for through Christ all the Gentiles should have the blessing, as was promised to Abraham [Gen. 12:3].

The third thing to be seen in Moses

In the third place we read Moses for the beautiful examples of faith, of love, and of the cross, as shown in the fathers, Adam, Abel, Noah, Abraham, Isaac, Jacob, Moses, and all the rest. From them we should learn to trust in God and love him. In turn there are also examples of the godless, how God does not pardon the unfaith of the unbelieving; how he can punish Cain, Ishmael, Esau, the whole world in the flood, Sodom and Gomorrah, etc. Examples like these are necessary. For although I am not Cain, yet if I should act like Cain, I will receive the same punishment as Cain. Nowhere else do we find such fine examples of both faith and unfaith. Therefore we should not sweep Moses under the rug. Moreover the Old Testament is thus properly understood when we retain from the prophets the beautiful texts about Christ, when we take note of and thoroughly grasp the fine examples, and when we use the laws as we please to our advantage.

Conclusion and Summary

I have stated that all Christians, and especially those who handle the word of God and attempt to teach others, should take heed and learn Moses aright. Thus where he gives commandment, we are not to follow him except so far as he agrees with the natural law. Moses is a teacher and doctor of the Jews. We have our own master, Christ, and he has set before us what we are to know,

---

[16] The iconoclasm of the radical leftists, who took Moses literally and destroyed images, windows, and other church art, aroused Luther's indignation. Cf. his fuller treatment of this subject, also during 1525, in *Against the Heavenly Prophets. LW* 40, 84-101.

observe, do, and leave undone. However it is true that Moses sets down, in addition to the laws, fine examples of faith and unfaith— punishment of the godless, elevation of the righteous and believing— and also the dear and comforting promises concerning Christ which we should accept. The same is true also in the gospel. For example in the account of the ten lepers, that Christ bids them go to the priest and make sacrifice [Luke 17:14] does not pertain to me. The example of their faith, however, does pertain to me; I should believe Christ, as did they.

Enough has now been said of this, and it is to be noted well for it is really crucial. Many great and outstanding people have missed it, while even today many great preachers still stumble over it. They do not know how to preach Moses, nor how properly to regard his books. They are absurd as they rage and fume, chattering to people, "God's word, God's word!" All the while they mislead the poor people and drive them to destruction. Many learned men have not known how far Moses ought to be taught. Origen,[17] Jerome,[18] and others like them, have not shown clearly how far Moses can really serve us. This is what I have attempted, to say in an introduction to Moses how we should regard him, and how he should be understood and received and not simply be swept under the rug. For in Moses there is comprehended such a fine order, that it is a joy, etc.

God be praised.

---

[17] Origen (ca. 185-254), Alexandrian theologian and ascetic, always sought in his exegesis the deeper, hidden spiritual meaning that lay back of the unspiritual grammatical-historical meaning of the text. See p. 403, n. 7.
[18] On Jerome see p. 117, n. 1.

ON TRANSLATING:
AN OPEN LETTER

1530

Translated by Charles M. Jacobs
Revised by E. Theodore Bachmann

INTRODUCTION

During the sessions of the imperial diet at Augsburg Luther was lodged at Coburg castle nearly seventy miles north of Nürnberg, both for safekeeping and for possible consultation, since Coburg was relatively more accessible to Augsburg than was Wittenberg. Like the Wartburg earlier, the Coburg castle—which Luther called "The Wilderness"—became his temporary home from April 23 to October 4, 1530.

Understandably anxious and apprehensive about the outcome of the evangelical cause at Augsburg, Luther kept characteristically busy. His correspondence was weighty and voluminous, and his writings included a number of longer works in addition to what he had set as his foremost task while at the Coburg, that of translating. On the day of his arrival he wrote to Melanchthon, "Out of this Sinai we shall make a Zion and build three tabernacles: One to the Psalter, one to the Prophets, and one to Aesop."[1]

Luther set to work immediately on the Prophets, first of all—in view of the continuing threat of the Turks against the empire—translating and preparing for special publication chapters 39 and 40 of Ezekiel, in which he interpreted Gog and Magog to be the Turks, hoping that all the faithful might thereby draw courage and comfort from this passage.[2] In the same letter of May 12, 1530, in which Luther announced his treatise on Ezekiel 38—39 concerning Gog, he also told of his intention of finishing the Prophets by Ascension and how it had been thwarted by severe illness.[3] By June 10 he was finished with Jeremiah and working on Ezekiel which proved—with the recurrent headaches—impossible to complete while at the Coburg. Meanwhile he had taken up Hosea and completed all the Minor Prophets by early September. His wife Kate had heard

---

[1] Margaret A. Currie (trans.), *The Letters of Martin Luther* (London: Macmillan, 1909), p. 208.

[2] See the text of this brief treatise in WA 30^{II}, (220) 223-236.

[3] Currie, *op. cit.*, 211-212.

that he was ill, and his letter of September 8 reassured her that he was well, had finished all the Prophets except one, and was working on Ezekiel again.[4]

Meanwhile doctrinal issues central to the Reformation kept coming into his thoughts and writing, giving added pertinence to his task of translating. What was on his mind needed telling. Resorting to an open letter, Luther formulated his thoughts on translating and sent them to his friend, Wenceslaus Link, at Nürnberg on September 12 to have them published. Link turned the letter over to the Nürnberg printer, Johann Petreius,[5] together with his own brief introduction[6] dated September 15, 1530, indicating that this was a letter of Luther which Link had received "through a good friend."

Luther used this open letter to answer two questions which had apparently been put to him by some other "friend." Who that friend may have been we do not know. Nor does it matter, for the letter itself may well have been merely a literary device[7] for airing two doctrinal issues: the matter of justification by faith alone and the question of intercessory prayer by the saints. Both issues had again come to the fore during the summer at Augsburg, notably in Melanchthon's encounter with Johann Eck on the *sola fides*.[8] Luther's treatment of the second question is here so cursory (see page 198 where he announces his intention of treating it more fully elsewhere) that we have omitted mention of it in the title altogether.

His treatment of the first issue involved him in a direct discussion of a basic principle of translation. Luther readily admits that at times it is necessary for the translator to depart from the literal meaning of the words of the original in order to clarify in

---

[4] *Ibid.*, pp. 246-247. *WA*, DB 2, xii-xiii.

[5] *MA*[3] 6, 431. *WA* 30[II], 632 incorrectly names Johann Stüchs as the printer.

[6] We have here included in our translation Link's own introduction, which was omitted at *PE* 5, 10.

[7] This interpretation is suggested by the editors in both *WA* 30[II], 627 and *CL* 4, 179.

[8] See Eck's *Four Hundred and Four Articles for the Diet in Augsburg*, Michael Reu, *The Augsburg Confession* (Chicago: Wartburg, 1930), pp. 58ff., *97-*121. On the saints see the Augsburg Confession, Article 21.

the new language their actual sense, and that a careful translation will sometimes therefore convey a meaning quite different from the one conventionally held.[9] His much criticized translation of Rom. 3:28 is defended as being both theologically and linguistically just and necessary. By way of illustrating and buttressing this claim Luther also touches on the problems of relinquishing the letters and rendering the sense of Matt. 12:34, 26:8, and the angelic salutation to Mary in Luke 1:28.

Ever since its first publication in 1522 Luther's translation of the New Testament had been drawing not only wide approval but also certain narrow and often envious criticism. Among his sharpest critics was the notorious Jerome Emser (1478-1527), theologian, lawyer, and for over twenty years secretary to Duke George of Saxony. Like certain other rulers in the empire, Duke George had forbidden the circulation of Luther's German New Testament in his territory. However not to be left without a New Testament in German, the Duke had commissioned Emser to provide a reliable Roman version. Emser obliged and, in the year of his death, lived to see the publication of his traditionalist version of the New Testament in German.

Outwardly it looked almost identical with the folio edition of Luther's translation, even down to some of the Cranach woodcuts. But its introductions and glosses were all designed to cancel out those which accompanied Luther's version. The text of Emser's New Testament was based not on the original Greek text of Erasmus, which Luther had used, but on the Latin Vulgate and the late medieval German Bible. With these traditional sources as his base, Emser proceeded to "correct" the errors in Luther's German New Testament; he did not claim to offer wholly a "new" version.

Emser's translation, however, was not as traditional as might be supposed. Actually he had plagiarized much of Luther's translation and then palmed off the finished product as his own. Hence

---

[9] Cf. *Defense of the Translation of the Psalms,* in this volume, pp. 209, 216, 222, where the principle here enunciated with respect to translation of the New Testament is further illustrated in terms of the Old Testament.

the deep scorn and hostility which surges through Luther's open letter, here before us.

The following is a revision of the translation by Charles Michael Jacobs in *PE* 5, 10-27, in which he had followed *CL* 4, 180-193. Ours is based on the original text as given in *WA* 30^{II}, (627) 632-646: *Ein sendbrieff D. M. Luthers. Von Dolmetzschen und Fürbit der heiligenn.*

ON TRANSLATING:
AN OPEN LETTER

Wenceslaus Link:[1] *to all Believers in Christ*

God's grace and mercy. Solomon the Wise says, in Proverbs 11[:26], "The people curse him who holds back grain, but a blessing is on the head of him who sells it." This verse should really be understood to apply to everything that can serve the common good and well-being of Christendom. This is why the master in the gospel scolds the unfaithful servant as a slothful rogue for having buried and hidden his money in the ground [Matt. 25:25-26]. In order to avoid this curse of the Lord and of the whole church, I just had to publish this letter which came into my hands through a good friend. I could not hold it back. For there has been much talk about the translation of the Old and New Testaments.[2] The enemies of the truth charge that in many places the text has been modified or even falsified, whereby many simple Christians, even among the learned who do not know the Hebrew and Greek languages, have been startled and shocked. With this publication it is devoutly to be hoped that, at least in part, the slander of the godless will be stopped and the scruples of the devout removed. Perhaps it may even give rise to further writing on questions and matters such as these. I therefore ask every lover of the truth to take this work seriously to

---

[1] Wenceslaus Link (1483-1547), formerly dean of the theological faculty at Wittenberg and successor to Staupitz as vicar-general of the Augustinian Order, as a close friend of Luther, was acting on Luther's instruction in releasing this open letter for publication. We have here included the brief foreword appended to it by Link himself, which was omitted at *PE* 5, 10. See the Introduction, p. 178.

[2] Having published the first German New Testament in 1522 and promptly begun on the Old Testament—which he published serially in installments— Luther's work of translating the entire Bible was by this time far advanced; he was almost finished with the Prophets. See the Introduction pp. 177-178 and see pp. 228-229.

heart and faithfully to pray God for a right understanding of the divine Scriptures, to the improvement and increase of our common Christendom. Amen.

Nürnberg, September 15, 1530.

To the honorable and worthy N., my esteemed lord and friend.

Grace and peace in Christ, honorable, worthy, and dear lord and friend. I have received your letter with the two questions, or inquiries, to which you ask my reply. First you ask why in translating the words of Paul in Romans 3[:28], *Arbitramur hominem justificari ex fide absque operibus,*[3] I rendered them thus: "We hold that a man is justified without the works of the law, by faith alone."[4] You tell me, besides, that the papists are making a tremendous fuss, because the word *sola* (alone) is not in Paul's text, and this addition of mine to the words of God is not to be tolerated. Second you ask whether the departed saints too intercede for us, since we read that angels indeed do intercede for us?

With reference to the first question, you may give your papists the following answer from me, if you like.

First if I, Dr. Luther, could have expected that all the papists taken together would be capable enough to translate a single chapter of the Scriptures correctly and well, I should certainly have mustered up enough humility to invite their aid and assistance in putting the New Testament into German.[5] But because I knew—and still see with my own eyes—that none of them knows how to translate, or to speak German, I spared them and myself that trouble. It is evident, indeed, that from my German translation they are learning to speak and write German, and so are stealing from me my language, of which they had little knowledge before. They do not thank me for it, however, but prefer to use it against me. How-

---

[3] In Jerome's Vulgate the Latin actually was: *per fidem sine operibus legis.* Luther retained this reading unembellished in his 1529 revision of the Vulgate. *WA*, DB 5, 636.

[4] Luther inserted the word "alone" in his 1522 (and his 1546) translation, even though it did not originally appear in either the Latin or the Greek texts. *WA*, DB 7, 38-39.

[5] Luther regularly availed himself of the best technical consultants he could assemble for assistance in the work of translating. See for example p. 206.

ever I readily grant them this, for it tickles me[6] that I have taught my ungrateful pupils, even my enemies, how to speak.

Second you may say that I translated the New Testament conscientiously and to the best of my ability. I have compelled no one to read it, but have left that open, doing the work only as a service to those who could not do it better. No one is forbidden to do a better piece of work.[7] If anyone does not want to read it, he can let it alone. I neither ask anybody to read it nor praise anyone who does so. It is my Testament and my translation, and it shall continue to be mine. If I have made some mistakes in it—though I am not conscious of any and would certainly be most unwilling to give a single letter a wrong translation intentionally—I will not allow the papists [to act] as judges. For their ears are still too long, and their hee-haws[8] too weak, for them to criticize my translating. I know very well—and they know it even less than the miller's beast[9]—how much skill, energy, sense, and brains are required in a good translator. For they have never tried it.

There is a saying, "He who builds along the road has many masters."[10] That is the way it is with me too. Those who have never even been able to speak properly, to say nothing of translating, have all at once become my masters and I must be the pupil of them all. If I were to have asked them how to put into German the first two words of Matthew's Gospel, *Liber Generationis*,[11] none of them would have been able to say Quack![12] And now they sit in judgment

---

[6] *Es thut mir doch sanfft.*

[7] Cf. pp. 221-223 and pp. 249-251.

[8] *Ycka, ycka:* the braying of an ass.

[9] The ass.

[10] The sense of the proverb is that whoever undertakes to do anything publicly will have everybody looking on to judge and instruct. Cf. Wander (ed.), *Sprichwörter-Lexikon*, IV, 1851, "Weg," No. 228.

[11] Matt. 1:1, "The book of the genealogy" (RSV), was rendered by Luther both in 1522 and in 1546, "This is the book of the birth [of Jesus Christ]." *WA*, DB 6, 14-15. Emser's itemized critique of Luther's New Testament began with this very verse. His point, however, was that Luther's translation introduced a new idea in making David—rather than Jesus Christ—to be "the son of Abraham." *Annotationes Hieronimi Emsers vber Luthers Newe Testament* (4th edition; 1529), p. xviii.

[12] *Gack* is the cackle of the mother hen which has just laid an egg. It represented the simplest nonsense syllable that could be uttered by those fowl generally regarded to be models of stupidity. Grimm, *Deutsches Wörterbuch*, IV, 1128.

on my whole work! Fine fellows! That is the way it was with St. Jerome too when he translated the Bible. Everybody was his master. He was the only one who was totally incompetent. And people who were not worthy to clean his shoes criticized the good man's work.[13] It takes a great deal of patience to do a good thing publicly, for the world always wants to be Master Know-it-all.[14] It must always be putting the bit under the horse's tail,[15] criticizing everything but doing nothing itself. That is its nature; it cannot get away from it.

I should like to see a papist who would come forward and translate even a single epistle of St. Paul or one of the prophets without making use of Luther's German translation. Then we should see a fine, beautiful, praiseworthy German translation! We have seen the Dresden scribbler[16] who played the master to my New Testament. I shall not mention his name[17] again in my books as he has his Judge now,[18] and is already well known anyway. He admits that my German is sweet and good.[19] He saw that he could not im-

---

[13] In about the year 382 Jerome was commissioned by Damasus, the bishop of Rome (d. 384), to prepare an authoritative revision of the Latin Bible. In accepting the task Jerome spoke of the harsh criticism he anticipated both of himself and of his work. His expectations were fulfilled. Jerome's Vulgate version drew criticism even from Augustine, Rufinus, and others, criticism which had ceased, however, by the time of his death in 420. Jackson (ed.), *The New Schaff-Herzog Encyclopedia of Religious Knowledge*, II, 123-124; Hauck (ed.), *Realencyklopädie für protestantische Theologie und Kirche*, III, 36-40.

[14] *Meister Klüglin* is a favorite expression of Luther for someone who always knows everything better than the next fellow.

[15] Cf. Wander (ed.), *Sprichwörter-Lexikon*, III, 579, "*Meister*," No. 8; "The real Master Know-it-all is the one who can bridle the horse at the rear and ride it backward."

[16] *Sudler* was a choice bit of invective. Derived from the term to "dirty" or "deal in dirt" and "handle dirty things," it had come to be used of any craftsman—even an author—whose work was poor, clumsy, unreliable, and superficial. Grimm, *Deutsches Wörterbuch*, X, 972.

[17] Jerome Emser. . . .

[18] Jerome Emser had died November 8, 1527, after nearly a decade of literary hostility against Luther which called forth little response from Luther subsequent to his bitter polemical treatises of 1521. *PE* 3, (277) 282-401. See also the Introduction, pp. 179-180.

[19] Emser had admitted that Luther's translation "was nicer and sounded better" than the old version, but added, "This is why the common folk prefer to read it, and amid the sweet words they swallow the hook before they know it." Arnold E. Berger, *Luthers Werke* (Leipzig: Bibliographisches Institut [no date]), III, 172, n. 2.

prove on it. But eager to discredit it, he went to work and took my New Testament almost word for word as I had written it. He removed my introductions and explanations, inserted his own, and thus sold my New Testament under his name. Oh my, dear children, how it hurt me when his prince,[20] in a nasty preface, condemned Luther's New Testament and forbade the reading of it; yet commanded at the same time that the scribbler's New Testament be read, even though it was the very same one that Luther had produced!

That no one may think I am lying, just take the two Testaments, Luther's and the scribbler's, and compare them; you will see who is the translator in both of them. He has patched and altered it in a few places. And though not all of it pleases me, still I can let it go; it does me no particular harm, so far as the text is concerned. For this reason I never intended to write against it either. But I did have to laugh at the great wisdom that so terribly slandered, condemned, and forbade my New Testament, when it was published under my name, but made it required reading when it was published under the name of another. What kind of virtue that is, to heap slander and shame on somebody else's book, then to steal it and publish it under one's own name—thus seeking personal praise and reputation through the slandered work of somebody else—I leave that for his Judge to discover. Meanwhile I am satisfied and glad that my work (as St. Paul also boasts [Phil. 1:18]) must be furthered even by enemies; and that Luther's book, without Luther's name but under that of his enemies, must be read. How could I avenge myself better?

But to return to the matter in hand! If your papist wants to make so much fuss about the word *sola* (alone) tell him this, "Dr. Martin Luther will have it so, and says that a papist and an ass are the same thing." *Sic volo, sic jubeo; sit pro ratione voluntas.*[21] We

[20] Duke George, "The Bearded," of Saxony (1471-1539), had affixed his name to the 1527 Preface to Emser's New Testament (see the text in *St. L.* 19, 494-501). However, Luther suspected that Emser was its real author; cf. his letter to Justus Jonas of December 10, 1527, in Smith and Jacobs, *Luther's Correspondence*, II, 426-427.

[21] "I will it; I command it; my will is reason enough" is line 223 from the famous sixth satire of the Roman poet Juvenal (*ca.* A.D. 60-140), directed against the female sex. Luther used the quotation when he wanted to characterize the capricious unlimited power of the pope.

are not going to be the pupils and disciples of the papists, but their masters and judges. For once, we too are going to be proud and brag with these blockheads; and as St. Paul boasts over against his mad raving saints [II Cor. 11:21ff.], so I shall boast over against these asses of mine. Are they doctors? So am I. Are they learned? So am I. Are they preachers? So am I. Are they theologians? So am I. Are they debaters? So am I. Are they philosophers? So am I. Are they dialecticians? So am I. Are they lecturers? So am I. Do they write books? So do I.

I will go further with my boasting. I can expound psalms and prophets; they cannot. I can translate; they cannot. I can read the Holy Scriptures; they cannot. I can pray; they cannot. And, to come down to their level, I can use their own dialectics[22] and philosophy better than all of them put together; and besides I know for sure that none of them understands their Aristotle.[23] If there is a single one among them all who correctly understands one *proemium* [preface] or chapter in Aristotle, I'll eat my hat.[24] I am not saying too much, for I have been trained and practiced from my youth up in all their science and am well aware how deep and broad it is. They are very well aware, too, that I can do everything they can. Yet these incurable fellows treat me as though I were a stranger to their field, who had just arrived this morning for the first time and had never before either seen or heard what they teach and know. So brilliantly do they parade about with their science, teaching me what I outgrew[25] twenty years ago, that to all their blatting

---

[22] The art of debate was highly developed in the later Middle Ages.

[23] For Luther's view of Aristotle, and for a bibliography on the subject, see Peter Petersen, *Geschichte der aristotelischen Philosophie im protestantischen Deutschland* (Leipzig: Meiner, 1921), pp. 33-38. Cf. also Luther's own judgment of Aristotle's several works in *An Open Letter to the Christian Nobility.* PE 2, 146-147.

[24] *So will ich mich lassen prellen.* The meaning may be roughly equivalent to a seriously intended, "I'll be hanged." Apparently derived from the sport of fox hunting, the expression was taken over by boisterous groups, such as students, for a certain hazing procedure: their victim was thrown roughly and repeatedly up into the air by means of a tightly stretched blanket or net. Cf. WA 17I, 117, n. 1; Grimm, *Deutsches Wörterbuch,* VII, 2101; MA³ 6, 432, n. 12, 26; and BG, 7, 30, n. 2.

[25] *An den schuhen zu rissen.* Cf. Wander (ed.), *Sprichwörter-Lexikon,* IV, 357-359, "*Schuh,*" Nos. 184, 229.

and shouting I have to sing, with the harlot, "I have known for seven years that horseshoe-nails are iron."[26]

Let this be the answer to your first question. And please give these asses no other and no further answer to their useless braying[27] about the word *sola* than simply this, "Luther will have it so, and says that he is a doctor above all the doctors of the whole papacy." It shall stay at that! Henceforth I shall simply hold them in contempt, and have them held in contempt, so long as they are the kind of people—I should say, asses—that they are. There are shameless nincompoops among them who have never learned their own art of sophistry—like Dr. Schmidt[28] and Doctor Snotty-Nose,[29] and their likes—and who set themselves against me in this matter, which transcends not only sophistry, but (as St. Paul says [I Cor. 1:19-25]), all the world's wisdom and understanding as well. Truly an ass need not sing much; he is already well known anyway by his ears.[30]

To you and to our people, however, I shall show why I chose to use the word *sola*—though in Romans 3[:28] it was not *sola*, but *solum* or *tantum* that I used,[31] so sharply do the asses look at my

---

[26] *Mit jhener metzen . . . Ich habs fur siben jaren gewist, das hüffnegel eysen sind.* This obscure expression may possibly derive from a popular folk song.

[27] *Unnütze geplerre.*

[28] This was Luther's name for Johann Faber of Leutkirch (1478-1541); once sympathetic and friendly toward the humanist cause, he had switched in 1520-1521 to become an energetic opponent of the Reformation. With this name a pun may have been intended since Faber's father was a *Schmied* or smith.

[29] *Rotzlöffel* was a widely current term of opprobrium for some young or inexperienced person. Grimm, *Deutsches Wörterbuch*, VIII, 1330. Luther frequently used it, as here, as an abusive name for Johann Cochlaeus (1479-1552), whose "productivity and zeal" in polemic against Luther "was unmatched by any other Catholic theologian of his time." His publications, however, "were written in haste and bad temper, without . . . theological thoroughness" (*The Catholic Encyclopedia*, IV, 79). Having won little recognition while he lived, several of them were put on the Index by Pope Paul IV (1555-1559) (*Schaff-Herzog* III, 151). Again a pun was intended: while *Rotz* meant nasal mucus, *löffel* was the equivalent of the Latin *cochlear* meaning spoon. Both Faber and Cochlaeus had participated a few months earlier in preparing the first refutation of the Augsburg Confession (*Schaff-Herzog*, I, 362).

[30] Wander (ed.), *Sprichwörter-Lexikon*, I, 860, "*Esel*," No. 150.

[31] Luther's point is that the adverb which he supplied in his German New Testament of 1522 (*WA*, DB 7, 38)—*allein* (alone)—would have presupposed in Latin not a *sola fide* but a *solum* or *tantum fide*, and should be referred to in Latin as an adverb rather than an adjective (*MA*³ 6, 432, n. 13, 10). Luther did not himself emend the Latin text however (cf. p. 182, n. 3).

text! Nevertheless I have used *sola fide* elsewhere,[32] and I want both: *solum* and *sola*. I have constantly tried, in translating, to produce a pure and clear German, and it has often happened that for two or three or four weeks we have searched and inquired for a single word and sometimes not found it even then. In translating Job,[33] Master Philip,[34] Aurogallus,[35] and I labored so, that sometimes we scarcely handled three lines in four days. Now that it is translated and finished, everybody can read and criticize it. One now runs his eyes over three or four pages and does not stumble once—without realizing what boulders and clods had once lain there where he now goes along as over a smoothly-planed board. We had to sweat and toil there before we got those boulders and clods out of the way, so that one could go along so nicely. The plowing goes well when the field is cleared.[36] But rooting out the woods and stumps, and getting the field ready—this is a job nobody wants. There is no such thing as earning the world's thanks. Even God himself can earn no thanks, with the sun, indeed with heaven and earth, or with his own Son's death. It simply is and remains world, in the devil's name, because it just will not be anything else.

Here, in Romans 3[:28], I knew very well that the word *solum* is not in the Greek or Latin text; the papists did not have to teach me that. It is a fact that these four letters *s o l a* are not there. And these blockheads stare at them like cows at a new gate.[37] At the same time they do not see that it conveys the sense of the text; it belongs there if the translation is to be clear and vigorous. I wanted

---

[32] Cf. Luther's *Praefatio in epistolam Pauli ad Romanos* as published in his 1529 revision of the Vulgate: *Hinc et sola fides justificat, solaque legem implet*. WA, DB 5, 621.

[33] Luther mentions his difficulties with the translation of Job in a letter to Spalatin of February 23, 1524. Smith and Jacobs, *op. cit.*, II, 221. Cf. also his Preface to the book of Job, in this volume, pp. 251-253.

[34] Philip Melanchthon (1497-1560) had been professor of Greek at the University of Wittenberg since 1518.

[35] Matthew Aurogallus (1490-1543), teacher of Hebrew at Wittenberg since 1521, was one of Luther's chief assistants in translating the Old Testament. Cf. p. 206.

[36] Wander (ed.), *Sprichwörter-Lexikon*, III, 1334, "*Pflügen*," No. 5.

[37] The proverb has reference to the silent amazement which unthinkingly gapes at something new. Wander (ed.), *Sprichwörter-Lexikon*, I, 100, "*Ansehen*," No. 37.

to speak German, not Latin or Greek, since it was German I had undertaken to speak in the translation. But it is the nature of our German language that in speaking of two things, one of which is affirmed and the other denied, we use the word *solum (allein)*[38] along with the word *nicht* [not] or *kein* [no]. For example, we say, "The farmer brings *allein* grain and *kein* money"; "No, really I have now *nicht* money, but *allein* grain"; "I have *allein* eaten and *nicht* yet drunk"; "Did you *allein* write it, and *nicht* read it over?" There are innumerable cases of this kind in daily use.

In all these phrases, this is the German usage, even though it is not the Latin or Greek usage. It is the nature of the German language to add the word *allein* in order that the word *nicht* or *kein* may be clearer and more complete. To be sure, I can also say, "The farmer brings grain and *kein* money," but the words *"kein* money" do not sound as full and clear as if I were to say, "The farmer brings *allein* grain and *kein* money." Here the word *allein* helps the word *kein* so much that it becomes a complete, clear German expression.

We do not have to inquire of the literal Latin, how we are to speak German, as these asses do. Rather we must inquire about this of the mother in the home, the children on the street, the common man in the marketplace. We must be guided by their language, the way they speak, and do our translating accordingly. That way they will understand it and recognize that we are speaking German to them.

For example, Christ says: *Ex abundantia cordis os loquitur* [Matt. 12:34, Luke 6:45]. If I am to follow these asses, they will lay the original before me literally and translate thus: "Out of the abundance of the heart the mouth speaks."[39] Tell me, is that speaking German? What German could understand something like that? What is "the abundance of the heart"? No German can say that; unless, perhaps, he was trying to say that someone was altogether too magnanimous or too courageous,[40] though even that

---

[38] This adverb would be rendered in idiomatic English by either "alone" or "only."

[39] *Aus dem uberfluss des hertzen redet der mund.* This was Emser's translation of the passage. MA³ 6, 432, n. 14, 21.

[40] *Es sey das einer allzu ein gros hertz habe oder zu viel hertzes habe.*

would not yet be correct. For "abundance of the heart" is not German, any more than "abundance of the house," "abundance of the stove," or "abundance of the bench" is German. But the mother in the home and the common man say this, "What fills the heart overflows the mouth."[41] That is speaking good German, the kind that I have tried for—and unfortunately not always reached or hit upon. For the literal Latin is a great hindrance to speaking good German.

So, for example, Judas the traitor says, in Matthew 26[:8], *Ut quid perditio haec?*[42] and in Mark 14[:4], *Ut quid perditio ista unguenti facta est?*[43] If I follow these literalistic asses I would have to translate it thus: "Why has this loss of ointment happened?"[44] But what kind of German is that? What German says, "Loss of the ointment has happened"? If he understands that at all, he thinks that the ointment is lost and must be looked for and found again; though even that is still obscure and uncertain. Now if that is good German, why do they not come out and make us a fine, pretty, new German Testament like that, and let Luther's Testament lie? I think that would really bring their talents to light! But a German would say *Ut quid,* etc., thus: "Why this waste?"[45] Or, "Why this extravagance [*schade*]?" Indeed, "It's a shame about the ointment." That is good German, from which it is understood that Magdalene[46] had wasted the ointment that she poured out and been extravagant. That was what Judas meant, for he thought he could have used it to better advantage.

Again, when the angel greets Mary, he says, "Hail Mary, full

---

[41] *Wes das hertz vol ist, des gehet der mund über.* This was Luther's translation of the passage in both his 1522 and 1546 German Testaments (*WA,* DB 6, 58-59 and 238-239). Herman Haupt says this was a "truly popular" expression, current among the common people at the turn of the sixteenth century (*Zeitschrift für deutsche Philologie* [Halle: Waisenhaus, 1897], XIX, 109-110). The sense of the proverb, current in many languages, is that the nature or state of the heart or soul is disclosed through words (Wander [ed.], *Sprichwörter-Lexikon,* II, 615, "*Herz,*" No. 341).

[42] "Why this waste?" (RSV).

[43] "Why was the ointment wasted?" (RSV).

[44] *Warumb ist dise verlierung der salben geschehen?*

[45] *Was sol doch solcher unrat?* This was Luther's translation of the Mark 14:4 passage in both his 1522 and 1546 German Testaments. *WA,* DB 6, 192-193.

[46] Tradition had so identified the woman in the house of Simon the leper at Bethany.

of grace, the Lord is with you!"[47] [Luke 1:28]. Up to now that has simply been translated according to the literal Latin.[48] Tell me whether that is also good German! When does a German speak like that, "You are full of grace"? What German understands what that is, to be "full of grace"? He would have to think of a keg "full of" beer or a purse "full of" money. Therefore I have translated it, "Thou gracious one,"[49] so that a German can at least think his way through to what the angel meant by this greeting. Here, however, the papists are going wild about me, because I have corrupted the Angelic Salutation;[50] though I have still not hit upon the best German rendering for it. Suppose I had taken the best German, and translated the salutation thus: "Hello there, Mary"[51]—for that is

---

[47] *Gegruesset seistu, Maria vol gnaden, der Herr mit dir.*

[48] The Latin Vulgate reads: *Ave gratia plena.* A New Testament History Bible of the fifteenth century, for example, written in German, simply retains these three untranslated Latin words for the opening of Gabriel's address to Mary, and follows them with a literal German paraphrase: *Ave gratia plena, Maria,* du pist vol aller gunadum. Doo tho complote toxt of the Annunciation from this particular Bible in M. Reu, *Luther's German Bible* (Columbus: Lutheran Book Concern, 1934), p. 60°.

[49] *Du holdselige* was Luther's rendering of the Vulgate *gratia plena*. WA, DB 6, 210-211.

[50] Emser said that the first part of the Ave Maria or Hail Mary prayer had been rendered by Luther in lewd terms of vulgar familiarity (*auff gut bulerisch*). While admitting that *gratia* does at times mean the favor one has with other people, Emser insisted that in this context it must mean the favor Mary had with God—in order to preserve the idea that "the grace which Eve had lost has been won for us again by Mary, and the malediction (*maledeyung*) of Eve has been turned into the benediction (*benedeyung*) of Mary." *Annotationes*, p. xLV. He ascribes Luther's divergent rendering to Luther's "untenable distinction" between grace and gift made in the Preface to Romans (see p. 369). *Ibid.*, pp. LXXVII-LXXVIII.

[51] The German *Gott grusse dich, du liebe Maria*, literally, "God greet you, you dear Mary," has no exact equivalent in English. "God greet you," used as a greeting on arrival, is comparable to the English "God be with you" (contracted to "good bye"), used as a parting salutation; in a sermon on the Annunciation, March 25, 1525, Luther held this same expression to be the equivalent of the Vulgate's *Dominus vobiscum* in Judg. 6:12 and Ruth 2:4, i.e., an informal Hebrew greeting. WA 17[I], 153, ll. 14-23. *Liebe* is frequently used quite formally in German modes of address without any connotations of the term's literal meaning of inner attachment, sympathy, and affection; it can be translated rather literally as "beloved," but also rather freely as "O" or "my"—or left untranslated, with the tone of voice alone conveying the particular connotation intended. What Luther here intended as a rather literal term of endearment, his critics construed as a meaningless formal term of common familiarity. Cf. Grimm, *Deutsches Wörterbuch*, VI, 896-898.

what the angel wanted to say, and what he would have said, if he had wanted to greet her in German. Suppose I had done that! I believe that they would have hanged themselves out of tremendous fanaticism for the Virgin Mary, because I had thus destroyed the salutation.

But what do I care if they rage or rave? I shall not prevent them from translating as they please. However I shall translate too, not as they please but as I please. Whoever does not like it can just leave it alone and keep his criticism to himself, for I shall neither look at nor listen to it. They do not have to answer for my translation, nor bear any responsibility for it. Listen well to this! I shall say "gracious [*holdselige*] Mary," and "dear [*liebe*] Mary," and let them say "Mary full of grace [*volgnaden*]." Whoever knows German knows very well what a fine, expressive [*hertzlich*] word that word *liebe* is: the dear Mary, the dear God, the dear emperor, the dear prince, the dear man, the dear child. I do not know whether this word *liebe* can be said in Latin or other languages with such fulness of sentiment, so that it pierces and rings through the heart,[52] through all the senses, as it does in our language.

I believe that with the Greek *kecharitomene* [Luke 1:28] St. Luke, a master of the Hebrew and Greek tongues, wanted to render and clarify the Hebrew word that the angel used. And I think that the angel Gabriel spoke with Mary as he speaks with Daniel, calling him *Chamudoth* and *Ish chamudoth, vir desideriorum*,[53] that is, "You dear Daniel";[54] for that is Gabriel's way of speaking as we see in the book of Daniel. Now if I were to translate the angel's words literally, with the skill of these asses, I should have to say this, "Daniel, thou man of desires."[55] That would be pretty German! A German would hear, of course, that *Man, Lueste*, and *begyrunge* are German words—though not altogether pure German words, for *lust* and *begyr* would be better. But when the words are thus put together: "thou man of desires," no German would know what is said. He would think, perhaps, that Daniel is full of evil desires.

---

[52] *Das also dringe und klinge ynns hertz.*
[53] Dan. 9:23; 10:11, 19, "Man greatly beloved."
[54] *Du lieber Daniel.*
[55] *Daniel, du man der begirungen oder: Daniel, du man der lüste.*

Well that would be fine translating! Therefore I must let the literal words go and try to learn how the German says that which the Hebrew expresses with *ish chamudoth*. I find then that the German says this, "You dear Daniel," "You dear Mary," or "You gracious maid," "You lovely maiden," "You gentle girl," and the like. For a translator must have a great store of words, so that he can have them on hand in the event that one word does not fit in every context.

And why should I talk so much about translating? If I were to point out the reasons and considerations back of all my words, I should need a year to write on it. I have learned by experience what an art and what a task translating is. Therefore I will tolerate no papal ass or mule to be my judge or critic, for they have never tried it. He who desires none of my translating may let it alone. If anyone dislikes it or criticizes it without my knowledge and consent, the devil repay him! If it is to be criticized, I shall do it myself. If I do not do it, then let them leave my translation in peace. Let each of them make for himself one that suits—what do I care?

This I can testify with a good conscience—I gave it my utmost in care and effort, and I never had any ulterior motives. I have neither taken nor sought a single penny for it, nor made one by it. Neither have I sought my own honor by it; God, my Lord, knows this. Rather I have done it as a service to the dear Christians and to the honor of One who sitteth above, who blesses me so much every hour of my life that if I had translated a thousand times as much or as diligently, I should not for a single hour have deserved to live or to have a sound eye. All that I am and have is of his grace and mercy, indeed, of his precious blood and bitter sweat. Therefore, God willing, all of it shall also serve to his honor, joyfully and sincerely. Scribblers[56] and papal asses may blaspheme me, but real Christians—and Christ, their Lord—bless me! And I am more than plentifully repaid, if even a single Christian acknowledges me as an honest workman. I care nothing for the papal asses; they are not worthy of acknowledging my work, and it would grieve me to the bottom of my heart if they blessed me. Their blasphemy is my

---

[56] Cf. p. 184, n. 16.

highest praise and honor. I shall be a doctor anyway, yes even a distinguished doctor; and that name they shall not take from me till the Last Day, this I know for certain.

On the other hand I have not just gone ahead anyway and disregarded altogether the exact wording of the original. Rather with my helpers[57] I have been very careful to see that where everything turns on a single passage, I have kept to the original quite literally and have not lightly departed from it. For example, in John 6[:27] Christ says, "Him has God the Father sealed [*versiegelt*]." It would have been better German to say, "Him has God the Father signified [*gezeichent*]," or, "He it is whom God the Father means [*meinet*]." But I preferred to do violence to the German language rather than to depart from the word.[58] Ah, translating is not every man's skill as the mad saints imagine. It requires a right, devout, honest, sincere, God-fearing, Christian, trained, informed, and experienced heart. Therefore I hold that no false Christian or factious spirit can be a decent translator. That becomes obvious in the translation of the Prophets made at Worms.[59] It has been carefully done and approaches my German[60] very closely. But Jews

---

[57] See pp. 188, 206.

[58] The Greek *esphragisen* of John 6:27 means literally to seal, mark with a seal, or set a seal upon (in the sense of confirm, accredit, or stamp with approval). The Latin *signavit*, however, by which it was accurately rendered in the Vulgate, may mean in addition tropologically to signify, indicate, or designate. Luther's preference was always for the native *zeichen* over the foreign *versiegeln*, which was derived from the Latin legal term *sigillum* (cf. Grimm, *Deutsches Wörterbuch*, IV, 6920). However, *zeichen*, being the equivalent of the Latin *signare*, was broader in meaning than the Greek *sphragisein*; while *versiegeln* was its exact equivalent. What was at stake in Luther's rendering, besides fidelity to the original, was the conveying of a meaning which Luther did not want to lose or obscure, a meaning which he set down as a marginal gloss to John 6:27 in his German Testament, "Sealed means endowed with the Holy Spirit, so that whoever 'eats of this food' (as in the following verses) also receives the Spirit and shall live." *WA*, DB 6, 348.

[59] The first Protestant translation of the Prophets from the Hebrew, made by Ludwig Haetzer (1500-1529) and Hans Denk (1495-1527), was published by Peter Schöffer at Worms on April 13, 1527. The translators were not only Anabaptists but also antitrinitarians, Denk denying the atonement of Christ and Haetzer disputing even Christ's deity, which may in part account for Luther's allegation that "Jews had a hand in it." Hauck (ed.), *Realencyklopädie*, IV, 576-580; VII, 325-329.

[60] Luther's translation of the Old Testament first began to appear with the publication of Isaiah late in 1528. *BG* 7, 36, n. 7. See pp. 228-229.

had a hand in it, and they do not show much reverence for Christ. Apart from that there is plenty of skill and craftsmanship there. So much for translating and the nature of the languages!

Now I was not relying on and following the nature of the languages alone, however, when, in Roman 3[:28] I inserted the word *solum* (alone). Actually the text itself and the meaning of St. Paul urgently require and demand it. For in that very passage he is dealing with the main point of Christian doctrine,[61] namely, that we are justified by faith in Christ without any works of the law. And Paul cuts away all works so completely, as even to say that the works of the law—though it is God's law and word—do not help us for justification [Rom. 3:20]. He cites Abraham as an example and says that he was justified so entirely without works that even the highest work—which, moreover, had been newly commanded by God, over and above all other works and ordinances, namely circumcision—did not help him for justification; rather he was justified without circumcision and without any works, by faith, as he says in chapter 4[:2], "If Abraham was justified by works, he may boast, but not before God." But when all works are so completely cut away—and that must mean that faith alone justifies—whoever would speak plainly and clearly about this cutting away of works will have to say, "Faith alone justifies us, and not works." The matter itself, as well as the nature of the language, demands it.

"But," they say, "it has an offensive sound, and people infer from it that they need not do any good works." Land, what are we to say? Is it not much more "offensive" that St. Paul himself does not use the term "faith alone," but spells it out even more bluntly, and puts the finishing touches on it[62] by saying, "Without the works of the law"? And in Galatians 1[2:16] and many other places he says, "Not by the works of the law," for the expression "faith alone"

---

[61] Cf. pp. 373-374.

[62] *Schuttets wol gröber eraus, und stosset dem fass den boden aus.* The latter phrase was a common expression meaning to bring matters to a head or to destroy utterly that which one felt was beyond saving. See p. 405, n. 85. Cf. Wander (ed.), *Sprichwörter-Lexikon*, I, 933-934, "*Fass*," Nos. 109, 114, *et al.*

is susceptible of another interpretation,[63] but the phrase "without the works of the law" is so blunt, offensive, and scandalous that no amount of interpreting can help it. How much more might people learn from this "that they need not do any good works," when they hear this preaching about the works themselves put in such plain, strong words, "No works," "without works," "not by works"! If it is not "offensive" to preach, "without works," "no works," "not by works," why should it be "offensive" to preach, "by faith alone"?

And what is still more "offensive," St. Paul is here rejecting not just ordinary works, but "works of the law." Now someone could easily take offense at that all the more and say that the law is condemned and accursed before God, and we ought to be doing nothing but evil—as they did in Romans 3[:8], "Why not do evil that good may come?" This is the very thing that one factious spirit[64] began to do in our time. Are we to deny Paul's word on account of such "offense," or stop speaking out freely about faith? Land, St. Paul and I want to give such offense; we preach so strongly against works and insist on faith alone, for no other reason than that the people may be offended, stumble, and fall, in order that they may learn to know that they are not saved by their good works but only by Christ's death and resurrection. Now if they cannot be saved by the good works of the law, how much less shall they be saved by bad works, and without the law! For this reason it does not follow that because good works do not help, therefore bad works do help, any more than it follows that because the sun cannot help a blind man to see, night and darkness must, therefore, help him to see.

I am amazed that anyone can take exception in a matter as evident as this. Just tell me: Is Christ's death and resurrection our work, that we do, or is it not? Of course it is not our work, nor the work of any law either. Now it is Christ's death and resurrection

---

[63] The inference referred to already in this very paragraph was early drawn by Luther's enemies, though he never intended to say that true faith is, or ever could be—much less should be—without good works. His point was not that faith is ever "alone," but that "only" faith without works—hence the term "faith alone"—is necessary for justification before God. Cf. the famous passage in Preface to Romans, in this volume, p. 370.

[64] *Rottengeyst* in Luther's usage frequently meant Thomas Münzer, as *Tyrann* meant Duke George. MA³ 6, 433, n. 18, 28.

alone that saves us and makes us free from sin, as Paul says in Romans 4[:25], "He died for our sins and rose for our justification." Tell me, further: What is the work by which we lay hold of Christ's death and resurrection? It cannot be any external work, but only the eternal faith that is in the heart. Faith alone, indeed, all alone, without any works, lays hold of this death and resurrection when it is preached by the gospel. Why then this raging and raving, this making of heretics and burning them at the stake, when the matter itself at its very core is so clear and proves that faith alone lays hold of Christ's death and resurrection, without any works, and that his death and resurrection [alone] are our life and our righteousness? Since, then, the fact itself is so obvious—that faith alone conveys, grasps, and imparts this life and righteousness—why should we not also say so? It is no heresy that faith alone lays hold on Christ, and gives life; and yet it must be heresy, if anyone mentions it. Are they not mad, foolish, and nonsensical? They admit that the thing is right, but brand the saying of it as wrong, though nothing can be both right and wrong at the same time.

Moreover I am not the only one, or even the first, to say that faith alone justifies. Ambrose said it before me, and Augustine and many others. And if a man is going to read St. Paul and understand him, he will have to say the same thing; he can say nothing else. Paul's words are too strong; they admit of no works, none at all. Now if it is not a work, then it must be faith alone. What a fine, constructive, and inoffensive doctrine that would be, if people were taught that they could be saved by works, as well as faith! That would be as much as to say that it is not Christ's death alone that takes away our sins, but that our works too have something to do with it. That would be a fine honoring of Christ's death, to say that it is helped by our works, and that whatever it does our works can do too—so that we are his equal in strength and goodness! This is the very devil; he can never quit abusing the blood of Christ.

The matter itself in its very core, then, demands that we say, "Faith alone justifies." And the nature of our German language also teaches us to express it that way. I have in addition the precedent of the holy fathers. And the danger of the people also compels it, so that they may not continue to hang upon works and wander away from faith and lose Christ, especially in these days, for they have been accustomed to works so long they have to be torn away from them by force. For these reasons it is not only right but also highly necessary to speak it out as plainly and fully as possible, "Faith alone saves, without works." I am only sorry that I did not also add the words *alle* and *aller,* and say, "without *any* works of *any* laws," so that it would have been expressed with perfect clarity. Therefore it will stay in my New Testament, and though all the papal asses go stark raving mad they shall not take it from me.

Let this be enough for the present. If God gives me grace, I shall have more to say about it in the tract *On Justification.*[65]

Coming to the second[66] question, whether the departed saints intercede for us, I shall give you only a brief answer now, for I am thinking of publishing a sermon on the angels in which, God willing, I shall treat this point more fully.[67]

In the first place you know that under the papacy it is not only taught that the saints in heaven intercede for us—though we cannot know this, since the Scriptures tell us no such thing—but the saints have also been made gods, so that they have to be our patrons, on whom we are to call—some of whom never even existed. To each of these saints some particular power and might has been ascribed. One has power over fire, another over water, another over pestilence, fever, and all kinds of disease. Indeed God has had to be altogether idle, and let the saints work and act in his stead. The papists themselves are now aware of this abomination; they are quietly putting up their pipes, and presently preening and primping themselves with this teaching about the intercession of the saints. I shall defer this subject for the present, but you can bet I shall not forget it and allow their preening and primping to go unpaid for.

In the second place you know that there is not a single word

---

[65] This tract was never completed. Extant fragments of it in the form of notes and outlines give some indication of what Luther at the time intended. WA 30^{II}, 657-676.

[66] Cf. p. 182.

[67] The sermon on the angels preached September 29, 1530, at Coburg Castle, however, did not deal at all with the matter of venerating the saints. WA 32, 111-121.

of God commanding us to call on either angels or saints to intercede for us, and we have no example of it in the Scriptures. For we find that angels spoke with the fathers and the prophets, but none was ever asked to intercede for them. Even the patriarch Jacob did not ask the angel with whom he wrestled for any intercession, but merely took from him the blessing [Gen. 32:24-29]. Actually we find in the Apocalypse the very opposite: the angel would not allow himself to be worshiped by John [Rev. 22:9]. Thus the worship of saints shows itself to be nothing but human twaddle, man's own invention apart from the word of God and the Scriptures.

Since in the matter of divine worship, however, it is not proper for us to undertake anything without God's command—whoever does so is tempting God—it is therefore neither to be advised nor tolerated that one should call upon the departed saints to intercede for him or teach others to call upon them. Rather this is to be condemned, and men should be taught to avoid it. For this reason I, too, shall not advise it and so burden my conscience with other people's iniquities. It was exceedingly bitter for me to tear myself away from [the worship of] the saints, for I was steeped and fairly drowned in it. But the light of the gospel is now shining so clearly that henceforth no one has any excuse to remain in darkness. We all know very well what we ought to do.

Moreover this is in itself a dangerous and offensive way of worship, because people are easily accustomed to turning from Christ; they quickly learn to put more confidence in the saints than in Christ himself. Our nature is, in any case, all too prone to flee from God and Christ and to trust in men. Indeed it is exceedingly hard for one to learn to trust in God and Christ, though we have vowed [in baptism][68] and are in duty bound to do so. Therefore this offense is not to be tolerated, whereby those who are weak and of the flesh engage in idolatry, against the first commandment and against our baptism. Even if you attempt nothing else but to switch men's confidence and trust from the saints to Christ, by both teaching and practice, that will be difficult enough to accomplish—that men should come to him and lay hold on him aright. There is no

---

[68] Cf. pp. 40-42.

need to paint the devil on the door; he will be on hand anyway.[69]

Finally we are certain that God is not angry with us, and that we are quite secure, even if we do not call upon the saints to intercede for us, for he has never commanded it. He says that he is a jealous God, visiting their iniquities on those who do not keep his commandments [Exod. 20:5-6]; but here there is no commandment, and hence no wrath to be feared either. Since, then, there is on this side security and on that side great danger and offense against God's word, why should we give ourselves over from security into danger, where we have no word of God to sustain, comfort, and save us in time of need? For it is written, "Whoever loves danger will perish by it" [Ecclus. 3:26], and God's command says, "You shall not tempt the Lord your God" [Matt. 4:7].

"But," they say, "that way you condemn the whole of Christendom, which till now has everywhere maintained this." I reply: I know very well that the priests and monks seek this cloak for their abominations. They want to impute to Christendom the damage wrought by their own negligence. Then when we say, "Christendom does not err," we shall be saying at the same time that they too do not err; that way they may not be accused of any falsehood or error, since Christendom holds it to be so. Thus no pilgrimage can be wrong, however manifestly the devil is a party to it; no indulgence can be wrong, however gross the lies that are involved—in a word, there is nothing there but holiness! Therefore to this you should reply, "It is not a question of who is and who is not condemned." They inject this extraneous subject in order to lead us away from the subject at hand. We are now discussing God's word. What Christendom is or does belongs elsewhere. The question here is: What is or is not God's word? What is not God's word does not make Christendom.

We read that in the days of Elijah the Prophet there was apparently no word of God and no worship of God in all Israel. For he says, "Lord, they have slain thy prophets and thrown down thy altars, and I am left completely alone" [I Kings 19:10, 14]. Here

---

[69] The sense of this popular proverb is that it is not necessary to ask for trouble—to entice the devil—since it comes of its own accord. Cf. Wander (ed.), Sprich-wörter-Lexikon, IV, 1087, "Teufel," No. 650.

King Ahab and others might have said, "Elijah, with talk like that you condemn the whole people of God." However God had at the same time kept seven thousand [I Kings 19:18]. How? Do you not think that God could now also, under the papacy, have preserved his own, even though the priests and monks within Christendom have been mere teachers of the devil and gone to hell? Many children and young people have died in Christ. For even under Antichrist, Christ has forcibly preserved baptism, the simple text[70] of the gospel in the pulpit, the Lord's Prayer, and the Creed; whereby he preserved many of his Christians, and hence also his Christendom, and said nothing about it to these devil's teachers.

And even though Christians have done some bits of the papal abomination, the papal asses have not yet thereby proved that they did it gladly; still less does it prove that they did the right thing. All Christians can err and sin, but God has taught them all to pray in the Lord's Prayer for forgiveness of sins. And God could very well forgive the sins they had to commit unwillingly, unknowingly, and under the compulsion of Antichrist—without saying anything about it to the priests and monks! This, however, can easily be proved, that in all the world there has always been a lot of secret murmuring and complaining against the clergy, that they were not treating Christendom properly. And the papal asses have valiantly withstood such murmuring with fire and sword, down to the present day. This murmuring proves how happy Christians have been over these abominations, and how right they have been in doing them!

So come right out with it you papal asses and say that this is the teaching of Christendom: these stinking lies which you villains and traitors have imposed by force upon Christendom, and for the sake of which you arch-murderers have slain many Christians. Why every letter of every papal law bears witness to the fact that nothing has ever been taught by the counsel and consent of Christendom. There is nothing there but *districte precipiendo mandamus*.[71] That has been their Holy Spirit. This tyranny Christendom has had to

---

[70] *Den blossen text* means the bare text, devoid of corrupting glosses or explanations.

[71] "We teach and strictly command" is a common phrase in papal bulls. *CL* 4, 193, n. 7.

endure; by it, it has been robbed of the sacrament, and, through no fault of its own, been held in captivity.[72] And the asses would palm off on us this intolerable tyranny of their own wickedness, as a willing act and example of Christendom—and so clear themselves!

But this is getting too long. Let this be answer enough to your questions this time. More another time. Pardon this long letter. Christ our Lord be with us all. Amen.

MARTIN LUTHER,

Your good friend.

The Wilderness,[73] September 8, 1530.

---

[72] This is the theme of *The Babylonian Captivity*. *LW* 36, 11-126.

[73] This manner of dating is common in Luther's Wartburg letters, and it recurs in those written from Coburg castle in 1530.

DEFENSE OF THE TRANSLATION OF THE PSALMS

1531

Translated by E. Theodore Bachmann

INTRODUCTION

As Luther's *On Translating: An Open Letter* provides us with insight into some of the problems faced in rendering the Greek New Testament into a living German, so his *Defense of the Translation of the Psalms* recites some of the difficulties encountered in bridging the gulf between Hebrew and German.

Though Luther usually spoke modestly of his competence in the Hebrew language,[1] his skill in it was not lightly regarded by his contemporaries.[2] He had begun his study of Hebrew as early as 1508 with a lexicon borrowed from his trusted friend Johann Lang, and had—as was the custom—availed himself of the opportunity for Jewish instruction in the language during his 1510 visit to Rome.[3]

This short treatise was prepared originally as an introduction to Luther's *Summaries of the Psalms*, short and pertinent guides to the understanding of each of the psalms. The latter title may have been borrowed from a book of "short summaries" written by his friend Wenceslaus Link at Nürnberg in 1527.[4] However the content was strictly Luther's own, and grew out of his long-standing preoccupation with the psalms.

He had opened his teaching career by lecturing on the psalms from 1513 to 1515. The first book Luther ever offered for publication was a German translation and exposition for the simple people of *The Seven Penitential Psalms*,[5] a book which went through at least eight editions before it was revised in 1525. Thus a half year before his posting of the Ninety-five Theses in 1517, Luther was already launched on his life-long task of making the Scriptures avail-

---

[1] Cf. his statement, " I do not know much Hebrew." *LW* 40, 120.
[2] See the laudatory estimates given by Sebastian Frank and by Melanchthon in *WA*, DB 9^I, x.
[3] *WA*, DB 9^I, x-xii.
[4] *Kurtz Summaria oder auszüge der Psalmen, was man auss einem yden nemen und die zu wercke zihen müge. WA* 38, 1.
[5] Psalms 6, 32, 38, 51, 102, 130, 143. *WA* 1, (154) 158-220; *WA* 18, (467) 479-530.

able to the people, a task that could never be regarded as finished but always called for further improvement.

During his stay at the Wartburg he occupied himself—as soon as his books were made available—with a translation and exposition of Psalm 68,[6] a psalm which here some ten years later receives considerable attention, and frequently divergent treatment. In all Luther had translated and published individually or in groups some nineteen separate psalms[7] prior to the year 1524 when he brought out his first complete translation of all the psalms. The entire Psalter appeared in a half dozen editions between 1524 and the publication of the complete German Bible a decade later,[8] the most significant edition being the Psalter of 1531 in which—with the help of an advisory commission—Luther essentially accomplished his goal of putting the psalms into acceptable German.

The *collegium biblicum* met in Luther's home for sixteen sessions, afternoon and evening, from mid-January to March 15, 1531.[9] Included in it were the skilled philologist, Melanchthon, whose specialty was Greek; the Wittenberg Hebraist, Matthew Aurogallus, who had joined the faculty in 1521 and remained Luther's trusted associate in Hebrew until his death in 1543;[10] Caspar Cruciger, professor of theology; and the faithful recorder of many of Luther's sermons and lectures, Georg Rörer. Present on occasion were also Justus Jonas, Veit Dietrich, and Bernhard Ziegler.[11] Rörer's protocol of the lengthy sessions of this revisory commission reveals the care with which passages of particular difficulty were handled.[12] Luther selected a number of these passages[13] for discussion in his *Defense of the Translation of the Psalms.*

---

[6] *LW* 13, 3-37.

[7] Psalms 10, 12, 20, 25, 37, 67, 68, 79, 103, 110, 119, and 120, in addition to the Penitential Psalms. WA, DB 10^I, 106; 10^{II}, xxiv.

[8] WA, DB 10^{II}, xi.

[9] WA, DB 3, xxii.

[10] WA, DB 9^I, xxiii-xxiv.

[11] WA, DB 3, xlv, and 10^{II}, lxi.

[12] WA, DB 3, (xviii) 1-166.

[13] Ps. 58:9; 68:30; 63:5; 65:8; 68:13, 15, 16, 18; 91:5-6, 9; 92:14; 118:27, 12 are treated in this order.

It had been Luther's intention to provide along with the 1531 Psalter an explanation of the principles and procedures whereby the revision was undertaken. The pressure of the publication schedule, however—the revisory commission itself was barely able to keep ahead of the printer[14]—made this impossible. Luther had to be satisfied for the moment with a brief postscript to the reader appended at the end of his 1531 Psalter,[15] in which he intimates that the critics of his Psalter will be answered later, "in the *Summaries.*" Apparently intending to handle both subjects in a single treatise, Luther actually tackled prior to the writing of his "summaries of the psalms" this other matter which was still very fresh in his mind, namely, a delineation of the task and the principles of the translator, together with a defense of specific renderings by way of illustrating those principles.

Very simply, the task of the translator is not that of reproducing in one language words exactly equivalent to the words of another language, but of reproducing in vigorous vernacular idiom the meaning originally expressed in the foreign tongue. To do this properly, philological skill is indispensable—only, however, as the hand-maiden of an even greater theological competence. Ultimately the sense itself in the original must determine whether the rendering in translation will be literal or relatively free. Hence the Jews themselves are our best instructors in the Hebrew language but Christians alone can truly translate the Bible.[16]

While written in 1531, this *Defense* was not actually published until December of 1532, along with the *Summaries* for which it was to serve as an introduction. The *Summaries,* together with the *Defense,* were regularly included as an introduction in separate Wittenberg printings of the complete Psalter beginning with one by Hans Lufft in 1533.[17] Our translation of this work, the first in

---

[14] *WA, DB* 10[II], lxii.
[15] See the text in *WA, DB* 10[I], 590 and *WA, DB* 3, xlii-xliii.
[16] See the theological-exegetical introduction of A. Schleiff in *WA, DB* 9[I], xxviii-xxxvii, and that of O. Reichert in *WA, DB* 3, xliii.
[17] *WA, DB* 10[II], xxxix, n. 24 and lxiv, n. 97.

English, is based on the Lufft printing of May 1, 1533: *Summarien uber die Psalmen, Und ursachen des dolmetschens*—we have given only the introductory portion dealing with Luther's "reasons for translating" as he translated—as that document is reproduced in *WA* 38, 9-17.

DEFENSE OF THE
TRANSLATION
OF THE PSALMS

To All Devout Christians

Grace and peace in Christ. Around Easter of this year, 1531, we again went over our little German Psalter and gave it some finishing touches.[1] We intend now to let it go at that. Nor does it bother us how this Psalter will please Master Know-it-all.[2] But because a number of good, devout persons who know the languages but are not versed in translating—some now living and others yet to come after us—might possibly find it offensive or take exception to the fact that at many places we have departed rather freely from the letter of the original and at times even followed an interpretation different from that taught by the Jewish rabbis and grammarians, we shall herewith give our reasons and clarify them with several examples— so they will see that in so translating we have not acted out of a misunderstanding of the languages nor out of ignorance of the rabbinical commentaries, but knowingly and deliberately.

For example, in Psalm 58 we have translated verse 9 like this, "Before your thorns have ripened on the thornbush, a wrath will tear them out while they are still green." We know very well that the Jewish rabbis read and interpret this text differently.[3] They take

---

[1] Luther's 1531 revision of the Psalter was prepared with the assistance of several faculty colleagues. See the Introduction, p. 206.

[2] *Meister klüglinge;* cf. p. 184, n. 14.

[3] The traditional rendering of Ps. 58:9 is found in the KJV, "Before your pots can feel the thorns, he shall take them away as with a whirlwind, both living, and in his wrath," and in the modern Jewish version, "Before your pots can feel your thorns, he will sweep it away with a whirlwind, the raw and the burning alike." With these compare the RSV, "Sooner than your pots can feel the heat of thorns, whether green or ablaze, may he sweep them away."
Luther's translation and interpretation, however, are actually supported by

the [Hebrew] word *sir* to means "pots," and the word for "wrath" to mean "fire," so that the verse is supposed to mean, "Before your pots are aware of the thorns, and while the meat in them is still raw, even then the wrath (the fire) will have burned them up." That is to say, when the godless rage they are like the thorns men put under pots [Eccles. 7:6] to boil the meat (that is, to ruin the devout); the thorns however, burn themselves up before the meat is done. This opinion is acceptable; it is even our own. But we have rendered it like this, "Before the thorns have ripened or can be noticed[4] on the thornbush, the wrath comes along—that is, a hatchet or an axe—and cuts them down while they are still green and fresh."[5] Thus the godless with their raging are like young thorns on a bush, growing and threatening to prick, but along comes a farmer with his hatchet, before they are hard and ripe enough to prick, and chops them down like a bolt of lightning. For God indeed permits the godless to rage, but not to implement their raging and threatening; he causes them to be destroyed before they can carry it out—just as happened to Saul,[6] Absalom, Pharaoh, and all the other tyrants.

---

the Targum; the medieval Jewish commentators, such as Rashi and Kimchi; and the *Midrash Tehillim.* The *Midrash* reads *ad loc.,* "*Before your briar shoots harden into brambles.* David said: The court ought to learn from the workman. When he finds a briar shoot in a vineyard, he destroys it with his mattock before it grows up and becomes thorns and brambles. *He cuts it down while it is unripe,* while the briar is green; and *while it is soft,* as soft as fresh bread. Here *charon* is read like *chori* in the phrase *Three baskets of fresh bread (chori)* (Gen. 40:16)." William G. Braude, *The Midrash on Psalms* (New Haven: Yale University Press, 1959), I, 507.

The problem roots in the fact that the Hebrew words as they stand in this verse can be rendered in more than one way. While the usual translation for *sir* is "pot" it may also be translated "thorn" or "briar." Again, *bin,* usually translated as "feel," "understand," or "instruct," may according to Kimchi have the meaning of "hardening" or "ripening." Similarly *sha'ar* may be rendered either as "sweep away" or "cut down," and *charon* as "wrath," "burning," or "soft."

[4] Luther's Psalter of 1524 read "noticed"; that of 1531 read "ripened." *WA, DB* 10¹, 284-285.

[5] Cf. the same verse (Ps. 57:10) in the Douay Version as based on the Vulgate, "Before your thorns could know the briar; he swalloweth them up, as alive, in his wrath."

[6] Luther felt that his interpretation illuminated better than the other the relationship between David and Saul. See Georg Rörer's protocol on the work of the revisory commission (referred to in the Introduction, p. 206). *WA, DB* 3, 1-166; especially (on Ps. 58:9) p. 61.

In Psalm 68 we have translated [part of] verse 30 like this, "Those who lust after money." We know, of course, that the rabbis interpret the [Hebrew] word *ratse* differently because of the dagesh.[7] Yet we [and they] are virtually agreed on the meaning:[8] the psalmist is praying God to rebuke and ward off the beast in the reeds, that beast which lusts after money, i.e., for the sake of money runs about and does everything contrary to God's word. What kind of beast this is the psalmist himself tells us: It is the band or herd of bulls among the calves. That is to say, it is the fat and rich band of the high and mighty,[9] who graze off the land like bulls in good pasture or tall grass, and who have quite a following—just as the bulls have many cows and calves near them when they go to pasture. Such tyrants (and the psalmist means especially the priests of the Jewish people) contend against and contravene God's word simply for the sake of money, because they are worried that wherever God's word flourishes their own ostentation and riches must be done away. This is what we mean[10] by translating [the phrase] thus: "Those who lust after money." The rabbis make it read, "Those who run with the tramplers for the sake of money."[11] That is to say, such beasts run along with the tyrants who are trampling the pious for

---

[7] Luther transliterates without the dagesh. In the pointed text the word appears *ratstse*, that is with dagesh forte indicating that the root of the word is *ratsats* and that the word is a form of the noun *rats*, meaning "piece" or "morsel." If the dagesh is removed then the consonants could be repointed either as *rotse*, a form of the participle of *ratsah*, "to take pleasure in," or "to be pleased with;" or as *ratse*, a form of the participle of *ruts* meaning "to run." Neither of these forms appears in biblical Hebrew.

[8] Luther's interpretation is perhaps suggested by the play on words given in the Midrash; there, however, the meaning is actually quite different. See Braude, *op. cit.*, I, 548 and II, 480, nn. 31, 32.

[9] *Grossen hansen*. Cf. WA 10^II, 507, n. 21, 22 and WA, DB 3, 78, ll. 10-11.

[10] Cf. Luther's interpretation of the entire verse in his 1521 translation and commentary on Psalm 68, where he had translated the phrase, "ruling over the lovers of silver." LW 13, 30-32.

[11] The rabbis, according to Luther, construed the Hebrew root to be *ruts*, while Luther took it as *ratsah*. Interestingly, the reading of *ratse* (from *ruts*) is found in nine Hebrew manuscrips and is perhaps also witnessed by Aquila and Jerome. Perhaps the reading from *ruts* was suggested by its syntactical connection with the word *raphas* ("trample")—a word which in its obscure form Luther left unrendered until the 1545 Psalter, where he not only included it but significantly provided a marginal gloss on it as well. WA, DB 10^I, 317. The difficulty, however, is that the pointed text does not permit either of the above readings.

say in such a situation?" Once he has the German words to serve the purpose, let him drop the Hebrew words and express the meaning freely in the best German he knows.

Thus here in [Psalm 68] verse 13 we could also easily have rendered the Hebrew quite literally, like this, "If you lie within the marked boundaries,[17] then the wings of the doves will be covered with silver and their pinions with gleaming gold," etc. But what German understands that? However the preceding verse [Ps. 68:12] sings of kings who make war and turn over the spoils to the housewives. So the meaning of this verse [13] is this: these kings have a fine, handsome, and well-armed force in the field which, from the distance, looks like a dove whose feathers glisten white and red (as if they were silver and gold). These kings are the apostles who here and there in the world, gloriously aglow with the manifold wondrous gifts and miracles of the Holy Spirit, have taken the field against the devil and won many people away from him, turning them over as booty to the mistress of the house—the church—to govern and teach.

And in verse 15 we might also easily have followed the rabbis and said, "The mountain of God is a mountain of Bashan or a fat[18] mountain" (which is how we had previously translated it). But it is better and clearer to call it a "fruitful mountain." That is to say, in Christendom—which is "the mountain of God"—many good things are always happening. There the trees are fruitful; that is, Christians are doing great works and miracles. For the word of God does not return empty [Isa. 55:11], and a sound tree bears good fruit [Matt.

---

[17] *Zwischen den marcken,* which is the reading here, had been rendered in an almost identical way as *zwischen den grentzen* in 1521 (*WA* 8, 14) and in the 1524 Psalter, but more idiomatically *zu felde* in the Psalters of 1531 and 1545 (*WA*, DB 10ᴵ, 312-313). *Mark,* originally sign or mark, was also used of boundary indicators, and hence also of the boundaries themselves and even of the field bounded by them. Grimm, *Deutsches Wörterbuch,* VI, 1633. Luther properly interpreted the Hebrew *shephattayim*—stalls or folds for livestock—in terms of a circumscribed area or field. WA, DB 3, 73 and 553. Cf. the RSV, "sheepfold."

[18] *Fett* is the German equivalent of the Latin *pinguis,* which the Vulgate uses at this point. The name of the mountain, however, is usually thought to be derived from a Hebrew root meaning smooth or soft, and—by extension—fruitful and fertile. Where Luther's 1521 translation (*WA* 8, 17) and the 1524 Psalter read "fat," the Psalters of 1531 and 1545 read "fruitful" [*fruchtbar*]. WA, DB 10ᴵ, 312-313. See Luther's 1521 rendering and interpretation in *LW* 13, 17-18.

7:17]. In German we call a good fruitful region a fat land and a lard pit,[19] not, however, that everything is smeared with lard or is dripping with fat.

Thus the following phrase, "a many-peaked mountain, a fat mountain," we have rendered in German as "a great[20] mountain." For the meaning is that just as a mountain is properly called great in which many peaks are joined together, one above another right up to the highest peak, so also is the church put together: one saint or flock is always joined to the next [Eph. 4:16], and one flock or one Christian is more richly blessed and outdoes the next. Paul says as much in I Corinthians 12 [:4], that in the church there must needs be a distinction of deeds, gifts, and services; and in I Corinthians 15 [:41], "One star differs from another in glory." We let it pass that the rabbis argue over the word *gabnunnim,* some of them making "humps on the back" out of it, others "the brows over the eyes."[21] We neither could nor would use such terms in translating.

Similarly in verse 16 we might have rendered that same word, *gabnunnim,* like this, "Why do you leap, you humped or arched mountains?" But who would call that German? However because the psalm is speaking of the authority, wisdom, and holiness of the world, especially of the Jews, it is thus rebuking them: they are setting themselves against this "mountain of God," boasting that they are great, mighty, and numerous; they are trying to defend their own authority, holiness, and wisdom over against the "mountain of God"—despite the fact that God does not dwell with them, as they think he does, but on this mountain which they have been

---

[19] *Schmaltz gruben* might approximate the English expression, "gold mine."

[20] In the 1531 and 1545 Psalters, *gros* ("great") had here replaced the *gehugelt* ("many-peaked") of 1524 (*WA, DB,* 10[I], 312-313) and 1521 (*WA* 8, 17). See Luther's 1521 interpretation of the word in *LW* 13, 17-18.

[21] The *Midrash* interprets the verse as referring to the commotion among the mountains as to which would best serve God as the holy mountain from which God could give his Torah, and connects the word *gabnunnim* ("many-peaked," or "peak-backed") with *gibben* ("humped-back"). (Both words have the same root [*gaban*] and may be translated similarly. A related Aramaic word suggests the meaning "eyebrow.") When Sinai is chosen and the other mountains thunder protests, God asks, "Why do you wish to contend with Sinai? Ye are all *peak-backed mountains!* Here 'peak-backed' has the sense of 'blemished,' as in the verse 'He that hath a blemish . . . shall not approach, . . . a man that is . . . peak-backed' (Lev. 21:18-20)." Braude, *op. cit.,* I, 543.

haughtily despising and assailing as the devil's mountain, the mountain of sheer heresy, etc.

On the other hand we have at times also translated quite literally—even though we could have rendered the meaning more clearly another way—because everything turns on these very words. For example, here in [Psalm 68] verse 18, "Thou hast ascended on high; thou hast led captivity captive,"[22] it would have been good German to say, "Thou hast set the captives free." But this is too weak, and does not convey the fine, rich meaning of the Hebrew, which says literally, "Thou hast led captivity captive." This does not imply merely that Christ freed the captives,[23] but also that he captured and led away the captivity itself, so that it never again could or would take us captive again; thus it is really an eternal redemption [Heb. 9:12]. St. Paul likes to speak in this way, as when he says, "I through the law died to the law" [Gal. 2:19]; again, "Through sin Christ condemned sin" [Rom. 8:3]; and again, "Death has been put to death by Christ."[24] These are the captivities that Christ has taken captive and done away: death can no longer hold us, sin can no longer incriminate us, the law can no longer accuse our conscience. On every hand St. Paul propagates such rich, glorious, and comforting doctrine. Therefore out of respect for such doctrine, and for the comforting of our conscience, we should keep such words, accustom ourselves to them, and so give place to the Hebrew language where it does a better job than our German.

Likewise, in Ps. 91:5-6 we have stuck to the Hebrew, "You will not fear the terror of the night, nor the arrow that flies by day, nor the pestilence that stalks in darkness, nor the destruction that wastes at noonday," etc. Since they are expressed in obscure and veiled words, one man might well interpret differently from another these four torments or misfortunes which a righteous person must endure for God's sake. Therefore we tried to leave room for each person

---

[22] In English the KJV conveys Luther's meaning better than the RSV.

[23] This was essentially Luther's earlier interpretation, as reflected in his 1521 rendering, "Thou has plundered the plunder." *LW* 13, 20-21.

[24] Cf. I Cor. 15:54; II Tim. 1:10.

to understand them according to the gifts and measure of his spirit. Otherwise we would have rendered them in such a way as to give fuller expression to our own understanding of the meaning.

Namely, the first evil which the righteous must suffer is fear of the night; that is, threats, hatred, envy, and harm. For the word of God constantly enkindles peril and hostility; this hostility the psalmist here calls fear of the night. The second evil is the arrows that fly by day; these are open slander, contradiction, reviling, backbiting, cursing, and condemning, the sort that is being done today in papal bulls and imperial edicts, the prohibitions of princes and lords, the sermons and books of the sophists, and the writings of the factious spirits. The third is pestilence or fever, which stalks in darkness; these are the secret intrigues, devices, stratagems, tricks, and pacts whereby the adversaries take counsel together in their rooms and closets (which no one is supposed to notice or understand) and agree on how they will suppress the word of God and exterminate the righteous. The fourth is the destruction or pestilence that wastes at noonday; this is the open persecution, where they actually hang, drown, garrote, burn, exile, dispossess, etc., trying openly to destroy the word and bring everything to ruination.

This is my understanding of the passage. I know, of course, that St. Bernard[25] has a different interpretation, which is all right, though in my own opinion, it savors all too strongly of monkishness,[26] and is too feeble for Christians or Christian churches who are being assailed more for the sake of the word and faith than for the sake of their life and works. Others may offer still different interpretations, and these (as already mentioned) we do not want to dissuade from their own views. Our interpretation is good too, if not actually the

---

[25] Bernard (1090-1153), abbot of Clairvaux, first and foremost a monk but also a prominent medieval mystic and early scholastic theologian, was renowned especially for his preaching. In the interpretation of Ps. 91:5-6, where Luther externalizes, Bernard internalizes the enemies of the Christian. He interprets the four here listed as weakness of the flesh; vainglory and pride; cupidity and secret ambition; and the Devil—disguised as an angel of light—making evil to appear under the guise of what is good. Migne 183, 197-200.

[26] *Münchentzen* is a colloquialism in the same category as Luther's *Jüdentzen* "to savor of Jewishness." WA 38, 14, n. 2. Cf. p. 284, n. 114.

best. For we indeed see and experience it daily, that the word of God is being attacked from these four quarters. For this reason the Holy Spirit brings us comfort so that our faith should not fear, even though it does have to endure the attack.

Again, in this same psalm [91], verse 9, we changed the pronoun *mea* into *tua,* making "your" out of "my,"[27] because the verse is obscure if one says, "For the Lord is my refuge," inasmuch as throughout the psalm the psalmist uses the word "your" and speaks to or about someone else. Even this very verse says, "The Most High is your refuge." Now since an ordinary German will hardly understand this sudden change in speaking [from second to first] person, we tried to put the matter clearly and plainly. After all, one is not so accustomed to speaking in this way in German as in Hebrew. In Hebrew it often happens that someone says now "you," now "he," even though he is speaking to but one and the same person; but the Hebrews know all about this. We have made changes of this sort several other times as well. That may perhaps irritate Master Know-it-all, who does not bother about how a German is to understand this text but simply sticks to the words scrupulously and precisely, with the result that no one understands the text. We do not care. We have taken nothing from the meaning, and we have rendered the words clearly.

Again, Psalm 92[:14], says, "Even when they grow old, they will nevertheless bloom, and be fruitful and flourishing." We know, of course, that [translated literally] word for word the text says this, "When their hair is gray they will still bloom and be fat and green." But what does this mean? The psalm had been comparing the righteous to trees, to palm trees and cedars [verse 14], which have no "gray hair," neither are they "fat" (by which a German means an oily or greasy substance [*schmaltz*], and thinks of a hefty paunch). But the prophet here intends to say that the righteous are such trees, which bloom and are fruitful and flourishing even when

---

[27] The RSV makes this same emendation, which Luther first made in his 1531 Psalter. The Psalter of 1524 had followed the original Hebrew—and the Latin Vulgate—in using the first person pronoun rather than the second. Cf. WA, DB 10^I, 406-407.

they grow old. They must abide for ever, for the word of God which they teach abides for ever [I Pet. 1:25]. Psalm 1[:3] says, "His leaf shall not wither," for the longer the righteous live, the more they gain both in the word and in life. But all other trees finally die away when they grow old, especially those factious spirits whom God has not planted, as Christ declares, "Every plant which my heavenly Father has not planted, must be rooted up" [Matt. 15:13].

Again, we knew very well that the Jewish rabbis read Ps. 118:27 like this, "Bind the paschal lamb with cords, up to the horns of the altar,"[28] where we translate it thus: "Adorn the festival with branches." They arbitrarily make a paschal lamb out of the word *chag* (which actually means a feast or festival). And even if it did mean that elsewhere,[29] as they contend, they cannot prove it means that here. For where is it written that the Jews are supposed to lead the paschal lamb up to the altar with cords? Actually everyone was obliged to roast it at home[30] and eat it with his household—as the Jews still do, even though they have no altar.

Because there is such a misleading Jewish slant to this text, then, and because we know that this psalm is singing of Christ and his kingdom,[31] and because the words of this verse by the very nature of the language mean to bind the festival with branches,[32] we have made it clear in this way, "Adorn the festival with branches (this is the spiritual 'Feast of Tabernacles' whose prototype was

---

[28] This rabbinical interpretation may be found in the Targum and in the medieval Jewish commentators, where, however, the sacrifical victim is not designated as the passover lamb. On the other hand the *Midrash Tehillim* interprets the passage in a way similar to Luther, "From inside, the men of Jerusalem will say, *The Lord is God, and hath given us light.* And from outside, the men of Judah will say *Order the festival procession with boughs, even unto the horns of the altar."* Braude, *op. cit.,* II, 245.

[29] Used frequently in the Old Testament, the word *chag* apparently means the festive sacrifice (rather than the feast itself) only in Mal. 2:3. The word *abothim*, from a root meaning to wind or weave, may be translated either as "cords," or as "branches," that is, interwoven foliage.

[30] Cf. Exod. 12:46. Throughout Luther has spoken quite specifically of the passover sacrifice, although the rabbinical understanding is only of a general "festive sacrifice." Cf. below, however, Luther's reference to the Feast of Tabernacles.

[31] Cf. the reference in Matt. 21:6-9 with Ps. 118:26. This is a good example of how Luther interprets the Old Testament in terms of the New Testament. See his fuller exposition of the entire verse in *LW* 14, 103-104.

[32] Cf. the RSV, "Bind the festal procession with branches."

the Jewish Feast of Tabernacles), up to the horns of the altar."
By "altar" the psalmist indicates that this should be a spiritual "Feast
of Tabernacles," for which an altar must be present. For the Jewish
Feast of Tabernacles no altar was required,[33] except at Jerusalem.
The meaning is that at the time of Christ every festival will be a
daily festival,[34] in which one joyfully preaches in faith and thereby
renders sacrifices of thanksgiving to God. This is what it means to
"adorn the festival with branches up to the altar," to be joyful in
word and faith, and thus, in Christ who is our altar, to glorify and
praise God.

Again, in [Psalm 118] verse 12 where we say in German, "They
are stamping and quenching [dempffen] as a fire in the thorns," the
rabbis put it this way, "They are dying out [verlesschen] or being
extinguished [werden gedempfft] like fire in the thorns."[35] Now this
is supposed to mean that the godless persecutors are like the thorns
ignited under a pot, which blaze and flash furiously. But before the
meat in the pot is done, the thorns have burned themselves out, been
extinguished, and left the meat quite raw.[36] So the persecutors perish
before they have consumed the righteous. Wherever they can, the
rabbis thus apply the Scriptures to their pots and sacrifices, as men
who build their holiness chiefly on such sacrifices and works.

But because the text goes on to say, "In the name of the Lord
I cut them off!" (the same words which occur also in the two preceding verses), and because these words tell us how the godless
shall perish, we hold the view given by our [rendering of the] text,
that here is expressed the great fury of the adversaries against the
righteous. Just as in this same verse the psalmist compares the godless to angry bees, so here he compares them also to people who
come running to put out a fire when a field-hedge or forest is burn-

---

[33] Cf. Lev. 23:39-43.
[34] Cf. pp. 165-166.
[35] The RSV's "blazed" (following the Septuagint) is based on an emended text and corresponds to Luther's own rendering, while the KJV's "are extinguished" (following the Hebrew) corresponds to the rendering Luther ascribes to the rabbis.
[36] Cf. pp. 209-210.

ing.[37] The original Hebrew,[38] where they have not—without any justification—interpolated their vowel points, actually calls for this sort of interpretation. Moreover if the thorns are burned up and extinguished, how does one reconcile this with the intention of cutting them off in the name of the Lord? Is one supposed to hack among the ashes, or finish off completely the godless who no longer exist?

Well there is no need to give such justification for every word. We have truly spared no energy or effort. Whoever can do it better, more power to him.[39] But I expect that if he does not make use of our little Psalter, he will translate the psalms in such a way that there will not be much German or Hebrew left in them. If you compare his psalter with this one of ours, you should be able to see that. You will discover his peculiar skill, that of stealing our words. He is a disgraceful and repulsive fellow, this Master Know-it-all. If he can find one little word that we have mistaken (for who would be so brash as to claim that he had not missed a single word—as if he were Christ and the Holy Spirit himself), then he becomes the expert and the light of the world,[40] even though he surely knows that, apart from that, we have translated the entire Psalter quite well, and that he himself could not translate right a single verse of it. Such men are scoffers and slanderers, that's what they are.

Besides how does it happen that they examine us alone so minutely, when in the ancient Psalter even St. Jerome and many others have missed a good deal more than we, in both the Greek

---

[37] See Luther's fuller exposition of this verse in LW 14, 72-73, where he makes reference to Exod. 22:6 by way of establishing the urgency for extinguishing a fire that might be destructive of the crops. The point of Luther's new rendering becomes clearer when one compares the marginal gloss on *verlosschen* in his 1524 Psalter—where he still followed the rabbinical interpretation—to that on the substitute word *dempffen* in his Psalter of 1531, "They all came running to extinguish it as if the whole world would be destroyed by my teaching." WA, DB 10^I, 492-493.

[38] *Ebreische Grammatica* refers to the unpointed Hebrew text. Cf. the contrasting expression at p. 213, n. 15.

[39] Cf. pp. 183-184 and pp. 249-251.

[40] *Lux mundi* may be a reference to the Vulgate version of John 8:12. Luther uses the term elsewhere in referring to the contemptuous antagonist of Job 12:5. WA, DB 3, 483, l. 9.

and the Latin?[41] Or if they can be so patient and generous there, where they find many deficiencies, why then are they so venomous and unsparing here, where they even find much that is good, which they have come upon nowhere else? Yet this is the abominable arrogance and great jealousy of Master Know-it-all. When he sees that he can do nothing well himself, he tries to play the expert and gather laurels by blaspheming and slandering the good work of somebody else. But time will tell; what God plants will abide.[42]

Now because we extolled the principle of at times retaining the words quite literally, and at times rendering only the meaning,[43] these critics will undoubtedly try out their skill also at this point. First and foremost they will criticize and contend that we have not applied this principle rightly, or at the right time—although they never knew anything about such a principle before. Yet they are the type who, the moment they hear about something, immediately know it better than anyone else. If they are so tremendously learned and want to display their skill, I wish they would take that single and very common word, *chen*,[44] and give me a good translation of it. I will give fifty gulden to him who translates this word appro-

---

[41] The Septuagint version of the psalms in Greek, known already in the second century B.C.—before the Hebrew text had taken its final form, or been provided with vowel points—is "often altogether at fault in difficult passages, and hopelessly astray as to the purport of the titles." It became the basis of the Old Latin version of North Africa which was twice revised by Jerome, very slightly in 383 as the *Roman Psalter* and quite thoroughly in 387 as the *Gallican Psalter*. The latter version forced its way into Jerome's Vulgate, prepared in 389-403, and was never displaced in general usage by the newer Psalter which Jerome had specifically prepared—as he did the rest of the Vulgate version—on the basis of the Hebrew text. A. F. Kirkpatrick, *The Book of Psalms* (New York: Cambridge University Press, 1910), pp. lxviii-lxxii.

[42] Cf. Matt. 15:13.

[43] Cf. Luther's discussion of the principle in WA, TR 2, No. 2771a; TR 3, No. 3794; TR 5, No. 5521, and other passages cited rather fully in Reu, *The Augsburg Confession,* pp. 267-270. See "Luther's Method as Translator" in D. Otto Albrecht's historical-theological introduction to Luther's translation of the New Testament, especially the section on Luther's own testimony concerning his way of translating. WA, DB 6, lxxv-lxxxiii.

[44] This Hebrew root may mean favor or grace, with respect either to form and appearance or to speech; it may also mean the favor or acceptance one has in the sight either of God or of men. Luther found that his favorite equivalent, *Gnade*, was not always adequate for every form, context, and usage; he also utilized such terms as *Gunst, lieblich, holdselig*, and others to render the word. Cf. p. 346, n. 33.

priately and accurately throughout the entire Scriptures. Let all the experts and know-it-alls pool their skill, in order at least to see that actually doing the translation is a wholly different art and task from that of simply criticizing and finding fault with someone else's translation. Whoever does not like our translation can just leave it alone. By it we are serving our own, and those who do like it.

Let this, then, be enough on translating.[45]

I request that if my poor service in these summaries should please anyone, let him not insert them into the Psalter between the psalms. For I prefer to see the text stand alone by itself, without any interpolations. Nor would it be appropriate that these summaries (of which some are simply a brief commentary) should loom larger there among the texts than the psalms themselves. With this, may God be with you. Amen.

---

[45] At this point Luther begins his actual *Summaries of the Psalms*, which concludes with the brief parag.aph here appended. WA 38, 17-69.

PREFACES TO THE BOOKS OF
THE BIBLE

INTRODUCTION

"The Holy Scriptures are a vast and mighty forest, but there is no single tree in it that I have not shaken with my own hand," said Luther.[1] The publication of his translation of the entire Bible into German in 1534 remains one of the celebrated events of the Reformation. Luther's achievement of providing the people with a trustworthy and highly readable rendition of the Bible from the original languages has received fitting attention elsewhere.[2] Here it is enough to note that while Luther's translation was by no means the first to appear in German,[3] it was by all standards the best and most widely influential. Indeed prior to the publication of his own complete version in 1534, portions of his translation of the Old Testament had already been embodied in the editions of the first complete Protestant Bibles appearing in 1529 in Zurich and Worms.[4]

The ready availability of the Bible in the language of the people was, in the deepest sense of the term, an integral part of the Reformation. One of the devices that helped to facilitate the new reader's understanding of the Bible was the provision of prefaces for most of its books. These prefaces came out with the books themselves, in the irregular sequence of published instalments. For Luther's work of translation extended over many years, from the first appearance of his German New Testament in 1522 to the complete Bible in 1534. Nor was this all. Simultaneously with the production of new translation, Luther and his colleagues revised and improved upon such as had already been published. The prefaces too in many instances underwent a corresponding process of revision.

In order to see these prefaces in perspective, one may profitably look at them from at least three different vantage points: (1)

---

[1] *WA*, TR 1, No. 674, from the early 1530's.

[2] For a discussion of the subject, see *WA*, DB 6, xvii-lxxxix, and the monograph by Michael Reu, *Luther's German Bible*, which is based in large part on *WA*, DB 1-6.

[3] Reu, *Luther's German Bible*, pp. 19-53.

[4] *Ibid.*, p. 207.

Luther's plan and procedure for translating the Bible; (2) his combining of translation and theology in a firm unity; and (3) his prefaces as such.

(1) With his experience before the Diet at Worms still vividly in mind, Luther resolved early in his stay at the Wartburg to translate the entire Bible into German.[5] He well knew the gigantic proportions of such an undertaking, the years that would be involved, and the extraordinary linguistic ability as well as the theological acumen, that such a venture required. Yet the demand was urgent, and the promise of the Bible in the vernacular lay implicit in Luther's *Brief Instruction*[6] which introduced his first book of published sermons. The New Testament translation, which he completed in less than three months—by the beginning of March, 1522—at the Wartburg, was published in September of the same year, by which time Luther was already busy with the Old Testament. To his confidant, Georg Spalatin, he wrote on November 3, of that same year: "In translating the Old Testament I am only in Leviticus. . . . I have now decided to shut myself up at home and hasten the work, so that Moses may be in press by January. We shall publish this separately, then the historical books, and finally the prophets, for the size and cost of the books makes it necessary to divide them and publish them a little at a time."[7]

Luther was actually able to follow this procedure, even though the Old Testament was eventually to take him over a decade. The first instalment was the Pentateuch, which was published already in 1523. The second, consisting in the remaining historical books—Joshua through Esther—was completed in translation before December 4, 1523, but was not off the press until April 1524.[8] The third instalment included Job, the Psalter, and the Books of Solomon (Proverbs, Ecclesiastes, and Song of Solomon), and appeared later in 1524. Within the first three years of intensive translation Luther had thus completed about three-fourths of the entire canonical Bible.

His work on the prophetic books went forward slowly and only

---

[5] WA, DB 6, xxxii ff.
[6] In this volume, pp. 113-124.
[7] Smith and Jacobs (eds. and trans.), *Luther's Correspondence*, II, 141. See also the introduction to the Prefaces by Charles M. Jacobs, *PE* 6, 365-366.
[8] WA, DB 9[I], ix.

against mounting difficulties. Outwardly the unrest that set in with the peasant uprisings during 1524 and 1525, as well as the gathering volume of theological controversy,[9] deprived Luther of time for translation. Inwardly the nature of the prophetic books was such that their language was harder to render into German than that of the other books. Nevertheless Jonah and Habakkuk were finished in 1526, Zechariah in 1527, Isaiah in 1528, and Daniel in 1530. The going was tough. To his friend, Wenceslaus Link, at Nürnberg, Luther exclaimed in June of 1528: "We are sweating over the work of putting the Prophets into German. God, how much of it there is, and how hard it is to make these Hebrew writers talk German! They resist us, and do not want to leave their Hebrew and imitate our German barbarisms. It is like making a nightingale leave her own sweet song and imitate the monotonous voice of a cuckoo, which she detests."[10] Finally, in 1532, Luther published all the prophetical books in *Die Propheten alle deutsch*.[11] From 1529-1534 he completed the Old Testament Apocrypha, and in 1534 all the biblical books were collected and published in one volume as Luther's complete German Bible.

Paralleling and then outlasting the work of translation was the task of revision into which Luther drew his colleagues from the very start.[12] The second edition of the New Testament was issued within three months of the first, in December, 1522, complete with numerous improvements in the text. The Old Testament books were similarly revised and reissued. A revised edition of the Psalter, in 1531, was not only the proof of an on-going process but also the product of a semi-formally constituted revision commission, or *collegium biblicum*, which Luther had gathered about him.[13] He promoted the task of revision and improvement to the very end of his life, all of it done in the recognition that final authority belongs only to the original text, and that Christ is the unity of Scripture.[14]

(2) Luther the translator was at the same time Luther the theologian, a fact which came out clearly in his prefaces to the bibli-

---

[9] See pp. 157-158.
[10] Smith and Jacobs, *op. cit.*, II, 445.
[11] *WA*, DB 2, 512. See p. 265, n. 78.
[12] *WA*, DB 8, xxi.
[13] See p. 206.
[14] Reu, *Luther's German Bible*, pp. 114-124, 133-135.

cal books. The prefaces are his personal testimony to the living and abiding dynamic of the Scriptures.[15] Luther regarded the Scriptures as a great gift of God. This gift had been made accessible to him in the midst of his deepest spiritual struggle. God's life-creating Spirit had suddenly permitted one short text—the word in Romans 1:17 on justification—to shine with a brightness that disclosed the wonders and secrets of Holy Scripture.

It became clear to Luther what the law and sin, what righteousness and faith, really are. To him Paul's letter to the Romans became "really the chief part of the New Testament, and . . . the purest gospel."[16] He thought of this epistle as standing at the center of all the other books of the Bible, like a burning light that shed its rays in all directions. To him, therefore, Romans became the standard by which all the other books of the New Testament are to be measured and ranked. Besides, "whoever has this epistle well in his heart, has with him the light and power of the Old Testament."[17]

Despite all its diversity, Luther saw the entire Bible as a great and awesome unity. Everything in it was to be grasped or understood in relation to Christ, the Lord and Sovereign of the Scriptures. Therefore the Old Testament and the New Testament belong inseparably together. For they both testify of that God who, veiling his majesty and glory, uses speech and history as well as the offense and preaching of the cross in order to discredit the wisdom of this world and to gather his expectant church in the hope of the great day of Christ.

The dedicated scholarship of the past century has made the historical reality of the Bible much more comprehensible to us than it was to the men of the Reformation era. Luther indeed availed himself of the best aids of his time, inadequate though these were, in order to ascertain the most accurate text of Scripture. His exposition especially of the prophetic books made it vividly clear to him how necessary are insights into the concrete historical situation of

---

[15] In this respect one of the best accounts of Luther's prefaces is that supplied by Georg Merz for the latest Munich Edition of Luther's works. The five paragraphs of this section 2 are taken directly from the introduction by Merz in MA^3 6, 435-436.

[16] See p. 365.

[17] See p. 380.

the prophets. In this respect the preface to Isaiah[18] is especially significant.

Nevertheless it could hardly have occurred to Luther to see in this historical perspective and approach something ultimate and decisive. That is to say the historical point of view can function only in a serving capacity; it cannot penetrate to the ultimate depth of the Scriptures. That the holy and wondrous, the speech and action of the living God, should break through into the diffuse realm of man's religiousness is a fact which eludes the attempts of all purely historical research to lay hold of. It is precisely in this wondrousness of Scripture that Luther is at home. Despite all deficiencies which may show up in the light of today's biblical scholarship, Luther's prefaces still carry a relevant message. For he is here speaking as a man who is himself aware of a prophetic mission, and whose entire life and work stand in the light of the coming kingdom of Christ.

(3) In providing prefaces for the books in the German Bible, Luther was simply following a traditional practice. The inclusion of a prologue illuminating the main thoughts of a treatise was a practice associated with the best in scholarly exposition as far back as Aristotle. Jerome's Vulgate had prefaces to almost every book in the Bible, plus others for groups of books such as Paul's epistles and the seven catholic epistles.[19] However Marcion, in the second century, seems to have been the church's trail blazer in this direction with his prologues to the letters of Paul.[20] The second edition of Erasmus' New Testament in 1518 began with one hundred twenty folio pages of introductory material.[21]

Luther's prefaces, however, brought something new by means of which he revealed his understanding of the Scriptures, namely a set of value judgments and a ranking of the books into categories. For him the Gospel of John and the epistles of Paul as well as I Peter, rank as "the true kernel and marrow of all the books."[22] As books of secondary rank come Hebrews, James, Jude, and Revela-

---

[18] See pp. 273-278.
[19] See p. 360, n. 9.
[20] Karl Holl, *Gesammelte Aufsätze zur Kirchengeschichte*, Vol. I, Luther (6th ed.; Tübingen: Mohr, 1932), p. 572.
[21] *WA*, DB 6, 535; *WA*, DB 7, 555.
[22] See p. 362.

tion.[23] While Luther's assigning of a standard of values to the New Testament books may have been simply an act of religious devotion, it proved to be also, as Holl readily points out, a pioneering step toward modern biblical scholarship.[24] Luther's prefaces are thus more than simply popular introductions for lay readers. They reveal a theological position of Christocentricity which inevitably affects his understanding of the New Testament canon.[25]

In keeping with early Christian tradition, Luther also included the Apocrypha of the Old Testament. Sorting them out of the canonical books, he appended them at the end of the Old Testament with the caption, "These books are not held equal to the Scriptures, but are useful and good to read."[26] Because they were not in the Septuagint, Luther omitted III and IV Maccabees as well as III and IV Esdras. But he also cut out I and II Esdras because "they contain nothing that one could not find better in Aesop or in still slighter works."[27]

In the Weimar Edition, on which our translations are based as far as possible, the prefaces are not gathered in one place but, as in the original German Bible, appear at their proper place at the beginning of the text of each biblical book. Complete with critical apparatus, those prefaces that have thus far appeared cover the New Testament books (WA, DB 6-7) and the Old Testament books from Genesis through Ezekiel (WA, DB 8-11[I]). Our translations of the prefaces to Daniel, the Minor Prophets, and the Apocrypha respectively are based on EA 41, 237-258, 321-324; EA 63, 74-90; and EA 63, 91-108, since the appropriate volumes in the WA, DB series have not yet been published. Our few references in WA, DB 11[II], are derived from WA, DB 11[I], which became available just before this volume went to press.

The following English translation of the prefaces to the canonical books is a revision of that by Charles Michael Jacobs in PE 6, 367-489. The prefaces to the Apocrypha are here rendered in English for the first time.

---

[23] See pp. 394-398, especially p. 394, n. 43.
[24] Holl, op. cit., p. 561.
[25] See Jaroslav Pelikan, Luther the Expositor (companion volume to LW 1-30), pp. 86-88.
[26] See p. 337, n. 1.
[27] See pp. 349-350.

PREFACES TO THE OLD TESTAMENT

Translated by Charles M. Jacobs

Revised by E. Theodore Bachmann

PREFACES TO THE
OLD TESTAMENT

Preface to the Old Testament[1]

1545 (1523)

There are some who have little regard for the Old Testament. They think of it as a book that was given to the Jewish people only and is now out of date, containing only stories of past times. They think they have enough in the New Testament and assert that only a spiritual sense[2] is to be sought in the Old Testament. Origen,[3] Jerome,[4] and many other distinguished people have held this view. But Christ says in John 5[:39], "Search the Scriptures, for it is they that bear witness to me." St. Paul bids Timothy attend to the reading of the Scriptures [I Tim. 4:13], and in Romans 1[:2] he declares that the gospel was promised by God in the Scriptures, while in I Corinthians 15[5] he says that in accordance with the Scriptures Christ came of the seed of David, died, and was raised from the dead. St. Peter, too, points us back, more than once, to the Scriptures.

They do this in order to teach us that the Scriptures of the Old

---

[1] Luther finished translating the five books of Moses by the middle of December, 1522. They were published as a group by Melchior Lotther in Wittenberg by early summer, 1523, and revised six times by 1528. In contradistinction to the New Testament, the Psalter, Jesus Sirach, and the Books of Solomon, the Pentateuch was never published in separate edition after its incorporation into the complete Bible of 1534 (WA, DB 8, xix-xxi). This preface, composed after completion of the translation of the Pentateuch and first published with the Pentateuch in 1523, was retained almost intact in the 1534 and later versions of the complete Bible. It has reference, of course, primarily to the first five books of the Old Testament (WA, DB 8, xli). Our translation is based on the 1545 text as given in WA, DB 8, 11-31. See pp. 227-232 for the general introduction to all of Luther's biblical prefaces.

[2] Geistliche sinn. The allegorical sense of Scripture was differentiated from its literal sense and its moral sense by the early exegetes.

[3] Origen (ca. 185-ca. 254) at Alexandria was the principal exponent of allegorical exegesis.

[4] Jerome (ca. 342-420) sought to combine the literal and the allegorical methods of interpretation, giving somewhat greater emphasis to the former than to the latter.

[5] I Cor. 15:3-4; cf. Rom. 1:3 and II Tim. 2:8.

Testament are not to be despised, but diligently read. For they themselves base the New Testament upon them mightily, proving it by the Old Testament and appealing to it, as St. Luke also writes in Acts 17[:11], saying that they at Thessalonica examined the Scriptures daily to see if these things were so that Paul was teaching. The ground and proof of the New Testament is surely not to be despised, and therefore the Old Testament is to be highly regarded. And what is the New Testament but a public preaching and proclamation of Christ, set forth through the sayings of the Old Testament and fulfilled through Christ?

In order that those who are not more familiar with it may have instruction and guidance for reading the Old Testament with profit, I have prepared this preface to the best of the ability God has given me. I beg and really caution every pious Christian not to be offended by the simplicity of the language and stories frequently encountered there, but fully realize that, however simple they may seem, these are the very words, works, judgments, and deeds of the majesty, power, and wisdom of the most high God. For these are the Scriptures which make fools of all the wise and understanding, and are open only to the small and simple, as Christ says in Matthew 11[:25]. Therefore dismiss your own opinions and feelings, and think of the Scriptures as the loftiest and noblest of holy things, as the richest of mines which can never be sufficiently explored, in order that you may find that divine wisdom which God here lays before you in such simple guise as to quench all pride. Here you will find the swaddling cloths and the manger in which Christ lies, and to which the angel points the shepherds [Luke 2:12]. Simple and lowly are these swaddling cloths, but dear is the treasure, Christ, who lies in them.

Know, then, that the Old Testament is a book of laws, which teaches what men are to do and not to do—and in addition gives examples and stories of how these laws are kept or broken—just as the New Testament is gospel or book of grace,[6] and teaches where one is to get the power to fulfil the law. Now in the New Testament there are also given, along with the teaching about grace, many other teachings that are laws and commandments for the control of the flesh—since in this life the Spirit is not perfected and grace alone

---

[6] Cf. p. 358.

cannot rule. Similarly in the Old Testament too there are, beside the laws, certain promises and words of grace, by which the holy fathers and prophets under the law were kept, like us, in the faith of Christ. Nevertheless just as the chief teaching of the New Testament is really the proclamation of grace and peace through the forgiveness of sins in Christ, so the chief teaching of the Old Testament is really the teaching of laws, the showing up of sin, and the demanding of good. You should expect this in the Old Testament.

We come first to the books of Moses. In his first book [Genesis] Moses teaches how all creatures were created, and (as the chief cause for his writing) whence sin and death came, namely by Adam's fall, through the devil's wickedness. But immediately thereafter, before the coming of the law of Moses, he teaches whence help is to come for the driving out of sin and death, namely, not by the law or men's own works (since there was no law as yet), but by "the seed of the woman," Christ, promised to Adam and Abraham, in order that throughout the Scriptures from the beginning faith may be praised above all works and laws and merits. Genesis,[7] therefore, is made up almost entirely of illustrations of faith and unbelief, and of the fruits that faith and unbelief bear. It is an exceedingly evangelical book.

Afterward, in the second book [Exodus], when the world was now full and sunk in blindness so that men scarcely knew any longer what sin was or where death came from, God brings Moses forward with the law and selects a special people, in order to enlighten the world again through them, and by the law to reveal sin anew. He therefore organizes this people with all kinds of laws and separates it from all other peoples. He has them build a tent, and begins a form of worship. He appoints princes and officials, and provides his people splendidly with both laws and men, to rule them both in the body before the world and in the spirit before God.

The special topic of the third book [Leviticus] is the appointment of the priesthood, with the statutes and laws according to which the priests are to act and to teach the people. There we see that a priestly office is instituted only because of sin, to disclose sin to the people and to make atonement before God, so that its entire

---

[7] Cf. p. 161, n. 1.

function is to deal with sin and sinners. For this reason too no temporal wealth is given to the priests; neither are they commanded or permitted to rule men's bodies. Rather the only work assigned to them is to care for the people who are in sin.

In the fourth book [Numbers], after the laws have been given, the princes and priests instituted, the tent and form of worship set up, and everything that pertains to the people of God made ready, then the whole thing begins to function; a test is made as to how well the arrangement operates and how satisfactory it is. This is why this very book says so much about the disobedience of the people and the plagues that came upon them. And some of the laws are explained and the number of the laws increased. Indeed this is the way it always goes; laws are quickly given, but when they are to go into effect and become operative, they meet with nothing but hindrance; nothing goes as the law demands. This book is a notable example of how vacuous it is to make people righteous with laws; rather, as St. Paul says, laws cause only sin and wrath.[8]

In the fifth book [Deuteronomy], after the people have been punished because of their disobedience, and God has enticed them a little with grace, in order that by his kindness in giving them the two kingdoms[9] they might be moved to keep his law gladly and willingly, then Moses repeats the whole law. He repeats the story of all that has happened to the people (except for that which concerns the priesthood) and explains anew everything that belongs either to the bodily or to the spiritual governing of a people. Thus Moses, as a perfect lawgiver, fulfilled all the duties of his office.[10] He not only gave the law, but was there when men were to fulfil it. When things went wrong, he explained the law and re-established it. Yet this explanation in the fifth book really contains nothing else than faith toward God and love toward one's neighbor, for all God's laws come

---

[8] Cf. Rom. 5:20; 7:7-9; 4:15.

[9] Cf. p. 164, pp. 289-290.

[10] Throughout this preface with but two exceptions we have rendered the German word *Amt* by its closest English equivalent, "office." We have done so for the sake of preserving the continuity in Luther's discussion of the law, even though *Amt* in various contexts is really susceptible of numerous more felicitous English renderings which may or may not be implied in the term "office," such as work, ministry, function, and even dispensation (the RSV term in II Cor. 3:7, which we have retained on p. 242). Cf. the use of the same term on p. 348, l. 19, in connection with the gospel as well as the law.

to that. Therefore, down to the twentieth chapter, Moses, in his explanation of the law, guards against everything that might destroy faith in God; and from there to the end of the book he guards against everything that hinders love.

It is to be observed in the first place that Moses provides so exactly for the organization of the people under laws as to leave human reason no room to choose a single work of its own or to invent its own form of worship. For Moses not only teaches fear, love, and trust toward God, but he also provides so many ways of outward worship—sacrifices, thanksgivings, fasts, mortifications, and the like —that no one needs to choose anything else. Besides he gives instructions for planting and tilling, marrying and fighting, governing children, servants, and households, buying and selling, borrowing and repaying, and for everything that is to be done both outwardly and inwardly. He goes so far that some of the prescriptions are to be regarded as foolish and useless.

Why, my friend, does God do that? In the end, because he has taken this people to be his own and has willed to be their God. For this reason he would so rule them that all their doings may surely be right in his eyes. For if anyone does anything for which God's word has not first given warrant, it counts for nothing before God and is labor lost. For in Deuteronomy 4[:2] and 12[:32] he forbids any addition to his laws; and in 12[:8] he says that they shall not do merely whatever is right in their own eyes. The Psalter, too, and all the prophets lament that the people are simply doing good works that they themselves have chosen to do and that were not commanded by God. He cannot and will not permit those who are his to undertake anything that he has not commanded, no matter how good it may be. For obedience, which depends on God's word, is of all works the noblest and best.

Since this life, however, cannot be without external forms of worship, God put before them all these forms and included them in his commandment in order that if they must or would do God any outward service, they might take one of these and not one they themselves had invented. They could then be doubly sure that their work was being done in obedience to God and his word. So they are prevented on every hand from following their own reason and free will in doing good and living aright. Room, place, time, person, work, and form are all more than adequately determined and prescribed, so that the people cannot complain and need not follow simply the example of alien worship.

In the second place it should be noted that the laws are of three kinds. Some speak only of temporal things, as do our imperial laws. These are established by God chiefly because of the wicked, that they may not do worse things. Such laws are for prevention rather than for instruction,[11] as when Moses commands that a wife be dismissed with a bill of divorce [Deut. 24:1] or that a husband can get rid of his wife with a "cereal offering of jealousy" [Num. 5:11-31] and take other wives besides. All these are temporal laws. There are some, however, that teach about the external worship of God, as has already been mentioned.

Over and above these two are the laws about faith and love. All other laws must and ought to be measured by faith and love. That is to say, the other laws are to be kept where their observance does not conflict with faith and love; but where they conflict with faith and love, they should be done away entirely. For this reason we read that David did not kill the murderer Joab [I Kings 2:5-6], even though he had twice deserved death [II Sam. 3:27; 20:10]. And in II Samuel 14[:11][12] David promises the woman of Tekoa that her son shall not die for having slain his brother. Nor did David kill Absalom [II Sam. 14:21-24]. Moreover David himself ate of the holy bread of the priests, I Samuel 21[:6]. And Tamar thought the king might give her in marriage to her stepbrother, Amnon [II Sam. 13:13]. From these and similar incidents one sees plainly that the kings, priests, and heads of the people often transgressed the laws boldly, at the demand of faith and love. Therefore faith and love are always to be mistresses of the law and to have all laws in their power. For since all laws aim at faith and love, none of them can be valid, or be a law, if it conflicts with faith or love.

Even to the present day, the Jews are greatly in error when they hold so strictly and stubbornly to certain laws of Moses. They

---

[11] *Nur Wehrgesetz, mehr denn Leregesetz.*

[12] Where Luther cites correctly the Vulgate, in which the four books of I and II Samuel and I and II Kings were numbered as I, II, III, and IV Kings, we have given the corresponding RSV reference.

would rather let love and peace be destroyed than eat and drink with us, or do things of that kind. They do not properly regard the intention of the law; but to understand this is essential for all who live under laws, not for the Jews alone. Christ also says so in Matthew 12,[13] that one might break the sabbath if an ox had fallen into a pit, and might rescue it. Now that was only a temporal necessity and injury. How much more ought one boldly to break all kinds of laws when bodily necessity demands it, provided that nothing is done against faith and love. Christ says that David did this very thing when he ate the holy bread, Mark 3[2:25-26].

But why does Moses mix up his laws in such a disordered way? Why does he not put the temporal laws together in one group and the spiritual laws in another and the laws of faith and love in still another? Moreover he sometimes repeats a law so often and reiterates the same words so many times that it becomes tedious to read it or listen to it. The answer is that Moses writes as the situation demands, so that his book is a picture and illustration of governing and of living. For this is the way it happens in a dynamic situation: now this work has to be done and now that. No man can so arrange his life (if he is to act in a godly way) that on this day he uses only spiritual laws and on that day only temporal. Rather God governs all the laws mixed together—like the stars in the heavens and the flowers in the fields—in such a way that at every hour a man must be ready for anything, and do whatever the situation requires. In like manner the writing of Moses represents a heterogeneous mixture.

That Moses is so insistent and often repeats the same thing shows also the nature of his office. For one who is to rule a people-with-laws [Gesetzuolck] must constantly admonish, constantly drive, and knock himself out struggling with the people as [he would] with asses. For no work of law is done gladly and willingly; it is all forced and compelled. Now since Moses is a lawgiver, he has to show by his insistence that the work of the law is a forced work. He has to wear the people down, until this insistence makes them not only recognize their illness and their dislike for God's law, but also long for grace,[14] as we shall show.

---

[13] Matt. 12:11; cf. Luke 14:5.
[14] Cf. Luther's Brief Explanation of the Ten Commandments, The Creed, and The Lord's Prayer. PE 2, 354-355.

In the third place the true intention of Moses is through the law to reveal sin and put to shame all presumption as to human ability. For this reason St. Paul, in Galatians 2[:17], calls Moses "an agent of sin," and his office "a dispensation of death," II Corinthians 3[:7]. In Romans 3[:20] and 7[:7] he says, "Through the law comes nothing more than knowledge of sin"; and in Romans 3[:20], "By works of the law no one becomes righteous before God." For by the law Moses can do no more than tell what men ought to do and not do. However he does not provide the strength and ability for such doing and not doing, and thus lets us stick in sin. When we then stick in sin, death presses instantly upon us as vengeance and punishment for sin. For this reason St. Paul calls sin "the sting of death" [I Cor. 15:56], because it is by sin that death has all its right and power over us. But if there were no law, there would be no sin.[15] Therefore it is all the fault of Moses, who by the law precipitates and stirs up sin; and then upon sin death follows with a vengeance. Rightly, then, does St. Paul call the office of Moses a dispensation of sin and death [II Cor. 3:7], for by his lawgiving he brings upon us nothing but sin and death.

Nevertheless this office of sin and death is good and very necessary. For where there is no law of God, there all human reason is so blind that it cannot recognize sin. For human reason does not know that unbelief and despair of God is sin. Indeed it knows nothing about man's duty to believe and trust in God. Hardened in its blindness, it goes its way and never feels this sin at all. Meanwhile it does some works that would otherwise be good, and it leads an outwardly respectable life. Then it thinks it stands well and the matter has been satisfactorily handled; we see this in the heathen and the hypocrites, when their life is at its best. Besides reason does not know either that the evil inclination of the flesh, and hatred of enemies, is sin. Because it observes and feels that all men are so inclined, it holds rather that these things are natural and right, and thinks it is enough merely to guard against the outward acts. So it goes its way, regarding its illness as strength, its sin as virtue, its evil as good; and never getting anywhere.

See, then! Moses' office is essential for driving away this blindness and hardened presumption. Now he cannot drive them away

---

[15] Cf. Rom. 4:15.

unless he reveals them and makes them known. He does this by the law, when he teaches that men ought to fear, trust, believe, and love God; and that, besides, they ought to have or bear no evil desire or hatred for any man. When human nature, then, catches on to this, it must be frightened, for it certainly finds neither trust nor faith, neither fear nor love to God, and neither love nor purity toward one's neighbor. Human nature finds rather only unbelief, doubt, contempt, and hatred to God; and toward one's neighbor only evil will and evil desire. But when human nature finds these things, then death is instantly before its eyes, ready to devour such a sinner and to swallow him up in hell.

See, this is what it means for sin to bring death upon us and kill us. This is what it means for the law to stir up sin and set it before our eyes, driving all our presumption into despondency and trembling and despair, so that a man can do no more than cry with the prophets, "I am rejected by God," or, as we say in German, "The devil has me; I can never be saved." This is to be really cast into hell. This is what St. Paul means by those short words in I Corinthians 15[:56], "The sting of death is sin, and the power of sin is the law." It is as if he were saying, "Death stings and slays us because of the sin that is found in us, guilty of death; sin, however, is found in us and gives us so mightily to death because of the law which reveals sin to us and teaches us to recognize it, where before we did not know it and felt secure."

Notice with what power Moses conducts and performs this office of his. For in order to put human nature to the utmost shame, he not only gives laws like the Ten Commandments that speak of natural and true sins, but he also makes sins of things that are in their nature not sins. Moses thus forces and presses sins upon them in heaps. For unbelief and evil desire are in their nature sins, and worthy of death. But to eat leavened bread at the Passover [Exodus 12–13] and to eat an unclean animal [Leviticus 11, Deuteronomy 14] or make a mark on the body [Lev. 19:28, Deut. 14:1], and all those things that the Levitical priesthood deals with as sin—these are not in their nature sinful and evil. Rather they became sins only because they are forbidden by the law. This law can be done away. The Ten Commandments, however, cannot be done away, for here there really is sin, even if there were no commandments, or if they were not known—just as the unbelief of the heathen is sin, even though they do not know or think that it is sin.

Therefore we see that these many laws of Moses were given not only to prevent anyone from choosing ways of his own for doing good and living aright, as was said above,[16] but rather that sins might simply become numerous and be heaped up beyond measure. The purpose was to burden the conscience so that the hardened blindness would have to recognize itself, and feel its own inability and nothingness in the achieving of good. Such blindness must be thus compelled and forced by the law to seek something beyond the law and its own ability, namely, the grace of God promised in the Christ who was to come. Every law of God is good and right [Rom. 7:7-16], even if it only bids men to carry dung or to gather straw. Accordingly, whoever does not keep this good law—or keeps it unwillingly—cannot be righteous or good in his heart. But human nature cannot keep it otherwise than unwillingly. It must therefore, through this good law of God, recognize and feel its wickedness, and sigh and long for the aid of divine grace in Christ.

For this reason then, when Christ comes the law ceases, especially the Levitical law which, as has been said, makes sins of things that in their nature are not sins. The Ten Commandments also cease, not in the sense that they are no longer to be kept or fulfilled, but in the sense that the office of Moses in them ceases; it no longer increases sin [Rom. 5:20] by the Ten Commandments, and sin is no longer the sting of death [I Cor. 15:56]. For through Christ sin is forgiven, God is reconciled, and man's heart has begun to feel kindly toward the law.[17] The office of Moses can no longer rebuke the heart and make it to be sin for not having kept the commandments and for being guilty of death, as it did prior to grace, before Christ came.

St. Paul teaches this in II Corinthians 3[:7-14], where he says that the splendor in the face of Moses is taken away, because of the glory in the face of Jesus Christ. That is, the office of Moses, which makes us to be sin and shame with the glare of the knowledge of

---

[16] Cf. pp. 239-240.

[17] Separate editions of the Pentateuch prior to the 1534 complete Bible here read, "For through the grace of Christ the heart has now become good, loving the law and satisfying it." WA, DB 8, 24, n. 25/26.

our wickedness and nothingness, no longer causes us pain and no longer terrifies us with death. For we now have the glory in the face of Christ [II Cor. 4:6]. This is the office of grace, whereby we know Christ, by whose righteousness, life, and strength we fulfil the law and overcome death and hell. Thus it was that the three apostles who saw Moses and Elijah on Mount Tabor were not afraid of them, because of the tender glory in the face of Christ [Luke 9:32]. Yet in Exodus 34[:29-35], where Christ was not present, the children of Israel could not endure the splendor and brightness in the face of Moses, so that he had to put a veil over it.

For the law has three kinds of pupils. The first are those who hear the law and despise it, and who lead an impious life without fear. To these the law does not come. They are represented by the calf worshipers in the wilderness, on whose account Moses broke the tables of the law [Exod. 32:19]. To them he did not bring the law.

The second kind are those who attempt to fulfil the law by their own power, without grace. They are represented by the people who could not look at the face of Moses when he brought the tables of the law a second time [Exod. 34:34-35]. The law comes to them but they cannot endure it. They therefore put a veil over it and lead a life of hypocrisy, doing outward works of the law. Yet the law makes it all to be sin where the veil is taken off. For the law shows that our ability counts for nothing without Christ's grace.

The third kind of pupils are those who see Moses clearly, without a veil. These are they who understand the intention of the law and how it demands impossible things. There sin comes to power, there death is mighty, there Goliath's spear is like a weaver's beam and its point[18] weighs six hundred shekels of brass, so that all the children of Israel flee before him unless the one and only David—Christ our Lord—saves us from all this [I Sam. 17:7, 24, 32]. For if Christ's glory did not come alongside this splendor of Moses, no one could bear the brightness of the law, the terror of sin and death. These pupils fall away from all works and presumption and learn from the law nothing else except to recognize sin and to yearn for

---

[18] *Stachel*, meaning a sharp point such as the head of a spear, has additional overtones in this context, for it was also the word Luther had used in I Cor. 15:56 to speak of the "sting"of death (cf. p. 243). WA, DB 7, 134.

Christ. This is the true office of Moses and the very nature of the law.

. So Moses himself has told us that his office and teaching should endure until Christ, and then cease, when he says in Deuteronomy 18[:15-19], "The Lord your God will raise up for you a prophet like me from among your brethren—him shall you heed," etc. This is the noblest saying in all of Moses, indeed the very heart of it all. The apostles appealed to it and made great use of it to strengthen the gospel and to abolish the law [Acts 3:22; 7:37]. All the prophets, as well, drew heavily upon it. For since God here promises another Moses whom they are to hear, it follows of necessity that this other one would teach something different from Moses; and Moses gives up his power and yields to him, so that men will listen to him. This [coming] prophet cannot, then, teach the law, for Moses has done that to perfection; for the law's sake there would be no need to raise up another prophet. Therefore this word was surely spoken concerning Christ and the teaching of grace.

For this reason also, St. Paul calls the law of Moses "the old testament" [II Cor. 3:14], and Christ does the same when he institutes "the new testament" [I Cor. 11:25].[19] It is a testament because in it God promised and bequeathed to the people of Israel the land of Canaan, if they would keep it. He gave it to them too, and it was confirmed by the death and blood of sheep and goats. But since this testament did not stand upon God's grace, but upon men's works, it had to become obsolete and cease, and the promised land had to be lost again—because the law cannot be fulfilled by works. And another testament had to come which would not become obsolete, which would not stand upon our deeds either, but upon God's words and works, so that it might endure for ever. Therefore it is confirmed by the death and blood of an eternal Person, and an eternal land is promised and given.[20]

Let this be enough about the books and office of Moses. What, then, are the other books, the prophets and the histories? I answer: They are nothing else than what Moses is. For they all propagate the office of Moses; they guard against the false prophets, that they

---

[19] Cf. Heb. 8:13: "In speaking of a new covenant he treats the first as obsolete." In Luther's Bible, as in the Vulgate, the adjective "new" appeared also in the synoptic accounts of the Last Supper, Matt. 26:28, Mark 14:24, and Luke 22:20.
[20] Cf. Heb. 9:11-12.

may not lead the people to works, but allow them to remain in the true office of Moses, the knowledge of the law. They hold fast to this purpose of keeping the people conscious of their own impotence through a right understanding of the law, and thus driving them to Christ, as Moses does. For this reason they also explicate further what Moses says of Christ, and furnish two kinds of examples, of those who have Moses right and of those who do not, and also of the punishments and rewards that come to both. Thus the prophets are nothing else than administrators[21] and witnesses of Moses and his office, bringing everyone to Christ through the law.

In conclusion I ought also to indicate the spiritual meaning[22] presented to us by the Levitical law and priesthood of Moses. But there is too much of this to write; it requires space and time and should be expounded with the living voice. For Moses is, indeed, a well of all wisdom and understanding, out of which has sprung all that the prophets knew and said. Moreover even the New Testament flows out of it and is grounded in it, as we have heard[23] It is my duty, however, to give at least some little clue[24] to those who have the grace and understanding to pursue the matter further.

If you would interpret well and confidently, set Christ before you, for he is the man to whom it all applies, every bit of it. Make the high priest Aaron, then, to be nobody but Christ alone, as does the Epistle to the Hebrews [5:4-5], which is sufficient, all by itself, to interpret all the figures of Moses. Likewise, as the same epistle announces [Hebrews 9–10], it is certain that Christ himself is the sacrifice—indeed even the altar [Heb. 13:10]—who sacrificed himself with his own blood. Now whereas the sacrifice performed by the Levitical high priest took away only the artificial sins,[25] which in their nature were not sins, so our high priest, Christ, by his own sacrifice and blood, has taken away the true sin, that which in its very nature is sin. He has gone in once for all through the curtain to God to make atonement for us [Heb. 9:12]. Thus you should

---

[21] *Handhaber* has the sense of uphold, support, or defend as well as of perform or execute. WA, DB 8, 29, n. 22; cf. Grimm, *Deutsches Wörterbuch*, IV, 393-396.

[22] *Geistliche Deutung;* cf. p. 235, n. 2.

[23] Cf. p. 235.

[24] *Grifflin* means a trick, device, or stratagem. Grimm, *Deutsches Wörterbuch*, IV, 312; cf. WA, DB 8, 29, n. 30.

[25] *Die gemachten sunde.* See pp. 243-244.

apply to Christ personally, and to no one else, all that is written about the high priest.

The high priest's sons, however, who are engaged in the daily sacrifice, you should interpret to mean ourselves. Here on earth, in the body, we Christians live in the presence of our father Christ, who is sitting in heaven; we have not yet passed through to him except spiritually, by faith. Their office of slaughter and sacrifice signifies nothing else than the preaching of the gospel, by which the old man is slain and offered to God, burned and consumed by the fire of love, in the Holy Spirit. This sacrifice smells really good before God; that is, it produces a conscience that is good, pure, and secure before God. This is the interpretation that St. Paul makes in Romans 12[:1] when he teaches that we are to offer our bodies to God as a living, holy, and acceptable sacrifice. This is what we do (as has been said) by the constant exercise of the gospel both in preaching and in believing.

Let this suffice for the present as a brief suggestion for seeking Christ and the gospel in the Old Testament.[26]

Whoever reads this Bible should also know that I have been careful to write the name of God which the Jews call "Tetragrammaton"[27] in capital letters thus, LORD [HERR], and the other name which they call Adonai[28] only half in capital letters thus, LOrd [HErr].[29] For among all the names of God, these two alone are

[26] In editions of the complete Bible from 1534 on, the preface ended at this point. The paragraphs which follow were found only in the earlier editions.

[27] Tetragrammaton, literally "four letters," is the technical term for the four-consonant Hebrew word for the name God, which is now commonly thought to be represented in English by the word "Yahweh." When the Hebrews came to this name in speaking or reading they avoided uttering it because of its sacred character, pronouncing instead the word Adonai (Lord) unless (as at Gen. 15:2) it immediately followed the word "Adonai" in the text, in which case "Elohim" (God) was read. In written Hebrew texts the vowel-points of Adonai were given to the consonants of the Tetragrammaton with the resultant rendering in English, "Jehovah."

[28] Adonai literally means "my lord," but by usage it was in effect a proper name.

[29] While the Hebrew YHWH always had reference to God alone, ADN could mean either the divine Lord, or a lord or ruler who was not divine. Luther distinguished clearly between the two words by rendering HERR for YHWH and either HErr or herr for ADN (cf. LW 12, 99-101 and LW 13, 230). The distinction between the divine and human within ADN, however, was not consistently maintained in translation by the use of HErr and herr (cf. WA, DB 6, 538-539, note on Matt. 1:20). Cf. Luther's HERR-HERR in Jer. 23:5-6 with the RSV LORD-LORD, Luther's HERR-herr in Gen. 24:12 with the RSV LORD-master,

applied in the Scriptures to the real, true God; while the others are often ascribed to angels and saints. I have done this in order that readers can thereby draw the strong conclusion that Christ is true God. For Jeremiah 23[:6] calls him LORD, saying, "He will be called: 'The LORD, our righteousness.'" The same thing is to be found in other passages. Herewith I commend all my readers to Christ and ask that they help me get from God the power to carry this work through to a profitable end. For I freely admit that I have undertaken too much, especially in trying to put the Old Testament into German.[30] The Hebrew language, sad to say, has gone down so far that even the Jews know little enough about it, and their glosses and interpretations (which I have tested[31]) are not to be relied upon. I think that if the Bible is to come up again, we Christians are the ones who must do the work, for we have the understanding of Christ without which even the knowledge of the language is nothing. Because they were without it, the translators of old, even Jerome,[32] made mistakes in many passages. Though I cannot boast of having achieved perfection, nevertheless, I venture to say that this German Bible is clearer and more accurate at many points than the Latin. So it is true that if the printers do not, as usual, spoil it with their carelessness, the German language certainly has here a better Bible than the Latin language—and the readers will bear me out in this.

And now, of course, the mud will stick to the wheel,[33] and there will be no one so stupid that he will not try to be my master in this work, and criticize me here and there. Let them go to it. I figured from the very beginning that I would find ten thousand to criticize my work before I found one who would accomplish one-twentieth

---

and Luther's *HERR-HErr* in Ps. 110:1 (1545 version only, the earlier versions being both *HERR-HERR* and *HERR-herr*, *WA*, DB 10^I, 476-477) with the RSV Lord-lord. In Luther's Matt. 22:44 rendering of the first "Lord" of the Psalm quotation he went from *Gott* in 1522 through *Herr* and *HErr* to *HERR* in 1539 and later editions (*WA*, DB 6, 100, note). See Gen. 15:2, 8 where Luther translates *ADN YHWH* as *HErr HERR* (*WA*, DB 8, 73). Cf. also *WA*, DB 10^{II}, xxiii, n. 26.
[30] Cf. Luther's statement, "It was necessary for me to undertake the translation of the Bible, otherwise I would have died under the mistaken impression that I was a learned man." *WA* 10^{II}, 60, ll. 13-15; cf. also *WA*, Br 2, 423, ll. 48-50.
[31] Cf. Luther's *Defense of the Translation of the Psalms*, in this volume, pp. 209-223.
[32] Cf. p. 117, n. 1.
[33] Cf. Wander (ed.), *Sprichwörter-Lexikon*, II, 1556, "Koth," Nos. 4 and 16.

of what I have done. I, too, would like to be very learned and give brilliant proof of what I know by criticizing St. Jerome's Latin Bible; but he in turn could also defy me to do what he has done. Now if anyone is so much more learned than I, let him undertake to translate the whole Bible into German, and then tell me what he can do.[34] If he does it better, why should he not be preferred to me? I thought I was well educated—and I know that by the grace of God I am more learned than all the sophists in the universities—but now I see that I cannot handle even my own native German tongue. Nor have I read, up to this time, a book or letter which contained the right kind of German. Besides no one pays any attention to speaking real German. This is especially true of the people in the chancelleries, as well as those patchwork preachers and wretched writers.[35] They think they have the right to change the German language and to invent new words for us every day, such as *behertzigen*,[36] *behendigen*,[37] *esprieslich*,[38] *erschieslich*,[39] and the like. Yes, my dear fellow, there are [and this is] also *bethoret* and *ernarret*.[40]

In a word, if all of us were to work together, we would have plenty to do in bringing the Bible to light, one working with the meaning, the other with the language. For I too have not worked at this alone,[41] but have used the services of anyone whom I could

---

[34] Cf. pp. 183-184 and pp. 221-223.

[35] *Lumpen prediger und puppen schreyber.*

[36] Deriving largely from Swabian origin, the term had been used frequently by Emser. Friedrich Kluge, *Etymologisches Wörterbuch der deutschen Sprache* (17th ed.; Berlin: de Gruyter, 1957), p. 61.

[37] In a letter from Luther and Karlstadt to Duke Frederick of Saxony dated August 18, 1519, Luther—or perhaps his co-author—had himself used the term *Behendigkeit*. WA Br 1, 477, 1. 410. The use of *behendigen* is documented as early as 1484 in Wetterau. Moritz Heyne, *Deutsches Wörterbuch* (3 vols.; Leipzig: Hirzel, 1890-1895), I, 324.

[38] Meaning originally to spring forth or sprout, *espriessen* early came to be used in New High German in the sense of "be useful, profitable, advantageous." The adjective too was given this derived meaning from about the beginning of the sixteenth century. Kluge, *op. cit.*, p. 173.

[39] Luther apparently was unaware that the intransitive verb *erschiessen* was used rather extensively in a sense synonymous with that of *espriessen*. Grimm, *Deutsches Wörterbuch*, III, 962.

[40] *Bethören* means to make a fool of, in the sense of infatuate, seduce, or deceive. *Ernarren* means to play the fool, in the sense of be silly, astonish, or amaze. The construction of Luther's sentence conveys a double meaning: not only that these words too are recent innovations, but also that all such innovating is sheer folly.

[14] See the Introduction, p. 229.

get. Therefore I ask everyone to desist from abuse and leave the poor people undisturbed, and help me, if he can. If he will not do that, let him take up the Bible himself and make a translation of his own. Those who do nothing but abuse and bite and claw are actually not honest and upright enough to really want a pure Bible, since they know that they cannot produce it. They would prefer to be Master Know-it-all[42] in a field not their own, though in their own field they have never even been pupils.

May God bring to completion his work that he began [Phil. 1:6]. Amen.

Preface to the Book of Job

1545 (1524)

The book of Job deals with the question,[43] whether misfortune comes from God even to the righteous. Job stands firm and contends that God torments even the righteous without cause other than that this be to God's praise, as Christ also testifies in John 9[:3] of the man who was born blind.[44]

Job's friends take the other side. They make a big and lengthy palaver trying to maintain God's justice, saying that he does not punish a righteous man, and if he does punish, then the man who is punished must have sinned. They have a worldly and human[45] idea of God and his righteousness, as though he were just like men and his justice like the justice of the world.

To be sure, when Job is in danger of death, out of human weakness he talks too much against God, and in his suffering sins. Nevertheless Job insists that he has not deserved this suffering more

---

[42] See p. 184, n. 14.

[43] Editions prior to the complete Bible of 1534 began this sentence differently: "The book of Job is not a difficult book so far as its meaning is concerned; it is difficult only so far as its language is concerned. For the writer deals with the question, . . ." WA, DB, 10I, 4, n. 2. On Luther's difficulties in translating Job, see his comments, p. 188, n. 33, WA 48, 686, and WA, Br 3, 249.

[44] Editions prior to 1534 simply ended this sentence at the word "praise," omitting the New Testament reference. WA, DB 10I, 4, n. 6.

[45] Editions prior to 1534 simply read, "fleshly," as over against "worldly and human." WA, DB 10I, 4, n. 9.

than others have, which is, of course, true. Finally, however, God decides that Job, by speaking against God in his suffering, has spoken wrongly, but that in contending against his friends about his innocence before the suffering came Job has spoken the truth. So the book carries this story ultimately to this conclusion: God alone is righteous, and yet one man is more righteous than another, even in the sight of God.

But this is written for our comfort, that God allows even his great saints to falter, especially in adversity. For before Job comes into fear of death, he praises God at the theft of his goods and the death of his children. But when death is in prospect and God withdraws himself, Job's words show what kind of thoughts a man—however holy he may be—holds toward God: he thinks that God is not God, but only a judge and wrathful tyrant, who storms ahead and cares nothing about the goodness of a person's life. This is the finest part of this book. It is understood only by those who also experience and feel what it is to suffer the wrath and judgment of God, and to have his grace hidden.[46]

The language of this book is more vigorous and splendid than that of any other book in all the Scriptures. Yet if it were translated everywhere word for word—as the Jews and foolish translators would have it done—and not for the most part according to the sense, no one would understand it. So, for example, when he says something like this, "The thirsty will pant after his wealth" [Job 5:5], that means "robbers shall take it from him"; or when he says, "The children of pride have never trodden it" [Job 28:8], that means "the young lions that stalk proudly"; and many similar cases. Again, by "light" he means good fortune, by "darkness" misfortune [Job 18:8], and so forth.

Therefore I think that this third part[47] will have to suffer and be accused by the know-it-alls of being an entirely different book from the Latin Bible. We just let them go. We have taken care to

---

[46] In editions after 1534 the preface ended here. The paragraphs which follow appeared only in the earlier editions. WA, DB 10I, 6, n. 1.

[47] This "Third Part of the Old Testament" was originally intended to include the twenty-one books from Job through Malachi. Difficulties encountered in the translating, however, resulted in postponed publication of all except the poetical books, Job, Psalms, Proverbs, Ecclesiastes, and Song of Solomon, which were published in the winter of 1524. WA, DB 10I, 2; 10II, xv-xvii.

use language that is clear and that everybody can understand, without perverting the sense and meaning. We can allow anyone to do it better.

Preface to the Psalter[48]

1545 (1528)

Many of the holy fathers prized and praised the Psalter above all the other books of the Scripture. To be sure, the work itself gives praise enough to its author;[49] nevertheless we must give evidence of our own praise and thanks.

Over the years a great many legends of the saints,[50] and passionals,[51] books of examples,[52] and histories have been circulated; indeed, the world has been so filled with them that the Psalter has been neglected.[53] It has lain in such obscurity that not one psalm was rightly understood. Still it gave off such a fine and precious fragrance that all pious hearts felt the devotion and power in the unknown words and for this reason loved the book.

I hold, however, that no finer book of examples or of the legends of the saints has ever come, or can come, to earth than the Psalter. If one were to wish that from all the examples, legends, and histories, the best should be collected and brought together and put

---

[48] On Luther's earlier preoccupation with the Psalms in lecturing and translating see p. 205. The preface to his first Psalter of 1524 is given in English in Reu, *Luther's German Bible*, pp. 202-203; it discusses such key concepts as mercy and truth, judgment and righteousness. The preface here given is that which accompanied the wholly new Psalter of 1528, and was included in all later Psalters and in all editions of the complete Bible beginning in 1534 (*WA*, DB 10^{II}, lxxxviii). Our translation is based on the 1545 version as reprinted in *WA*, DB 10^{I}, 99-105, which is essentially identical with that of 1528.

[49] See Wander (ed.), *Sprichwörter-Lexikon*, III, 579, "*Meister*," No. 17. Cf. Ecclus. 9:17.

[50] The most famous collection of such legends was probably that of Jacobus de Voragine compiled *ca.* 1230-1298. Granger Ryan and Helmut Ripperger (trans.), *The Golden Legend of Jacobus de Voragine* (New York, 1941). Cf. *LW* 36, 26, n. 52.

[51] *Passional* were picture books, with text, describing the life as well as the sufferings of Christ or the saints. *WA* 9, 687, n. 1.

[52] *Exempel Bücher* were books in which the lives of the saints were set forth as examples for devout Christians to follow. *BG* 7, 5, n. 2.

[53] *Unter der banck lag.* See *WA* 51, 724, n. 468, "shoved aside, despised, forgotten"; cf. p. 166, n. 7.

in the best form, the result would have to be the present Psalter. For here we find not only what one or two saints have done, but what he has done who is the very head of all saints. We also find what all the saints still do, such as the attitude they take toward God, toward friends and enemies, and the way they conduct themselves amid all dangers and sufferings. Beyond that there are contained here all sorts of divine and wholesome teachings and commandments.

The Psalter ought to be a precious and beloved book, if for no other reason than this: it promises Christ's death and resurrection so clearly—and pictures his kingdom and the condition and nature of all Christendom—that it might well be called a little Bible. In it is comprehended most beautifully and briefly everything that is in the entire Bible. It is really a fine enchiridion or handbook. In fact, I have a notion that the Holy Spirit wanted to take the trouble himself to compile a short Bible and book of examples of all Christendom or all saints, so that anyone who could not read the whole Bible would here have anyway almost an entire summary of it, comprised in one little book.

Beyond all that, the Psalter has this noble virtue and quality. Other books make much ado about the works of the saints, but say very little about their words. The Psalter is a gem in this respect. It gives forth so sweet a fragrance when one reads it because it relates not only the works of the saints, but also their words, how they spoke with God and prayed, and still speak and pray. Compared to the Psalter, the other legends and examples present to us nothing but mere silent saints; the Psalter, however, pictures for us real, living, active saints.

Compared to a speaking man, a silent one is simply to be regarded as a half-dead man; and there is no mightier or nobler work of man than speech. For it is by speech, more than by his shape or by any other work, that man is most distinguished from other animals. By the carver's art even a block of wood can have the shape of a man; and an animal can see, hear, smell, sing, walk, stand, eat, drink, fast, thirst—and suffer from hunger, frost, and a hard bed—as well as a man.

Moreover the Psalter does more than this. It presents to us not the simple, ordinary speech of the saints, but the best of their language, that which they used when they talked with God himself in great earnestness and on the most important matters. Thus the Psalter lays before us not only their words instead of their deeds, but their very hearts and the inmost treasure of their souls, so we can look down to the foundation and source of their words and deeds. We can look into their hearts and see what kind of thoughts they had, how their hearts were disposed, and how they acted in all kinds of situations, in danger and in need. The legends and examples, which speak only of the deeds and miracles of the saints, do not and cannot do this, for I cannot know how a man's heart is, even though I see or hear of many great deeds that he does. And just as I would rather hear what a saint says than see the deeds he does, so I would far rather see his heart, and the treasure in his soul, than hear his words. And this the Psalter gives us most abundantly concerning the saints, so that we can be certain of how their hearts were toward God and of the words they spoke to God and every man.

A human heart is like a ship on a wild sea, driven by the storm winds from the four corners of the world. Here it is stuck with fear and worry about impending disaster; there comes grief and sadness because of present evil. Here breathes a breeze of hope and of anticipated happiness; there blows security and joy in present blessings. These storm winds teach us to speak with earnestness, to open the heart and pour out what lies at the bottom of it. He who is stuck in fear and need speaks of misfortune quite differently from him who floats on joy; and he who floats on joy speaks and sings of joy quite differently from him who is stuck in fear. When a sad man laughs or a glad man weeps, they say, he does not do so from the heart;[54] that is, the depths of the heart are not open, and what is in them does not come out.

What is the greatest thing in the Psalter but this earnest speaking amid these storm winds of every kind? Where does one find finer words of joy than in the psalms of praise and thanksgiving? There you look into the hearts of all the saints, as into fair and pleasant gardens, yes, as into heaven itself. There you see what fine and pleasant flowers of the heart spring up from all sorts of fair and happy thoughts toward God, because of his blessings. On the

---

[54] See Wander (ed.), *Sprichwörter-Lexikon*, II, 608, "*Herz*," No. 175.

Preface to the Books of Solomon[59]

1545 (1534)

Three books bear the name of Solomon.[60] The first is *Proverbia*, "Proverbs" [*die Sprüche*]. It may properly be called a book of good works, for in it he teaches how to lead a good life before God and the world.

He pays special attention to the young people. In fatherly fashion he instructs them in God's commandments, with reassuring promises of how well things shall be with the righteous, and threats as to how the wicked will have to be punished. For young people are of themselves inclined to all evil. Because of their inexperience, they do not understand the wiles and wickedness of the world and the devil. They are far too weak to withstand bad examples and the causes of offense, neither are they able to govern themselves. If they are not instructed, they are ruined and lost even before they get their bearings.[61]

Therefore young people need and must have teachers and rulers who will exhort, warn, rebuke, and chastise them, who will hold them constantly to the fear of God and to his commandments in order to ward off the devil, the world, and the flesh. This, then, is what Solomon does abundantly and with all diligence in this book. He puts his teaching into proverbs, so that it can be grasped the more easily and kept the more readily. Anyone who intends to become righteous might well take this as a handbook or prayerbook for his daily use, read it often, and ponder his own life in it.

For a man must go one of two ways: either he must let his father chastise him or he must let the executioner punish him. As

---

[59] This preface to the entire group of three books appeared first not in 1524—as *PE* 6, 389 and *EA* 63, 35 wrongly indicate—but in the 1534 edition of the complete Bible and then in following editions of the Bible as well as in five separate Wittenberg editions of the books of Solomon alone between 1535 and 1546. It was intended to replace the two prefaces of 1524, which dealt in separate fashion with Proverbs and Ecclesiastes (see pp. 261-264). *WA*, DB 10^{II}, xii-xiii, xci. Our translation is based on the text in *WA* 10^{II}, 7-11, which is the 1545 version of the preface.

[60] Tradition had so ascribed to Solomon the authorship of Proverbs, Ecclesiastes, and Song of Solomon. For Luther's view of authorship see p. 263.

[61] *Ehe sie sich umbsihet.*

they say, "You may escape me, but you will not escape the hangman."[62] And it would be good to impress this constantly on the young people, so that they might know without any doubt that they must suffer either the father's rod or the executioner's sword, just as, in this book, Solomon is constantly threatening the disobedient with death. There is no other way out, for God leaves nothing unpunished. We see in our own experience that disobedient knaves perish in strange ways; they finally come into the executioner's hands just when they least expect it and feel most secure. Public testimony and signs of all this are the gallows, wheels, and places of execution at the gates of all the cities. Through his temporal government God has put them there to terrify all those who will not obey their elders and let themselves be instructed in God's word.

Therefore in this book Solomon calls all those who despise God's word "fools," and all those who deport themselves according to God's commandments "wise." This does not apply solely to young people—though it is primarily they whom he has undertaken to teach—but to people of all stations from the highest to the very lowest. For just as youth has its own particular offenses against God's commandments, so every other group has its vices as well; and these are worse than the vices of youth. As they say, "The older they are, the worse they get";[63] and again, "Age is no cure for folly."[64]

Even if there were nothing evil in the other and higher stations, no greed, pride, hatred, envy, etc., nevertheless this one vice would be bad enough, namely, that they try to be shrewd and smart when they ought not to be; everybody is inclined to do something else than what is committed to him, and to leave undone that which

---

[62] Cf. in the text Luther's marginal comments on the word "die" in Prov. 19:16, "He comes into the hands of the hangman, and to the gallows, for disobedient children cannot escape him;" and in Prov. 23:13, "If you flog him, the executioner will not have to. But the flogging must be done—if the father does not do it the hangman will—there is no other way; no one has ever escaped him yet, for it is the judgment of God." WA, DB 10^II 63, 77. Cf. also Wander (ed.), Sprichwörter-Lexikon, I, 812, "Eltern," No. 40; and IV, 1511, "Vater," No. 170.
[63] See Wander (ed.), Sprichwörter-Lexikon, I, 51, "Alt," No. 21; and cf. II, 1785, "Lange," No. 6.
[64] See WA 51, 708, n. 320; and Wander (ed.), Sprichwörter-Lexikon, I, 59, "Alter," No. 7.

is committed to him. For example, whoever is in the spiritual office tries to be wise and active in the worldly office, and there is no end to his wisdom in this regard; in turn, whoever is in the worldly office has a head too small to hold all his superfluous knowledge about the conduct of the spiritual office.

Of such fools all lands, all cities, all homes are full, and in this book they are diligently rebuked. Everyone is exhorted to take care of his own affairs and to do faithfully and diligently that which is committed to him; there is indeed no virtue beyond that of obedience, attending to that which is given him to do. Such people are called wise men; the disobedient are called fools, even though they do not want to be, or be called, disobedient men or fools.

The second book is called *Qoheleth,* the one we call "The Preacher."[65] It is a book of comfort. When a man would live an obedient life according to the teaching of the first book [Proverbs] and attend to his duty or office, then the devil, the world, and his own flesh put up so much resistance that he becomes weary and discouraged with his station in life and regrets everything he has begun, for things simply will not go as he wants them to. Everything becomes a struggle then; dissatisfaction, impatience, and murmuring arise until a man is ready to give up all hope and do nothing more. For if the devil cannot prevent obedience through covetousness and desire on the right hand, he will hinder it on the left hand through toil and trouble.

While in the first book [Proverbs] Solomon teaches obedience in the face of mad lust and desire, so in this book he teaches that men are to be patient and steadfast in obedience, in the face of unpleasantness and temptation [*anfechtung*], and ever to wait out the brief hour in peace and joy. What they cannot keep or alter, they are to let go; it will all work out, etc.

The third book [Song of Solomon] is a song of praise, in which Solomon praises God for obedience, as for a gift of God. For where God is not himself the householder and ruler, there is neither obedience nor peace in any station of life. But where there is obedience and good governing, there God dwells, he kisses and embraces his

---

[65] *Der Prediger* is the German title of Ecclesiastes.

dear bride with his word, which is the kiss of his lips. Therefore when things go in a land or a home as nearly as possible according to the first two of these books, then one may well sing this third book and thank God. For God has not only taught us this, but has himself also done it. Amen.

Preface to the Proverbs of Solomon[66]

1524

Because this book deals especially with fools and wise men, and everywhere praises wisdom and rebukes folly, it is necessary to consider its language and its words and to see what is meant by fools and wise men. Therefore in order that this useful book may become even plainer, I shall here briefly explain a few words as clearly as I can.

It is the way of King David in the Psalter, and especially of King Solomon—it may have been the nature of the language at that time—to give the name of fool[67] not to those whom the world calls fools, or who are born fools, but to all kinds of loose, frivolous, heedless people, and most of all to those who live without God's word, acting and speaking according to their own reason and purpose— though usually, in the eyes of the world, such people are considered the greatest, wisest, mightiest, richest, and holiest. For example, in the gospel Paul calls the Galatians,[68] and Christ the Pharisees, and even his own disciples,[69] fools. Therefore you may know that when Solomon speaks of fools, he is speaking not of plain or insignificant people, but precisely of the very best people in the world.

That which Solomon here calls wisdom is nothing else than the wisdom of God, which is taught in the words and works of God. This is also why he is constantly citing God's commandments and

---

[66] This preface was prepared and published in connection with the third part of the Old Testament which first appeared in 1524. Beginning in 1534 it was replaced by the preface given above on pp. 258-261. See p. 258, n. 59. Our translation is based on the text in WA 10^{II}, 2-4.

[67] *Narren odder thoren.*

[68] In actually translating Gal. 3:1 and 3, however, Luther used the term *unverstendig* rather than *narrisch*. WA, DB 7, 179 and 181.

[69] Matt. 23:17, 19; Luke 11:40; 12:20; 24:25.

works. Besides no proverbs have their origin anywhere else than in God's words and works, since all the plans of men are vain and false, and nothing turns out except as God wills and acts. As we put it in German, *Es ist dyr bedacht, aber nicht bescheret*,[70] and *Wer das glueck hat, fuehrt die braut heym*.[71] These and similar proverbs have their sole origin in the fact that men have been obliged to see and learn that human plans and hopes constantly fail—turning out otherwise than intended—and ultimately to discover that it is someone else who is really the driving power.[7] uis Other, some have called God, some rortune. Accordingly the proverbs in all tongues and languages are true and certain, since they are founded on God'.: works ᵃ᷉ᵈ ᵈerive from God's works, even though God's word is not there. In turn Solomon calls folly all that which proceeds without God's word and works. A wise man, then, is one who guides himself by God's word and works; a fool is one who presumptuously guides himself by his own mind and notions.

From this we see what a splendid, wise, and fine man King Solomon was. He took things so seriously that amid so many royal duties he still undertook to be a teacher, and particularly—as was most needful—to teach and train young people in the way they should act acceptably before God, according to the spirit, and wisely before the world, with body and possessions. For this is all-important, as King Solomon realized very well, that there be [such] people on earth; and they will not be unless they are instructed in their youth. This book, therefore, ought early to be impressed on the young people throughout the world and put into daily use and practice. Undoubtedly it was made and written by

---

[70] "It is intended for you, but not imparted." Cf. Wander (ed.), *Sprichwörter-Lexikon*, I, 320-321, "*Bescheren*," Nos. 7, 8.

[71] "Fortune gains the bride." Luther interprets the expression in his 1534 exposition of Psalm 101 (:5) (*LW* 13, 200-201) and in *Von Ehesachen*, 1530 (*WA* 30III, 224). The emphasis is on fortune or luck over against skill, merit, or justice, and on consummating the marriage over against simply contracting for it. *WA* 51, 684, n. 145; cf. Wander (ed.), *Sprichwörter-Lexikon*, I, 1768-1769, "*Glück*," No. 899.

[72] *Der das redlin treybt* means literally, "who makes the wheels go round." Implicit in the expression is a play on words whereby both *Rad* (*Rädlein*), or "wheel," and *Rede* (*Redlein*), or "talk," are involved—perhaps deriving from the parlor where the tempo of the spinning wheel often fluctuated with the pace of the conversation. Wander (ed.), *Sprichwörter-Lexikon*, III, 1458, "*Rädlein*," No. 7. Cf. *WA* 51, 681, n. 126.

King Solomon for this very purpose, as an example to all kings and lords that they too should take an interest in young people. To this end may God give his grace. Amen.

Preface to Solomon's "The Preacher"[73]

1524

This book is called in Hebrew *Qoheleth,* that is, "One who speaks publicly in a congregation." For *Qahal*[74] means a congregation assembled together, that which in Greek is called *ekklesia.* Now this book was certainly not written or set down by King Solomon with his own hand. Instead scholars put together what others had heard from Solomon's lips, as they themselves admit at the end of the book where they say, "These words of the wise are like goads and nails, fixed by the masters of the congregation and given by one shepherd" [Eccles. 12:11]. That is to say, certain persons selected by the kings and the people were at that time appointed to fix and arrange this and other books that were handed down by Solomon, the one shepherd. They did this so that not everyone would have to be making books as he pleased, as they also lament in that same place that "of the making of books there is no end" [Eccles. 12:12]; they forbid the acceptance of others.

These men here call themselves "masters of the congregation" [Eccles. 12:11], and books had to be accepted and approved at their hands and by their office. Of course the Jewish people had an external government that was instituted by God, which is why such a thing as this could be done surely and properly. In like manner too, the book of the Proverbs of Solomon has been put together by others, with the teaching and sayings of some wise men added at the end. The Song of Solomon too has the appearance of a book compiled by others out of things received from the lips of Solomon. For this reason these books have no particular order either, but one thing is mixed with another. This must be the character of

---

[73] Ecclesiastes, cf. p. 260, n. 65. Our translation of this 1524 preface is based on the text in WA 10[II], 104-106. See above p. 258, n. 59.

[74] Cf. Reuchlin's *Rudimenta linguae hebraicae* ([Pforzheim, 1506], p. 464) which defines the word as *"congregatio, concio, coetus hominum, ecclesia."*

such books, since they did not hear it all from him at one time but at different times.

Now this book ought really to have a title [to indicate] that it was written against the free will.[75] For the entire book tends to show that the counsels, plans, and undertakings of men are all in vain and fruitless, and that they always have a different outcome from that which we will and purpose. Thus Solomon would teach us to wait in confident trust[76] and to let God alone do everything, above and against and without our knowledge and counsel. Therefore you must not understand this book to be reviling God's creatures when it says, "All is vanity and a striving after wind."[77] For God's creatures are all good, Genesis 1[:31] and II Timothy 4[I Tim. 4:4]; and this book itself says that a man shall be happy with his wife and enjoy life, etc. [Eccles. 9:9]. It teaches, rather, that the plans and undertakings of men in their dealings with the creatures all go wrong and are in vain, if one is not satisfied with what is presently at hand but wants to be their master and ruler for the future. That's how it always goes—backward—so that a man has had nothing but wasted toil and anxiety; things turn out anyway as God wills and purposes, not as we will and purpose.

To put it briefly, Christ says in Matthew 6[:34], "Do not be anxious about tomorrow, for tomorrow will have its own anxiety; it is enough that every day has its own evil." This saying is really the interpretation and content of this book. Anxiety about us is God's affair; our anxiety goes wrong anyhow, and produces nothing but wasted toil.

---

[75] At about the same time Luther was writing this preface, in the latter part of September, 1524, Erasmus' famous treatise *De libero arbitrio*, published at the beginning of the month in Basel, was making its appearance in Wittenberg. *WA*, DB 10[II], 104, n. 2.

[76] *Gelassen stehen*, literally "stand resigned," was used by Luther not in the Stoic sense of passivity and rest, but in the sense of dispensing with one's own will and standing upon—entrusting oneself and all things to—the will of God. Grimm, *Deutsches Wörterbuch*, IV, 4[I], 2866-2867.

[77] *Eyttel und iamer etc.* Eccles. 1:14; 2:11, 26; 4:16, 6:9, etc.

Preface to the Prophets[78]

1545 (1532)

To human reason the prophets seem of very small account, and little of value is found in them. This is especially so when Master Know-it-all[78] comes along. He knows the Scriptures by heart right down to the minutest detail, and out of the riches of his own spirit he regards the writings of the prophets as worthless and dead talk. As a result the events and works are now no longer noticed, and only the words and stories are heard. This should be no surprise, when at present the word of God itself is despised, even though each day the signs and events, and the kingdom of Christ as well, are forcefully present and operative before men's eyes. How much more would it be despised, if the events and deeds were no longer present—just as the children of Israel despised God and his word when they still had before their eyes the bread from heaven, the fiery pillar, and the bright cloud, and in addition both the priesthood and the princedom.

Therefore we Christians ought not to be such shameful, satiated, ungrateful know-it-alls, but rather read and use the prophets with earnestness and profit. For, in the first place, the prophets proclaim and bear witness to the kingdom of Christ in which we now live, and in which all believers in Christ have heretofore lived, and will live until the end of the world. For us there is strong comfort and comforting strength in having for our Christian life such mighty and ancient witnesses. By them our Christian faith is greatly comforted in the confidence that before God it is the right station or stance [stand], over against all other wrong, false, human holiness and sects. For these all are a source of great offense and affliction [anfechten] to a weak heart, because they make such a good appearance and have such a multitude of adherents, and also because of

---

[78] This preface was written in February, 1532, as an introduction to the complete edition of the prophets which came out in March of that year, *Die Propheten alle deutsch*. Our translation is based on the text as it appeared—virtually unchanged—in the complete Bible of 1545 and is reprinted in *WA*, DB 11¹, 3-15.
[79] Cf. p. 184, n. 14.

the cross and of the small number of those who hold to Christian faith. So, in our days, the sects of the Turk,[80] the pope, and others are great and powerful snares.

For this, then, the prophets are useful to us, as St. Peter boasts in I Peter 1[:11-12] that the prophets were not serving themselves in the things which were revealed to them, but us. It was us, he says, that they were serving. For they have served us thus with their prophesying, in order that he who would be in Christ's kingdom might know that he himself must first suffer many things before he comes to glory, and govern himself accordingly. By this we become sure of two things: first, that the great glory of Christ's kingdom is surely ours, and will come hereafter; and, second, that it is nevertheless preceded by crosses, shame, misery, contempt, and all kinds of suffering for the sake of Christ. The purpose is that we shall not grow discouraged through impatience or unbelief, or despair of that future glory, which is to be so great that even the angels desire to see it [I Pet. 1:12].

In the second place the prophets show us many great examples and experiences which illustrate the first commandment. They explicate it in masterly fashion, in both words and examples, so as to drive us powerfully to the fear of God and to faith, and to keep us in them. For after they have prophesied of Christ's kingdom, all the rest is nothing but examples of how God has so strictly and severely confirmed his first commandment. So to read or hear the prophets is surely nothing else than to read and hear how God threatens and comforts. God threatens the godless, who feel proud and secure. And if threatening does not help, he backs it up with penalties, pestilence, famine, war, until they are destroyed. Thus does God make good his threat in the first commandment [Exod. 20:5]. But he comforts those who fear him, who are in all sorts of need, and backs it up also with aid and counsel, by means of all kinds of wonders and signs, against all the might of the devil and the world. Thus does God make good also his comfort in the first commandment [Exod. 20:6].

With sermons and examples like these the prophets repeatedly serve us more than abundantly, in order that we should not be offended when we see with what pride and assurance the godless

---

[80] Cf. p. 407, n. 89.

despise God's word and pay no attention to his threatenings, as though God were an utter nonenity. For in the prophets we see that things have never turned out well for any man who has despised God's threatening, even though they were the mightiest emperors and kings or the holiest and most learned people on whom the sun ever shone. On the other hand we see that no one has ever been deserted who has dared to rely upon God's comforts and promises, even though they were the most miserable and the poorest sinners and beggars that were ever on the earth, indeed, even though it were a slain Abel and a swallowed Jonah. By this the prophets prove to us that God holds fast to his first commandment and wills to be a gracious Father to the poor and believing, and that for him no one is too small or too despised. He wills, however, to be an angry Judge to the godless and the proud; and for him no one is too great, too mighty, too wise, too holy, be it emperor, pope, Turk, and the devil besides.

For this reason it is today profitable and necessary for us to read the prophets, so that by these examples and sermons we may be strengthened and comforted against the unspeakable, innumerable, and (if God so will) ultimate snares of the condemned world. How the Turk regards our Lord Jesus Christ and his kingdom as an utter nonentity, when compared with himself and his Mohammed![81] How greatly the poor gospel and word of God are despised on this side, among us and under the papacy, compared with the glorious show and riches of human commandments and holiness! With what assurance the sectarians, the Epicureans,[82] and others like them follow their own opinions, contrary to Holy Scripture! What an utterly audacious and wild life everyone now lives, following his own self-will and contrary to the clear truth which is now as plain as day! It appears as if neither God nor Christ amounted to anything, not to mention that the stringency of God's first commandment should be so watered down! So the watchword is "Wait a bit, wait a bit!" The question is whether the prophets are lying

---

[81] See p. 404, n. 81.

[82] For Luther the term "Epicurean" had reference to the followers of the ancient Athenian philosopher (see p. 392, n. 40), particularly their sixteenth century counterparts whose this-worldly orientation made them scornful and skeptical of God's eternal truth.

up a form of divine worship and service without God's bidding, simply out of one's own pious inclination. For God will not have us teach him how he is to be served. He wills to teach us and to prescribe for us. His word is supposed to be there; it is supposed to enlighten and guide us. Without his word all is idolatry and outright lies, however devout and beautiful it may appear to be. Of this we have often written.

Idolatry among Christians

From this it follows that among us Christians all those people are idolatrous—and to them the prophets' denunciations are truly applicable—who have invented or are following new ways of worshiping God, without his commission or command, simply out of their own pious inclination and, as they say, good intentions. They are thereby putting their reliance on works which they themselves have chosen, and not simply and exclusively on Jesus Christ. The prophets call such people adulteresses [Ezek. 16:32, 38; 23:45; Hosea 2:2ff.]; they are not satisfied with their own husband, Jesus Christ, but run after other men as well, as though Christ alone could be of no help without us and our works, or as though Christ alone had not redeemed us and we had to do something toward it ourselves. Still we know very well that we did absolutely nothing toward having him die for us, taking our sins upon himself and bearing them on the cross, not only before the whole world could even think of any such thing, but also before we were even born. Just as little, indeed even less, did the children of Israel do toward bringing the plagues upon Egypt and Pharaoh [Exodus 7—10], and toward setting themselves free through the death of the first-born of Egypt [Exodus 11—12]. God did this alone; in no case did they do anything at all toward it.

"Of course," they say, "with their worship the children of Israel served idols, and not the true God; but in our churches we serve the true God and the one Lord Jesus Christ. For we have nothing to do with idols." I answer: That is what the children of Israel said too. They all declared that their entire worship was devoted to the true God. They certainly would not allow anyone to call it the worshiping of idols any more than our clergy would allow it. On this account they killed and persecuted all the true prophets. For they too would truly have nothing to do with idols, as the histories tell us.

For thus we read in Judges 17[:2-3] that the mother of Micah, when he had taken from her the eleven hundred pieces of silver and again returned them, said to him, "Blessed be my son by the Lord. I vowed this silver to the Lord, that my son should take the silver and have a graven image and a molten image made of it," etc. Here one learns clearly and certainly that the mother is thinking of the true God, to whom she has vowed the silver, to have a graven image and a molten image made of it. For she does not say, "I have vowed this silver to an idol," but to the "Lord," a word which is known among all the Jews to mean the one true God.[86] The Turk also does the same thing; in his worship he names and has in mind the true God who created heaven and earth. So also do the Jews, Tartars,[87] and now all unbelievers. Nevertheless with them it is all sheer idolatry.

Again how strange was the fall of that wondrous man Gideon, in Judges 8[:22-27]. To the children of Israel who desired that he and his children should rule over them he said, "I will not rule over you, and my children will not rule over you; but the Lord (that is, the true God[88]) will rule over you." Yet in that selfsame moment he took the jewels that they gave him and made of them, not a graven image or an altar, but only a priest's garment.[89] His piety also inclined him to want a form of divine worship and service right in his own city. Nevertheless the Scripture says that thereby all Israel committed harlotry, and the house of Gideon went down to destruction because of it. Now this great and holy man was not thinking of any idol, but of the one true God, as his words—so rich in spirit—testify, when he says, "The Lord will rule over you, not I." By these

---

[86] Luther is here referring to the Tetragrammaton which appears twice in the woman's speeches in the Hebrew original of Judg. 17:2-3. Cf. pp. 248-249, especially p. 248, n. 27.

[87] See p. 409, n. 97.

[88] In the Hebrew of Judg. 8:23 Gideon designates their proper ruler by use of the Tetragrammaton. See p. 248, n. 27.

[89] *Priesterkleider* is obviously a reference to the ephod. The root meaning of the Hebrew word *ephod* is unknown. Although the term in some places meant an image, pouch, or other cult object, it is usually understood to be an apron-like garment worn over the robe and under the breastplate of the high priest. Luther so interprets the word in Judg. 8:27.

271

words he plainly gives honor to God alone and confesses the only true God and will have him alone held as God and Lord.

So, too, we heard above, that King Jeroboam in I Kings 12[:28] does not call his golden calves idols either. He calls them rather the God of Israel, who had brought them up out of Egypt. This is of course the one true God, for no idol had brought them up out of Egypt. Nor was it his intention to worship idols. Rather, because he feared (as the text says [I Kings 12:26-27]) that the people would fall away from him to the king of Judah if they were to engage in worship of God only at Jerusalem, he simply invented a worship service of his own in order to hold the people to himself. Yet by it he intended worship of the true God who dwelt at Jerusalem, except that it would not be necessary to worship God only at Jerusalem.

Why expend many words on it? God himself confesses that with their worship the children of Israel had in mind no idol, but him alone. He says so in Hosea 2[:16-17], "In that day, says the Lord, you will call me 'My husband' and no longer will you call me 'My Baal.' For I will remove the names of the Baals from her mouth, and they shall be mentioned by name no more." Here one must confess that it is true: with their worship the children of Israel had in mind no idol, but the one true God, as God plainly says here in Hosea, "You will no longer call me 'My Baal.'" Now among the people of Israel, Baal-worship was the greatest, commonest, and most glorious form of worship; yet it was utter idolatry, despite the fact that by it they intended to worship the true God.

Therefore it does not help our clergy at all to allege that in their churches and chapters they serve no idol, but only God, the true Lord. For here you learn that it is not enough to say or think, "I am doing it to God's glory; I have in mind the true God; I mean to be worshiping and serving the only God." All idolaters say and intend the very same thing. The thinking and intending is not what counts, otherwise those who martyred the apostles and the Christians would also have been God's servants. For they too thought that they were offering a service to God, as Christ says in John 16[:2]; and St. Paul in Romans 10[:2] bears witness to the Jews that they have a zeal for God, and adds in Acts 26[:7] that with their worship night and day they hope to attain to the promised salvation.

272

On the contrary let everyone see to it that he is certain his worship and service of God has been instituted by God's word, and not invented by his own pious notions or good intentions. Whoever engages in a form of worship to which God has not borne witness ought to know that he is serving not the true God but an idol that he has concocted for himself. That is to say, he is serving his own notions and false ideas, and thereby the devil himself; and the words of all the prophets are against him. For the God who would have us establish worship and service of him according to our own choice and inclination—without his commission and word—does not exist. There is only one God, he who through his word has abundantly established and commissioned all the various stations of life and the forms of worship and service in which it is his will to be served. We should abide by this and not turn aside from it either to the right or to the left,[90] doing neither more nor less, making it neither worse nor better. Otherwise there will be no end of idolatry, and it will be impossible to distinguish between true worship and idolatry, since all have the true God in mind, and all use his true Name. To this one and only God be thanks and praise, through Jesus Christ, his Son, our Lord blessed forever. Amen.

Preface to the Prophet Isaiah

1545 (1528)[91]

If anyone would read the holy prophet Isaiah with profit and understand him better, let him not ignore this advice and instruction of mine, unless he has better advice or is himself better informed. In the first place let him not skip the title, or beginning, of this book [Isa. 1:1], but learn to understand it as thoroughly as possible, in order that he may not imagine he understands Isaiah very well, and then have someone charge him with never having even under-

---

[90] Deut. 5:32; 28:14; Josh. 1:7; Prov. 4:27; *et al.*
[91] Luther lectured on Isaiah at various times in the years 1527-1530 (*WA* 31[II], (vii) 1-585; *WA* 25, 79-401). In a letter of May 22, 1528, to Spalatin he refers to his translation of Isaiah (De Wette, *Dr. Martin Luthers Briefe*, III, 326), which was published separately that same year (*WA*, DB 11[II], xxi f.). This preface, first published with that translation in 1528, is here given as it appeared—essentially unchanged—in the 1545 complete Bible. It is reprinted in *WA*, DB 11[I], 17-25.

stood the title and first line, let alone the whole prophet. For this title is to be regarded really as a gloss and a light upon the whole book. Isaiah himself, as though with his finger; points his readers to this title as stating the occasion and reason for his book. I say to him who ignores or does not understand the title that he should let the prophet Isaiah alone, or at least that he will not understand him thoroughly. For it is impossible to mark or perceive the prophet's words and meaning properly and clearly without this thorough understanding of the title.

When I speak of the title [1:1], I do not mean only that you should read or understand the words "Uzziah, Jotham, Ahaz, Hezekiah, kings of Judah," etc., but that you should take in hand the last book of Kings and the last book of Chronicles[92] and grasp them well, especially the events, the speeches, and the incidents that occurred under the kings named in the title [of Isaiah], clear to the end of those books. For if one would understand the prophecies, it is necessary that one know how things were in the land, how matters lay, what was in the mind of the people—what plans they had with respect to their neighbors, friends, and enemies—and especially what attitude they took in their country toward God and toward the prophet, whether they held to his word and worship or to idolatry.

Lands Surrounding Israel and Judah

In addition it would be well also to know how these lands were situated with reference to one another, so that the strange and unfamiliar words and names might not make reading unpleasant and impede or obscure understanding. To do my simple Germans a service, I shall briefly describe the country surrounding Jerusalem or Judah, where Isaiah lived and preached, so that they may better see whither the prophet turned when he prophesied to the south or the north, etc.

Toward the east the nearest thing to Jerusalem or Judah is the Dead Sea, where Sodom and Gomorrah stood in ancient times.[93]

---

[92] II Kings 15, 16, 18—20; II Chronicles 26—32.
[93] Gen. 10:19; 13:10-12; 19:24-28. The site of these ancient cities, though not certain, may be submerged under the waters of the Dead Sea. See G. E. Wright and F. V. Filson (eds.), *The Westminster Historical Atlas to the Bible* (Philadelphia: Westminster, 1945), p. 20b and Plate X, H-3.

Beyond the Dead Sea lies the land of Moab, and of the children of Ammon. Farther beyond lies Babylon, or Chaldea, and farther still the land of the Persians, of which Isaiah speaks so much.

Toward the north lies Mount Lebanon, and beyond it Damascus and Syria. Farther on to the northeast lies Assyria, of which Isaiah also treats a good deal.

Toward the west, along the Great Sea, are situated the Philistines, the worst enemies of the Jews. Along the shore to the north of them lie Sidon and Tyre, which border on Galilee.

Toward the south are many lands: Egypt, the land of the Moors, the Red Sea, Edom, and Midian, so situated that in this southern region Egypt lies to the west.

These are really the lands and the names about which Isaiah prophesies, the neighbors—enemies and friends—surrounding the land of Judah like wolves around a sheepfold. With some of them Judah made alliances and counter-alliances, but it did not help her at all.

What the Prophet Isaiah Treats

After this, you must divide the prophet Isaiah into three parts. In the first part, like the other prophets, he handles two things. First he preaches a good deal to his people and rebukes their many sins, especially the manifold idolatry which has got the upper hand among the people. As godly preachers now and always do and must do with their people, so Isaiah too keeps the people in check with threats of punishment and promises of good.

Second he prepares and disposes them to expect the coming kingdom of Christ, of which he prophesies more clearly and in more ways than any other prophet. In chapter 7 he even describes the mother of Christ, the Virgin Mary, how she is to conceive and bear him with her virginity intact.[94] In chapter 53 Isaiah even describes Christ's passion together with his resurrection from the dead, proclaiming his kingdom as powerfully and plainly as if it had just

---

[94] *Mit unversehrter Jungfrauschaft* does not admit of the ambiguity concerning chastity which the German word *Jungfrau* standing alone has in common with the Hebrew *almah*. Luther rendered the *almah* of Isa. 7:14 with *Jungfrau*, but by it—following Matt. 1:23—he meant a "virgin," not as in the RSV a "young woman." See *LW* 1, 193-194. Cf. Grimm, *Deutsches Wörterbuch*, IV, 2388-2390 and 2393.

happened, already at that time. This must have been a splendid and highly enlightened prophet. For all the prophets do the same: they teach and rebuke the people of their time, and they proclaim the coming and the kingdom of Christ, directing and pointing the people to him as the common Savior of both those who have gone before and those who are yet to come. Only, one of the prophets does more of this than another, one does it more extensively than another. Isaiah, however, does it most of all, and more extensively than any of the others.

In the second part Isaiah has to do especially with the empire of Assyria and the Emperor Sennacherib. He also prophesies more and at greater length about this than does any other prophet, namely, about how the emperor would subdue all neighboring lands, including the kingdom of Israel, and inflict much misfortune on the kingdom of Judah. But there he stands like a rock, with his promise that Jerusalem shall be defended and freed by him from Sennacherib. And this is one of the greatest miracles to be found in the Scripture, not only because of the event, that so mighty an emperor should be defeated before Jerusalem, but also because of the faith with which men believed it. It is a miracle, I say, that anyone at Jerusalem could have believed him in such an impossible thing. Isaiah must, without doubt, have heard many bad words from unbelievers. Yet he did it; he defeated the emperor and defended the city. He must have stood well with God and been a precious man in his sight!

In the third part Isaiah has to do with the empire at Babylon. Here he prophesies of the Babylonian captivity, whereby the people were to be punished and Jerusalem destroyed by the emperor at Babylon. It is here that he does his greatest work, comforting and upholding a people yet to be, in this destruction and captivity yet to come, in order that they might not despair, as if they were vanquished and Christ's kingdom would not be coming and all prophecy were false and vain. How rich and full his preaching: Babylon shall in turn be destroyed, and the Jews will be released and will return to Jerusalem. With proud defiance of Babylon, Isaiah even gives the names of the kings who shall destroy it, namely the Medes and Elamites, or Persians. He mentions particularly the king who shall release the Jews and help them back to Jerusalem, namely

Cyrus, whom Isaiah calls "God's anointed" [Isa. 45:1]. He does all this long before there is a kingdom in Persia. For he is concerned altogether with the Christ, that his future coming and the promised kingdom of grace and salvation shall not be despised or be lost and in vain because of unbelief and great misfortune and impatience amongst his people. This, indeed, would be the case, unless the people expected it and believed confidently that it would come. These, then, are the three things with which Isaiah deals.

The Order of the Prophecies

He does not, however, treat them in sequence or give each of them its own place, with its own chapters and pages. Instead they are so completely interwoven that much of the first part is brought in along with the second and third, and once the third is discussed somewhat earlier than the second. Now whether this was done by those who collected and wrote down the prophecies (as is thought to have happened with the Psalter[95]) or whether Isaiah himself arranged them this way as time, occasion, and persons suggested, I do not know. These times and occasions were not always alike, and had no order. Isaiah has at least this much order: he brings in the first part as the most important thing and deals with it from beginning to end, all the way through the second and third parts as well. This is what we ought also to do in our sermons. Our most important matter—the rebuking of the people and the preaching of Christ—ought always to run concurrently, even though as occasion arises we may at times undertake to preach on other subjects, such as the Turk, the emperor, etc.

Remembering this, anyone can readily comprehend the prophet and be at home in him without becoming confused or exasperated by the order of the prophecies, as may happen to those who are not accustomed to this book. We have done our best to make Isaiah speak good, clear German, although he has not lent himself easily to it and has strongly resisted it.[96] Those who know German and Hebrew well will readily see that, especially the wiseacres who

---

[95] See Luther's Preface to the Psalter, in this volume, pp. 253-257. Cf. also pp. 263-264.

[96] On the difficulty of translating Isaiah see Luther's comments to Link in the Introduction, p. 229.

persuade themselves that they know everything. Isaiah was really so eloquent in Hebrew that the stiff German language just did not set well with him. [This is what occasioned our publishing of Isaiah separately,[97] to see how in this barren, wild, and ungrateful time he would fare among the people, in order that, God willing, we might with greater assurance let the other prophets follow after.][98]

What profit there may be in reading Isaiah, I prefer to let the reader discover for himself, rather than to tell him here. For one who does not, or will not discover it for himself, there is not much gained by speaking about it. The book is truly full of living, comforting, tender sayings for all poor consciences and miserable, disturbed hearts. There are also plenty of words of threatening and terror in it against the stubborn, proud hardheads—if that may be of any help.

Now you should see that among the Jewish people Isaiah was nothing but a man despised as a fool and madman. For they did not regard him as we regard him now. As he himself testifies in chapter 58,[99] they put out their tongues at him and pointed their fingers at him; and except for a few devout children of God in the crowd, such as King Hezekiah, they all regarded his preaching as foolishness. For it was the custom among the people to mock the prophets and consider them madmen, II Kings 9[:11]—as has always happened to all servants of God and preachers, is happening every day, and will continue to happen.

As one can readily observe, the thing for which Isaiah rebukes the people most of all is idolatry. The other vices, such as gaudy display, drunkenness, greed, he hardly touches on three times. But all the way through he rebukes the people for reliance on their self-appointed worship of idols and on their own works, their confidence in kings and alliances. This was intolerable to the people, for they thought that in this they were right. For this reason too he is supposed to have been slain as a heretic and a deceiver by King Manasseh and, as the Jews say, to have been sawn apart.[100]

---

[97] On the separate edition of Isaiah in 1528 see WA, DB 11[II], xxi f.

[98] This bracketed sentence appeared in the 1528 edition but was dropped in 1532 and later editions. WA, DB 11[I], 22, n. 19/22.

[99] Isa. 57:4; cf. 58:9.

[100] Cf. II Kings 21:16; 24:3-4. See The Martyrdom of Isaiah, which has survived

Preface to the Prophet Jeremiah[101]

1545 (1532)

Few comments are needed for an understanding of the prophet Jeremiah, if one will only pay attention to the events that took place under the kings in whose time he preached. For his preaching had reference to the condition of the land at that time.

In the first place the land was full of vices and idolatry. The people slew the prophets and would have their own vices and idolatry go unrebuked. Therefore the first part, down to the twentieth chapter, is almost entirely rebuke and complaint of the wickedness of the Jews.

In the second place Jeremiah also foretold the punishment that was at hand, namely, the destruction of Jerusalem and of the whole land, and the Babylonian captivity, indeed the punishment of all nations as well. Yet, along with this, he gives comfort and promises that at a definite time, after the punishment is over, they shall be released and shall return to their land and to Jerusalem, etc. And this is the most important thing in Jeremiah. It was for this very thing that Jeremiah was raised up, as is indicated in the first chapter [1:11, 13], by the vision of the rod and the boiling pots coming from the north.

And this was highly necessary; for since this cruel hardship was to come upon the people, and they were to be uprooted and carried away out of their land, many pious souls—such as Daniel [Dan. 9:2] and others—would have been driven to despair of God and his prom-

---

only as a constituent part of the pseudepigraphical *Ascension of Isaiah*, especially 1:7-9 and 5:1-14; of Jewish origin, its account of Isaiah's death conforms closely to that given in the Babylonian Talmud (*Jebamoth* 49b) and the Jerusalem Talmud (*Sanhedrin* x). R. H. Charles (ed.), *The Apocrypha and Pseudepigrapha of the Old Testament* (Oxford: Clarendon), II (1919), 155-162. Cf. *The Jewish Encyclopedia* (12 vols.; New York: Funk and Wagnalls, 1901-1906), VI, 636 and 642-643. Tertullian, Origen, Jerome, and other early fathers readily believed the legend, finding in Hebrews 11:37 an allusion to it. *The Catholic Encyclopedia*, VIII, 180-181. See also further references to this tradition, particularly to portrayals of it in art, in *WA, DB* 11¹, 24, n. 1.

[101] Though not published until the 1532 *Propheten alle deutsch*, this preface may have been completed by the end of June, 1530, at the Coburg when Luther completed his translation of the book of Jeremiah. Cf. Reu, *Luther's German Bible*, p. 208.

ises. For they would not have been able to think otherwise than that it was all over with them, that they were utterly cast off by God, and that no Christ would ever come, but that God, in great anger, had taken back his promises because of the people's sin.

Therefore Jeremiah had to be there and proclaim the punishment and the wrath, telling the people that it would not last forever, but for a fixed time, such as seventy years [25:11-12; 29:10], and that afterward they would come into grace once again. With this promise he had also to comfort and sustain himself, or he would have had little consolation and happiness. For he was a sad and troubled prophet and lived in miserably evil days. Besides he had a peculiarly difficult ministry. For over forty years,[102] down to the captivity, he had to say hard things to obstinately wicked people. Still it did little good. He had to look on while the people went from bad to worse, always wanting to kill him, and putting him to much hardship.

On top of that he had to experience and see with his own eyes how the land was destroyed and the people carried away captive, amid great misery and bloodshed. Nor does this include what he had afterward to preach and suffer in Egypt, for it is believed that he was stoned to death by the Jews in Egypt.[103]

In the third place like the other prophets, Jeremiah too prophesies of Christ and his kingdom, especially in the twenty-third and thirty-first chapters [23:5-6; 31:31-34]. There he clearly prophesies of the person of Christ, of his kingdom, of the new testament, and of the end of the old testament.

Now these three things do not follow one another in sequence; they are not separated from one another in the book in the way that they actually came along. Frequently in the first part there is something in a later chapter which really took place before that which is spoken of in an earlier chapter. So it seems as though Jeremiah did

---

[102] Jeremiah was called to prophesy about the year 626 B.C. Jerusalem was destroyed about the year 586 B.C. Cf. Jer. 1:2-3.

[103] Mention of Jeremiah's death by stoning at the hands of his own people is made by Tertullian in his *Scorpiace,* chap. VIII. Alexander Roberts and James Donaldson (eds.), *The Ante-Nicene Fathers* (10 vols.; Grand Rapids: Eerdmans, 1951-1953), III, 640; and by Jerome in his *Adversus Jovinianum* ii, 37. Migne 23, 335. Whether this information is pure legend or derives from genuine tradition is uncertain. Hauck (ed.), *Realencyklopädie für protestantische Theologie und Kirche,* VIII, 649.

not compose these books himself, but that the parts were taken piecemeal from his utterances and written into a book. For this reason one must not worry about the order or be hindered by the lack of it.

We learn from Jeremiah among others that, as usual, the nearer the punishment, the worse the people become; and that the more one preaches to them, the more they despise his preaching. Thus we understand that when it is God's will to inflict punishment, he makes the people to become hardened so they may be destroyed without any mercy and not appease God's wrath with any repentance. So the men of Sodom long ago had to not only despise the righteous Lot, but even afflict him because he taught them—even though their own affliction was at the door [Gen. 19:1-13]. Likewise Pharaoh, when about to be drowned in the Red Sea, had to oppress the children of Israel twice as much as before [Exod. 5:6-21]. And Jerusalem had to crucify God's Son when its own final destruction was on the way.[104]

So it goes everywhere even now. Now that the end of the world is approaching, the people rage and rave most horribly against God. They blaspheme and damn God's word, though they well know that it is God's word and the truth. Besides so many fearful signs and wonders are appearing, both in the heavens and among all creatures, which threaten them terribly.[105] It is indeed a wicked and miserable time, even worse than that of Jeremiah.

But so it will be, and must be. The people begin to feel secure and sing, "Peace; all is well."[106] They simply persecute everything that accords with the will of God and disregard all the threatening

---

[104] The Romans under Titus destroyed Jerusalem in A.D. 70.

[105] This may be a reference to the plague and pestilence that ravaged the country at least twice during the years Luther was translating the Prophets. The siege of 1527 which sent his colleagues of the university into exile at Jena for several months did not allow Luther's own person and household to go unscathed. Out of this period of terror came the hymn, "A Mighty Fortress is our God." Julius Köstlin, *Martin Luther—Sein Leben und Seine Schriften* (3rd ed.; Elberfeld: Friderichs, 1883), II, 175-183. The reference may also be to Halley's comet, visible from August 18 to September 3, 1531, which Luther mentions in letters of August 18 and October 10 of that year (*WA*, Br 6, 165, 204; cf. *WA*, TR 2, No. 2100), and to a meteor of January 22, 1532 (*WA*, Br 6, 173 and *WA*, TR 2, No. 2438).

[106] See p. 268, nn. 83, 84.

signs, until (as St. Paul says [I Thess. 5:3]) destruction suddenly surprises them and destroys them before they know it.

But Christ will be able to sustain his own, for whose sake he causes his word to shine forth in this shameful time of ours, just as at Babylon he sustained Daniel and those like him, for whose sake Jeremiah's prophecy had to shine forth. To the same dear Lord be praise and thanks, with the Father and the Holy Spirit, one God over all and to eternity. Amen.

Preface to the Prophet Ezekiel

1545 (1532)

Ezekiel, like Daniel and many more following the counsel of Jeremiah, went willingly into captivity in Babylon along with King Jeconiah.[107] Jeremiah constantly advised that the people should surrender to the king of Babylon—and thus live; they should not resist—and thus be destroyed, Jeremiah 21.[108]

Now when the people had arrived in Babylon, as Jeremiah shows in chapter 24 with his kind words of encouragement, they became impatient and regretted beyond measure that they had surrendered. For they saw that those who had stayed in Jerusalem and had not surrendered still possessed the city and everything else, and were hoping to make Jeremiah a liar and to defend themselves against the king of Babylon and remain in their own land.

There at Jerusalem the false prophets helped this notion along by constantly consoling the people that their city would not be captured, and that Jeremiah had to be a lying heretic and a traitor. Along with this (as it usually does) went the fact that those at Jerusalem boasted that they were holding honestly and firmly to God and fatherland. They claimed that the others who had surrendered had deserted God and fatherland and were thus faithless traitors who were unable to trust or hope in God, but had gone over to the enemy because of the vile talking of Jeremiah, the liar. This hurt and embittered greatly those who had surrendered to Babylon,

---

[107] The name Jeconiah is a variant of the name Jehoiachin (see Jer. 24:1, et al.).
[108] Jer. 21:8-9; cf. 27:11-17, 38:2.

and their captivity became a double one. O how many a hefty curse they must have wished on Jeremiah, whom they had followed and who had led them astray so miserably!

For this reason God raises up at Babylon this prophet Ezekiel, to encourage the captives and to prophesy against the false prophets at Jerusalem, as well as to substantiate the word of Jeremiah. Ezekiel does this thoroughly; he prophesies much harder and far more than Jeremiah that Jerusalem shall be destroyed and the people perish, along with the king and princes. Yet he promises also that the captives shall return home to the land of Judah. This is the most important thing that Ezekiel did in his time; he deals with this matter down to chapter twenty-five.

After that, to chapter thirty-four, he extends his prophecy also to all the other lands round about, which the king of Babylon was to afflict. There follow in addition[109] four chapters [34–37] on the spirit and kingdom of Christ, and after that on the last tyrant in Christ's kingdom, Gog and Magog [38–39].[110] At the end Jerusalem is rebuilt, and Ezekiel encourages the people to believe that they shall go home again [40–48]. Yet in the Spirit he means the eternal city, the heavenly Jerusalem, of which the Apocalypse also speaks [Revelation 21].

---

[109] *Feiner* may have been intended as *ferner* according to *EA* 63, 64, n. 5.
[110] See p. 407, n. 89.

A New Preface to the Prophet Ezekiel

1545 (1541)

St. Jerome[111] and others[112] write that it was, and still is, forbidden among the Jews for any man under thirty years of age to read the first and last parts of the Prophet Ezekiel [1:4-28; 40:2–48:35] and the first chapter of Genesis. To be sure, there was no need of this prohibition among the Jews, for Isaiah 29[:11-12] prophesies that the entire Holy Scriptures are sealed and closed to the unbelieving Jews.[113] St. Paul says as much in II Corinthians 3[:14-16], that the veil of Moses remains over the Scriptures, so long as they do not believe in Christ.

Their works prove that too. For like filthy swine wallowing and rolling in a beautiful garden, they rip and torture the Scriptures in their interpretations of them. So it would be preferable if they were to quit meddling in the Scriptures, even though many of our own people cling so tightly to the rabbis and have such confidence in them, that they Judaize[114] more than the ancient Jews themselves.

This vision in the first part of Ezekiel [1:4-28], however, is nothing else than a revelation of the kingdom of Christ in faith here upon earth, in all four corners of the whole world as said in Psalm

---

[111] In his *Commentary on the Prophet Ezekiel* (I, i) Jerome writes, "*Nam nisi quis apud eus aetatem sacerdotalis ministerii, id est, tricesimum annum impleverit, nec principia Geneseos, nec Canticum Canticorum, nec hujus voluminis exordium et finem legere permittitur, ut ad perfectam scientiam, et mysticos intellectus, plenum humanae naturae tempus accedat.*" Migne 25, 17.

[112] Cf. The Babylonian Talmud (*Hagiga* II, 1), "The laws on incest may not be discussed among three; the story of creation, among two; and the doctrine of the heavenly circles not even by oneself alone—unless one is learned and understands it on the basis of his own knowledge." In commenting on this passage, the rabbis discussed the actual length of the Ezekiel passage referred to (through 1:26 or through 1:28a?) as well as the kind of maturity, dignity, skill, and rank one must possess before he is eligible to know the mysteries of this passage. *Ibid.*, Gemara 13a.

[113] Luther cited this verse frequently about this time in his criticism of Jewish exposition of Scripture. See, e.g., *WA, TR* 5, No. 5324; *WA* 53, 645; *WA* 54, 30.

[114] *Jüdentzen* means actually to interpret in Jewish fashion. Luther was thinking particularly of the Dominican Santes Pagninus (*ca.* 1470-1541) at Lyon who prepared a literal Latin translation of the Bible in 1528 and a Hebrew lexicon in 1529, and of Sebastian Münster (1489-1552), Hebraist at Basel who published a literal Latin translation along with his Hebrew text edition of the Old Testament in 1534-1535. *WA, DB* 11¹, 394, n. 3. Cf. p. 217, n. 26.

19[:4]: *In omnem terram.*[115] This is how I understand it (let someone else improve on it[116]). For no one can be a prophet, as St. Peter testifies, unless he have the Spirit of Christ [II Pet. 1:21]. But to give an interpretation of the entire vision is too long a matter for a preface. To put it briefly: this vision is the spiritual chariot of Christ in which he rides here in the world, meaning thereby his entire holy church.

There are the four living creatures, which Ezekiel calls in chapter 10 "cherubim," for Christ sits, rides, and travels on cherubim, as the Scriptures often declare. Each living creature has four faces. They stand foursquare like four horses, but inside and between the wheels. For about the living creatures there are also four perfect wheels, by each beast a wheel. All is so arranged that they can go to the four corners of the world—that is, forward, backward, and to both sides—without needing to turn.

In this same way the living creatures go on calves' feet toward the four corners of the world without having to turn. There is no axle, wagon tongue, undercarriage, pin, rack, whipple tree, strap, or trace, but the Spirit drives it all surely from within. Overhead is the firmament, like a saddlecloth, and in it a throne for a saddle. And on the throne sits God, that is, Christ.

The four wheels run alike, for all churches in the four corners of the earth, that is, throughout the world, have one and the same harmonious course, in faith, hope, love, the cross, and all spiritual things; they are not driven from without by doctrines of men, but from within by one Spirit, Romans 8[:2-27], I Corinthians 12[:3-13], Ephesians 4[:4].

Now the four living creatures go with the wheels—or rather the wheels with them—forward, backward, upward, and to both sides. For the apostles, or the preaching ministry, the word of God, baptism, sacrament, keys, and all that belongs to the spiritual government of the church are also one and the same, and harmonious throughout the world. And the living creatures and the wheels hold firmly and surely together, so that the chariot is one, without any external hitching, fastening, or yoking. Thus there is nothing but fours: four living creatures, four faces to each living creature, four

---

[115] "Through all the earth." Vulgate Ps. 18:5.
[116] Cf. WA, DB 11[II], 124, l. 19.

feet to each living creature, four hands to each living creature, four wings to each living creature, four wheels, and four spokes to a wheel. This signifies, as said, that Christendom, or the kingdom of Christ in faith, is to go to the four corners, that is, into all the world.

This vision, moreover (as Ezekiel himself shows in chapters 8–9), signified the end and destruction of the synagogue, or of Judaism, that is, of the priesthood, the worship, and the church organization instituted and given them by Moses. For all of these were instituted only until Christ should come, as St. Paul says in Romans 8[:2-3] and II Corinthians 3[:6], as Christ himself says in Matthew 11[:13], and as the Epistle to the Hebrews says repeatedly. The Jews have taken terrible offense at this; it has been a stumbling block to them even to this day.

Over against the blindness of the Jews, it should be known especially that all the prophecies which say that Israel and Judah shall return to their lands[117] and possess them in a physical way forever, have been long since fulfilled, so that the hopes of the Jews are utterly vain and lost.[118]

For this prophecy contains two things. The first is that Israel and Judah shall return to their land after their captivity. This came to pass through King Cyrus[119] and the Persians, before the birth of Christ, at the time when the Jews returned to their land and to Jerusalem from all countries. They also came to Jerusalem every year to the feasts, even from foreign countries where they maintained their residence, drawing many Gentiles with them and to them.

But the hope of the Jews that there shall yet be another physical return, when all of them together shall come back into the land and set up again the old Mosaic order of things, this is something they have dreamed up themselves. There is not a letter in the prophets or in Scripture which says or signifies anything of the kind. It is written,[120] indeed, that they shall return out of all lands whither they have been driven; not all of them, however, but only some of them out of all lands. There is a great difference between a return of all

---

[117] Jer. 15:16; 23:3, 8; 32:37.
[118] Cf. Luther's 1543 treatise, *Von den Juden und ihren Lügen.* WA 53, 449-511.
[119] Ezra 1:1-8; II Chron. 36:22-23. See pp. 276-277.
[120] Jer. 15:16; 23:3, 8; 32:37.

Jews and a return out of all lands. The return out of all lands is fulfilled; the return of all Jews was never prophesied, but rather the opposite, just as at Jerusalem, while it was yet standing, both before and after the captivity, not all the people were the people of God, but the majority of them were people of the devil, idolatrous murderers and the worst people on earth.

The second thing, and the best thing in this prophecy—that which the Jews will neither see nor heed—is that God promises to create something new in the land, to make a new covenant unlike the old covenant of Moses that they dream about. This is plain from Jeremiah 31[:31-32] and from many more passages. No longer are there to be two kingdoms but one kingdom, under their King David who is to come; and his shall be an everlasting kingdom, even in that same physical land.

This, too, has been fulfilled. For when Christ came and found the people of both Israel and Judah gathered again out of all lands so that the country was full, he started something new: he established the promised new covenant. He did this not at a spiritual place, or at some other physical place, but exactly in that same physical land of Canaan, and at that same physical Jerusalem—as had been promised—to which they had been brought back out of all lands.

And although the Jews did not want this covenant—or at least not many of them would accept it—it has, nevertheless, remained an everlasting covenant, and not only at Jerusalem and in that land. It has broken forth from there into all the four corners of the world, and remains to the present day, both at Jerusalem and everywhere. For the place, Jerusalem, is still there, and Christ is Lord and King there as he is in all the world. He helps and hears all who are there or who come there, as he does those in all the world. Meanwhile he lets Mohammed[121] with his tyranny and the pope with his trickery do what they do; Christ is and remains Lord over all.

The Jews make a point of the name Israel and claim that they alone are Israel and that we are Gentiles. Now this is true so far as the first part of the prophecy and the old covenant of Moses are concerned, though this has long since been fulfilled. But according to the second part of the prophecy and the new covenant, the Jews

---

[121] Cf. p. 404, n. 81.

287

are no longer Israel, for all things are to be new, and Israel too must become new. Those alone are the true Israel who have accepted the new covenant which was established and begun at Jerusalem.

For according to the old covenant I am no Israelite, or Jew. But I claim now that I am the son of St. Paul, and an Israelite or Benjamite. For Paul is my father, not the old Paul but the new Paul. He is still the old Paul, but out of the old Paul there has arisen a new Paul in Christ; and he has begotten me in Christ by the gospel [I Cor. 4:15], so that I am in his likeness according to the new covenant.[122] Thus all the Gentiles who are Christians are the true Israelites and new Jews, born of Christ, the noblest Jew. Everything, therefore, depends upon the new covenant, which the Messiah was to found, making all things new, as he has done.

And this rule is to be noted well: when the prophets say of Israel that it is to return or to be gathered in its entirety, as in Micah 2[:12], Ezekiel 20[:40], etc., they are certainly speaking of the new covenant, and of the new Israel from which no one will be excluded, the everlasting kingdom of Christ. It cannot possibly be understood to mean the old Israel, for the majority of them remained in Assyria and Babylonia, both living and dead, and only a very few returned; Ezra [2:1-65] numbers them all.

The Jews, however, want to have a Messiah according to the old covenant and pay no attention to this new covenant. So they miss both covenants and hang between heaven and earth. The new covenant they do not want, the old they cannot have. Therefore the Scriptures are sealed against them, Isaiah 29,[123] and they understand none of the prophets. Besides they are without any government, either physical or spiritual. The physical, earthly government they have not, for they have neither king nor lord, neither kingdom nor princedom; the spiritual too they have not, for they will not accept the new covenant, and must thus remain without a priesthood. In a word they not only despised this new covenant, but persecuted it. They tried to eradicate it, not wanting to put up with it; and on that account they have been destroyed, and their covenant along with them.

Even though Jerusalem and the whole ancient order could have

---

[122] Cf. Gen. 5:3; I Cor. 4:16.
[123] Isa. 29:11-12; cf. p. 284, n. 113.

remained, nevertheless, in order to fulfil the Scriptures, the new covenant would have had to come and make all things new, as it now is in Christendom. There would have had to be at Jerusalem an apostle, bishop, or preacher—as Christ himself made a beginning—who would have had to rule Christ's church there, preach the gospel, baptize, administer the sacrament, absolve, bind,[124] etc. If the high priest—Caiaphas, or somebody else—had been unwilling to do this, an apostle would have had to do it, or one of the successors to the apostles, as has happened heretofore and must happen. Thus the eternal kingdom of Christ would have had to rule all the same, even in old Jerusalem as well as in all the world, as the prophecy intends and had promised. The old kingdom of Moses would then have remained as a temporal government.

For so the old, worldly, temporal government remains in all the world, and does not at all prevent the establishment upon earth of the new, spiritual, everlasting rule and kingdom of Christ under it and within it, a kingdom that has its own peculiar nature, as we clearly see.[125] Especially is this the case where there are righteous kings and princes, who in their old government tolerate this new everlasting kingdom of Christ, or who themselves accept it, promote it, and desire as Christians to be in it. Otherwise the greater part of the kings, princes, and lords of the old government hate the new covenant and kingdom of Christ as poisonously and bitterly as the Jews at Jerusalem. They persecute it and would wipe it out; and, like the Jews, they go to destruction because of it. That is what happened to Rome; it will happen to others also. Christ's new kingdom must abide for it is promised it shall be an everlasting kingdom, and the old kingdom must perish in the end.

It is well to remember, too, that since God himself calls this kingdom a new kingdom, it must be a far more glorious kingdom than the old kingdom was or is. It was God's will to make it a far better kingdom than the old one. Even if this new kingdom had no other glory, this alone would be enough to make it glorious beyond measure: that it is to be an everlasting kingdom that will not come to an end like the old, worldly kingdom.

---

[124] The reference is to Matt. 16:19 and the office of the keys. See *The Sacrament of Penance*, in this volume, pp. 3-27.
[125] On the two kingdoms see p. 164.

This everlasting kingdom, however, contains in addition such immeasurable, glorious blessings as forgiveness of sins, peace with God, security against everlasting death and all evil, communion with the Divine Majesty and with all angels and saints, joy and pleasure in the whole creation, even in a physical sense. For this same body, which is now the old body, shall also become new, together with the whole creation, as the soul has already begun to become new in faith.

Therefore the Jews do themselves wrong and injury when they desire through the Messiah not the new kingdom but the former, old, transitory kingdom, where they will possess silver, gold, riches, power, honor, pleasure, and joy according to the mortal flesh, all of which count before God as very minor things, indeed, as nothing at all. For if God had willed to promise such a kingdom, he would not have called it a new, different, and better kingdom.

Beyond the goods of this world nothing else can be called new and better, except only the spiritual, everlasting blessings in heaven, among which there can be nothing bad or evil. But among the earthly, old, temporal goods, however glorious they may be—as the Jews envision those coming from their Messiah—there must always be and remain much that is bad, much that is evil, at least death must be there, and the end of these goods.

These two things Ezekiel teaches us when he comforts the people concerning the return from Babylon, but even more when he prophesies the new Israel and the kingdom of Christ. That is his vision of the chariot,[126] and also really his temple, in the last part of his book [40:2–48:35].[127]

Guide to the Understanding of Ezekiel's Building in the Closing Chapters, from the Fortieth to the End of the Prophecy

He would understand this building of the temple, altar, city, and land, which Ezekiel [40–48] describes, must take up Lyra,[128]

---

[126] Ezek. 1:4-28; cf. pp. 284-286.

[127] MA^3 6, 62 concludes the 1541 preface at this point, without reproducing the following "Guide." This "Guide" appeared after the text of Ezekiel in the 1541 Bible but before the text in the Bibles from 1543 on. WA, DB 11^{II}, lxxxvi, n. 11.

[128] Nicholas of Lyra (1270-1340), a Franciscan and teacher at the Sorbonne in

with his figures and glosses; otherwise he will toil and labor on the matter in vain. Since we have not known how better to put the figures on paper, we have not attempted it but have referred the reader to Lyra. Besides it is not possible to plot out a building on paper, but a carved model would have to be constructed.

About the significance of it, one scholar has thought one way, another a different way. But the understanding of it that is held by the Jews and others like them is most certainly to be rejected. They think it is supposed to be the third temple, which must be built by their Messiah who is to come; in their foolish and vain hope they claim for it much great glory. The blind and ignorant people do not see that the text does not admit of their fanciful interpretation, as Lyra too has impressively shown.[129] For Ezekiel says neither that this city shall be called Jerusalem, nor that it shall stand at the place where Jerusalem was situated. Jerusalem was situated on the northern slope of the mountain with the temple standing in the midst of it on the hill of Mount Moriah, and the stronghold of Zion on the height south of it.[130]

But this city of Ezekiel is supposed to lie to the south[131] [of the temple] and he says, "It shall be called *Dominus ibi*," "There God," or "God there," that is, "Where God himself is."[132] The temple shall

Paris, was noted for his commentaries. His *Postillae perpetuae in Vetus et Novum Testamentum* was the most popular of all pre-Reformation works of its kind and the first biblical commentary ever printed. Luther used it extensively but was also highly critical of it because of its obvious reliance upon rabbinical interpretations. See Luther's *Commentary on Genesis*, LW 1, 93, 169, 184, 191, 223, 226, 231, 302, 353, and especially pp. 32, 101, 303, where Luther scores Lyra's frequent dependence on Rashi (Rabbi Solomon ben Isaac of Troyes, 1040-1105). The various editions of Lyra's *Postillae* containing woodcut sketches and outlines of Ezekiel's temple installation, beginning with Koberger's Nürnberg edition of 1481, are listed in WA, DB 11¹ 406, n. 1. See Luther's criticism of a Lyra illustration in the 1541 protocol of the Bible revision in WA, DB 4, 175 l. 18. On the new picture of Ezekiel's vision—very similar to that of Lyra—which appeared in the Luther Bibles from 1541 on, see WA, DB 11¹¹, lxxxiii-lxxxiv, especially note 102, and plates VIII a and b at the end of the volume.

[129] See the conclusion of the exposition of the prophet Ezekiel in Lyra's *Postillae*.
[130] Moriah and Zion were two distinct eminences in the "mountain of the Lord" (Isa. 2:2-3, Mic. 4:1-2), that "holy mountain, beautiful in elevation" (Ps. 48:2) which was Jerusalem. See I Chron. 11:5, and cf. II Chron. 3:1 with 5:2.
[131] Luther follows the Vulgate rather than the Septuagint in Ezek. 40:2, reading in the Hebrew *minegeb* (cf. KJV, "on the south") rather than *mineged* (cf. RSV, "opposite me").
[132] Ezek. 48:35, "The Lord is there" (RSV).

not be in the city but—as the reckoning shows[133]—seven good, big German miles[134] to the north of it. And the city on the high mountain shall be about nine good, big German miles both in length and breadth, so that the encircling wall shall be approximately thirty-six German miles around.[135] We may call that a little city, and the hill on which it lies, a little hill!

If a townsman living at the southern end of the city wanted to go to church, or to the temple, he would have to walk sixteen [German] miles, nine through the city and seven to the temple. The blind Jews do not see the absurdity. This cannot be any physical building; still less can it be at the place where Jerusalem was situated,[136] as they falsely hope.

There shall also be a great flow of water out of the temple into the Dead Sea [Ezek. 47:1-12] (which the papists—fools that they are!—take to be their holy water[137]); but this in no way squares with the topography of Israel.[138]

Besides the tribes and the land of Israel are very differently divided and arranged,[139] so that the city and the temple shall not lie in the land of any tribe of Israel, though Jerusalem was previously located in the land of the tribe of Benjamin [Josh. 18:28]. All this and much more is plainly given in the text.

The altar shall be eleven cubits high and fourteen cubits wide at the top [Ezek. 43:13-17], so that even if a priest manages to

---

[133] Luther assumes the measurements in Ezek. 45:1-6 and 48:8-22 to have been given in reeds (cf. KJV) rather than cubits (cf. RSV).
[134] The German geographical mile of the sixteenth century was perhaps equal to about 7420 meters, or 4½ statute miles in terms of modern English and American linear measure. *Der Grosse Brockhaus* (16th ed., 12 vols.; Wiesbaden: Brockhaus, 1952-1958), VII, 650. Cf. Grimm, *Deutsches Wörterbuch*, VI, 1907.
[135] This may be a reference to Ezek. 48:35. WA, DB 11[I], 408, n. 1, assumes that Luther borrowed from Lyra the equation five hundred reeds equals one German mile, but hence necessarily also admits ignorance as to the derivation of Luther's figure of "seven German miles" for the distance between city and temple.
[136] Despite possible misinterpretation or miscalculation, Luther's point is correct: the massive dimensions given by Ezekiel hardly conform to those of the ancient capital, where temple and city together (Moriah and Zion) measured only about ⅛ mile by ½ mile in terms of modern English and American linear measure.
[137] Luther is referring to the antiphon intoned each Sunday during the Easter season just prior to the weekly sprinkling with holy water. WA, DB 11[I] 409, n. 3.
[138] The Valley of the Kidron, however, did drain from the watershed near Jerusalem southeastward into the Dead Sea near Qumran. George Adam Smith, *Jerusalem* (2 vols.; London: Hodder and Stoughton, 1907), I, 10.
[139] Ezek. 47:13-20, 48:1-29; cf. Joshua 13—22 and Numbers 32, 34.

mount the steps, he must have an arm seven cubits long to reach onto the altar and arrange the sacrifice. That would have to be a pretty small priest too, to be fifteen or sixteen good, big cubits tall![140]

Therefore this building of Ezekiel is not to be understood to mean a physical building, but like the chariot at the beginning [1:4-28] so this building at the end [40—48] is nothing else than the kingdom of Christ, the holy church or Christendom here on earth until the last day.

As to how all the parts of the prophecy are to be interpreted and arranged, we will leave that until that life in which we shall see the whole building finished and complete. We cannot see it all now, since it is still under construction, and much of the stone and wood that belong to it is not yet born, let alone prepared for use in building. It is enough that we know it to be the house of God, his own building in which we all are.

Whoever has the leisure and the inclination can look into it and investigate it extensively, if he will take up the word of God and the sacraments, with their powers and the effects which the Holy Spirit works in the church through them, and bring these things into agreement. The Revelation of John can also be of help in this regard.[141]

---

[140] As a measure of length the cubit was based on the length of the forearm. In Ezek. 43:13 and 40:5 the long cubit may have been approximately 20.67 inches, the shorter cubit about 17.72 inches, which would make Luther's hypothetical priest about 27 feet tall with arms 12 feet long.
[141] See the Preface to the Revelation of St. John, in this volume, pp. 399-411.

Preface to the Prophet Daniel[142]

1530

In this preface I desire to provide a short instruction on this book of St. Daniel in order that the simple people and those who do not know and cannot read the histories may nevertheless get the gist of its meaning. Before proceeding, let me point out that Daniel came to Babylon some years before the destruction of Jerusalem, during the reign of King Jehoiakim. King Nebuchadnezzar had had Jehoiakim captured and bound, and would have brought him to Babylon too, had he not changed his mind and let him remain. As it was, Nebuchadnezzar brought some of the best people back with him (including Daniel) as well as vessels from the temple in Jerusalem. We can read all about this in II Kings 24, and in II Chronicles 36.[143]

The first chapter brings us a fine example from Daniel's life. We see how holy, how God-fearing, and how possessed he was of a great and noble faith in God; and all this in the very midst of the wild and pagan life and the abominable offenses which he had to listen to and look upon every day at Babylon. In spite of it all, he remained firm and steadfast, and conquered all these temptations in his heart. For this reason there follows almost immediately [the account of] how God showed him great mercy, first highly honoring him in things of the spirit by granting him wisdom and understanding beyond that of other men, and then by elevating him also in worldly affairs and doing nothing but great and mighty deeds and miracles

---

[142] This preface accompanied Luther's translation of the Book of Daniel which was published separately in 1530 under the title *Der Prophet Daniel Deudsch*, together with a letter of dedication to John Frederick of Saxony (Smith and Jacobs, *Luther's Correspondence*, II, 516-618, give only a portion of that letter: the complete text is given in *EA* 41, 233-237). In the dedicatory letter Luther expressed his conviction that the end of the world was near at hand. At the urging of Rörer, Luther prepared early in 1541 an extensive antipapistic commentary on Daniel 12 which in the 1541 edition of the complete Bible he then appended to his 1530 preface. *WA, DB* 6, lxxxix. We have translated here for the first time in English the entire 1530 preface (exclusive of the 1541 commentary), as it is given in *EA* 41, 237-258, 294, and 321-324, rather than merely the concluding paragraphs as was done in *PE* 6, 420-423.

[143] Cf. Dan. 1:20.

through him. God did this to show us all how much he loves and cherishes those who fear and trust in him; with such an impressive example he prods us in a kindly way to faith and the fear of God.

In the second chapter the honoring of Daniel begins; it is occasioned by the king's dream which Daniel, with the help of divine revelation, discerns and interprets. As a result Daniel becomes a ruler of the entire Babylonian realm and a bishop or chief prefect over all the priests and learned men. This takes place also for the comforting of the whole Jewish community, that despite their wretched condition they should neither despair nor grow impatient, as if God had abandoned them or withdrawn his promise of Christ. This is why a captured Jew must rule in such a great kingdom, while no Babylonian can enjoy similar honor. It is just as though Daniel had been led away captive for the express purpose of being made a great ruler, even over those who had captured him and were now holding him. So wondrously does God lead his faithful ones; he bestows upon them far more than anyone could wish.

The dream, however, and the image is clearly interpreted in the text by Daniel himself in terms of the four kingdoms. The first kingdom is that of the Assyrians or Babylonians; the second, that of the Medes and Persians; the third, that of Alexander the Great and the Greeks; the fourth, that of the Romans. Everyone agrees on this view and interpretation; subsequent events and the histories prove it conclusively.

Daniel has most to say about the Roman empire. Therefore we must pay close attention. At the end [2:41-45], where the iron legs begin to divide into the toes of the feet, Daniel points out three things about the Roman empire.

The first is that the toes are divided, although they retain their origin in the iron foot. Just as in the human body the toes separate while projecting from and belonging to the foot, so also was the Roman empire split, as Spain, France, England, and other parts came out of it. Nevertheless it has continued to grow and, like a plant, has been transplanted or (as they say) transferred [*translatum*] from the Greeks to the Germans.[144] Yet this has occurred in such a way that its nature as iron was retained, for the empire still has its estates, offices, laws, and statutes as of old. Therefore Daniel

---

[144] See p. 406, n. 88.

says here that even though it will be a divided kingdom the root, plant, or trunk of iron will nevertheless be in it.

The second thing—that these divided toes are dissimilar, partly iron and partly clay—Daniel himself interprets in terms of this divided kingdom: now it is mighty, now weak. This too has come to pass. Often there have been numerous brave emperors like Charlemagne,[145] the three Ottos,[146] and others, who were unconquerable; and in turn there have often been weak and unfortunate emperors who were frequently defeated. All this is said, however, in order that we might know that the Roman empire is to be the last, and that no one will be able to destroy it save Christ alone and his kingdom. Therefore, even though many monarchs may have risen against the German empire and the Turks may rage against it, and even though all such enemies may perhaps win an occasional battle, they are nevertheless unable to conquer an iron root or plant like this, or to destroy it. It must remain until the Last Day, no matter how weak it may be. For Daniel does not lie, and up until now experience —with respect to both the popes themselves and the kings—has borne this out.

The third thing—that such divided and dissimilar toes are mixed or interchanged—Daniel himself interprets in terms of this weak kingdom seeking strength and support by means of alliances and intermarriages here and there among other kings. But this will not help, neither will it secure peace and concord. If the kingdom is to endure, it must find its strength and victory in God's providence alone.

The mountain, from which the stone is cut without human hands [2:45], is interpreted by some as signifying the blessed Virgin Mary, from whom Christ was born without human co-operation. This is not an un-Christian interpretation. Yet it may also be that the mountain signifies the whole Jewish people from whom Christ sprang. He is their flesh and blood but has been torn from them and has come among the Gentiles. Among the Gentiles he has become a

---

[145] Charles the Great, king of the Franks from A.D. 768-814, was crowned head of the Holy Roman Empire in the year 800.

[146] Under the three generations of Saxon Ottos the Holy Roman Empire became a strong power; Otto I, the Great, ruled A.D. 936-973; Otto II, 973-983; Otto III, 983-1002.

296

Lord in all the world—in all four of these kingdoms [to which Daniel refers]—and will so remain.

In the third chapter Daniel again records a great miracle of faith. There the three men are preserved in the fiery furnace, so that God is confessed and praised by the king [Nebuchadnezzar] throughout the entire realm, even in writing. This, too, happened for the consolation of the Jews who, along with their God, were despised nobodies at Babylon under the tyrants and false gods. But now' their God is highly honored above all gods, in order that they may firmly believe that at the proper time he can and will indeed save them, and meanwhile hold fast to and console themselves with this honor he receives and this miracle he performs.

In the fourth chapter a pointed example is directed against the bloodthirsty and the tyrants. For the great and mighty king [Nebuchadnezzar] is here robbed of his reason. He becomes so raving mad that he has to be treated like a mad dog, chained and put out in the field because people cannot stand his presence. Today, because we simply read this in a book, it may appear as a minor matter. If we had been present, however, and seen something like this, we would have been witnessing a terrifying and horrible judgment of God. Everyone would have been moved with compassion for all the overlords and evil tyrants, that they have to expect such gruesome judgment when they abuse their position as rulers.

This too, however, happened for purposes of consolation—at that time the consolation of the wretched captive Jews, today and evermore the consolation of those who are plagued by tyrants or who suffer injustice—that men may see how God intends and is able to avenge us against our enemies even more fully than we dare to dream. As Psalm 58[:10] declares, "The righteous will rejoice when he sees the vengeance; he will bathe his feet in the blood of the wicked." For this reason we should not only put up patiently with such tyrants but also pity them for the judgment that they have coming to them, and pray for them earnestly just as the righteous Daniel does here. For Daniel is troubled that things were to go so badly for the king (who, after all, had captured the Jews and destroyed their land); Daniel wished such evil rather upon the king's enemies.

However, for the righteous lords and princes this is also a comforting and lovely image, that God the Lord depicts even this tyrannical king as a beautiful tree which nourishes all the beasts and lets them rest in its shade. Hereby God makes it clear that through civil authority [Oberkeit] he provides and maintains peace and tranquillity, protection and defense, sustenance and possessions, and this entire temporal life, and that it is pleasing to him wherever a lord or prince practices his office conscientiously. For these are fine fruits, fine leaves, fine foliage, Daniel [4:21-22] says; that is, these are precious, noble, good works. Because it is so pleasing to God himself that he thus portrays, praises, and adorns it, a lord should indeed exercise his office with all eagerness and delight, even though it be full of toil and trouble. By the same token, we too ought not to pay attention to how evil the tyrants may be but to how precious and useful is the office which they have from God, instituted for our benefit and welfare.

In the fifth chapter, however, comes another example against the tyrants. The example in the previous chapter is still bearable because the king permits himself to be rebuked and then turns to God with proper repentance, humility, and confession; so that, undoubtedly, this is a case of a tyrant becoming a great saint. But here [in this fifth chapter] the hardened and unrepentant tyrant [Belshazzar] is punished mercilessly for his evil. At one blow he loses everything, land, people, and his own life. This is surely written to terrify all similar tyrants.

The sixth chapter brings us the fine and precious example of a good and righteous king [Darius] who loved Daniel. As far as the other high moguls[147] were concerned, Daniel had to pay for this favor [he enjoyed with the king]; they prove him guilty of a petty intrigue and he is finally thrown into the den of lions. Once again the captive and wretched Jews were undoubtedly grieved. But once again God proves himself righteous and comforting; for he so marvelously reverses the plot that that which Daniel's enemies had prepared for him they had to swallow themselves. This is just as Psalm 7[:14, 16] declares, "[The wicked] are pregnant with mischief and bring forth lies. Their mischief returns upon their own head, and on their own pate their violence descends." Thus Daniel's life is nothing but a fine, clear mirror. In it we see the conflict and vic-

---

[147] Grossen Hansen; see p. 211, n. 9.

tory of faith, which, by the grace of God, triumphs over all men and devils; we see too the great fruit and use of faith, which it produces through patience and cross-bearing, before both God and the world.

In the seventh chapter begin the visions and prophecies of the future kingdoms, especially of the kingdom of Christ, for whose sake all these visions came to pass. To begin with, the four kingdoms, which he pointed out above in chapter 2[:31-43] in the great image, he now sees again in another form, namely in the four beasts. Most of his attention centers on the fourth beast, the Roman empire, about which he wants to say something more. For under that very Roman empire the greatest event on earth was supposed to take place, namely, that Christ should come and redeem men, and the world should come to its end.

So, then, the first beast is here the kingdom of Assyria and Babylon, which is the lion with the two wings of an eagle; for this is the noblest and best of all, the golden kingdom, as was said above.[148] The two wings are the two parts of the kingdom, Assyria and Babylon. To it is given a human heart, and it stands upon its feet. The other kingdoms had no such king [as Nebuchadnezzar], who came so wondrously to the knowledge of God; neither did the others have so many great, holy, and wise men at court as did this kingdom.

The second beast, the bear, is the kingdom in Persia and Media, which destroyed the preceding kingdom of Babylon and tore out its wings. Among its teeth it has three ribs, that is three big and long teeth. These are the foremost kings, Cyrus, Darius, and Xerxes,[149] who accomplished the most in this kingdom and devoured much flesh, that is to say, won great lands.

The third beast, the leopard with four wings and four heads, is the kingdom of Alexander the Great in Greece, which later broke up into four kingdoms—as we shall hear in the next chapter.[150]

---

[148] Cf. p. 295.

[149] The Persian Empire had ten kings: Cyrus (538-529), Cambyses (529-522), Darius I Hystapsis (522-486), Xerxes I (485-465), Artaxerxes I Longimanus (464-424), Xerxes II (a few months in 424-423), Darius II Nothus (423-404), Artaxerxes II Mnemon (404-359), Artaxerxes III Ochus (359-338), Darius III Codomannus (338-331). W. O. E. Oesterley, A History of Israel (Oxford: Clarendon, 1932), II, 466.

[150] See pp. 300-303.

The fourth beast, with the iron teeth, is now the really guilty one. This is the last, the Roman empire; with it the world should have an end, as Daniel here has much to say about the Final Judgment and about the kingdom of the saints that is to follow this one. However he portrays this Roman empire in such a way that it should first be broken up into ten kingdoms. These are the ten horns: Syria, Egypt, Asia [Minor], Greece, [North] Africa, Spain, Gaul, Italy, Germany, England, etc. He also indicates that one small horn shall knock off three among the top ten horns—meaning Mohammed[151] or the Turk who now holds Egypt, Asia, and Greece—and that this same little horn will fight the saints and blaspheme Christ, something that we are all experiencing and seeing before our very eyes.[152] For the Turk has had great victories against the Christians, yet denies Christ while elevating his Mohammed over all. Certainly we have nothing to wait for now except the Last Day, for the Turk will not knock off more than these three horns.

In the eighth chapter Daniel experiences a special vision. Unlike the former, this one pertains not to the whole world but to his own people, the Jews; it shows how they were to fare prior to the Roman empire and before the coming of Christ, namely, under the third empire, that of Alexander the Great. Once again the purpose is to console the Jews, that they may not despair amid the wretchedness that is to engulf them, as if Christ would leave them again and not come.

Daniel himself interprets this vision as follows. The ram with the two horns is the king of Media and Persia. The he-goat is Alexander the Great, who defeated Darius [III], the last king of Persia, and took away his kingdom. Daniel also says that the he-goat flew, so that he did not even touch the ground. For Alexander went so fast that in twelve years he conquered the world; he had begun at the age of twenty and died at the age of thirty-two.[153] Indeed,

---

[151] See p. 404, n. 81.

[152] The Ottoman Turks captured Constantinople in 1453, and soon held all of Greece. In 1517 under Selim I they took Egypt. The campaigns of Suleiman the Magnificent, 1520-1566, up the Danube valley led to the first—unsuccessful —siege of Vienna in 1529, and instilled in Luther and his central European contemporaries a proverbial dread of the Turk. William L. Langer (ed.), *An Encyclopaedia of World History*, (Boston: Houghton Mifflin, 1948), pp. 327, 422. Cf. p. 407, n. 89.

[153] Cf. I Macc. 1:1-7. Alexander was born in 356 B.C. and succeeded his father,

humanly speaking, no greater person than Alexander has come or will come on this earth. But whatever rises rapidly also falls rapidly;[154] Alexander's empire crumbled as soon as he died, and these four kingdoms came in its place: Syria, Egypt, Asia, Greece.

Now Daniel skips over two of them, Asia and Greece, and centers attention on the two others, Syria and Egypt. For it is between these latter two that the land of the Jews is located. Syria lies to the north and Egypt to the south, and the two stood in perpetual conflict against each other. This is why the Jews were bedeviled from both sides, being caught between two fires.[155] Now they fell to the Egyptians, now to the Syrians, depending on which of these kingdoms was the stronger. So they had to pay dearly for their location, just as always happens in the course of war. This was especially true when that wanton man, whom the histories call Antiochus the Noble, was king of Syria.[156] He manhandled the Jews gruesomely, and raved and raged in their midst like a demon. He abolished the worship of God in Jerusalem, desecrated the temple, plundered its treasures, set up idols and idolatry in it, and chased out and murdered the priests and everyone else whose will was opposed to his own. He was bent on mixing all kinds of faith into a single faith, and this was to be the faith of the Greeks. To that end he had the help of a number of traitorous rascals among the Jews, fellows who could not otherwise get ahead, as we find further in I Maccabees 1[:41-53].[157] Antiochus, of course, could not carry on this way for long.

Now concerning this Antiochus, Daniel [8:9] says that following Alexander, a small horn would be coming out of one of the four big horns. This is Antiochus the Noble, coming out of the horn of Syria. He was mighty against the south and the east, and against the glorious land, that is, the land of the Jews. By means of treachery and deceit this Antiochus snatched much land and many cities from

---

Philip, as ruler of the Macedonian empire in 337. His twelve years of actual campaigning, 334-323, included an early triumph over Darius III (see p. 299, n. 149) at the Battle of Issus in 333. Langer, *An Encyclopaedia of World History* p. 65.

[154] Cf. Wander (ed.), *Sprichwörter-Lexikon*, I, 223, "Bald," Nos. 11, 12.

[155] *Zwischen Thur und Angel steckten.* See Wander (ed), *Sprichwörter-Lexikon*, IV, 1200, "Thür," No. 221.

[156] See the chart, p. 307.

[157] See Luther's Preface to I Maccabees in this volume, pp. 350-352.

the king of Egypt, as we shall learn in chapter 11.[158] Thus he also cast many stars to the ground, so that many saintly people among the Jews were put to death. He devastated and desecrated the worship of the God in heaven in the temple [at Jerusalem] and placed idols in it. Against such a devil God raised up Judas Maccabaeus and his brothers. They fought, and performed valiant and righteous deeds. In five years they had killed some two hundred thousand men, as we read in II Maccabees.[159] They cleansed the land and the temple, and made everything right again. The text here [Dan. 8:14] tells us that after twenty-three hundred days—which makes six and one-quarter years—the temple would be cleansed. For this length of time Antiochus vented his fury on the Jews, but he died in the seventh year. These figures readily agree, as the book of [I] Maccabees [1:20-24; 6:16] proves.

Therefore the angel here warns that King Antiochus will do great harm, and that he is an impudent and insolent monarch. For as the histories tell us, he led an immoral and disgraceful life, being a completely lewd person. However he shall be broken, as the angel says [8:25], by no human hand. For since he wanted to go after gold in Persia, he gave orders to his field commander, Lysias, to destroy and wipe out the Jews. But when Antiochus was unable to get any gold, and received the news that Judas Maccabaeus had defeated and put to rout Lysias and his army, he became ill with rage and impatience because things had not turned out for him as he had planned, and died after intense suffering and misery in a strange land.[160]

This is what must happen to tyrants. For Antiochus is here set up as an example of all evil kings and princes, especially those who rage against God and his Word. It is for this reason that the earlier teachers have designated and interpreted Antiochus as a figure of the Antichrist,[161] and rightly so. For such a wild and filthy fellow,

---

[158] See pp. 306-313.
[159] This round figure Luther probably attained by totaling those given in II Macc. 8:24, 30; 10:17, 23, 31; 11:11; 12:19, 23, 26, 28; 13:15; 15:27.
[160] I Macc. 6:1-16; cf., II Macc. 9:1-28.
[161] Building on the interpretation given already in II Thess. 2:3-4, most of the early fathers—Irenaeus, Clement, Tertullian, Origen, Eusebius, Jerome—continued to rely in varying degrees on an apocalyptic rather than an historical exegesis. James A. Montgomery, A Critical and Exegetical Commentary on the Book of Daniel ("The International Critical Commentary" [New York: Scribner's, 1927]), pp. 398-399, 469.

such a raving tyrant, is supposed to be chosen to represent and portray the ultimate abomination, as several words in this chapter [8] and in chapter 12[162] suggest and secretly disclose.

The ninth chapter opens with a splendid prayer in which Daniel prays for his people who are held captive in Babylon, and for the city of Jerusalem and the temple. He prays that the Jews might return to Jerusalem and there resume their worship of God. The prayer is answered, and to Daniel is revealed the number of years until Christ should come and begin his eternal kingdom. Now this is a remarkable and great revelation of Christ which sets the time so surely and accurately.

These seventy weeks, as decreed by the angel,[163] are unanimously regarded by all teachers as weeks of years and not as weeks of days; that is, one week denotes seven years and not seven days. Experience also demands this interpretation, for seventy weeks of days add up to less than two years, and this would be no remarkable [span of] time for such a glorious revelation. But seventy weeks of years total four hundred and ninety years. This is how long men were still supposed to wait for Christ, and then his kingdom was to begin.

Here, of course, we must inquire as to where and when these seventy weeks begin. The angel explains them; he begins in the year that a command goes out for the rebuilding of Jerusalem. For he speaks thus, "From the going forth of the word to restore and build Jerusalem," etc. [9:25], which some have badly stretched and twisted. But in order that we may proceed correctly in this matter we must begin these seventy weeks with the second year of King Darius, who was called Longimanus.[164] For in that same year the Word of God came through the prophets Haggai [1:1-15] and Zechariah [1:1-17], and Zerubbabel gave orders to build the temple; as we read in the first chapter of both of these prophets.[165] This same Darius commanded the very same thing, and his commandment was executed accordingly, Ezra 6[:6-15].

---

[162] For Luther—according to the chapter divisions in his translation of the prophet (EA 41, 287-294)—Dan. 11:2b-35 constitute the eleventh chapter and Dan. 11:36—12:13 constitute the twelfth chapter.

[163] In Dan. 9:24 the "seventy weeks" in the KJV is literal, the "seventy weeks of years" in the RSV represents the interpretation which Luther describes as universal.

[164] The epithet Longimanus (Langhand) was applied historically to Artaxerxes I (464-424), the grandson of Darius I (522-486).

[165] Cf. below pp. 329-330.

Now the calculation [of the years] agrees with this. From the commandment or word spoken through Haggai, up to the baptism of Christ when he took up his office and when his kingdom or the New Testament began—the angel here speaks of him as a "prince" —is incidentally 483 years. This makes sixty-nine of these weeks, of which the angel says, "Unto Christ, the prince, there shall be seven weeks, and threescore and two weeks," that is, sixty-nine weeks.[166] The calculation is as follows: from the second year of Darius to Alexander the Great are 145 years, according to Metasthenes; from Alexander to the birth of Christ are 311 years, as the histories attest;[167] and from the birth of Christ to his baptism are thirty years, according to Luke 3[:23]. That makes a total of 486 years; these are the sixty-nine weeks. There is a remainder of three years. These we must ignore in our calculations because it often happens in such calculations and histories that a half-year is called a whole year. It is impossible to account for every day and hour when writing history. It is good enough for us to come this close, especially since we have such specific scriptural information concerning the main items.

This opinion approximates that of those who begin the seventy weeks with the twentieth and last year of Cambyses, the father of Darius, who gave permission to Nehemiah to return and restore Jerusalem, Nehemiah 2,[168] for the twentieth year of Cambyses is actually two years before the second year of Darius.[169] Now when a great event happens within [a matter of] three years, one must really understand it as comprising one year, that is, a single period of time, and say: it happened about such and such a time. So here one must say: The word of God—that Jerusalem should be restored and built—went forth in the second year of Darius, about the time that Nehemiah came from Cambyses and began to rebuild Jerusalem, etc. For this was a great event, begun by many—and even promoted by angels, as Zechariah 1[:7-17] declares—yet not by everybody at once on the same day or at the same hour [Ezra 1-6].

Now the angel further divides these seventy weeks into three

---

[166] In Dan. 9:25 Luther follows Jerome's Vulgate (cf. KJV) rather than the Masoretic Text (cf. RSV) in combining the figures "seven weeks and sixty-two weeks" as one numeral.

[167] See p. 299, n. 149; and p. 300, n. 153.

[168] According to Neh. 2:1-8 the permission was granted by Artaxerxes, in the twentieth year of his reign.

[169] See p. 299, n. 149.

parts. In the first seven weeks—that is, in forty-nine years—(he says) the wall and streets shall be rebuilt, in troublous times.[170] And he really had trouble too, because of the intense opposition in the neighboring countries [Neh. 2:10; 4; 6]. This agrees with the statement of the Jews to Christ in John 2[:20], "It has taken forty-six years to build this temple, and will you raise it up in three days?" Then after sixty-two weeks (he says) Christ shall be put to death.

Here he shows what is to happen when these sixty-nine weeks are up, and Christ has begun [his ministry], namely, that Christ shall be crucified (which happened in the fourth year after the sixty-nine weeks and after the beginning [of his ministry]), and that the city of Jerusalem shall therefore finally be destroyed, and Judaism come to an end (which afterward happened at the hands of the Romans). The one last week—that is, seven years—is the time which follows the sixty-nine weeks, during which (as has been said) Christ was supposed to be put to death. And that took place in this way (as the angel states [9:27]): He shall make a covenant with many for one week. For the preaching of Christ spread mightily during those seven years, both through Christ himself up into the fourth year, and thereafter through the apostles, proclaiming to the people the promised grace. In the midst of that same week— that is, during the fourth year after his baptism—Christ was put to death. And then the sacrifice ceased; that is, through Christ's death, which is the true sacrifice, the Jewish sacrifice and worship were abolished. Then the Romans under Emperor Caius Caligula[171] placed an idol in the temple (as the angel says here [9:27] as a sign that the temple and Judaism were to be at an end.

The tenth chapter is a prologue to the eleventh. Yet in it Daniel writes something special about the angels, the like of which we find nowhere else in the Scriptures, namely, that the good angels do battle with the evil angels in defense of men. Besides Daniel calls also the evil angels princes, as when he speaks of "the prince of Greece" [10:20]. Hence we may understand why things are so wild and dissolute at the courts of kings and princes, and why they hinder the good and bring on war and unhappiness. For there are devils there, hounding and goading, or hindering to such an extent

---

[170] Luther follows the Vulgate in rendering Dan. 9:25 (cf. KJV).
[171] Cf. pp. 341-342, especially p. 341, n. 18.

that nothing goes as it should. For example, though the Jews were supposed to get out of Babylon by the help of the Persian kings, nothing happened despite the willingness of the kings; as a result this [good] angel here says that he has his hands full and must fight against the prince of Persia, and expresses the concern on departing that the prince of Greece will come in the meanwhile. It is as if he were to say, "Where we parry one misfortune the devil produces another; if you get liberated from Babylon, then the Greeks will bedevil you." Now that is enough on this, for it would require more space and time to speak of it further.

In the eleventh chapter[172] Daniel prophesies to his people, the Jews—almost exactly as he does in the eighth chapter[173]—concerning Alexander the Great and the two kingdoms, Syria and Egypt, chiefly on account of Antiochus (called the Noble) who is to plague the Jews. But he describes Antiochus in such a way that his words ultimately tend under the figure of Antiochus to portray the very Antichrist. And so Daniel is actually referring here to these last times of ours just before the Last Day.[174] For all teachers are unanimously agreed that these prophecies about Antiochus point to the Antichrist.[175] Daniel's words too show compellingly that he does not mean exclusively Antiochus but is actually mixing together Antiochus and the Antichrist, and thus purposely scrambling his otherwise clear and transparent words.

There shall stand up yet (he says [11:2]) three kings in Persia. He does not mean this in the sense in which the Jews interpret it, that Persia should have so few kings; for the Persians have had at least ten kings.[176] Rather these four are said to be standing up in Persia because they were especially distinguished beyond the others. Thus after Cyrus came Cambyses, Darius, and Xerxes; and these are the four most important. Of the four, Xerxes was the richest; he campaigned with innumerable forces against the Greeks, but was disgracefully defeated[177] and barely escaped with his life. After

---

[172] See p. 303, n. 162.
[173] See pp. 300-303.
[174] See p. 294, n. 142.
[175] See p. 302, n. 161.
[176] See p. 299, n. 149.
[177] Xerxes I (486-465) was defeated by the Greeks on the sea at Salamis (480) and on the land at Plataea and Mycale (479). Langer, *An Encyclopaedia of World History*, p. 40.

that comes Alexander and his four successors who, however, were neither of his lineage nor blood.

Then come the two kingdoms, Syria and Egypt, and how they fall to tearing and mauling each other. Here we must really set down the names of the kings on a sheet of paper, so that we do not become confused in the histories and in the text before us.

Alexander the Great [337-323][178]

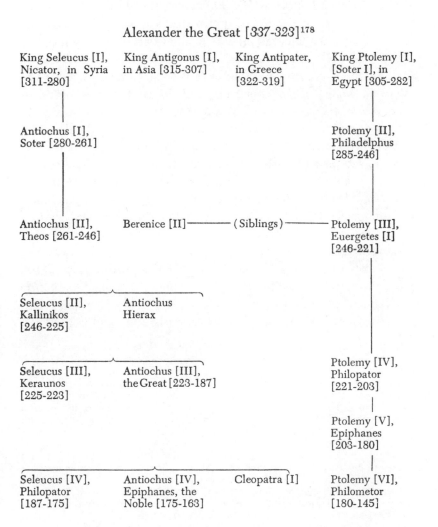

King Seleucus [I], Nicator, in Syria [311-280]	King Antigonus [I], in Asia [315-307]	King Antipater, in Greece [322-319]	King Ptolemy [I], [Soter I], in Egypt [305-282]
Antiochus [I], Soter [280-261]			Ptolemy [II], Philadelphus [285-246]
Antiochus [II], Theos [261-246]	Berenice [II] ——— (Siblings) ———		Ptolemy [III], Euergetes [I] [246-221]
Seleucus [II], Kallinikos [246-225]	Antiochus Hierax		
Seleucus [III], Keraunos [225-223]	Antiochus [III], the Great [223-187]		Ptolemy [IV], Philopator [221-203]
			Ptolemy [V], Epiphanes [203-180]
Seleucus [IV], Philopator [187-175]	Antiochus [IV], Epiphanes, the Noble [175-163]	Cleopatra [I]	Ptolemy [VI], Philometor [180-145]

[178] Dates and titles given in brackets in this table are taken from Oesterly, *A History of Israel*, II, 466, supplemented as needed by Langer, *An Encyclopaedia of World History*, passim.

After Alexander the kingdom in Egypt became very strong, as Daniel [11:5] here indicates. The same was true of the kingdom in Syria. Neither was able to conquer or subjugate the other, though each of them tried often and would have liked nothing better.

The first war[179] took place between Antiochus [II] Theos and Ptolemy [II] Philadelphus; after prolonged campaigning they finally reached an accord. Ptolemy [II] Philadelphus was an especially fine king, for he sought peace and patronized the arts. He supported many learned men and gathered a splendid library[180] from all parts of the world. He also did many fine things for the Jews, gloriously adorning the temple and worship in Jerusalem. In fact, I would even count him among the saintly kings.[181] In order to make the peace more secure, he gave his only daughter, Berenice, in marriage to Antiochus Theos; and then he died. Berenice, however, the daughter of a mighty monarch and now herself a powerful queen and lady at court, schemed that her [infant] son should inherit the kingdom of Syria. But the plot failed, for Laodice, the [divorced] former queen of Antiochus Theos, and her two sons, Seleucus Kallinikos and Antiochus Hierax, hated Berenice and her son and desired themselves to inherit the kingdom. Laodice poisoned her lord, Antiochus Theos, and then stirred up her two sons against Berenice, their stepmother. They chased her out and finally murdered not only her but also her child and all her retinue. It is to this situation that Daniel has reference when he says [11:6], "She shall not retain the strength of her arm, and her offspring shall not endure; but she

---

[179] In this "Second Syrian War" (260-255) Ptolemy II lost to Antiochus II some of the territory he had taken earlier in the "First Syrian War" (276-272) from Antiochus I. Langer, *An Encyclopaedia of World History,* pp. 81, 84.

[180] See p. 348. The idea of founding at Alexandria a "Museum"—a temple of the Muses—with library attached was probably first conceived by Demetrius of Phalerum and implemented by Ptolemy I. All of the early Ptolemies fostered the enterprise until it became the largest collection of Greek books in the world. Edwyn Bevan, *A History of Egypt under the Ptolemaic Dynasty* (London: Methuen, 1927), pp. 124-125.

[181] Cf. pp. 297, 300, and Dan. 4:34-37. Luther appears to base his high opinion of Ptolemy II on the *Letter of Aristeas,* one of the pseudepigraphic writings composed by an Alexandrine Jew some time between 200-93 B.C., but attributed to Aristeas, an officer at the court of Ptolemy Philadelphus. This letter contains the famous story of the translation of the Septuagint by the seventy-two translators sent down from Jerusalem to Alexandria at Ptolemy's request; in return for which rich gifts were sent to Jerusalem. It was first printed in a Latin Bible at Rome in 1471 and at Nürnberg in 1475, and in a separate edition at Erfurt in 1483. See Charles, *op. cit.,* II (1919), 83-122.

shall be given into death, with her child, and her attendants, indeed also with her lord king through whom she had become mighty."

Ptolemy [III] Euergetes, the brother of Berenice, then avenges and punishes this crime by making war on the two brothers, Seleucus [II] and Antiochus [Hierax].[182] He drove them out, plundered their kingdom, and returned home [to Egypt]. Shortly thereafter, as befits those guilty of matricide, these two brothers finally came to a wretched and miserable end. Daniel speaks about all this here [11:7], saying that the king of the south shall move with an army against the king of the north and shall prevail.

After the death of Ptolemy Euergetes, Seleucus [III] Keraunos and Antiochus the Great, sons of the deceased Seleucus [II] Kallinikos, prepared for war. In the midst of these preparations, however, Seleucus Keraunos died. Consequently Antiochus [III] had to hurry back from Babylon and direct the campaign which had already begun against Ptolemy [IV] Philopator, the son of Ptolemy Euergetes. Ptolemy, however, defeated Antiochus the Great and his army.[183] This is what Daniel is saying here [11:10-12], that the sons of Kallinikos shall be stirred up and move against Ptolemy Philopator, but Philopator will defeat them, and through his victory become proud. For this same Philopator subsequently fell into vice, and at last, for the sake of a prostitute, murdered his queen Euridice, who was also his sister.

Following the death of Philopator, however, Antiochus [III] the Great armed himself more powerfully [than before] against Philopator's son, known as Ptolemy [V] Epiphanes, who was still a mere child of four or five years. Now, as often happens when [infant] monarchs must have guardians, other kings—such as Philip of Greece[184] —conspired against him along with Antiochus and were eager to divide among themselves the land of the boy-king, Epiphanes. Moreover there was also dissension in the country itself, and the Jews too defected from Epiphanes to Antiochus. For this reason

---

[182] Ptolemaic power reached its height during this "Third Syrian War" (246-241). Langer, An Encyclopaedia of World History, p. 84.

[183] Despite initial successes in the "Fourth Syrian War" (221-217) Antiochus III the Great ultimately lost all but one of the cities he had taken from Ptolemy IV. Langer, An Encyclopaedia of World History, pp. 81, 84.

[184] In 203 B.C. Philip V of Macedon allied himself with Antiochus III against Egypt. The "Fifth Syrian War" (201-195) was decided by Antiochus' victory at Panium in 200. Langer, An Encyclopaedia of World History, pp. 80-81.

Daniel says here [11:13-16] that King Antiochus shall come again and that many shall turn against the child, Epiphanes, that the forces of the south—that is, the picked troops of Epiphanes which he had in the lands of Phoenicia and Judea, and at Jerusalem—could not stand before him. Instead Antiochus conquered all these lands, entering also the glorious land of Jerusalem. It was there that the Jews helped him to rout completely the picked troops of Epiphanes. In return for this help, Antiochus highly honored the Jews, giving them ample goods and much freedom.[185]

When, however, Antiochus planned to move on and to capture Egypt itself, Ptolemy Epiphanes called on the Romans [for help]. Thereupon Antiochus had to cancel his plans. He made a treaty with Ptolemy Epiphanes and gave him his daughter, Cleopatra, in marriage—not in good faith, however, but as Daniel[186] says here [11:17], to destroy him. For by means of his daughter, Antiochus thought to take the young man's kingdom away from him. But the queen [Cleopatra][187] and the Egyptians themselves frustrated these plans.

Next Antiochus waged war against the islands of Asia Minor (as Daniel [11:18-19] relates) and took many of them. But in the process he ran into the Romans, who drove him back and stripped him of a fine cloak—nearly the whole of Asia Minor.[188] After that Antiochus turned back to his home and undertook an expedition to Persia, aiming there to make a big haul of gold from the temple at Elymais [I Macc. 6:1-3]. But the inhabitants were on the alert and brought death to him and to his army. So he remained in a strange land and was never found.

Prior to this, however, when the Romans still had him on the

---

[185] On the friendship of Antiochus for the Jews see Flavius Josephus, *The Antiquities of the Jews*, XII, iii, 3-4.

[186] The original in *EA* 41, 255—"*David*"—is obviously a mistake.

[187] Arriving in Egypt about 194 B.C., following the peace treaty of 197, Antiochus' daughter found the place to her liking, promoted her husband's cause, supported the Egyptian alliance with Rome, and dashed her father's hopes for the absorption of Egypt into the Syrian realm. She was the first of what became a line of Egyptian Cleopatras. See *The Interpreter's Bible* (New York: Abingdon-Cokesburg Press, 1952-1957), VI, 521-522.

[188] Antiochus waged war against Rome in 192-189. After a decisive defeat at the hands of the Roman forces at Magnesia (190), he paid a large indemnity, surrendering Asia Minor, which was divided between Rhodes and Pergamum. Langer, *An Encyclopaedia of World History*, p. 81.

run, he had sent his son, Antiochus—later called the Noble, though he was actually the lowest and most contemptible—to Rome as a hostage and pledge [I Macc. 1:10]. Now that the elder Antiochus [III] was dead, another of his sons, Seleucus [IV] Philopator, became king. But he was quite incompetent and, as Daniel [11:20] says, better fitted to be a constable or bailiff than a king. Actually, he accomplished nothing noble or honest, and soon died.

Thereupon Antiochus [IV] the Noble secretly escaped from Rome. Although he too was contemptible and the kingdom was not intended for him (as Daniel [11:21] says) he nevertheless sneaked in and made such a good pretense that by craftiness he became king. This is the last king about whom Daniel writes, that noble and pious child who did everything with stealth and craftiness, with lies and deceit, as befits not a king but a wanton scoundrel. His schemes were so boorish, crude, and impudent, that—as we shall see—he showed not the slightest interest in [maintaining] even the appearance of respectability and honor. It was primarily on account of this knave and wanton fellow that the vision [8:2-14] took place, as a solace for the Jews whom he was to plague with all sorts of misery.

Now when he had craftily taken over the kingdom, he proceeded with the same cunning to other things. Inasmuch as the king of Egypt, Ptolemy [VI] Philometor, the son of his sister [Cleopatra], was still too young, Antiochus made a pretense of being a faithful guardian of his nephew; he took over the cities in Syria, Phoenicia, and Judea. When the Egyptian prefects demanded them back, Antiochus refused to withdraw. Then the conflict broke out, of which Daniel here [11:21-22] says that he shall overwhelm like a flood the Egyptian armies (that is, the prefects and picked troops of Philometor); for Antiochus won the victory.

Not satisfied with that coup, he schemed underhandedly to take over the whole land of Egypt as well. He made an alliance with Philometor's chief officers and pretended that he was doing everything as a faithful guardian in the best interests of the nephew. By means of such deceit (as Daniel here [11:23-24] says) he came to Egypt with a small people; for the Egyptians opened all the gates to this dear kinsman. He seized the crown and made himself king of Egypt. By such deceitfulness he robbed, plundered, and despoiled the entire country (as the text here [11:24] declares), something

311

his forebears had never been able to do by force. And then he returned home.

Meanwhile, since King Philometor had now become of age and assumed the kingship, he was bent on recovering by force what actually belonged to him. The two kings thus began to arm against each other. But when that noble child, Antiochus, realized that Philometor had probably grown too powerful for him, he resorted again to his innate virtue and used money to arrange treason. Philometor's own people defected to the enemy, and in the ensuing struggle many fell down slain. Yet Antiochus did not succeed in capturing the country. So he made peace once again with his kinsman. Eating and speaking with Philometor at the table, Antiochus expressed the desire to see Egypt once again; but nobody trusted him any more. As Daniel here [11:27] declares, each king was bent on the undoing of the other, under the guise of peace. Thus Antiochus returned home with great substance, and on the way he was admitted into Jerusalem by craftiness and deceit. He shamefully plundered the temple and the city as I Maccabees 1[:20-28] reports, and as Daniel says here [11:28] also: he shall set his heart against the holy covenant.

Some two years later, since his lies and skulduggery were no longer effective, Antiochus determined to take Egypt by force. He confronted his nephew no longer as a guardian but as an enemy. But as Daniel [11:29] declares, he was not to succeed as he had before. For the Romans—who had been designated as the guardians and protectors of Ptolemy Philometor by terms of his father's last will and testament—sent to Antiochus with an armed force an ambassador, Marcus Popilius, who gave him orders to get out of Egypt.[189] Artfully as ever, Antiochus tried to put the Romans off with smooth words, pretending that he simply wanted to take counsel with his relatives. Thereat Marcus Popilius, with the staff he carried in his hand, drew a circle in the sand—Antiochus was standing by the sea—and declared in the name of the Roman senate, "You do not leave this circle until you answer whether you want peace or war!" In disgrace Antiochus had to withdraw and thus returned home.

---

[189] Caius Popilius Laenas was the Roman ambassador who prevented Antiochus IV from attacking Egypt. Langer, *An Encyclopaedia of World History*, p. 89.

Retiring via Jerusalem, he vented his wrath on the temple, the worship, and the people. For he had no other outlet for his defiance than against God and his kingdom. Many scoundrels among the Jews lent him a hand and joined his side, until God raised up against him Judas Maccabaeus and his brothers, as was indicated above in chapter 8,[190] and as Daniel here relates in the text [11:30-35].[191]

The twelfth chapter[192] of Daniel—as all teachers unanimously interpret it—under the name of Antiochus has to do wholly with the Antichrist and with these last times in which we are living.[193] For this reason we do not have to consult the histories any longer at this point. Rather it is the clear gospel which now indicates and discloses plainly to everyone just who the real Antiochus is. It identifies clearly him who has magnified himself above every god, who has not simply failed to regard the love of women—that is, the estate of marriage—but actually forbidden it, in its place filling the world with the idolatrous worship of his own god and with carnal unchastity, and who has parceled out the treasures and possessions upon earth, etc. [11:36-39]. For the love of women [*Frauenliebe*] does not mean here [11:37] fornication or impure love. It must mean that pure and honorable love of women [*liebe zu Weibern*] which God created and commanded, namely, married love, since the prophet here reckons among the foremost crimes of the Antichrist that he does not regard the love of women. We shall also drop the matter at this point, for only in experience can this chapter be understood and Antiochus spiritually discerned; and as he says [12:2] the resurrection of the dead and the true redemption shall follow immediately thereafter.[194]

From this book we see what a splendid, great man Daniel was

---

[190] See pp. 300-303.
[191] At this point *EA* 41, 285-294—presumably following the arrangement given in the 1541 complete edition of Luther's Bible—breaks off the 1530 preface to insert Luther's German translation of the book of Daniel. That translation is then followed in *EA* 41, 294-321 by the 1541 antipapistic commentary on Daniel 12 (see p. 294, n. 142), of which we here give next only the first paragraph since it alone was originally a part of the earlier 1530 preface. The original German text of this paragraph is to found in *EA* 41, 294, including n. 3.
[192] See p. 303, n. 162.
[193] See p. 294, n. 142.
[194] The concluding paragraphs which follow were appended to the extended commentary on Daniel 12 in Luther's 1541 Bible, but are included here—based on the text in *EA* 41, 321-324—because they were originally a part of his earlier 1530 preface. See p. 294, n. 142.

in the sight of both God and the world. First in the sight of God, he above all other prophets had this special prophecy to give. That is, he not only prophesies of Christ, like the others, but also reckons, determines, and fixes with certainty the times and years. Moreover he arranges the kingdoms with their doings so precisely and well, in the right succession down to the fixed time of Christ, that one cannot miss the coming of Christ unless one does it wilfully, as do the Jews. In addition, from that point on until the Last Day, Daniel also depicts the condition and state of the Roman Empire and the affairs of the world in such an ordered way that one cannot miss the Last Day or have it come upon him unawares, unless one does this too wilfully, as our Epicureans[195] are doing just now.

Therefore it seems to me that St. Peter had Daniel especially in mind when he says in I Peter 1[:11], "The prophets searched what, and what manner of time the Spirit of Christ did signify," etc. The "what" means that he definitely reckons and determines the time, how long and how many years it was to be until then. The "what manner" means that he depicts well how things are to be in the world at that time, who is to exercise supreme rule, or where the empire is to be. Thus Daniel proclaims not only the time but also the activity, shape, and nature of that time. And this strengthens our Christian faith immeasurably and makes us sure and firm in our consciences. For we see in operation before our very eyes that which he described and depicted for us so plainly and correctly in his book so long ago.

For Daniel freely prophesies and plainly declares that the coming of Christ and the beginning of his kingdom (that is, Christ's baptism and preaching ministry) is to happen five hundred and ten years after King Cyrus (Daniel 9),[196]—when the empire of the Persians and of the Greeks is at an end, and the Roman Empire in force (Daniel 7 and 9)[197]—and that therefore Christ assuredly had to come at the time of the Roman Empire, when it was at its height, the empire which was also to destroy Jerusalem and the Temple, since after Rome there is to be no other empire but only the end of the world as Daniel 2 and 7[198] clearly state.

[195] See p. 392, n. 40.
[196] Cf. pp. 303-305.
[197] Cf. pp. 299-300, 303-305.
[198] Cf. pp. 295-297, 299-300.

In the sight of the world, too, Daniel was a splendid and great man. For we see here that he rules the first two kingdoms[199] as their chief prefect. It is as though God were to say, "I must provide leaders [Leute] for these kingdoms, even if I have to let my Jerusalem and my people be destroyed in order to do so." Though Daniel was never a king, and never had great wealth or honor out of it, nevertheless, he did possess and perform the functions, duties, and offices of a king. That is the way the world operates: those who work most about the place have the least, and those who do nothing get the most; in the words of the gospel saying, "One sows and another reaps" (John 4[:37]). Indeed, what is worse, he had to take hatred, envy, perils, and persecution as his reward for it all, for that is the reward with which the world is accustomed to repay all services and benefits.

However this does not hurt Daniel. He is the dearer to God because of it, and God rewards him all the more bountifully, looking upon Daniel as king in Babylon and Persia. For God reckons and judges according to the deed and fruit, not according to the person and name. Daniel is therefore, in deed the true king of Babylon and Persia, even though he lacks the royal person and name, and gets out of it no wealth but only unhappiness and all kinds of peril. Behold how God is able to console and to honor his captive Jews, by taking the son of a townsman from destroyed Jerusalem and making him a twofold emperor, in Babylon and Persia. In short, among all the children of Abraham, none was so highly exalted in the world as Daniel. Joseph was indeed great in Egypt with King Pharaoh. David and Solomon were great in Israel. But they were all little kings and lords compared with the kings of Babylon and Persia; and it was among these that Daniel was the chief ruler. He miraculously converted them to God, and doubtless produced great fruit among the people in both empires; through him they came to a knowledge of God and were saved. This is well indicated by the documents and decrees of these emperors that the God of Daniel was to be honored in every land (Daniel 2 and 6).[200]

This Daniel we commend to the reading of all good Christians, to whom he is comforting and useful in these wretched, last times.

---

[199] The four kingdoms of Daniel 2 are interpreted on pp. 295-297.
[200] Cf. pp. 295-297, 298-299.

But to the wicked he is of no use, as he himself says at the end [12:10], "The wicked shall remain wicked and shall not understand." For the prophecies of Daniel, and others like them, are not written simply that men may know history and the tribulations that are to come, and thus satisfy their curiosity, as with a news report, but in order that the righteous shall be encouraged and made joyful, and strengthened in faith and hope and patience. For here the righteous see and hear that their misery shall have an end, that they are to be freed from sins, death, the devil, and all evil—a freedom for which they yearn—and be brought into heaven, to Christ, into his blessed, everlasting kingdom. This is how Christ too, in Luke 21[:28], comforts his own by means of the terrible news, saying, "When you shall see these things, look up and raise your heads, because your redemption is near," etc. For this reason we see that here too Daniel always ends all his visions and dreams, however terrible, with joy, namely, with Christ's kingdom and advent. It is on account of this advent, the last and most important thing, that these visions and dreams were given, interpreted, and written.

Whoever would read them with profit must not depend entirely on the histories or stick exclusively to history, but rather refresh and comfort his heart with the promised and certain advent of our Savior Jesus Christ, who is the blessed and joyful redemption from this vale of misery and wretchedness. To this may he help us, our dear Lord and Savior, to whom with the Father and the Holy Spirit be praise for ever and ever. Amen.

Preface to the Prophet Hosea[201]

1532

Hosea lived and preached, as he himself indicates in the title [1:1], at the time of the second and last Jeroboam, king of Israel. This was the same time in which Isaiah and also Amos and Micah were living in Judah;[202] but Hosea was the oldest of them.[203]

Jeroboam too was a fine and prosperous king who did much for the kingdom of Israel, as II Kings 14[:23-27] testifies. Nevertheless he persisted in the old idolatry of his ancestors, the kings of Israel. Thus although there were truly many fine men in the nation at that time, they still could not make the people righteous. For the devil had to inflict this misery on the people, that they always killed the prophets and sacrificed their children to the idols, and so filled the land with bloodguiltiness, because of which he here in chapter 1[:5] threatens Jezreel.

It appears, however, as though this prophecy of Hosea was not fully and entirely written, but that pieces and sayings were taken out of his preaching and brought together into a book. Nevertheless we can trace and discover in it this much at least, that he performed the two offices[204] fully and boldly. First he preached vigorously against the idolatry of his time and bravely rebuked the people, together with the king and his princes and priests. It was surely for this reason that he, like the others, tasted death. He had to die as a heretic against the priests and as a rebel against the king, for that is a prophetic and apostolic death, and in this way Christ himself had to die. Second he also prophesied powerfully and most comfortingly about Christ and his kingdom, as is shown particularly in chapters 2, 13, and 14.

But no one should think because he uses the words "harlot"

---

[201] Our translation of the prefaces to the Minor Prophets from Hosea to Malachi has been based on the text given in EA 63, 74-90, since the appropriate volume of the superior Weimar Edition (WA, DB 11ᴵᴵ) has unfortunately not yet been published.

[202] Cf. Hos. 1:1, Isa. 1:1, Amos 1:1, and Mic. 1:1.

[203] Actually the ministry of Amos probably began a number of years before that of Hosea, though they were contemporaries.

[204] See pp. 265-267 and pp. 275-276.

and "harlotry" many times, and in chapter 1[:2-3] takes a "wife of harlotry," that he was unchaste in words and deeds. For Hosea is speaking allegorically; this "wife of harlotry" is his lawfully wedded wife, and with her he begot legitimate children. The wife and children, however, had to bear those shameful names as a sign and rebuke to the idolatrous nation. For it was full of spiritual harlotry, that is, idolatry, as Hosea himself says in the text, "The land commits great harlotry by forsaking the Lord" [1:2]. In the same way Jeremiah wore the wooden yoke and carried the cup [Jer. 27:2; 25:17]. Indeed it was common for all the prophets to be doing some strange thing as a sign to the people. So here Hosea's wife and children had to have names of harlotry as a sign against the whoring, idolatrous nation. For it is incredible that God should order a prophet to practice harlotry, as some interpret this passage in Hosea to mean.[205]

Preface to the Prophet Joel

1532

Joel does not specify the time at which he lived and preached, but the ancients say that it was in the days of Hosea and Amos. We are satisfied with that and have no better suggestion.

Joel was a kindly and gentle man. He does not denounce and rebuke as do the other prophets, but pleads and laments; he tried with kind and friendly words to make the people righteous and to protect them from harm and misfortune. But it happened to him as to the other prophets: the people did not believe his words and held him to be a fool.

---

[205] Augustine (354-430), Cyril of Alexandria (d. 444), and Theodoret (ca. 393-458) held that the events described in Hosea 1–3 were actual and historical; their occurrence was both real and external. Thomas Aquinas (ca. 1225-1274) shared this view, explaining that the law of God was suspended in this special case because of the particular divine command involved. Jerome (ca. 342-420) and, according to Rufinus (ca. 345-410), the disciples of Origen (ca. 185-254) in Palestine and Egypt held the events to be real, but internal rather than external; the marriage took place in the spirit. Luther's view had few supporters before or after him, except for Calvin (1509-1564) who similarly regarded it as a parabolic presentation, a kind of theatrical performance, neither real nor external. E. W. Hengstenberg, *Christologie des Alten Testaments* (Berlin: Oehmigke, 1835), III, 14-19.

Nevertheless Joel is highly praised in the New Testament, for in Acts 2 St. Peter quotes him.[206] Thus Joel had to provide the first sermon ever preached in the Christian Church, the one on Pentecost at Jerusalem when the Holy Spirit was given [Acts 2:1-16]. St. Paul too makes glorious use of the saying, "Everyone who calls upon the name of the Lord will be saved" [Rom. 10:13], which is also in Joel 2[:32].

In the first chapter he prophesies the punishment which is to come upon the people of Israel. They are to be destroyed and carried away by the Assyrians; and he calls the Assyrians cutting, swarming, hopping, and destroying locusts [1:4]. For the Assyrians devoured the kingdom of Israel bit by bit until they had completely destroyed it. In the end, however, King Sennacherib had to suffer defeat before Jerusalem; Joel touches on that in chapter 2[:20] when he says, "I will remove the northerner far from you."

In the second place, at the end of the second chapter and from that point on [2:28-3:21] he prophesies of the kingdom of Christ, and of the Holy Spirit, and speaks of the everlasting Jerusalem.

He speaks of the valley of Jehoshaphat [3:12] and says that the Lord will summon all the nations thither for judgment. The ancient fathers understand that to refer to the Last Judgment. I do not condemn this interpretation, but hold, nevertheless, that this is really Joel's meaning: even as he calls the Christian Church the everlasting Jerusalem, so he calls it also the valley of Jehoshaphat. He does so because through the word all the world is summoned to the Christian Church and is there judged, and by the preaching is reproved as being all together sinners in the sight of God, as Christ says, "The Spirit of truth will reprove the world of sin" [John 16:8]. For valley of Jehoshaphat means valley of judgment.[207] Thus also does Hosea call the Christian Church the valley of Achor.[208]

---

[206] Acts 2:17-21 is a quotation from Joel 2:28-32.
[207] The name Jehoshaphat is built on the Hebrew root *shaphat* meaning to judge.
[208] Hos. 2:15. The Hebrew root *akar* means to trouble or disturb.

Preface to the Prophet Amos

1532

Amos [1:1] does specify his time: he lived and preached in the days of Hosea and Isaiah. He attacks the same vices and idolatry, or false sanctity, as does Hosea, and he also forewarns of the Assyrian captivity.

He is violent too, and denounces the people of Israel throughout almost the entire book until the end of the last chapter, where he prophesies of Christ and his kingdom and closes his book with that. No prophet, I think, has so little in the way of promises and so much in the way of denunciations and threats. He can well be called Amos, that is, "a burden," one who is hard to get along with and irritating,[209] particularly because he is a shepherd and not one of the order of prophets (as he himself says in chapter 7[:14]). Besides he comes out of the land of the tribe of Judah, from Tekoa, into the kingdom of Israel, and preaches there as a foreigner. It is for this reason that they say the priest Amaziah, whom he rebukes in chapter 7[:10-17], beat him to death with a club.[210]

In the first chapter Amos is difficult and obscure, where he speaks of three and four sins. Many have knocked themselves out over it, struggling with it at great length. But the text, I believe, shows clearly that these three and four sins are but one sin. For he always names and cites only one sin. Against Damascus, for example, he names only the sin that "they have threshed Gilead with iron chariots," etc. [1:3].

But Amos calls this sin "three and four" because the people do not repent of the sin or acknowledge it; rather they boast of it

---

[209] Derived from the Hebrew root *amas* meaning to lift or carry, the name Amos may possibly mean a burden-bearer; or it may perhaps be a shortened form of the Hebrew *amasyah* meaning the Lord has borne.

[210] A tradition deriving from the *Historia de prophetarum vita* which was long falsely ascribed to Epiphanius (*ca.* 315-403), bishop of Salamis, holds that Amos was beaten to death with a club by the son of Amaziah because of controversy over the two golden calves. See the text in *D. Epiphanii Episcopi Constantiae Cypri . . . continens . . . tomus siue sectiones ex toto septem* (Basel: *ex officina hervagiana*, 1578), p. 423. Cf. *The Jewish Encyclopedia*, I, 533, for a divergent tradition as well concerning the prophet's death.

and rely upon it as though it were a good deed, as false saints always do. For a sin cannot become more grave, great, or weighty than when it tries to be a holy and godly work, making the devil God and God the devil. So, too, three and four make seven, which is the completeness of numbers in the Scriptures, where one turns back and begins to count again, both the days and the weeks.[211]

Amos is quoted twice in the New Testament. The first time is in Acts 7[:42-43], where Stephen cites Amos 5[:25-27] against the Jews and shows by it that the Jews have never kept God's law from the time they first came out of Egypt. The second time is in Acts 15[:16-17], where St. James in the first council of the apostles quotes from the last chapter of Amos [9:11-12] as a proof of Christian liberty, that the Gentiles under the New Testament are not bound to keep the laws of Moses which the Jews themselves have never kept and could not keep, as St. Peter preaches in Acts 15[:10]. These are the two most important bits in Amos, and they are two very good bits.

Preface to the Prophet Obadiah

1532

Obadiah does not specify the time when he lived. However his prophecy applies to the time of the Babylonian captivity, for he comforts the people of Judah that they shall return to Zion.

His prophecy is directed especially against Edom, or Esau, which bore a special and everlasting hatred against the people of Israel and Judah, as usually happens when friends turn against each other; especially when brothers fall into hatred and hostility against each other, such hostility knows no measure.

So here the Edomites hated the Jewish people beyond all meas-

---

[211] Seven was a sacred number for many ancient peoples. Its importance for the Hebrews derived from God's own hallowing of the seventh day in the Creation (Gen. 2:3) and the laws concerning the sabbath (Exod. 20:8-11; Deut. 5:12-15). Certain festivals like the Passover (Exod. 12:15-19) lasted seven days. The date for the Feast of Weeks was set by counting seven weeks after the consecration of the harvest season (Deut. 16:9-10). The Feast of Tabernacles was held in the seventh month (Lev. 23:39). The sabbatical year was celebrated every seven years, and the year of jubilee every seven times seven years.

ure, and had no greater joy than to see the captivity of the Jews, boasting and mocking them in their misery and wretchedness. Almost all the prophets denounced the Edomites because of their hateful wickedness. Even Psalm 137[:7] complains of them and says, "Remember, O Lord, against the Edomites the day of Jerusalem, how they said, 'Rase it, rase it! Down to its foundations!'"

This hurts beyond measure when men mock and laugh at those who are wretched and troubled, defying them and boasting against them. It constitutes a great and strong assault [*Anfechtung*] upon their faith in God and a powerful incentive to despair and unbelief. Therefore God here appoints a special prophet against such vexatious mockers and tempters, and comforts those who are troubled, strengthening their faith with threats and denunciations against such hostile Edomites—those who mock the wretched—and with promises and assurances of future help and rescue. In such distress this is truly a needed comfort, and [the one who brings it] a veritable Obadiah.[212]

At the end he prophesies of Christ's kingdom, that it shall not be at Jerusalem only, but everywhere. For he mixes all the nations together, Ephraim, Benjamin, Gilead, the Philistines, the Canaanites, Zarephath. This cannot be understood to refer to the temporal kingdom of Israel, for according to the law of Moses these tribes and people had to remain separate and distinct in the land.

The Jews interpret Zarephath to mean France and Sepharad to mean Spain.[213] I dismiss that and believe none of it. On the contrary, I let Zarephath be a town near Sidon [I Kings 17:9; Luke 4:26] and Sepharad a town or district in Assyria where the captives from Jerusalem were. This is what the text plainly says, "And the exiles of Jerusalem who are in Sepharad" [20]. But let anyone believe about this what he chooses.

---

[212] From the Hebrew root *abad* meaning to serve, the name Obadiah means literally "servant of the Lord."

[213] The Targum Jonathan 4:6 and the Peshitta Syriac wrongly interpret Sepharad to mean Spain; hence the name "Sephardim" for the entire group of Spanish Jews. C. J. Ellicott (ed.), *An Old Testament Commentary* (New York: Dutton, n. d.), V, 479.

Preface to the Prophet Jonah[214]

1532

As Jerome indicates,[215] there are some[216] who contend that this prophet was the son of the widow at Zarephath near Sidon, who fed Elijah in the famine, as described in I Kings 17[:8-24] and Luke 4[:26]. The reason they give is that Jonah [1:1] here calls himself a son of Amittai, that is, a son of the True One, because his mother said to Elijah when he had raised him from the dead, "Now I know that the word of your mouth is true" [I Kings 17:24].

Let anyone believe this who will; I do not believe it. Jonah's father's name was Amittai,[217] in Latin *Verax*, in German *Wahrhaftig;* he was from Gath-hepher, a town in the land of the tribe of Zebulun, Joshua 19[:13]. For it is written in II Kings 14[:25], "King Jeroboam restored again the border of Israel from Hamath as far as the Sea of the Arabah, according to the word of the Lord, the God of Israel, which he spoke by his servant Jonah, the son of Amittai, the prophet of Gath-hepher." Moreover the widow at Zarephath was a Gentile, as Christ indicates in Luke 4[:25-26]. But Jonah here in chapter 1[:9] confesses that he is a Hebrew.

So we gather then that this Jonah lived at the time of King Jeroboam [II], the great grandson of King Jehu, at the time when

---

[214] In 1524-1526 Luther had lectured on the Minor Prophets. In 1526, intending to counterbalance his heavy preoccupation with polemics, he set about to prepare an exposition of Jonah, Habbakuk, and Zechariah. His first preface to Jonah—wholly different from the one given in the 1532 *Propheten alle deutsch* here translated—was written in that connection (see the text in WA 19, 185-187) in February of 1526. Hence the date of 1526 falsely ascribed to this later preface by *PE* 6, 429 (following *EA* 63, 80); *MA*³ 6, 441. Cf. p. 327, n. 226; p. 330, n. 235.

[215] In the prologue to his commentary on Jonah, Jerome writes that Hebrew tradition indentified this prophet with the son of the widow at Zarephath, the dead boy whom Elijah revived. It did so, he says, on the grounds of his mother's subsequent statement that "the word of the Lord in your mouth is truth": because Elijah spoke the truth, the one whom he revived is called "the son of truth," which is the meaning of the name Amittai. Migne 25, 1118.

[216] A Haggadic-midrashic work ascribed to Rabbi Eliezer, son of Hyrcanus, and composed in Italy shortly after 833, in chapter 33 on *Elisha and the Shunammite* says, "She [the widow of Zarephath] was the mother of Jonah." Gerald Friedlander (trans.), *Pirke de Rabbi Eliezer* (New York: Bloch, 1916), p. 240.

[217] From the Hebrew *emeth* meaning true, the name Amittai means truthful.

King Uzziah reigned in Judah. This was also the time at which the prophets Hosea, Amos, and Joel were living in the same kingdom of Israel in other places and towns. From this we can readily gather what a splendid and valuable man this Jonah was in the kingdom of Israel. God did great things through him, for it was through his preaching that King Jeroboam was so successful and won back all that Hazael, king of Syria, had taken from the kingdom of Israel [II Kings 10:32-33; 13:3, 7; 14:25].

But greater than all he did in his own nation were his attacks upon the great and mighty kingdom of Assyria and his fruitful preaching among the Gentiles; among them he accomplished more than could have been accomplished among his own people with many sermons. It was as though God willed to demonstrate by him the word of Isaiah, "He who has not heard, shall hear it,"[218] as an illustration of the fact that they who have the word richly despise it thoroughly, and they who cannot have it accept it gladly. Christ himself says, in Matthew 21[:43], "The kingdom of God will be taken away from you and given to the nations producing the fruits of it."

Preface to the Prophet Micah

1532

The prophet Micah lived at the time of Isaiah. Micah [4:1-3] even uses the words of Isaiah 2[:2-4], and thus one notes that these prophets who lived at the same time preached almost the very same word concerning Christ, as though they had consulted one another on the matter.

Micah is one of the fine prophets who rebukes the people severely for their idolatry and constantly refers to the coming Christ and to his kingdom. In one respect he is unique among the prophets, in that he points with certainty to Bethlehem, naming it as the town where Christ was to be born [5:2]. For this reason he was famous under the Old Covenant, as Matthew certainly shows in chapter 2[:3-6].

---

[218] Isa. 52:15; cf. the Vulgate.

In short he denounces, he prophesies, he preaches, etc. Ultimately, however, his meaning is that even though Israel and Judah have to go to pieces, Christ will yet come and make all things good. So, too, we now have to rebuke, denounce, comfort, and preach, etc., and then say, "Even though all be lost, Christ will yet come at the Last Day and help us out of all misfortune."

In the first chapter Micah is difficult, a fact to which the original Hebrew[219] contributes. He makes numerous plays on words, such as *Zaanan* for *shaanan,* and *Achzib* and *Mareshah,* etc.,[220] twisting the words to give them an ominous meaning. It is as if I were to say, "Rome, you shall become a *room* full of emptiness"; or, "Wittenberg, you shall become a *weiter Berg,*"[221] etc. The grammarians will surely notice this and also observe the pains we have taken.

---

[219] See p. 229.

[220] The meaning of Micah's cry of alarm in 1:10-16 has been obscured in transmission since copyists of the text failed to see that it involved a play on words in which the meaning of each town's name—in slightly modified form—was utilized to describe what would happen to that town. The play on the name Zaanan was probably in the word actually used in Micah 1:11 *yatsa* (to go forth)—the people of the town did not "come forth" for fear of the enemy—rather than in Luther's suggested *shaanan* (at ease or rest) which is phonetically closer. Certainly the play on Achzib was in the word immediately following it in Micah 1:14, *akzab* (lying or failing)—the town would be like a stream whose waters fail when they are most needed (cf. Jer. 15:18). And the play on Mareshah involved the word in Micah 1:15, *yarash* (to possess or occupy; cf. RSV), which Luther interprets in the sense of inherit (cf. KJV)—the first to inherit the town were the Israelites who dispossessed the Canaanites, the next heir or conqueror will be the enemy. Cf. C. F. Keil, *Biblischer Commentar über die Zwölf Kleinen Propheten* (3rd ed.; Leipzig: Dörffling and Franke, 1888), pp. 313-317. T. H. Robinson and F. Horst, *Die Zwölf Kleinen Propheten* ("Handbuch zum Alten Testament," Vol. XIV [2nd rev. ed.; Tübingen: J. C. B. Mohr, 1954]), pp. 132-133. G. W. Wade, *The Books of the Prophets Micah, Obadiah, Joel, and Jonah* (London: Methuen and Co., 1925), pp. 8-12.

[221] Wittenberg, the town where Luther lived most of his life as teacher and reformer, had derived its name from two Flemish words meaning "white mountain." The phonetically similar *weiter Berg* means a mountain far removed. Luther's pun might be approximated in English thus: "Radiant mountain, you shall become a remote mountain." The play on the words *Roma* and *Raum* in the same sentence is as apparent in English as in the original German.

Preface to the Prophet Nahum

1532

The prophet Nahum prophesies about the destruction that the Assyrians were to inflict upon the people of Israel and Judah, as it was then actually accomplished by Shalmaneser and Sennacherib. This destruction took place because of the people's great sins. It was limited, however, in that the righteous remnant were to be preserved, as Hezekiah and those like him then experienced.[222] Therefore it seems that Nahum came before Isaiah, or was at least his contemporary.

Next Nahum announces the destruction of the kingdom of Assyria, especially of Nineveh. While this city was very righteous in the time of Jonah,[223] it afterward became full of wickedness again, and greatly afflicted the captives of Israel. Therefore even Tobit announces the final ruin of Nineveh's wickedness, and says, "Its iniquity will bring it to destruction."[224] True to his name (for Nahum means *consolator*, or comforter,[225]) he comforts God's people, telling them that their enemies, the Assyrians, shall in turn be destroyed.

At the end of chapter 1[:15], he talks like Isaiah 52[:7] of the good preachers who proclaim peace and salvation on the mountains, and bids Judah joyfully to celebrate. Though that can be understood to refer to the time of Hezekiah, after Sennacherib, when Judah was rescued and survived against King Sennacherib, nevertheless, this is a general prophecy referring also to Christ. It declares that the good news and the joyous worship of God, taught and confirmed by God's word, shall remain in Judah. Thus he is, and is properly called, a real *Nahum*.

---

[222] Shalmaneser V, king of Assyria (*ca.* 728-722), commenced the siege which led to the capture of Samaria, capital of the Northern Kingdom, in 722 B.C. under his successor, Sargon II (II Kings 17:1-7; 18:9-12). Sennacherib, son of Sargon, conquered the neighbors of Judah and in 701 forced Hezekiah to pay tribute, but failed to capture Jerusalem (II Kings 18:13–19:36). Jerusalem fell in 586, not to the Assyrians, but to Nebuchadnezzar whose father had joined the Medes in destroying Nineveh, the Assyrian capital, in 612 and founded the Neo-Babylonian Empire (II Kings 24–25).

[223] Cf. pp. 323-324; Jonah 3:5-10.

[224] Tob. 14:13 (Vulgate).

[225] The name Nahum is from the Hebrew root *nacham* meaning to comfort.

Preface to the Prophet Habakkuk[226]

1526

This Habakkuk is a prophet of comfort, who is to strengthen and support the people, to prevent them from despairing of the coming of Christ, however strangely things may go. This is why he uses every device and stratagem that can serve to keep strong in their hearts the faith in the promised Christ. His message is as follows.

It is indeed true that because of the people's sins the lands shall have to be destroyed by the king of Babylon. But Christ and his kingdom shall not fail to come on that account. On the contrary, the destroyer, the king of Babylon, shall have little good out of his conquest, for he too shall perish. For it is God's nature and work to help when there is need and to come in the midst of the proper season. As Habakkuk's song says, "In wrath he remembers mercy" [3:2]; or as the proverb puts it, "When the rope holds tightest, it breaks."[227]

In the same way we must support Christians with the word of God in anticipation of the Last Day, even though it appears that Christ is delaying long and will not come. For Christ himself says that he will come when men least expect it—when they are building and planting, buying and selling, eating and drinking, marrying and giving in marriage [Luke 17:27-28]—in order that at least some, though not all, can be preserved in faith. For in this matter preaching and believing are essential, as we see every day.

From all this we observe that Habakkuk lived before the Babylonian captivity, possibly in the time of Jeremiah; and the meaning and purpose of his writing is also easy to understand.

Some books say that Habakkuk brought food from the land of Judah to the prophet Daniel, when he lay in prison in Babylon.[228]

---

[226] Following his exposition of Jonah (cf. p. 323, n. 214), Luther had prepared and published in June of 1526 a translation of and a detailed commentary on the book of Habakkuk. Included in it was a rather extensive introduction—dealing in a general way with all the prophets—which ended with a few paragraphs specifically on Habakkuk, here given (following EA 63, 84-85) as they were retained intact in the 1532 Propheten alle deutsch. See the identical text in the 1526 Habakkuk commentary in WA 19, 353-354.

[227] Wander (ed.), Sprichwörter-Lexikon, IV, 911, "Strick," No. 39.

[228] Bel and Dragon 33-39. Cf. p. 354, n. 68.

However there is no evidence or basis for this. Besides it does not agree with the reckoning of time since, so far as Habakkuk's prophecy indicates, Habakkuk is older than Jeremiah—who lived through the destruction of Jerusalem of which Habakkuk had prophesied—but Daniel came after Jeremiah, and had already been living quite a while before he was thrown into prison.

Habakkuk certainly has a name appropriate to his office, for Habakkuk means an embracer, one who embraces another and takes him in his arms.[229] This is what he does in his prophecy: he embraces his people and takes them in his arms. That is, he comforts them and supports them, as one embraces a weeping child or person to quiet and compose him with the assurance that things will go better, if God so will.

Preface to the Prophet Zephaniah

1532

Zephaniah lived in the time of the prophet Jeremiah, for as the title [1:1] shows, he prophesied under King Josiah, as did Jeremiah. For that reason he prophesies the very same things as Jeremiah, namely, that Jerusalem and Judah shall be destroyed and the people carried away because of their wicked life, devoid of repentance.

Unlike Jeremiah, however, he does not name the king of Babylon as the one who is to inflict this destruction and captivity. He says simply that God will bring misfortune and affliction upon the people so that they may be moved to repentance. For none of the prophets was ever able even once to persuade this people that God was angry with them. They relied continually on the claim that they were, and were called, God's people; and whoever preached that God was angry with them had to be a false prophet and had to die, for they would not believe that God would leave his people. It was then as it is today: all who teach that the church errs and sins, and that God will punish her, are denounced as heretics and killed.

---

[229] Luther takes the name Habakkuk to be derived from the Hebrew root *chabaq* meaning to caress or embrace.

Now Zephaniah prophesies this disaster not only for Judah, but also for all the surrounding and neighboring lands, such as the Philistines, Moab, the Ethiopians, and Assyria. The king of Babylon is to be God's rod upon all lands.

In the third chapter Zephaniah prophesies gloriously and clearly of the happy and blessed kingdom of Christ, which shall be spread abroad in all the world. Although he is a minor prophet, he speaks more about Christ than many other major prophets, almost more than Jeremiah even. He does so in order to give the people abundant comfort, so that they would not despair of God because of their disastrous captivity in Babylon, as if God had cast them off forever, but rather be sure that after this punishment they would receive grace again and get the promised Savior, Christ, with his glorious kingdom.

Preface to the Prophet Haggai

1532

Haggai is the first prophet given to the people after the Babylonian captivity, and by his prophecy the temple and the worship of God were set up again. In addition Zechariah was later given to him as a companion for a period of two months,[230] so that by the mouth of two witnesses the word of God might the more surely be believed.[231] For the people had fallen into great doubt whether the temple would ever be rebuilt.

It is our opinion that Daniel is speaking of this prophet, where he says in chapter 9, "From the going forth of the commandment to restore and rebuild Jerusalem to the coming of Christ, the prince, there shall be seven weeks, and three score and two weeks,"[232] etc. For although a decree had gone out earlier from King Cyrus that the temple should be rebuilt at Jerusalem at his (the king's) expense, yet it was hindered until the time of Haggai and Zechariah. When God's commandment went out through their prophesying, then the work went ahead [Ezra 1:1-4; 4:4–6:15].

Haggai denounces the people, however, because they had given

---

[230] Cf. Hag. 1:1 and 2:10-23 with Zech. 1:1.
[231] Cf. Deut. 17:6; Matt. 18:16; II Cor. 13:1; *et al.*
[232] See p. 304, n. 166.

no thought to setting up the temple and the worship of God, but had feverishly grubbed and scraped only for their own property and houses. For this reason they were afflicted with famine and with loss of produce, wine, grain, and all sorts of crops. This was an example to all the godless, who pay no heed to God's word and worship and are always filling their own bags. It is to them alone that this text applies, when he says, "Their bag shall be full of holes" [1:6].

So we find in all the histories that when men will not support God's servants or help to maintain his word, he just lets them go and grub for themselves, and scrape incessantly. However in the end he punctures the bag full of holes; he blows into it so that it disintegrates and vanishes, and no one knows what has become of it. God intends to share their food or they'll not have any.

He prophesies also of Christ in chapter 2[:6-7], that he shall soon come as a "comfort of all nations," by which he indicates in a mystery that the kingdom and the laws of the Jews shall have an end, and the kingdoms of all the world shall be destroyed and become subject to Christ. This has already taken place, and continues to take place until the Last Day when it will all be fulfilled.

Preface to the Prophet Zechariah[233]

1532

This prophet lived after the Babylonian captivity. With his colleague, Haggai,[234] he helped to rebuild Jerusalem and the temple and to bring the scattered people together again, so that government and order might be set up in the land again. He is truly one of the most comforting of the prophets. He presents many lovely and reassuring visions, and gives many sweet and kindly words, in order to encourage and strengthen the troubled and scattered people to proceed with the building and the government despite the great

---

[233] Following his exposition of Jonah and Habakkuk (cf. p. 323, n. 214, and p. 327, n. 226), Luther prepared a translation of, preface to, and commentary on Zechariah, which was not finally completed and published until late in 1527 (see the text in WA 23, 485-664). The 1527 preface, however, was totally different from that provided in the 1532 Propheten alle deutsch, here translated according to the version given in EA 63, 88-89.
[234] See p. 329.

and varied resistance which they had till then encountered. He does this down to the fifth chapter.

In the fifth chapter, under the vision of the scroll and the bushel, he prophesies of the false teachers who are later to come among the Jewish people, and who will deny Christ; and this still applies to the Jews at the present day.

In the sixth chapter he prophesies of the gospel of Christ and the spiritual temple to be built in all the world, because the Jews denied him and would not have him.

In the seventh and eighth chapters a question arises which the prophet answers, encouraging and exhorting them once more to build the temple and organize the government. And with this he concludes the prophecy about the rebuilding in his time.

In the ninth chapter he proceeds to the coming times, and prophesies first in chapter ten [9:1-6] of how Alexander the Great[235] shall conquer Tyre, Sidon, and the Philistines, so that the whole world shall be opened to the coming gospel of Christ; and Zechariah [9:9] has the King Christ coming into Jerusalem on an ass.

In the eleventh chapter, however, he prophesies that Christ shall be sold by the Jews for thirty pieces of silver [11:12-13], for which cause Christ will leave them, so that Jerusalem will be destroyed and the Jews will be hardened in their error and dispersed. Thus the gospel and the kingdom of Christ will come to the Gentiles, after the sufferings of Christ, in which he, as the Shepherd, shall first be beaten, and the apostles, as the sheep, be scattered. For Christ had to suffer first and thus enter into his glory [Luke 24:26].

In the last chapter [14], when he has destroyed Jerusalem, he abolishes also the Levitical priesthood along with its organization and utensils and festivals, saying that all spiritual offices shall be held in common, for the worship and service of God, and shall not belong to the tribe of Levi only. That is, there shall be other priests, other festivals, other sacrifices, other worship, which other tribes could observe, indeed, even the Egyptians and all the Gentiles. Surely that is the outright abolition and removal of the Old Covenant.

---

[235] Alexander the Great, king of Macedonia 336-323, defeated Darius at the Battle of the Issus in southeastern Asia Minor in October of 333. Instead of pursuing the Persians to the east, he moved south in the direction of Egypt and within a year had taken all of Syria.

Preface to the Prophet Malachi

1532

The Hebrews believe that this Malachi was Ezra.[236] We let that pass, because we can know nothing certain about him except that, so far as we can gather from his prophecy, he lived not long before Christ's birth and was certainly the last prophet. For he says in chapter 2[3:1] that Christ the Lord shall come soon.[237]

He is a fine prophet, and his book contains beautiful sayings about Christ and the gospel. He calls it "a pure offering in all the world," for by the gospel the grace of God is praised, and that is the true pure thank-offering. Again he prophesies of the coming of John the Baptist, as Christ himself in Matthew 11[:10, 14] interprets that of which Malachi [3:1; 4:5] writes, calling John his messenger and Elijah.

Beyond that he also denounces his people severely because they do not give the priests their tithes and other services [3:8-10]. Even when they gave them, they did it faithlessly; sick and blemished sheep, for example, whatever they did not want themselves, had to be good enough for the poor priests and preachers [1:8-14]. This is the way it usually goes. Those who are true preachers of the word of God must suffer hunger and privation, while false teachers must always have their fill. To be sure, the priests too are denounced along with the offerings, because they accepted those offerings and sacrificed them. Such was the work of dear Sir Avarice.

But God here declares that he is greatly displeased with this.

---

[236] The Targumist Jonathan states on the basis of the spirit and contents of the prophecy that Ezra the scribe is the author of the book (James Martin [trans.], C. F. Keil's *The Twelve Minor Prophets* [Edinburgh: T. and T. Clark, 1874], II, 423). The Babylonian Talmud (*Megilla* 15a) adduces an old tradition, "Rabbi Yehoshua ben Korcha [first or second century A.D.] says Malachi is the same as Ezra; the sages say Ezra's name was Malachi," and adds that Rabbi Nahman finds the view illuminating from the standpoint of a comparison between Mal. 2:11 and Ezra 10:2.

[237] *Bald*, the word Luther used to translate the Hebrew *pithom*, can also mean unexpectedly or suddenly (cf. RSV); however in this context Luther is clearly following the false lead of Jerome's Vulgate (*statim*) by taking the word to mean immediately or presently (cf. Douay).

He calls such faithlessness and wickedness an offense against himself. On account of it God threatens to leave them and to take the Gentiles as his people.

Afterward he denounces the priests particularly because they falsified the word of God and taught it faithlessly and thereby deceived many [2:6-10] and because they abused their priestly office by not rebuking those who offered blemished things or were otherwise unrighteous, and by praising them instead and calling them righteous, just to gain contributions and profit from them. In this way avarice and concern for the belly have always injured the word and worship of God; they always turn preachers into hypocrites.

He denounces them also because they grieved [betrübten] their wives and despised them, and thereby defiled their own sacrifices and worship [2:13-16]. For the law of Moses forbade the offering of impure [betrübte]²³⁸ sacrifies to God; and those who were impure dared not sacrifice or eat of the sacrifice.²³⁹ This is what they brought about who grieved their wives and made them weep, and tried to justify their actions by the example of Abraham, who had to cast out and grieve his Hagar [Gen. 21:9-14]. However Abraham had not done this because of ill will, just as he had not taken Hagar to wife because of a whim [Gen. 16:1-4].

---

²³⁸ This last paragraph involves a play on the word *Betrüben*, which means both to trouble or afflict and to tarnish or polute. Grimm, *Deutsches Wörterbuch*, I, 1719-1720.

²³⁹ Cf. the laws of purification and the Holiness Code in Leviticus 11–15 and 17–22.

PREFACES TO THE APOCRYPHA

Translated by E. Theodore Bachmann

PREFACES TO THE APOCRYPHA[1]

Preface to the Book of Judith

1534[2]

If one could prove from established and reliable histories that the events in Judith really happened, it would be a noble and fine book, and should properly be in the Bible. Yet it hardly squares with the historical accounts of the Holy Scriptures, especially Jeremiah and Ezra. For these show how Jerusalem and the whole country were destroyed, and were thereafter laboriously rebuilt during the time of the monarchy of the Persians who occupied the land.

Against this the first chapter of Judith[3] claims that King Nebuchadnezzar of Babylon was the first one to set about conquering this territory; it creates the impression that these events took place before the captivity of the Jews, and before the rise of the Persian monarchy. Philo, on the contrary, says that they happened after the release and return of the Jews from Babylon under King Ahasuerus,[4] at which time the Jews had rebuilt neither the temple nor Jerusalem,

---

[1] These prefaces are here given in the order in which they were arranged in the complete Bible of 1534 where the title appears for the first time: "Apocrypha: these books are not held equal to the Scriptures but are useful and good to read." WA, DB 2, 547; cf. Ibid., p. 519. Earlier editions of the Pentateuch had contained a catalogue of Old Testament books listing all twenty-four of them (the last one of which included the twelve Minor Prophets) in the order in which they still appear in our English Bibles, and numbering them consecutively, after which were listed—without title or number—"Tobit, Judith, Baruch, Ezra, the Book of Wisdom, Wise Man, and Maccabees." WA, DB 8, 34. Actually Luther's translation of the Apocrypha was selective in that he omitted some of the books or portions that had been included in the Septuagint and the Vulgate. Our translation of these prefaces to the Apocrypha is based on the text given in EA 63, 91-108. See pp. 227-232 for the general introduction to all of Luther's biblical prefaces.

[2] On the date, cf. WA, DB 2, 547 and Reu, Luther's German Bible, p. 211, over against EA 63, 91.

[3] Cf., however, Jth. 4:3 and 5:19.

[4] Ahasuerus was the Cambyses of secular history, King of Persia 529-522 B.C.; cf. p. 299, n. 149.

337

and had no government. Thus as to both time and name, error and doubt are still present, so that I cannot reconcile [the accounts] at all.[5]

Some people think this is not an account of historical events [Geschichte] but rather a beautiful religious fiction [Gedicht] by a holy and ingenious man who wanted to sketch and depict therein the fortunes of the whole Jewish people and the victory God always miraculously granted them over all their enemies. This would be similar to the way Solomon in his Song poetizes and sings of a bride, yet means thereby not some specific person or event but the whole people of Israel. St. John, in his Apocalypse, and Daniel likewise sketch many pictures and beasts; yet these pertain not to specific persons but to the totality of Christian churches and [to the various] empires. And Christ our Lord himself likes to make use of parables and fictions like this in the gospel. He compares the kingdom of heaven to ten maidens [Matt. 25:1-13], or to a merchant and pearls [Matt. 13:45], a baker woman [Matt. 13:33], a grain of mustard seed [Matt. 13:31-32], or to fishermen and nets [Matt. 13:47-49], or to shepherds and sheep [Matt. 18:12-14], and the like.

Such an interpretation strikes my fancy, and I think that the poet deliberately and painstakingly inserted the errors of time and name in order to remind the reader that the book should be taken and understood as that kind of a sacred, religious, composition.

Now the names fit into this sort of an interpretation extraordinarily well. Judith means Judea,[6] (that is) the Jewish people. She is a chaste and holy widow; that is, God's people is always a forsaken widow who is nevertheless chaste and holy, remaining pure and holy in the Word of God and in the true faith, mortifying herself and praying. Holofernes means worldly leader or governor, a heathen, godless, or un-Christian lord or prince—as all enemies of

---

[5] The historical problems of the book—far more complicated than even Luther indicates, though he was among the first to recognize them—are well summarized in Robert H. Pfeiffer, History of New Testament Times, with an Introduction to the Apocrypha (New York: Harper, 1949), pp. 291-297.

[6] The Latin word Judaea used here can mean either a Jewish woman (Jewess) or the land of Judah. Luther uses it in the latter sense. The Hebrew Yehudith means simply "Jewess" and then by allegory the Jewish people. It should be noted, however, that it is the personal name of Esau's wife who was not a Jew but a Hittite (Gen. 26:34).

the Jewish people are. Bethulia (a city nobody knows[7]) means a virgin,[8] indicating that at that time the believing and devout Jews were the pure virgin, free from idolatry and unbelief, as described in Isaiah [37:22] and Jeremiah [14:17; 18:13; 31:4], which is also why they remained unconquerable, though they were in distress.

It may even be that in those days they dramatized literature like this, just as among us the Passion and other sacred stories are performed. In a common presentation or play they conceivably wanted to teach their people and youth to trust God, to be righteous, and to hope in God for all help and comfort, in every need, against all enemies, etc.

Therefore this is a fine, good, holy, useful book, well worth reading by us Christians. For the words spoken by the persons in it should be understood as though they were uttered in the Holy Spirit by a spiritual, holy poet or prophet who, in presenting such persons in his play, preaches to us through them. Next after Judith, therefore,[9] like a song following a play, belongs the Wisdom of Philo,[10] a work which denounces tyrants and praises the help which God bestows on his people. The song [that follows] may well be called an illustration of this book [of Judith].

---

[7] The location of the actual city intended by this allegorical name has never been determined, though the author undoubtedly had some well-known and important site in mind as the scene of the story's main action. Cf. Charles (ed.), *The Apocrypha and Pseudepigrapha of the Old Testament,* I (1913), 251. Cf. *The Jewish Encyclopedia,* III, 125. Robert H. Pfeiffer (*op. cit.,* p. 297, n. 15) concurs with C. C. Torrey in identifying Bethulia with Shechem.

[8] Luther connects the name of the city with the Hebrew *bethulah,* meaning virgin.

[9] Luther's ordering of the apocryphal books is his own. It does not follow the sequence in which they appeared either in the Vulgate or in the Septuagint where they were interspersed among the canonical books in positions which varied with the different manuscripts. In the older German Bibles, Judith had followed Tobit and preceded Esther; Wisdom had followed Song of Solomon and preceded Ecclesiasticus. Reu, *Luther's German Bible,* p. 36.

[10] The Wisdom of Solomon. Cf. p. 341, n. 17.

Preface to the Wisdom of Solomon[11]

1529

[Because the present meeting of the Diet at Spires[12] has separated us, so that we who had intended to translate the prophets completely could not all get together—and because, hindered by an unexpected weakness, I was unfit to attend to these and other matters, yet did not want to sit here altogether idle—I have in the meanwhile picked up this little block of wood, the book of Wisdom, and begun whittling away. With the help of my good friends I have translated it and, insofar as God has granted it, we have brought it out of its Latin and Greek[13] obscurity into the German daylight. Even though others have translated it before,[14] I think their German will just have to stand comparison with ours; indeed, it may even need ours.]

For a long time this book has stood in the cross fire of controversy as to whether or not it should be included among the

---

[11] The opening paragraph, here set in brackets, appeared in the 1529 edition of Wisdom but not in the 1545 Wittenberg edition of the entire Bible, on which this translation is otherwise based. *EA* 63, 93, n. 3. The 1529 edition also carried a subtitle: "To the Tyrants."

[12] At the Diet of Spires on April 19, 1529, the Lutheran princes presented the epoch-making "protest" by which they received the name their descendants still bear—Protestants. For the text of their "protest" see Reu, *The Augsburg Confession*, pp. 487-498, especially p. 487.

[13] The book was probably written originally in Greek. The Latin version antedates Jerome, and he did not revise it in preparing the Vulgate. Joseph Reider, *The Book of Wisdom* ("Dropsie College Edition of Jewish Apocryphal Literature" [New York: Harper, 1957]), pp. 6, 22-29; Charles, *op. cit.*, I, 520, 524-525.

[14] Numerous translators preceded Luther in rendering the Latin Vulgate Bible into German. There were four complete translations already in the fourteenth century. Cf. Reu, *Luther's German Bible*, p. 35. Between 1466 and 1521 a total of eighteen translations of the complete Bible, including the Apocrypha, appeared in German. Leo Jud's translation of the Apocrypha, which immediately preceded Luther's (*WA, DB* 2, xii), was published in 1530 in one of the "composite Bibles" of Wolf Köpphl at Strassburg. Luther's relation to the earlier German translators has been described as ranging from ignorance of their work to outright plagiarism. Neither charge is valid, but his own native ability to produce a living translation was undoubtedly sharpened by the example of other men's work. While individually undertaken, his task actually became a concerted effort, and his translation the product of concerted effort. Thus many improvements were made on the first edition of 1534 by means of Luther's *collegium biblicum*. Cf. Hauck (ed.), *Realencyklopädie für protestantische Theologie und Kirche*, III, 65, 70-73. On Luther's assistants in translating see pp. 188, 206, 229.

sacred Scriptures of the Old Testament, especially in view of the fact that the author suggests in chapter 9[:7] that throughout the book it is King Solomon speaking—he whose wisdom is also extolled in the Book of Kings [I Kings 4, 10].

The ancient church fathers,[15] however, excluded it outright from the sacred Scriptures. They believed it was made to appear like the work of King Solomon, so that the name and fame of such a renowned king would gain for the book greater attention and reputation among the mighty men on earth, for whom it was mainly written. Perhaps it would long since have disappeared had its author —if he were a man of small reputation—let it come out under his own name.

They contend, however, that Philo[16] is the author of this book.[17] Undoubtedly he was one of the most learned and wisest men the Jewish people have had since the prophets, as he demonstrated in other books and deeds of his.

For during the reign of the emperor, Caligula,[18] when the Jews were most disgracefully maligned in blasphemous pamphlets and abusive speeches by Apion[19] and others in Alexandria, and then were most poisonously denounced and accused before the emperor,

---

[15] Jerome, e.g., characterized the Wisdom as pseudepigraphical (making an unsubstantiated and false claim of authorship) in his Preface to the Books of Solomon in the Vulgate. Cf. Reider, op. cit., p. 1.

[16] Philo Judaeus (ca. 20 B.C.-A.D. 50) was a Hellenistic Jewish philosopher and exegete, of a prosperous priestly family in Alexandria. In A.D. 40 he led an embassy of five Jews, described in his Treatise on the Virtues and on the Office of Ambassadors: Addressed to Caius to plead with the Emperor Caius Caligula for the uninterrupted exercise of their religion, a privilege that had been suspended because the Jews refused to give the emperor divine homage.

[17] Jerome says that some of the ancient writers affirm the author to be Philo. However, Philonic authorship—and certainly Solomonic authorship—is rejected by modern scholars. Cf. Charles, op. cit., I, 525; also Reider, op. cit., pp. 15-18. The reference by Luther is also to certain commentators of the high Middle Ages, especially to the Parisian Franciscan scholar, Nicholas of Lyra (see p. 290, n. 128).

[18] Caligula, a great-grandson of Antony, was the third emperor of Rome (A.D. 37-41). Unbalanced and given to megalomania, he had himself worshiped as a god, but was foiled in a scheme to place his statue in the temple at Jerusalem by the legate of Syria, Petronius. He died by assassination.

[19] Apion, a contemporary of Philo, was a Greek grammarian and sophist of note. Probably because of his great reputation, he was chosen to head the delegation from Alexandria to the emperor Caligula, A.D. 40, bringing complaints of disloyalty against the Jews in that city. The Jewish historian, Josephus, wrote a belated rebuttal to his polemic against the Jews, Against Apion, which has preserved for posterity the most important account of anti-Semitism in Roman times.

it was this same Philo whom the Jewish people sent to the emperor to defend their cause and plead their case. When the emperor was so embittered against the Jews that he turned them away and would not even hear them,[20] then Philo—a man of courage and confidence— spoke up and said to his fellow Jews, "Well, then, dear brethren, do not be afraid but take heart; just because human help fails us, God's help will surely be with us!"[21]

In my estimation, this book must have come out of such a situation or cause. When the case and rights of Philo and the Jews could no longer gain a hearing before the emperor, Philo turned to God and threatened the mighty and the evil-tongued with God's judgment. This is also why the author speaks so vehemently in chapters 1[:6-11] and 2[:10-20] against the poisonous and evil tongues who on account of the truth persecute and destroy the righteous and innocent, and then goes on to cite the great example of the divine judgment which God meted out to Pharaoh and the Egyptians for the sake of the children of Israel [10:15-19; 18:5-19; 19:1-16]. He does this with such incisiveness and forcefulness as though he were eagerly seeking to make every word strike the emperor, the Romans, and the poisonous tongues of the Greeks who were raving against the Jews. Through powerful examples he would frighten off [the opponents] and comfort the Jews.

[Finally, when one considers the times, history, and writings of Philo and compares this book with them, then it appears so intensely Jewish, and corresponds so fully, that the holy fathers were not without considerable justification when they held Philo to be its author.][22]

Afterward, however, it came to be regarded by many as a genu-

---

[20] Caligula received the embassy, but only to insult them. They were obliged to follow at his heels while he interspersed orders to his gardeners with ribald remarks on the Jewish religion. *The Jewish Encyclopedia*, III, 515. See Philo's own account of their audience with the emperor in Philo's *Treatise on the Virtues and on the Office of Ambassadors: Addressed to Caius*. C. D. Yonge (trans.), *The Works of Philo Judaeus* (London: Bohn, 1855), IV, 175-180.

[21] Cf. Flavius Josephus, *The Antiquities of the Jews*, XVIII, viii, 1, "So Philo, being thus affronted, went out and said to those Jews who were about him, that they should be of good courage, since Caius's words indeed showed anger at them, but in reality had already set God against himself." William Whiston (trans.), *The Life and Works of Flavius Josephus* (Philadelphia: Winston, 1957 [reprint of eighteenth century translation]), p. 550.

[22] This bracketed paragraph appeared in the 1529 edition of Wisdom, but not in the 1545 edition of the Bible. *EA* 63, 95, n. 7.

ine book of sacred Scripture. This has been particularly true in the Roman Church, which has esteemed it so highly that there is hardly another book of Scripture about which so much fuss[23] has been made. Perhaps it is because in this book tyrants are explicitly attacked and condemned so sharply, while saints and martyrs are so superbly consoled. In Rome, where Christians were persecuted and martyred more than anywhere else in the world, this book has been stressed most of all, as the one that perfectly fit the case with its threats against the tyrants and comfort for the saints. Of course there were many passages they did not understand, but simply dragged in by the hair, as has often happened also to the whole of sacred Scripture, and still happens daily.

Be that as it may, there are many good things in this book, and it is well worth reading. Especially the great lords, who take it out on their subjects and who, on account of God's Word, rage against the innocent, should read this book. For [the author] addresses himself to them in chapter 6[:1-2] and affirms that the book is written for them, saying, "To you, O tyrants, my words are directed," etc. [6:9]. And he testifies very well that the worldly overlords have their power from God and are really God's agents [6:3], yet warns them against using such a divincly entrusted office tyrannically [6:4-6].

This book is timely for our day, because tyrants are now cocksurely abusing their authority against him from whom they have it. And they are living just as disgracefully in their idolatry and un-Christian holiness as the Romans and heathen, whom Philo here describes, [lived] in their own idolatry. So in every respect it really fits our present times.

It is called the Wisdom of Solomon because (as has been pointed out) it was brought forth under his name and character; and it exalts wisdom quite royally, namely, for what it is, what it can accomplish, and from whence it comes [6:22]. It pleases me beyond measure that the author here extols the Word of God so highly, and ascribes to the Word all the wonders God has performed, both on enemies and in his saints.

From this it can be clearly seen that what the author here calls

---

[23] In *EA* 63, 95, n. e, Luther's *viel Gesanges* is said to mean *viel Kirchengesang*. But Luther apparently had a more figurative meaning in mind. Cf. Grimm, *Deutsches Wörterbuch*, IV, 3798.

wisdom is not the clever or lofty thoughts of pagan teachers and human reason, but the holy and divine Word. Mark well that whatever praise and glory you hear ascribed herein to wisdom is said of nothing other than the Word of God. For even [the author] himself says, in chapter 16[:12], that the children of Israel were not sustained by manna, nor saved by the bronze serpent, but by the Word of God. Just as in Matthew 4[:4] Christ says, "Man shall not live by bread alone," etc. This is why [the author] teaches that wisdom comes from nowhere else than from God, and brings many illustrations from Scripture.[24] So he ascribes to wisdom what Scripture ascribes to the Word of God.

Because one commonly understands the word "wisdom" in a sense different from that in which it is used in Scripture, I have spoken all the more readily about this matter. When one hears mention of the word, one usually jumps at conclusions and imagines that the reference is to nothing but thoughts lying hidden in the hearts of wise people; at the same time one does not regard the external Word or Scripture as wisdom, even though all human thoughts without the Word of God are lies and false dreams. To refer to this book as the Wisdom of Solomon is as much as to call it: A Book of Solomon about the Word of God. So the spirit of wisdom is nothing other than faith, our understanding of that same Word; this, however, the Holy Spirit imparts.[25] Such faith or spirit can do all things, and does do all things, as this book glories in chapter 7[:27].

Finally, this book is a proper exposition and illustration of the first commandment. For here you see that the author throughout is teaching you to fear and trust God; he terrifies with examples of divine wrath those who are not afraid and who despise God, and he comforts with examples of divine grace those who believe and trust him. All of this is simply a correct understanding of the first commandment.

From this one can also see that all wisdom wells up and flows forth from the first commandment, as from a central spring. Indeed this same commandment is the true sun by which all wise men see what they see. For whoever fears and believes God is full of wisdom, master of all the world, mighty over all words and deeds, judge of

---

[24] E.g., Wisd. of Sol. 10:1—11:1.
[25] Cf. Wisd. of Sol. 7:7.

all such teaching and living as are valid and worthful in the sight of God. Again, whoever does not have the first commandment, and neither fears nor trusts God, he is full of foolishness; he can do nothing and is nothing. This is the foremost reason why it is well to read this book: that one may learn to fear and trust God. To that end may he graciously help us. Amen.

Preface to the Book of Tobit

1534[26]

What was said about the book of Judith may also be said about this book of Tobit.[27] If the events really happened, then it is a fine and holy history. But if they are all made up, then it is indeed a very beautiful, wholesome, and useful fiction or drama by a gifted poet. It may even be assumed that beautiful compositions and plays like this were common among the Jews. On their festivals and sabbaths they steeped themselves in them; and through them, especially in times of peace and good government, they liked to instill God's Word and work into their young people. For they had outstanding people—prophets, bards, poets, and the like—who in all sorts of ways diligently set forth the Word of God.

It may even be that the Greeks picked up from the Jews their art of presenting comedies and tragedies, as well as a lot of other wisdom and worship, etc.[28] For Judith presents a good, serious, heroic tragedy, and Tobit presents a fine, delightful, devout comedy. The book of Judith shows how a land and people may often fare miserably, and how the tyrants who rave proudly in the beginning end in disgraceful ruin. Similarly, the book of Tobit shows how things may go badly with a pious peasant or townsman, and there may be much suffering in married life, yet God always graciously helps and finally crowns the outcome with joy, in order that married

---

[26] On the date cf. WA, DB 2, 547 and Reu, *Luther's German Bible*, p. 211, over against *EA* 63, 98.
[27] Cf. pp. 337-339.
[28] It was widely assumed in Hellenistic Judaism, as the writings of Philo demonstrate, that in significant respects Greek culture was dependent upon Jewish traditions. Arnold E. Berger, *Luthers Werke* (Leipzig: Bibliographisches Institut [n. d.]), III, 251, n. 4.

folk should learn to have patience and, in a genuine fear of God and firm faith, put up gladly with all sorts of hardships because they have hope.[29]

Now the Greek version[30] almost looks as though it had been a play. For Tobit [1:1–3:6] speaks of everything in the first person, just as characters in a drama customarily do. Afterward some writer came along and cast the drama in the form of a regular discourse. The names also bear this out very well. For Tobit signifies a righteous man; and he begets another "Tobit."[31] He has to live in peril and anxiety because of both the tyrants and his own neighbors. In addition (that no misfortune should be alone[32]), he becomes blind. Finally, he falls out with his dear wife Anna, sends their son away, and life becomes miserable. But Tobit remains steadfast in faith, patience, and good works. Anna signifies amiable,[33] that is, a dear housewife who lives in love and friendship with her husband. The demon Asmodeus signifies destroyer or spoiler,[34] that is, the domestic demon[35] who obstructs and spoils everything, so that one can no longer get along with the children or the rest of the household. Sarah means a champion or victor, one who wins, comes out on top, triumphs.[36] The archangel Raphael, i.e., physician or healer,[37] is here also and calls himself Azarias, i.e., helper or aid, son of the

---

[29] *Auf künftig Hoffnung.*
[30] The story was probably written originally in Aramaic, but survived in Greek texts based on older Hebrew versions. Cf. Frank Zimmermann, *The Book of Tobit* ("Dropsie College Edition of Jewish Apocryphal Literature" [New York: Harper, 1958]), pp. 139-149.
[31] *Tobias* is the Greek form of the Hebrew *Tobiyyahu* or *Tobiyyah* and means "the Lord is my good." Luther, following the Vulgate, uses the single name Tobias for both father and son. The RSV, following the Septuagint, spells the two names differently: Tobit for the father and Tobias for the son.
[32] Cf. Wander (ed.), *Sprichwörter-Lexikon,* V, 1783, "Welcome, misfortune, if you come alone."
[33] This Greek name is from the Hebrew *channah* (Hannah) which is based on the root *chen* meaning grace or favor. Cf. p. 222, n. 44.
[34] Asmodeus, according to many scholars, is to be derived from the Persian *Aeshma daeva;* others, however, take it as Hebraic, being derived from the root *shamad* meaning to destroy. Cf. Zimmermann, *op. cit.,* p. 63.
[35] *Hausteufel,* in contrast to the *Hausfrau* (housewife) just described, commonly meant the bad wife—though it could also refer to the husband—who disrupts the peace and harmony of the home. Cf. Grimm, *Deutsches Wörterbuch,* IV, 692.
[36] The Hebrew word *sarah* means "princess," corresponding to the masculine *sar,* "prince" or "leader." The meaning of the root is uncertain.
[37] Literally "God has healed," the name Raphael is from the Hebrew root *rapha* meaning to heal.

great Azarias,[38] in other words an aid, emissary, or messenger of the Most High God.[39] For God helps keep the home, and stands by married folk; else they would never have a chance against Asmodeus.

Therefore this book is useful and good for us Christians to read. It is the work of a fine Hebrew author who deals not with trivial but important issues, and whose writing and concerns are extraordinarily Christian. It is appropriate that the book of Jesus Sirach[40] should follow a work such as this.[41] For this next book is for the common man and housefather a true teacher and comforter in all things. And Tobit is an illustration of just such a book.

Preface to the Book of Jesus Sirach

1533[42]

This book has heretofore carried the Latin title, *Ecclesiasticus*,[43] which has been understood in German to mean "spiritual discipline." Through reading, singing, and preaching it has been extensively used and inculcated in the churches, yet with little understanding or profit except to exalt the estate of the clergy and the pomp of the churches.

Its real name is otherwise Jesus Sirach, after its author as its own prologue[44] and the Greek [50:27] indicate. This is how the books of Moses, Joshua, Isaiah, and all the prophets are named, after their authors. Yet the ancient fathers did not include this one among the books of sacred Scripture, but simply regarded it as the fine work of a wise man. And we shall let it go at that.

---

[38] Cf. Tob. 5:12: Ananias.

[39] Literally "the Lord has helped," the name Azariah (in Greek form, Azarias) is from the Hebrew root *azar* meaning to help.

[40] Ecclesiasticus.

[41] Cf. p. 339, n. 9.

[42] On the date cf. *WA*, DB 2, 528 and Reu, *Luther's German Bible*, p. 211, over against *EA* 63, 100.

[43] The Latin version carried this title even in the Vulgate, possibly because among the *libri ecclesiastici*—books not regarded as canonical but read nonetheless for edification in the churches—this one was the "church book" par excellence, possibly because the book itself was patterned after one of similar title, Ecclesiastes. W. O. E. Oesterley, *An Introduction to the Books of the Apocrypha* (London: S. P. C. K., 1935), pp. 224-225.

[44] In the Greek prologue to his Greek version, the author's grandson states explicitly that his grandfather's name was Jesus.

Since [the translator] admits in the prologue that he came to Egypt in the reign of King Euergetes[45] and that he there completed this book (which his grandfather had originally begun), it seems to us that he has compiled the best from as many books as he could find. After all, there was a valuable library in Egypt which had been founded by the father of Euergetes, King Philadelphus.[46] Moreover in those days both books and learned men were held in high esteem; and, having come from all over, especially from Greece, they constituted one great school of learning [in Alexandria]. There, too, the Jews had built a temple and instituted divine worship.

That the book must be a compilation is suggested also by the fact that in it one part is not fitted neatly to the next, as in the work of a single author. Instead it draws on many books and authors and mixes them together, much as a bee sucks juices out of all sorts of flowers and mixes them. Moreover, as one may deduce from Philo, it appears that Jesus Sirach was descended from the royal line of David, and was either a nephew or grandson of Amos Sirach, the foremost prince in the house of Judah, living some two centuries before the birth of Christ, about the time of the Maccabees.

This is a useful book for the ordinary man. The author concentrates all his effort on helping a citizen or housefather to be God-fearing, devout, and wise; and on showing what the relationship of such a man should be to God, the Word of God, priests, parents, wife, children, his own body, his servants, possessions, neighbors, friends, enemies, government, and anyone else. So one might well call this a book on home discipline or on the virtues of a pious householder. This indeed is the proper "spiritual discipline," and should be recognized as such.

Should anyone like to know what labor it cost us to translate

---

[45] Luther interprets this as a reference to Ptolemy III (246-221 B.C.), who was called Euergetes (see the table on p. 307). Since his reign lasted only twenty-five years, however, most scholars interpret the prologue's mention of the "thirty-eighth year of the reign of Euergetes" as a reference to Ptolemy VII, also called Euergetes, whose reign lasted fifty-four years (170-145 B.C. as joint king with Ptolemy VI, 145-116 B.C. as sole king), which would give a date of *ca.* 180 B.C. for the original work of Jesus Sirach. Oesterley, *An Introduction to the Books of the Apocrypha,* pp. 225-229. Luther's translation of that same phrase from the prologue makes "thirty-eighth year" refer to the writer's age rather than the king's tenure in office. Cf. *EA* 63, 103.

[46] Ptolemy II (285-246 B.C.); see the table on p. 307; see also p. 308, n. 181.

this book,[47] let him compare our German with all the other versions, be they Greek, Latin, or German, old or new—the product will bear sufficient testimony concerning those who produced it.[48] In all languages so many wiseacres have gone at this book that—quite apart from its inherent lack of order from the very outset—one should not be surprised if it turned out completely unrecognizable, unintelligible, and in every respect worthless. But we have put it together again like a torn, trampled, and scattered letter, and washed off the mud; we have brought it into shape as anyone can see for himself. God be praised and thanked. Amen. Christians will not criticize us for this, but the world will; in keeping with its virtues, it will manage to thank us as it has always done.[49]

Preface to the Book of Baruch

1534[50]

Whoever the good Baruch may be, this book is very skimpy. It is hardly credible that the servant of St. Jeremiah, whose name is also Baruch[51] (and to whom this letter is attributed), should not be richer and loftier in spirit than this Baruch. Furthermore, the book's chronology does not agree with the [accepted] histories.[52] Thus I very nearly let it go with the third and fourth books of Esdras,[53]

---

[47] Cf. pp. 184-189.

[48] Cf. Wander (ed.), *Sprichwörter-Lexikon*, III, 579, "*Meister*," Nos. 15-17.

[49] *EA* reproduces here the prologue to Jesus Sirach as it appeared in the 1545 Wittenberg edition of the Bible. We have not translated it since it is readily accessible in various English versions, such as that of *The Apocrypha*, Revised Standard Version of the Old Testament (New York: Nelson, 1957), p. 110.

[50] On the date cf. *WA, DB* 2, 547 and Reu, *Luther's German Bible*, p. 211, over against *EA* 63, 103.

[51] Jer. 36:4. Many Greek and Latin fathers in the ancient church regarded Baruch as part of the writings of Jeremiah, and thus considered it authentic Scripture. Jerome, however, rejected its canonicity. Charles, *op. cit.*, I, 580.

[52] The historical discrepancies between Baruch and the canonical books, which point to a date of composition sometime after A.D. 70, are listed in Oesterley, *An Introduction to the Books of the Apocrypha*, pp. 258-260.

[53] According to the terminology of the Vulgate, which Luther is here using, I and II Esdras are called III and IV Esdras, while the canonical Ezra and Nehemiah are called I and II Esdras (Esdras being the Latin name for Ezra). Even the Council of Trent on April 8, 1546, excluded III and IV Esdras from the list of apocryphal books which it officially declared to be "sacred and canonical" Scripture for the Roman Catholic Church; it did not exclude Baruch. Cf. Luther's negative estimate of IV Esdras in his 1522 Preface to Revelation, p. 398.

books which we did not wish to translate into German because they contain nothing that one could not find better in Aesop[54] or in still slighter works. As to the Fourth Book of Esdras, St. Jerome says it contains vain fancies;[55] nor did Lyra[56] want to comment on it. Besides, it does not exist in Greek.[57]

Whoever is so inclined may and should translate them; only let him not include them among these [recognized] books. Baruch, however, we shall let run with the pack because he writes so vigorously against idolatry and sets forth the law of Moses.

Preface to the First Book of Maccabees

1533[58]

This is another book not to be found in the Hebrew Bible.[59] Yet its words and speech adhere to the same style as the other books of sacred Scripture. This book would not have been unworthy of a place among them, because it is very necessary and helpful for an understanding of chapter 11 of the prophet Daniel.[60] For the fulfilment of Daniel's prophecy in that chapter, about the abomination and misfortune which was going to befall the people of Israel, is here described—namely, Antiochus Epiphanes—and in much the same way that Daniel [11:29-35] speaks of it: a little help and great persecution by the Gentiles and by false Jews, which is what took place at the time of the Maccabees. This is why the book is good for us Christians to read and to know.

---

[54] Luther's high regard for Aesop's *Fables* led to his translating fourteen of them, also in the year 1530. Berger, *op. cit.*, III, 99-114. *WA* 50 (432), 440-460.

[55] See Jerome's preface to Ezra. Migne 28, 1403.

[56] In his monumental *Postillae perpetuae,* Nicholas of Lyra significantly avoided IV Esdras. Cf. p. 290, n. 128.

[57] Apart from some reminiscences and three direct quotations in early church writings, no traces of the Greek version of IV Esdras have been preserved. Oesterley, *An Introduction to the Books of the Apocrypha,* p. 159.

[58] On the date cf. *WA, DB* 2, 531, and Reu, *Luther's German Bible,* p. 211, over against *EA* 63, 104.

[59] Except for some parts of I Esdras, none of the Apocrypha mentioned by Luther is found in the Hebrew Bible. Except for II Esdras all of them are found, however, in the Septuagint, a Greek translation of the Hebrew Scriptures. Oesterley, *An Introduction to the Books of the Apocrypha,* p. 6.

[60] See Luther's interpretation of Daniel 11 in his Preface to Daniel in this volume, pp. 306-313.

In the first place, since Antiochus is regarded as a figure or image of the Antichrist who perpetrated the abomination and desolation of the worship of God in Jerusalem and in Judea not long before the birth and first coming of Christ, we learn from this to recognize the real Antichrist who is to devastate Christendom and destroy the worship of God [sometime] before the second and final coming of Christ. Therefore we should not be terrified when we experience such things and see them happening before our very eyes. Rather, be the chaos ever so great, and the devil as angry as he knows how, we should hold fast to this and take comfort in it, that we and all Christendom must nevertheless be sustained and finally saved.

For we too see the help, though small and slight, which God the Almighty has begun to grant us. The dear and holy gospel is the sword with which God's own can nevertheless valiantly attack the Antichrist of our day and actually accomplish something—even though it cost much suffering and bloodshed—just as God aided his people with the sword of the Maccabees in that day. Although it did not happen without persecution and great heartache, they nevertheless cleansed the temple, restored the worship of God [4:36-61], and brought the people together again under their former government. Today, in this same way, the gospel is sweeping out idolatry—as Christ says, that his angels will purge out of his kingdom all causes of offense [Matt. 13:41]—and is bringing the real Christians together again into the old true Christian faith and unto genuine good works and worship of God.

In the second place we should take heart that God helped those people not only against Antiochus and the Gentiles but also against the traitorous and disloyal Jews who had gone over to the Gentiles and were helping to persecute, kill, and torment their own people and brethren. We should be sure of [God's help] and remain unafraid even when false Christians and rabble-rousers—who have now become our betrayers—turn against us and plague and harm us as much as, if not more than, our Antiochus or Antichrist. For Daniel [11:32-34] has said it, and for our comfort proclaimed it, that things must happen this way; that the children of our people would deal treacherously with us and blithely help to persecute us. Therefore we shall not fare much better than those pious children

351

But the texts of Susanna, and of Bel, Habakkuk,[68] and the Dragon, seem like beautiful religious fictions, such as Judith and Tobit,[69] for their names indicate as much. For example, Susanna means a rose,[70] that is, a nice pious land and folk, or a group of poor people among the thorns; Daniel means a judge,[71] and so on. Be the story as it may, it can all be easily interpreted in terms of the state, the home, or the devout company of the faithful.

---

[68] The subordinate role of the prophet Habakkuk in Bel and the Dragon (verses 33-39), as well as the reference to him in the opening verse of the Septuagint text (Oesterley, *An Introduction to the Books of the Apocrypha*, p. 290) may have led to Luther's inclusion of the name in the title.

[69] Cf. pp. 337-339, 345.

[70] Susanna is a Greek adaptation of the Hebrew *shoshannah*, a lily or lily-like flower.

[71] Daniel is traditionally derived from the Hebrew word *din* meaning to judge, and so means "God is my judge."

PREFACES TO THE NEW TESTAMENT

Translated by Charles M. Jacobs
Revised by E. Theodore Bachmann

PREFACES TO THE
NEW TESTAMENT

Preface to the New Testament[1]

1546 (1522)

[It would be right and proper for this book to go forth without any prefaces or extraneous names attached and simply have its own say under its own name. However many unfounded [*wilde*] interpretations and prefaces[2] have scattered the thought of Christians to a point where no one any longer knows what is gospel or law, New Testament or Old. Necessity demands, therefore, that there should be a notice or preface, by which the ordinary man can be rescued from his former delusions, set on the right track, and taught what he is to look for in this book, so that he may not seek laws and commandments where he ought to be seeking the gospel and promises of God.

Therefore it should be known, in the first place, that the notion must be given up that there are four gospels and only four evangelists.[3] The division of the New Testament books into legal, historical, prophetic, and wisdom books is also to be utterly rejected. Some make this division,[4] thinking thereby (I know not how) to compare

---

[1] Prior to the 1534 edition of the complete Bible this preface—intended perhaps as a preface to the entire New Testament or at least to the first part of the New Testament including the gospels and Acts (see WA, DB 7, xxxi)—carried as a title the single word, "Preface." We have based our translation on the version which appeared in the 1546 edition of the complete Bible, noting significant variations from earlier versions, particularly from the first version as it appeared in the September Testament of 1522. WA, DB 6, 2-11. See pp. 227-232 for the general introduction to all of Luther's biblical prefaces.

[2] On the ancient practice of providing prefaces, see the Introduction, p. 231. On the prefaces which appeared in early printed German Bibles, including the text of that to the book of Romans in the Mentel Bible—the first printed Bible in High German published by Johann Mentel in Strassburg about 1466—see Reu, *Luther's German Bible*, pp. 35 and 305, n. 71.

[3] Limiting the number of gospels to four was an ancient practice going back at least to Jerome, who based his position on the existence of but four living creatures in Ezekiel 1 and Revelation 4—the man, lion, ox, and eagle. Migne 30, 531-534. WA, DB 6, 536, n. 2, 12. Cf. p. 360, n. 9.

[4] This division had been made, e.g., in the 1509 Vulgate printed at Basel, which Luther had probably used. WA, DB 6, 537, n. 2, 14.

357

the New with the Old Testament. On the contrary it is to be held firmly that]⁵

Just as the Old Testament is a book in which are written God's laws and commandments, together with the history of those who kept and of those who did not keep them,⁶ so the New Testament is a book in which are written the gospel and the promises of God, together with the history of those who believe and of those who do not believe them.⁷

For "gospel" [*Euangelium*] is a Greek word and means in Greek a good message, good tidings, good news, a good report, which one sings and tells with gladness. For example, when David overcame the great Goliath, there came among the Jewish people the good report and encouraging news that their terrible enemy had been struck down and that they had been rescued and given joy and peace; and they sang and danced and were glad for it [I Sam. 18:6].

Thus this gospel of God or New Testament is a good story and report, sounded forth into all the world by the apostles, telling of a true David who strove with sin, death, and the devil, and overcame them, and thereby rescued all those who were captive in sin, afflicted with death, and overpowered by the devil. Without any merit of their own he made them righteous, gave them life, and saved them, so that they were given peace and brought back to God. For this they sing, and thank and praise God, and are glad forever, if only they believe firmly and remain steadfast in faith.

This report and encouraging tidings, or evangelical and divine news, is also called a New Testament. For it is a testament when a dying man bequeaths his property, after his death, to his legally

---

⁵ The portions here set in brackets did not appear in any editions of the complete Bible, nor in editions of the New Testament after 1537. Divergences from the original 1522 text were due primarily to Luther's desire to accommodate the text of the New Testament prefaces to that of the Old Testament prefaces with which they were—in the 1534 complete Bible—to appear for the first time, rather than to criticism on the part of Emser or other opponents. That these divergences were not taken into account in the 1534-1537 separate editions of the New Testament was probably due to the carelessness of the printer, Luther having likely given no personal attention to these particular editions. WA, DB 6, 536.
⁶ Cf. p. 236.
⁷ The editions prior to the 1534 complete Bible here add, "Thus one may be sure that there is only one gospel, just as there is only one book—the New Testament—one faith, and one God who gives the promise" (Eph. 4:4-6).

defined heirs.[8] And Christ, before his death, commanded and ordained that his gospel be preached after his death in all the world [Luke 24:44-47]. Thereby he gave to all who believe, as their possession, everything that he had. This included: his life, in which he swallowed up death; his righteousness, by which he blotted out sin; and his salvation, with which he overcame everlasting damnation. A poor man, dead in sin and consigned to hell, can hear nothing more comforting than this precious and tender message about Christ; from the bottom of his heart he must laugh and be glad over it, if he believes it true.

Now to strengthen this faith, God has promised this gospel and testament in many ways, by the prophets in the Old Testament, as St. Paul says in Romans 1[:1], "I am set apart to preach the gospel of God which he promised beforehand through his prophets in the holy scriptures, concerning his Son, who was descended from David," etc.

To mention some of these places: God gave the first promise when he said to the serpent, in Genesis 3[:15], "I will put enmity between you and the woman, and between your seed and her seed; he shall bruise your head, and you shall bruise his heel." Christ is this woman's seed, who has bruised the devil's head, that is, sin, death, hell, and all his power. For without this seed, no man can escape sin, death, or hell.

Again, in Genesis 22[:18], God promised Abraham, "Through your descendant shall all the nations of the earth be blessed." Christ is that descendant of Abraham, says St. Paul in Galatians 3[:16]; he has blessed all the world, through the gospel [Gal. 3:8]. For where Christ is not, there is still the curse that fell upon Adam and his children when he had sinned, so that they all are necessarily guilty and subject to sin, death, and hell. Over against this curse, the gospel now blesses all the world by publicly announcing, "Whoever believes in this descendant of Abraham shall be blessed." That is, he shall be rid of sin, death, and hell, and shall remain righteous, alive, and saved forever, as Christ himself says in John 11[:26], "Whoever believes in me shall never die."

Again God made this promise to David in II Samuel 7[:12-14] when he said, "I will raise up your son after you, who shall build

---

[8] Cf. pp. 87-90.

a house for my name, and I will establish the throne of his kingdom forever. I will be his father, and he shall be my son," etc. This is the kingdom of Christ, of which the gospel speaks: an everlasting kingdom, a kingdom of life, salvation, and righteousness, where all those who believe enter in from out of the prison of sin and death.

There are many more such promises of the gospel in the other prophets as well, for example Micah 5[:2], "But you, O Bethlehem Ephrathah, who are little to be among the clans of Judah, from you shall come forth for me one who is to be ruler in Israel"; and again, Hosea 13[:14], "I shall ransom them from the power of hell and redeem them from death. O death, I will be your plague; O hell, I will be your destruction."

The gospel, then, is nothing but the preaching about Christ, Son of God and of David, true God and man, who by his death and resurrection has overcome for us the sin, death, and hell of all men who believe in him. Thus the gospel can be either a brief or a lengthy message; one person can write of it briefly, another at length. He writes of it at length, who writes about many words and works of Christ, as do the four evangelists. He writes of it briefly, however, who does not tell of Christ's works, but indicates briefly how by his death and resurrection he has overcome sin, death, and hell for those who believe in him, as do St. Peter and St. Paul.

See to it, therefore, that you do not make a Moses out of Christ, or a book of laws and doctrines out of the gospel, as has been done heretofore and as certain prefaces put it, even those of St. Jerome.[9] For the gospel does not expressly demand works of our own by which we become righteous and are saved; indeed it condemns such works. Rather the gospel demands faith in Christ: that he has overcome for us sin, death, and hell, and thus gives us righteousness, life, and salvation not through our works, but through his own works, death, and suffering, in order that we may avail ourselves of his death and victory as though we had done it ourselves.

To be sure, Christ in the gospel, and St. Peter and St. Paul besides, do give many commandments and doctrines, and expound the law. But these are to be counted like all Christ's other works and

---

[9] Each of the four gospels had its own preface in Jerome's Vulgate. Luther's concern for the "one gospel" kept him from ever writing four such separate prefaces. Indeed at the beginning it seems likely that he envisioned but one preface for the entire New Testament. WA, DB 6, 537, n. 8, 5; WA, DB 7, xxi. Cf. pp. 117-124.

good deeds. To know his works and the things that happened to him is not yet to know the true gospel, for you do not yet thereby know that he has overcome sin, death, and the devil. So, too, it is not yet knowledge of the gospel when you know these doctrines and commandments, but only when the voice comes that says, "Christ is your own, with his life, teaching, works, death, resurrection, and all that he is, has, does, and can do."

Thus we see also that he does not compel us but invites us kindly and says, "Blessed are the poor," etc. [Matt. 5:3]. And the apostles use the words, "I exhort," "I entreat," "I beg," so that one sees on every hand that the gospel is not a book of law, but really a preaching of the benefits of Christ, shown to us and given to us for our own possession, if we believe. But Moses, in his books, drives, compels, threatens, strikes, and rebukes terribly, for he is a lawgiver and driver.

Hence it comes that to a believer no law is given by which he becomes righteous before God, as St. Paul says in I Timothy 1[:9], because he is alive and righteous and saved by faith, and he needs nothing further except to prove his faith by works. Truly, if faith is there, he cannot hold back; he proves himself, breaks out into good works, confesses and teaches this gospel before the people, and stakes his life on it. Everything that he lives and does is directed to his neighbor's profit, in order to help him—not only to the attainment of this grace, but also in body, property, and honor. Seeing that Christ has done this for him, he thus follows Christ's example.

That is what Christ meant when at the last he gave no other commandment than love, by which men were to know who were his disciples [John 13:34-35] and true believers. For where works and love do not break forth, there faith is not right, the gospel does not yet take hold, and Christ is not rightly known. See, then, that you so approach the books of the New Testament as to learn to read them in this way.

[Which are the true and noblest books of the New Testament][10]
[From all this you can now judge all the books and decide among them which are the best. John's Gospel and St. Paul's epis-

---

[10] See p. 358, n. 5.

tles, especially that to the Romans, and St. Peter's first epistle are the true kernel and marrow of all the books. They ought properly to be the foremost books, and it would be advisable for every Christian to read them first and most, and by daily reading to make them as much his own as his daily bread. For in them you do not find many works and miracles of Christ described, but you do find depicted in masterly fashion how faith in Christ overcomes sin, death, and hell, and gives life, righteousness, and salvation. This is the real nature of the gospel, as you have heard.

If I had to do without one or the other—either the works or the preaching of Christ—I would rather do without the works than without his preaching. For the works do not help me, but his words give life, as he himself says [John 6:63]. Now John writes very little about the works of Christ, but very much about his preaching, while the other evangelists write much about his works and little about his preaching. Therefore John's Gospel is the one, fine, true, and chief gospel, and is far, far to be preferred over the other three and placed high above them. So, too, the epistles of St. Paul and St. Peter far surpass the other three gospels, Matthew, Mark, and Luke.

In a word St. John's Gospel and his first epistle, St. Paul's epistles, especially Romans, Galatians, and Ephesians, and St. Peter's first epistle are the books that show you Christ and teach you all that is necessary and salvatory for you to know, even if you were never to see or hear any other book or doctrine. Therefore St. James' epistle is really an epistle of straw,[11] compared to these others, for it has nothing of the nature of the gospel about it. But more of this in the other prefaces.][12]

---

[11] On the term "straw" cf. Luther's reference on p. 395 to I Cor. 3:12. Luther's sharp expression may have been in part a reaction against Karlstadt's excessive praise of the book of James. Cf. WA, DB 6, 537, n. 10, 6-34, and the literature there listed.

[12] See especially the Preface to James in this volume, pp. 395-398. Cf. also Luther's negative estimate of the book of James already in his 1520 Babylonian Captivity of the Church in LW 36, 118, and in his Resolutiones of 1519 in WA 2, 425.

Preface to the Acts of the Apostles[13]
1546 (1533)

Contrary to what has sometimes been the practice, this book should not be read or regarded as though St. Luke had written about the personal work or history of the apostles simply as an example of good works or good life. Even St. Augustine and many others have looked upon the fact that the apostles had all things in common with Christians [Acts 2:44-45; 4:32-37] as the best example which the book contains. Yet this practice did not last long and in time had to stop. Rather it should be noted that by this book St. Luke teaches the whole of Christendom, even to the end of the world, that the true and chief article of Christian doctrine is this: We must all be justified alone by faith in Jesus Christ, without any contribution from the law or help from our works.

This doctrine is the chief intention of the book and the author's principal reason for writing it. Therefore he emphasizes so powerfully not only the preaching of the apostles about faith in Christ, how both Gentiles and Jews must thereby be justified without any merits or works, but also the examples and the instances of this teaching, how the Gentiles as well as Jews were justified through the gospel alone, without the law.

As St. Peter testifies in chapters 10[:34-47] and 15[:7-11], in this matter God made no distinction between Jews and Gentiles; just as he gave the Holy Spirit through the gospel to the Gentiles who were living without the law, so he gave him to the Jews through the gospel, and not through the law or because of their own works

---

[13] In his 1522 Testament the opening preface (see p. 357, n. 1) was intended to apply to Acts as well as the four gospels. Luther first envisioned a separate preface in connection with his 1530 plan for a book on justification, a book which never reached the stage of publication (see the plan for that book, including many passages from Luke and Acts in support of Luther's fundamental teaching, in WA 30[II], 657-676). It was then he determined to provide a preface to Acts for his New Testament (see his 1530 outline for such a preface in WA, DB 4, 457). The resulting preface was written sometime between 1530 and 1533. It first appeared in the 1533 edition of the New Testament and was retained, essentially unchanged, in editions of the New Testament and of the entire Bible from 1534 on. Our translation is based on the version in the 1546 full Bible as it appears in WA, DB 6, 415-417.

and merits. Thus in this book St. Luke puts side by side both the doctrine about faith and the examples of faith.

Therefore this book might well be called a commentáry on the epistles of St. Paul. For what Paul teaches and insists upon with words and passages of Scripture, St. Luke here points out and proves with examples and instances to show that it has happened and must happen in the way St. Paul teaches, namely, that no law, no work justifies men, but only faith in Christ. Here, then, in this book you find a beautiful mirror in which you can see that this is true: *Sola*[14] *fides justificat,* "faith alone justifies." For all the examples and incidents contained in this book are sure and comforting testimonies to this doctrine; they neither deceive nor lie to you.

For consider how St. Paul himself was converted [Acts 9:1-19], and how the Gentile, Cornelius, was converted through St. Peter's word—the angel telling him beforehand that Peter would preach to him and that thereby he would be saved [Acts 10:1-8, 30-33]. Look at the proconsul Sergius [Acts 13:7] and at all the cities where Paul and Barnabas preached. Look at the first council of the apostles at Jerusalem, in chapter 15; look at all the preaching of SS. Peter, Paul, Stephen, and Philip. You will find that it all adds up to one thing: we must come into grace and be justified only through faith in Christ, without law and works.

By means of this book, used in this way, we can silence in a masterly and effective way the loquacity of opponents who [keep on] pointing us to the law and to our own works, and reveal their foolish unwisdom before all the world. Therefore St. Luke says too that these illustrations of faith amazed the pious Jews who had become believers, and that the unbelieving Jews became maddened and foolish over it. And this was no surprise, for they had been raised in the law and had been accustomed to it ever since Abraham. So it was bound to vex them that the Gentiles, who were without law and God, should be equal to themselves in God's grace.

But that our people [today]—we being all Gentiles—should slander and persecute this doctrine is ten times worse. For here we see, and cannot deny, that the grace of God and the knowledge of Christ came to our forebears without law and merit, indeed, [when they themselves lived] in horrible idolatry and blasphemy. But [the

---

14 Cf. pp. 185-189, 195-202.

papists] will gain no more by their slander and persecution than the Jews gained by their raging and raving. For he who of old threatened the Jews and had Moses intone, "I will provoke you with those who are not my people, and make you mad with an ignorant nation" [Deut. 32:21]; and who said in Hosea 2[:23], "I will call 'my people' those are not my people" (that is, who live without law and works), and then did what he said, even this very One threatens these slanderers of ours with the same warnings. And he will surely keep his word, as he has already begun to do. But [the papists] will not believe this until, like the Jews, they experience it. Amen.

Preface to the Epistle of St. Paul to the Romans[15]

1546 (1522)

This epistle is really the chief part of the New Testament, and is truly the purest gospel. It is worthy not only that every Christian should know it word for word, by heart, but also that he should occupy himself with it every day, as the daily bread of the soul. We can never read it or ponder over it too much; for the more we deal with it, the more precious it becomes and the better it tastes.

Therefore I too will do my best, so far as God has given me power, to open the way into it through this preface, so that it may

---

[15] For the second part of the New Testament—designated in the 1546 separate version of the New Testament as "The Epistles of Paul: to the Revelation of St. John"—Luther had apparently planned from the outset to provide separate prefaces. He postponed until just prior to publication of his September Testament of 1522 the composition of this most important Preface to the Epistle to the Romans, envisioning it as a recapitulation and continuation of that comprehensive preface to the gospels (see above pp. 357-362). Back of this famous preface, in which Luther sets forth the basic concepts of Paul's theology and of his own evangelical teaching, stands of course his thorough study of the epistle reflected in his 1515-1516 lectures on Romans (published in Latin by Johannes Ficker, *Vorlesung über den Römerbrief* [2nd ed.; Leipzig, 1923] and in German by Eduard Ellwein, MA³, Er 2 [München, 1957]), as well as the recently completed *Loci communes* of Melanchthon and the latter's Annotations on Romans for which Luther was the instigator and also provided the foreword. This was the preface which was being read in John Wesley's hearing when, by his own account, he felt his heart "strongly warmed" at the time of his conversion May 24, 1738. WA, DB 7, xxxi-xxxiv.

Our translation is based on the 1546 version appearing in the complete Bible of that year, as given in WA, DB 7, 3-27.

be the better understood by everyone. Heretofore it has been badly obscured by glosses[16] and all kinds of idle talk, though in itself it is a bright light, almost sufficient to illuminate the entire holy Scriptures.

To begin with we must have knowledge of its language and know what St. Paul means by the words: "law," "sin," "grace," "faith," "righteousness," "flesh," "spirit," and the like. Otherwise no reading of the book has any value.

The little word "law" you must here not take in human fashion as a teaching about what works are to be done or not done. That is the way with human laws; a law is fulfilled by works, even though there is no heart in the doing of them. But God judges according to what is in the depths of the heart. For this reason, his law too makes its demands on the inmost heart; it cannot be satisfied with works, but rather punishes as hypocrisy and lies the works not done from the bottom of the heart. Hence all men are called liars in Psalm 116[:11],[17] because no one keeps or can keep God's law from the bottom of the heart. For everyone finds in himself displeasure in what is good and pleasure in what is bad. If, now, there is no willing pleasure in the good, then the inmost heart is not set on the law of God. Then, too, there is surely sin, and God's wrath is deserved, even though outwardly there seem to be many good deeds and an honorable life.

Hence St. Paul concludes, in chapter 2[:13], that the Jews are all sinners, saying that only the doers of the law are righteous before God. He means by this that no one, in terms of his works, is a doer of the law. Rather, he speaks to them thus, "You teach one must not commit adultery, but you yourself commit adultery" [2:22]; and again, "In passing judgment upon another you condemn yourself, because you, the judge, are doing the very same things" [2:1]. This is as if to say, "You live a fine outward life in the works of the law, and you pass judgment on those who do not so live. You know how to teach everyone; you see the speck that is in the eye of

---

[16] For an alphabetical listing of commentaries on Romans, including a considerable number from periods prior to the Reformation, see William P. Dickinson (trans.), H. A. W. Meyer's *Critical and Exegetical Handbook to the Epistle to the Romans* (New York: Funk and Wagnalls, 1884), pp. xv-xxiii.

[17] Vulgate version, Ps. 115:11; cf. KJV.

another, but do not notice the log that is in your own eye" [Matt. 7:3].

For even though you keep the law outwardly, with works, from fear of punishment or love of reward, nevertheless you do all this unwillingly, without pleasure in and love for the law, but with reluctance and under compulsion. For if the law were not there, you would prefer to act otherwise. The conclusion is that from the bottom of your heart you hate the law. What point is there then in your teaching others not to steal, if you yourself are a thief at heart, and would gladly be one outwardly if you dared? Though, to be sure, the outward work does not lag far behind among such hypocrites! So you teach others, but not yourself; nor do you yourself know what you are teaching—you have never yet understood the law correctly. Moreover the law increases sin, as St. Paul says in chapter 5[:20], because the more the law demands of men what they cannot do, the more they hate the law.

For this reason he says, in chapter 7[:14], "The law is spiritual." What does that mean? If the law were for the body, it could be satisfied with works; but since it is spiritual, no one can satisfy it— unless all that you do is done from the bottom of your heart. But such a heart is given only by God's Spirit, who fashions a man after the law, so that he acquires a desire for the law in his heart, doing nothing henceforth out of fear and compulsion but out of a willing heart. The law is thus spiritual in that it will be loved and fulfilled with such a spiritual heart, and requires such a spirit. Where that spirit is not in the heart, there sin remains, also displeasure with the law and hostility toward it even though the law itself is good and just and holy.

Accustom yourself, then, to this language, that doing the works of the law and fulfilling the law are two very different things. The work of the law is everything that one does, or can do, toward keeping the law of his own free will or by his own powers. But since in the midst of all these works and along with them there remains in the heart a dislike of the law and compulsion with respect to it, these works are all wasted and have no value. That is what St. Paul means in chapter 3[:20], when he says, "By works of the law will no man be justified in God's sight." Hence you see that the wranglers and sophists practice deception when they teach men to pre-

pare themselves for grace by means of works.[18] How can a man prepare himself for good by means of works, if he does good works only
with aversion and unwillingness in his heart? How shall a work
please God if it proceeds from a reluctant and resisting heart?

To fulfil the law, however, is to do its works with pleasure and
love, to live a godly and good life of one's own accord, without the
compulsion of the law. This pleasure and love for the law is put
into the heart by the Holy Spirit, as St. Paul says in chapter 5[:5].
But the Holy Spirit is not given except in, with, and by faith in
Jesus Christ, as St. Paul says in the introduction. Faith, moreover,
comes only through God's Word or gospel, which preaches Christ,
saying that he is God's Son and a man, and has died and risen again
for our sakes, as he says in chapters 3[:25], 4[:25], and 10[:9].

So it happens that faith alone makes a person righteous and fulfils the law. For out of the merit of Christ it brings forth the Spirit.
And the Spirit makes the heart glad and free, as the law requires that

---

[18] Two elements dominate the scholastic conception of grace: infusion and merit.
By grace, Thomas (1225-1274) meant not God's love, favor, or forgiveness but
"a certain supernatural thing in man, coming into existence from God"—an infused condition, a supernatural ethical nature which makes man capable of
good. Man's free will is thereby moved to prepare itself for or dispose itself
toward further grace. Thomas always referred grace, and with it everything
good in man, back to the agency of God as Prime Mover. Despite his emphasis
on divine causality, however, his conception of grace as an infused substantial
gift required—in order that the personal element not be lost entirely—that the
personal agency of man and his free will be constantly brought to the fore. Thus
Bonaventura taught that the purpose of God's infusing of grace is to make the
sinner capable of merit; this merit can be attained, however, only through the
free will.

The scholastics distinguished between two kinds of merit: the merit of
worthiness (*meritum de condigno*—conduct insofar as it is purely a product of
grace, and is deserving of eternal life) and the merit of fitness (*meritum de
congruo*—conduct insofar as it results from the exercise of the free will, and
merits from God a reward commensurate with its particular excellence). In the
process of salvation God bestows initially a "grace gratuitously given." The resultant movements of the human will merit (congruously, by fitness) through
co-operation God's next gift of the "grace which makes acceptable." Again, the
resultant movements of the human will merit (condignly, by worthiness) through
co-operation the gift of eternal life.

Without grace, of course, no merit is possible. To the attainment of justification, however, man can nevertheless dispose or prepare himself by fitness. Thus
Gabriel Biel (*ca.* 1425-1492) says, "Good works morally performed without love
merit by fitness . . . the grace of justification." So the idea of merit was made
tolerable by the pious interpretation given to it in the appeal to prior grace;
while into the conception of infused grace there was introduced through the
scheme of merits that element which it otherwise lacked, namely, an element of
personal relationship to God. Cf. Seeberg, *History of Doctrines,* II, 118-123.

it shall be. Thus good works emerge from faith itself. That is what St. Paul means in chapter 3[:31]; after he has rejected the works of the law, it sounds as if he would overthrow the law by this faith. "No," he says, "we uphold the law by faith"; that is, we fulfil it by faith.

Sin, in the Scripture, means not only the outward works of the body but also all the activities that move men to do these works, namely, the inmost heart, with all its powers. Thus the little word "do"[19] ought to mean that a man falls all the way and lives in sin. Even outward works of sin do not take place, unless a man plunges into it completely with body and soul. And the Scriptures look especially into the heart and single out the root and source of all sin, which is unbelief in the inmost heart. As, therefore, faith alone makes a person righteous, and brings the Spirit and pleasure in good outward works, so unbelief alone commits sin, and brings forth the flesh and pleasure in bad outward works, as happened to Adam and Eve in paradise, Genesis 3.

Hence Christ calls unbelief the only sin, when he says in John 16[:8-9], "The Spirit will convince the world of sin . . . because they do not believe in me." For this reason too, before good or bad works take place, as the good or bad fruits, there must first be in the heart faith or unbelief. Unbelief is the root, the sap, and the chief power of all sin. For this reason, in the Scriptures it is called the serpent's head and the head of the old dragon, which the seed of the woman, Christ, must tread under foot, as was promised to Adam, Genesis 3[:15].

Between grace and gift there is this difference. Grace actually means God's favor, or the good will which in himself he bears toward us, by which he is disposed to give us Christ and to pour into us the Holy Spirit with his gifts. This is clear from chapter 5[:15], where St. Paul speaks of "the grace and gift in Christ," etc. The gifts and the Spirit increase in us every day, but they are not yet perfect since there remain in us the evil desires and sins that war against the Spirit, as he says in Romans 7[:5ff.] and Galatians 5[:17], and the conflict between the seed of the woman and the seed of the serpent, as foretold in Genesis 3[:15]. Nevertheless grace

---

[19] *Thun,* i.e., "commit sin."

does so much that we are accounted completely righteous before God. For his grace is not divided or parceled out, as are the gifts, but takes us completely into favor for the sake of Christ our Intercessor and Mediator. And because of this, the gifts are begun in us.

In this sense, then, you can understand chapter 7. There St. Paul still calls himself a sinner; and yet he can say, in chapter 8[:1], that there is no condemnation for those who are in Christ, simply because of the incompleteness of the gifts and of the Spirit. Because the flesh is not yet slain, we are still sinners. But because we believe in Christ and have a beginning of the Spirit, God is so favorable and gracious to us that he will not count the sin against us or judge us because of it. Rather he deals with us according to our faith in Christ, until sin is slain.

Faith is not the human notion and dream that some people call faith. When they see that no improvement of life and no good works follow—although they can hear and say much about faith—they fall into the error of saying, "Faith is not enough; one must do works in order to be righteous and be saved." This is due to the fact that when they hear the gospel, they get busy and by their own powers create an idea in their heart which says, "I believe"; they take this then to be a true faith. But, as it is a human figment and idea that never reaches the depths of the heart, nothing comes of it either, and no improvement follows.

Faith, however, is a divine work in us which changes us and makes us to be born anew of God, John 1[:12-13]. It kills the old Adam and makes us altogether different men, in heart and spirit and mind and powers; and it brings with it the Holy Spirit. O it is a living, busy, active, mighty thing, this faith. It is impossible for it not to be doing good works incessantly. It does not ask whether good works are to be done, but before the question is asked, it has already done them, and is constantly doing them. Whoever does not do such works, however, is an unbeliever. He gropes and looks around for faith and good works, but knows neither what faith is nor what good works are. Yet he talks and talks, with many words, about faith and good works.

Faith is a living, daring confidence in God's grace, so sure and certain that the believer would stake his life on it a thousand times.

This knowledge of and confidence in God's grace makes men glad and bold and happy in dealing with God and with all creatures. And this is the work which the Holy Spirit performs in faith. Because of it, without compulsion, a person is ready and glad to do good to everyone, to serve everyone, to suffer everything, out of love and praise to God who has shown him this grace. Thus it is impossible to separate works from faith, quite as impossible as to separate heat and light from fire. Beware, therefore, of your own false notions and of the idle talkers who imagine themselves wise enough to make decisions about faith and good works, and yet are the greatest fools. Pray God that he may work faith in you. Otherwise you will surely remain forever without faith, regardless of what you may think or do.

Righteousness, then, is such a faith. It is called "the righteousness of God" because God gives it, and counts it as righteousness for the sake of Christ our Mediator, and makes a man to fulfil his obligation to everybody. For through faith a man becomes free from sin[20] and comes to take pleasure in God's commandments, thereby he gives God the honor due him, and pays him what he owes him. Likewise he serves his fellow-men willingly, by whatever means he can, and thus pays his debt to everyone. Nature, free will, and our own powers cannot bring this righteousness into being. For as no one can give himself faith, neither can he take away his own unbelief. How, then, will he take away a single sin, even the very smallest? Therefore all that is done apart from faith, or in unbelief, is false; it is hypocrisy and sin, Romans 14[:23], no matter how good a showing it makes.

Flesh and spirit you must not understand as though flesh is only that which has to do with unchastity and spirit is only that which has to do with what is inwardly in the heart. Rather, like Christ in John 3[:6], Paul calls everything "flesh" that is born of the flesh—the whole man, with body and soul, mind and senses—because everything about him longs for the flesh. Thus you should learn to call him "fleshly" too who thinks, teaches, and talks a great

---

[20] *Wird on sünde.*

371

deal about lofty spiritual matters, yet does so without grace. From the "works of the flesh" in Galatians 5[:19-21], you can learn that Paul calls heresy and hatred "works of the flesh." And in Romans 8[:3] he says that "the law is weakened by the flesh"; yet this is said not of unchastity, but of all sins, and above all of unbelief, which is the most spiritual of all vices.

On the contrary, you should call him "spiritual" who is occupied with the most external kind of works, as Christ was when he washed the disciples' feet [John 13:1-14], and Peter when he steered his boat and fished. Thus "the flesh" is a man who lives and works, inwardly and outwardly, in the service of the flesh's gain and of this temporal life. "The spirit" is the man who lives and works, inwardly and outwardly, in the service of the Spirit and of the future life.

Without such a grasp of these words, you will never understand this letter of St. Paul, nor any other book of Holy Scripture. Therefore beware of all teachers who use these words in a different sense, no matter who they are, even Origen, Ambrose, Augustine, Jerome, and others like them or even above them. And now we will take up the epistle.

It is right for a preacher of the gospel in the first place by revelation of the law and of sin to rebuke and to constitute as sin everything that is not the living fruit of the Spirit and of faith in Christ, in order that men should be led to know themselves and their own wretchedness, and to become humble and ask for help. This is therefore what St. Paul does. He begins in chapter 1 to rebuke the gross sins and unbelief that are plainly evident. These were, and still are, the sins of the heathen who live without God's grace. He says: Through the gospel there shall be revealed the wrath of God from heaven against all men because of their godless lives and their unrighteousness. For even though they know and daily recognize that there is a God, nevertheless nature itself, without grace, is so bad that it neither thanks nor honors God. Instead it blinds itself, and goes steadily from bad to worse until, after idolatry, it blatantly commits the most shameful sins, along with all the vices, and also allows others to commit them unreprimanded.

In chapter 2 he extends his rebuke to include those who seem outwardly to be righteous and who commit their sins in secret. Such were the Jews and such are all the hypocrites who without desire or love for the law of God lead decent lives, but at heart hate God's law, and yet are quick to judge other people. This is the nature of all hypocrites, to think of themselves as pure, and yet to be full of covetousness, hatred, pride, and all uncleanness, Matthew 23[:25-28]. These are they who despise God's goodness, and in their hardheartedness heap wrath upon themselves. Thus St. Paul, as a true interpreter of the law, leaves no one without sin, but proclaims the wrath of God upon all who would live well simply by nature or of their own volition.[21] He makes them to be no better than the obvious sinners; indeed, he says they are stubborn and unrepentant.

In chapter 3 he throws them all together in a heap, and says that one is like the other: they are all sinners before God. Only, the Jews have had the word of God. Though not many have believed that word, this does not mean that the faith and truth of God are exhausted. He quotes incidentally a verse from Psalm 51[:4], that God remains justified in his words. Afterward he comes back to this again and proves also by Scripture that all men are sinners, and that by the works of the law nobody is justified, but that the law was given only that sin might be known.

Then he begins to teach the right way by which men must be justified and saved. He says: They are all sinners making no boast of God; but they must be justified without merit [of their own] through faith in Christ, who has merited this for us by his blood, and has become for us a mercy-seat by God. God forgives all former sins to demonstrate that we are helped only by his righteousness, which he grants in faith, and which was revealed at that time through the gospel and was witnessed to beforehand by the law and the prophets. Thus the law is upheld by faith, though the works of the law are thereby put down, together with the boasting of them.

After the first three chapters, in which sin is revealed and faith's way to righteousness is taught, St. Paul begins in chapter 4 to meet certain remonstrances and objections. First he takes up the one that all men commonly make when they hear that faith justifies without works. They say, "Are we, then, to do no good works?" Therefore he himself takes up the case of Abraham, and asks, "What did Abraham accomplish, then, with his good works?

---

[21] *Aus natur oder freiem willen.*

Were they all in vain? Were his works of no use?" He concludes that Abraham was justified by faith alone, without any works, so much so that the Scriptures in Genesis 15[:6] declare that he was justified by faith alone even before the work of circumcision. But if the work of circumcision contributed nothing to his righteousness, though God had commanded it and it was a good work of obedience, then surely no other good work will contribute anything to righteousness. Rather, as Abraham's circumcision was an external sign by which he showed the righteousness that was already his in faith, so all good works are only external signs which follow out of faith; like good fruit, they demonstrate that a person is already inwardly righteous before God.

With this powerful illustration from the Scriptures, St. Paul confirms the doctrine of faith which he had set forth in chapter 3. He cites also another witness, David, who says in Psalm 32[:1-2] that a man is justified without works—although he does not remain without works when he has been justified. Then he gives the illustration a broader application, setting it over against all other works of the law. He concludes that the Jews cannot be Abraham's heirs merely because of their blood, still less because of the works of the law; they must inherit Abraham's faith, if they would be true heirs. For before the law—before the law of Moses and the law of circumcision—Abraham was justified by faith and called the father of all believers. Moreover the law brings about wrath rather than grace, because no one keeps the law out of love for it and pleasure in it. What comes by the works of the law is thus disfavor rather than grace. Therefore faith alone must obtain the grace promised to Abraham, for these examples too were written for our sakes [Rom. 15:4], that we too should believe.

In chapter 5 he comes to the fruits and works of faith, such as peace, joy, love to God and to every man, as well as confidence, assurance, boldness, courage, and hope amid tribulation and suffering. For all this follows, if faith be true, because of the superabundant goodness that God shows us in Christ, causing Christ to die for us before we could ask it of him, indeed, while we were still enemies. Thus we have it that faith justifies without any works; and yet it does not follow that men are therefore to do no good works, but rather that the genuine works will not be lacking. Of these the work-righteous saints know nothing. They dream up works of their own in which there is no peace, joy, confidence, love, hope, boldness, or any of the qualities of true Christian work and faith.

After this he digresses and makes a pleasant excursion, telling whence come sin and righteousness, death and life, and comparing Adam and Christ. He means to say that Christ had to come as a second Adam bequeathing his righteousness to us through a new spiritual birth in faith, just as the first Adam bequeathed sin to us through the old fleshly birth. Thus he declares and proves that no one by his own works can raise himself out of sin into righteousness, any more than he can prevent the birth of his own body. This is proved also by the fact that the divine law—which ought to assist toward righteousness, if anything can—has not only not helped, but has even increased sin. For the more the law forbids, the more our evil nature hates the law, and the more it wants to give reign to its own lust. Thus the law makes Christ all the more necessary, and more grace is needed to help our nature.

In chapter 6 he takes up the special work of faith, the conflict of the spirit with the flesh for the complete slaying of the sin and lust that remain after we are justified. He teaches us that we are not by faith so freed from sin that we can be idle, slack, and careless, as though there were no longer any sin in us. Sin is present; but it is no longer reckoned for our condemnation, because of the faith that is struggling against it. Therefore we have enough to do all our life long in taming the body, slaying its lusts, and compelling its members to obey the spirit and not the lusts. Thus we become like the death and resurrection of Christ, and complete our baptism—which signifies the death of sin and the new life of grace—until we are entirely purified of sin, and even our bodies rise again with Christ and live forever.

All this we can do, he says, because we are under[22] grace and not under law. He himself explains what this means. To be without the law is not the same thing as to have no laws and to be able to do what one pleases. Rather we are under the law when, without grace, we occupy ourselves with the works of the law. Then sin certainly rules [us] through the law, for no one loves the law by nature; and that is great sin. Grace, however, makes the law dear

[22] Editions prior to 1546 read "in" rather than "under." *WA*, DB 7, 19, n. 29/30.

to us; then sin is no longer present, and the law is no longer against us but one with us.

This is the true freedom from sin and from the law. He writes about this down to the end of the chapter, saying that it is a freedom only to do good with pleasure and to live well without the compulsion of the law. Therefore this freedom is a spiritual freedom, which does not overthrow the law but presents what the law demands, namely, pleasure [in the law] and love [for it] whereby the law is quieted and no longer drives men or makes demands of them. It is just as if you owed a debt to your overlord and could not pay it. There are two ways in which you could rid yourself of the debt: either he would take nothing from you and would tear up the account, or some good man would pay it for you and give you the means to satisfy the account. It is in this latter way that Christ has made us free from the law. Our freedom is, therefore, no carefree fleshly freedom which is not obligated to do anything, but a freedom that does many works of all kinds, and is free of the demands and obligations of the law.

In chapter 7 he supports this with an analogy from married life. When a man dies, his wife is also alone, and thus the one is released entirely from the other. Not that the wife cannot or ought not take another husband, but rather that she is now for the first time really free to take another—something which she could not do previously, before she was free from her husband. So our conscience is bound to the law, under the old man of sin; when he is slain by the Spirit, then the conscience is free, and the one is released from the other. Not that the conscience is to do nothing, but rather that it is now for the first time really free to hold fast to Christ, the second husband, and bring forth the fruit of life.

Then he depicts more fully the nature of sin and of the law, how by means of the law sin now stirs and becomes mighty. The old man comes to hate the law all the more because he cannot pay what the law demands. Sin is his nature and of himself he can do nothing but sin; therefore the law to him is death and torment. Not that the law is bad, but the old man's evil nature cannot endure the good, and the law demands good of him; just as a sick man cannot stand it when he is required to run and jump and do the works of a well man.

Therefore St. Paul here concludes that the law, correctly understood and thoroughly grasped, does nothing more than to remind us of our sin, and to slay us by it, making us liable to eternal wrath. All this is fully learned[23] and experienced by our conscience, when it is really struck by the law. Therefore a person must have something other than the law, something more than the law, to make him righteous and save him. But they who do not correctly understand the law are blind. They go ahead in their presumption, thinking to satisfy the law by means of their deeds, not knowing how much the law demands, namely, a willing and happy heart. Therefore they do not see Moses clearly; the veil is put between them and him, and covers him [Exod. 34:29-35; II Cor. 3:12-16].

Then he shows how spirit and flesh struggle with one another in a man. He uses himself as an example, in order that we may learn how properly to understand the work of slaying sin within us. He calls both the spirit and the flesh "laws"; for just as it is in the nature of the divine law to drive men and make demands of them, so the flesh drives men and makes demands. It rages against the spirit, and will have its own way. The spirit, in turn, drives men and makes demands contrary to the flesh, and will have its own way. This tension lasts in us as long as we live; though in one person it is greater, in another less, according as the spirit or the flesh is stronger. Nevertheless the whole man is himself both spirit and flesh, and he fights with himself until he becomes wholly spiritual.

In chapter 8 he comforts these fighters, telling them that this flesh does not condemn them. He shows further what the nature of flesh and spirit is, and how the Spirit comes from Christ. Christ has given us his Holy Spirit; he makes us spiritual and subdues the flesh, and assures us that we are still God's children, however hard sin may be raging within us, so long as we follow the spirit and resist sin to slay it. Since, however, nothing else is so good for the mortifying of the flesh as the cross and suffering, he comforts us in suffering with the support of the Spirit of love, and of the whole creation, namely, that the Spirit sighs within us and the creation longs with us that we may be rid of the flesh and of sin. So we see

---

[23] *Leret* may have been introduced for the sake of rhyming with the following word *erferet;* in editions prior to 1530 the word had been *lernt.* WA, DB 7, 21, n. 34.

that these three chapters (6–8) drive home the one task of faith, which is to slay the old Adam and subdue the flesh.

In chapters 9, 10, and 11 he teaches of God's eternal predestination—out of which originally proceeds who shall believe or not, who can or cannot get rid of sin—in order that our salvation may be taken entirely out of our hands and put in the hand of God alone. And this too is utterly necessary. For we are so weak and uncertain that if it depended on us, not even a single person would be saved; the devil would surely overpower us all. But since God is dependable—his predestination cannot fail, and no one can withstand him—we still have hope in the face of sin.

Here, now, for once we must put a stop to those wicked and high flying spirits who first apply their own reason to this matter. They begin at the top to search the abyss of divine predestination, and worry in vain about whether they are predestinated. They are bound to plunge to their own destruction, either through despair, or through throwing caution to the winds.[24]

But you had better follow the order of this epistle. Worry first about Christ and the gospel, that you may recognize your sin and his grace. Then fight your sin, as the first eight chapters here have taught. Then, when you have reached the eighth chapter, and are under the cross and suffering, this will teach you correctly of predestination in chapters 9, 10, and 11, and how comforting it is. For in the absence of suffering and the cross and the perils of death, one cannot deal with predestination without harm and without secret anger against God. The old Adam must first die before he can tolerate this thing and drink the strong wine. Therefore beware that you do not drink wine while you are still a suckling. There is a limit, a time, and an age for every doctrine.

In chapter 12 he teaches what true worship is, and makes all Christians priests. They are to offer not money or cattle, as under the law, but their own bodies, with slaying of the lusts. Then he describes the outward conduct of Christians, under the spiritual government, telling how they are to teach, preach, rule, serve, give, suffer, love, live, and act toward friend, foe, and all men. These are the works that a Christian does; for, as has been said, faith takes no holidays.

---

[24] *Sich in die freie schantz schlahen.*

In chapter 13 he teaches honor and obedience to worldly government. Although worldly government does not make people righteous before God, nevertheless it is instituted in order to accomplish at least this much, that the good may have outward peace and protection and the bad may not be free to do evil in peace and quietness, and without fear. Therefore the good too are to honor it even though they themselves do not need it. Finally, he comprehends it all in love, and sums it up in the example of Christ: as he has done for us, we are also to do, following in his footsteps.

In chapter 14 he teaches that consciences weak in faith are to be led gently, spared, so that we do not use our Christian freedom for doing harm, but for the assistance of the weak. For where that is not done, the result is discord and contempt for the gospel; and the gospel is the all-important thing. Thus it is better to yield a little to the weak in faith, until they grow stronger, than to have the teaching of the gospel come to nothing. And this work is a peculiar work of love, for which there is great need even now, when with the eating of meat and other liberties, men are rudely and roughly—and needlessly—shaking weak consciences, before they know the truth.

In chapter 15 he sets up Christ as an example: we are to tolerate also those other weak ones who fail in other ways, in open sins or in unpleasing habits. We are not to cast them off, but to bear with them until they too grow better. For so Christ has done with us, and still does every day; he bears with our many faults and bad habits, and with all our imperfections, and helps us constantly.

Then, at the end, he prays for them, praises them, and commends them to God. He speaks of his own office and of his preaching, and asks them kindly for a contribution to the poor at Jerusalem. All that he speaks of or deals with is pure love.

The last chapter is a chapter of greetings. But he mingles with them a noble warning against the doctrines of men,[25] which break in alongside the teaching of the gospel and cause offense. It is as if he had certainly foreseen that out of Rome and through the Romans would come the seductive and offensive canons and decretals and the whole squirming mass of human laws and commandments,

---

[25] Cf. Luther's treatise *Avoiding the Doctrines of Men* (1522) in this volume, pp. 125-153.

which have now drowned the whole world and wiped out this epistle and all the Holy Scriptures, along with the Spirit and faith itself; so that nothing remains anymore except the idol, Belly,[26] whose servants St. Paul here rebukes. God save us from them. Amen.

In this epistle we thus find most abundantly the things that a Christian ought to know, namely, what is law, gospel, sin, punishment, grace, faith, righteousness, Christ, God, good works, love, hope, and the cross; and also how we are to conduct ourselves toward everyone, be he righteous or sinner, strong or weak, friend or foe—and even toward our own selves. Moreover this is all ably supported with Scripture and proved by St. Paul's own example and that of the prophets, so that one could not wish for anything more. Therefore it appears that he wanted in this one epistle to sum up briefly the whole Christian and evangelical doctrine, and to prepare an introduction to the entire Old Testament. For, without doubt, whoever has this epistle well in his heart, has with him the light and power of the Old Testament. Therefore let every Christian be familiar with it and exercise himself in it continually. To this end may God give his grace. Amen.[27]

Preface to the First Epistle of Paul to the Corinthians[28]

1546 (1530)

In this epistle St. Paul exhorts the Corinthians to be one in faith and love, and to see to it that they learn well the chief thing, namely, that Christ is our salvation, the thing over which all reason and wisdom stumbles.

For it was as in our day, when the gospel has come to light. There are many mad saints (we call them factious spirits, fanatics, and heretics) who have become wise and learned all too quickly and, because of their great knowledge and wisdom, cannot live in

---

[26] Phil. 3:19; cf. Rom. 16:18.

[27] In editions prior to 1539 the order of these last two paragraphs is exactly reversed, so that the one here given last comes before rather than after the one which here immediately precedes it.

[28] Luther's first preface to this book, from 1522, was considerably enlarged in the essentially new preface of 1530. Our translation is of the later, longer preface as it appeared in the 1546 edition of the complete Bible, and is reprinted in WA, DB 7, 83-87.

harmony with anybody. One wants to go this way, another that way, as though it would be a great shame if each were not to undertake something special and to put forth his own wisdom. No one can make them out to be fools—though at bottom they neither know nor understand anything about that which is really the chief thing, even though they jabber much about it with their mouths.

So it was with St. Paul too. He had taught his Corinthians Christian faith and freedom from the law. But then the mad saints came along, and the immature know-it-alls. They broke up the unity of the doctrine and caused division among the believers. One claimed to belong to Paul, the other to Apollos; one to Peter, the other to Christ. One wanted circumcision, the other not; one wanted marriage, the other not; one wanted to eat food offered to idols, the other not. Some wanted to be outwardly free [leiblich frey]; some of the women wanted to go with uncovered hair, and so on. They went so far that one man abused his liberty and married his father's wife,[29] some did not believe in the resurrection of the dead, and some thought lightly of the sacrament.

In short, things got so wild and disorderly that everyone wanted to be the expert and do the teaching and make what he pleased of the gospel, the sacrament, and faith. Meanwhile they let the main thing drop—namely, that Christ is our salvation, righteousness, and redemption—as if they had long since outgrown it.[30] This truth can never remain intact when people begin to imagine they are wise and know it all.

This is exactly what is now happening to us. Now that we, by God's grace, have opened the gospel to the Germans, everyone claims that he is the top expert and alone has the Holy Spirit—as if the gospel had been preached in order that in it we should show off our cleverness and reason, and strive for a reputation. Those Corinthians may well be an example or illustration of our people in these days, who also certainly need an epistle of this kind. But this is the way things have to go with the gospel; mad saints and immature know-it-alls have to create disturbances and offenses, so that those who are "tested," as St. Paul also says here [I Cor. 3:13], may be revealed.

Therefore St. Paul most severely rebukes and condemns this

---

[29] *Stiffmutter,* literally, "stepmother."
[30] See p. 186, n. 25.

shameful wisdom, and makes these connoisseur saints out to be fools. He says outright that they know nothing of Christ, or of the Spirit and gifts of God given to us in Christ, and that they had better begin to learn. It takes spiritual folk to understand this. The desire to be wise and the pretense of cleverness in the gospel are the very things that really give offense and hinder the knowledge of Christ and God, and create disturbances and contentions. This clever wisdom and reason can well serve to make for nothing but mad saints and wild Christians. Yet such people can never know our Lord Christ, unless they first become fools again and humbly let themselves be taught and led by the simple word of God. This is what St. Paul deals with in the first four chapters.

In chapter 5 he rebukes the gross unchastity of the man who had married his father's wife. He would put this man under the ban[31] and give him over to the devil. Thus he points out the right way of using the ban,[32] that it should be laid with the consent of the believing congregation upon obvious transgressions, as Christ also teaches in Matthew 18[:17].

In chapter 6 he rebukes contention and disputing in the courts, especially before heathen and unbelievers. He teaches them that they should settle their cases among themselves, or suffer wrong.

In chapter 7 he gives instruction concerning chastity and married life. He praises chastity and virginity, saying that these are helpful in allowing closer attentiveness to the gospel, as Christ also teaches in Matthew 19[:12] concerning celibates who are chaste for the sake of the gospel or the kingdom of heaven. But Paul wills that it be practiced without force or compulsion, or the risk of greater sin; otherwise, marriage is better than a chastity which is continually aflame with passion.

In chapters 8 to 12 he discusses many different ways in which weak consciences are to be guided and regarded in external matters such as eating, drinking, apparel, and receiving the sacrament. Everywhere he forbids the strong to despise the weak, since he himself, even though he is an apostle, has refrained from many things to which he really had a right. Moreover the strong may well be afraid, because in ancient Israel so many were destroyed, all of

---

[31] Cf. p. 51, n. 11.
[32] Cf. p. 17, n. 16.

whom had been led out of Egypt by miracles. Besides this, he makes several digressions into worthwhile teachings.

In chapters 12 and 13 he discusses the many different gifts of God, among which love is the best. He teaches the people not to exalt themselves but to serve one another in unity of spirit, since there is one God, one Lord, one Spirit, and everything is one, however great the diversity.

In chapter 14 he teaches the preachers, prophets, and singers to use their gifts in an orderly manner; they are to display their preaching, skill, and understanding for edification only, and not in order to gain honor for themselves.

In chapter 15 he takes those to task who had taught and believed wrongly concerning the resurrection of the body.

In the last chapter he exhorts the people to give brotherly assistance to the needy in the form of material aid.

Preface to the Second Epistle to the Corinthians

1546 (1522)

In the first epistle, St. Paul rebuked the Corinthians severely for many things, pouring sharp wine into their wounds [Luke 10:34] and frightening them. But an apostle should be a preacher of comfort, to raise up terrified and fearful consciences, rather than to frighten them. Therefore in this epistle he praises them once more and pours oil into their wounds [Luke 10:34]. He shows himself wonderfully kind to them and bids them to receive the sinner back with love.

In chapters 1 and 2 he shows his love toward them, how all that he said, did, and suffered was for their profit and benefit, and how they ought to trust him for the best.

After that he praises the office of the gospel, which is the highest and most comforting of all works and is for the profit and benefit of men's consciences. He shows how it is nobler than the office of the law, also how it is persecuted, and yet increases among believers and produces through the cross a hope of eternal glory. But with all this he touches the false apostles, who were inculcating the law over against the gospel, teaching mere outward holiness—that is, hypocrisy—and allowing the inner shame of unbelief to continue.[33] This he does in chapters 3, 4, and 5.

In chapters 6 and 7 he exhorts them to implement this kind of preaching in the things they do and suffer. He concludes by praising them, so that he may encourage them to carry on.

In chapters 8 and 9 he exhorts them to contribute also material aid and help in time of scarcity to the saints in Jerusalem, who from the outset had given over all their possessions, Acts 4[:34-35].

In chapters 10, 11, and 12 he deals with the false apostles.

In chapter 13 he threatens those who had sinned and not reformed.

Preface to the Epistle of St. Paul to the Galatians

1546 (1522)

The Galatians had been brought by St. Paul to the true Christian faith, from the law to the gospel. After his departure, however, false apostles came along. They were disciples of the true apostles, but they so turned the Galatians around that they believed they had to be saved by works of the law and were committing sin if they did not keep the law—as even several dignitaries in Jerusalem maintained, Acts 15.

To refute them, St. Paul magnifies his office; he will not take a back seat to any other apostle. He boasts that his doctrine and office are from God alone, in order that he might silence the boast of the false apostles who helped themselves to the works and reputation of the true apostles. He says it is not true, even if an angel were to preach differently, or he himself, to say nothing of disciples of apostles, or of apostles themselves. This he does in chapters 1 and 2, and concludes that everyone must be justified without merit, without works, without law, through Christ alone.

In chapters 3 and 4 he proves all this with passages of Scripture, examples, and analogies. He shows that the law brings sin and a curse rather than righteousness. Righteousness is promised by God, fulfilled by Christ without the law, given to us—out of grace alone.

In chapters 5 and 6 he teaches the works of love that ought to follow faith.

---

[33] This sentence did not occur in editions prior to 1530.

Preface to the Epistle of St. Paul to the Ephesians

1546 (1522)

In this epistle St. Paul teaches, first, what the gospel is, how it was predestined by God alone in eternity, and earned and sent forth through Christ, so that all who believe on it become righteous, godly, living, saved men, and free from the law, sin, and death. This he does in the first three chapters.

Then he teaches that false teachings and the commandments of men are to be avoided, so that we may remain true to one Head, and become sure and genuine and complete in Christ alone. For in him we have everything, so that we need nothing beside him. This he does in chapter 4.

Then he goes on to teach that we are to practice and prove our faith with good works, avoid sin, and fight with spiritual weapons against the devil, so that through the cross we may be steadfast in hope.

Preface to the Epistle of St. Paul to the Philippians

1546 (1522)

In this epistle St. Paul praises and admonishes the Philippians that they abide and carry on in the true faith and increase in love. But since injury is always done to faith by false apostles and teachers of works, he warns them against these men and points out to them many different preachers—some good, some bad—including even himself and his disciples, Timothy and Epaphroditus. This he does in chapters 1 and 2.

In chapter 3 he rejects that human righteousness not based on faith, which is taught and held by the false apostles. He offers himself as an example: he had lived gloriously in this kind of righteousness, and yet now holds it to be nothing, for the sake of the righteousness of Christ. For human righteousness makes the belly its god, and makes men enemies of the cross of Christ.

In chapter 4 he exhorts them to peace and good outward conduct toward each other, and thanks them for the gift they sent him.

Preface to the Epistle of St. Paul to the Colossians
1546 (1522)

Just as the Epistle to the Galatians resembles and is modeled on the Epistle to the Romans, comprising in outline the same material that is more fully and richly developed in Romans; so this epistle resembles that to the Ephesians and comprises also in outline the same contents.

First he praises and wishes for the Colossians, that they continue and increase in faith. He delineates what the gospel and faith are, namely, a wisdom which recognizes Christ as Lord and God, crucified for us, which has been hidden for ages but now brought into the open through his ministry. This is the first chapter.

In chapter 2 he warns them against the doctrines of men, which are always contrary to faith. He depicts these doctrines more clearly than they are depicted anywhere else in Scripture, and criticizes them in a masterly way.

In chapter 3 he exhorts them to be fruitful in the pure faith, doing all sorts of good works for one another, and he describes for some various stations in life the works which are appropriate to them.

In chapter 4 he commends himself to their prayers and gives them greetings and encouragement.

Preface to the First Epistle of St. Paul to the Thessalonians
1546 (1522)

This epistle St. Paul writes out of especial love and apostolic solicitude. For in the first two chapters he praises them because they received the gospel from him with such earnestness that they remained steadfast in it despite suffering and persecution, and became a beautiful example of faith to all congregations everywhere, and suffered persecution from their own kinsfolk like Christ and his apostles did from the Jews—as St. Paul by way of example had himself also suffered and led a holy life when he was with them. For this he thanks God, that his gospel had borne such fruit among them.

In chapter 3 he shows his care and solicitude that this labor of his and their praiseworthy beginning not be brought to nothing by the devil and his apostles through the doctrines of men. For this reason he sent Timothy to them beforehand to make sure about this. And he thanks God that things were still right among them and hopes that they continue to increase.

In chapter 4 he exhorts them to guard against sin and to do good to one another. He also answers a question which they had presented to him through Timothy concerning the resurrection of the dead, whether all would rise at once, or whether some after others.

In chapter 5 he writes of the Last Day, how it shall come suddenly and quickly. He gives them some good directions for governing other people and tells them what attitude they are to take toward the lives and teachings of others.

Preface to the Second Epistle of St. Paul to the Thessalonians

1546 (1522)

In the first epistle [5:2], Paul had resolved for the Thessalonians the question of the Last Day, telling them that it would come quickly, as a thief in the night. Now as is likely to happen—that one question always gives rise to another, because of misunderstanding—the Thessalonians understood that the Last Day was already at hand. Thereupon Paul writes this epistle and explains himself.

In chapter 1 he comforts them with the eternal reward of their faith and of their patience amid sufferings of every kind and with the punishment of their persecutors in eternal pain.

In chapter 2 he teaches that before the Last Day, the Roman Empire must first pass away, and Antichrist set himself up as God in Christendom and seduce the unbelieving world with false doctrines and signs—until Christ shall come and destroy him by his glorious coming, first slaying him with spiritual preaching.

In chapter 3 he gives some admonitions, especially that they rebuke the idlers who are not supporting themselves by their own labor. If the idlers will not reform, then the faithful shall avoid them. And this is a stiff rebuke to the clergy of our day.

Preface to the First Epistle of St. Paul to Timothy
1546 (1522)

This epistle St. Paul writes in order to provide a model to all bishops of what they are to teach and how they are to rule Christendom in the various stations of life, so that it may not be necessary for them to rule Christians according to their own human opinions.

In chapter 1 he charges that a bishop keep true faith and love and resist the false preachers of the law who, beside Christ and the gospel, would also insist on the works of the law. In a brief summary, he comprehends the entire Christian doctrine concerning the purpose of the law and the nature of the gospel. He offers himself as an example to comfort all sinners and those with troubled conscience.[34]

In chapter 2 he charges that prayer be made for all stations of life. He also commands that women are not to preach or wear costly adornment, but are to be obedient to men.

In chapter 3 he describes the kind of persons that bishops, or priests, and their wives ought to be, and also the deacons[35] and their wives. He praises those who desire to be bishops of this kind.

In chapter 4 he prophesies of false bishops and the spiritual estate which is opposed to that spoken of above, who will not be persons of that kind, but instead will forbid marriage and foods, and with their doctrines of men inculcate the very opposite of the things Paul has described.

In chapter 5 he gives orders as to how widows and young women should be looked after, and which widows are to be supported from the common funds; also how godly bishops or priests are to be held in honor, and blameworthy ones punished.

In chapter 6 he exhorts the bishops to hold fast to the pure gospel and to promulgate it by their preaching and living. They are to avoid senseless and meddlesome controversies which are only raised for gaining worldly reputation and riches.

---

[34] This sentence did not occur in editions prior to 1530.
[35] *Kirchendiener*. Editions prior to 1530 read *Diacon*.

Preface to the Second Epistle of St. Paul to Timothy
1546 (1522)

This epistle is a farewell letter, in which St. Paul exhorts Timothy to go on propagating the gospel, even as he has begun. This is quite necessary, since there are many who fall away; and false spirits and teachers keep springing up all around. Therefore it is incumbent upon a bishop always to be alert and to work at the gospel.

But he prophesies especially, in chapters 3 and 4, concerning the perilous time at the end of the world. It is then that a false spiritual life will lead all the world astray, with an outward show, under which every sort of wickedness and wrong will have its fling. Sad to say! we now see this prophecy of St. Paul all too amply fulfilled in our clergy.

Preface to the Epistle of St. Paul to Titus
1546 (1522)

This is a short epistle, but a model of Christian doctrine, in which is comprehended in a masterful way all that is necessary for a Christian to know and to live.

In chapter 1 he teaches what kind of man a bishop, or pastor, ought to be, namely, one who is pious and learned in preaching the gospel and in refuting the false teachers of works and of man-made laws, those who are always warring against faith and leading consciences away from Christian liberty into the captivity of their own man-made works, [as if these works,] which are actually worthless, [should make them righteous before God.][36]

In chapter 2 he teaches the various estates—the older, the younger, wives, husbands, masters, and slaves—how they are to act, as those whom Christ, by his death, has won for his own.

In chapter 3 he teaches Christians to honor worldly rulers and to obey them. He cites again the grace that Christ has won for us,

---

[36] The bracketed words in this sentence did not occur in any editions prior to 1530.

so that no one may think that obeying rulers is enough, since all our righteousness is nothing before God. And he forbids association with the obstinate and with heretics.

Preface to the Epistle of St. Paul to Philemon
1546 (1522)

This epistle gives us a masterful and tender illustration of Christian love. For here we see how St. Paul takes the part of poor Onesimus and, to the best of his ability, advocates his cause with his master. He acts exactly as if he were himself Onesimus, who had done wrong.

Yet he does this not with force or compulsion, as lay within his rights; but he empties himself of his rights in order to compel Philemon also to waive his rights. What Christ has done for us with God the Father, that St. Paul does also for Onesimus with Philemon. For Christ emptied himself of his rights [Phil. 2:7] and overcame the Father with love and humility, so that the Father had to put away his wrath and rights, and receive us into favor for the sake of Christ, who so earnestly advocates our cause and so heartily takes our part. For we are all his Onesimus's[37] if we believe.

Preface to the First Epistle of St. Peter
1546 (1522)

This epistle St. Peter wrote to the converted heathen; he exhorts them to be steadfast in faith and to increase through all kinds of suffering and good works.

In chapter 1 he strengthens their faith through the divine promise and power of the salvation to come. He shows that this salvation has not been merited by us but was first proclaimed by the prophets. Therefore they ought now to live new and holy lives, and forget the old life, as those who have been born anew through the living and eternal Word of God.

In chapter 2 he teaches them to know Christ as the Head and

---

[37] The name Onesimus in Greek means profitable, helpful, or useful.

the Cornerstone, and like true priests to sacrifice themselves to God as Christ sacrificed himself. And he sets about giving instructions to the various estates. First he teaches in general subjection to temporal rulership; afterward he teaches in particular that servants are to be subordinate to their masters and [even] to suffer wrong from them, for the sake of Christ who also suffered wrong for us.

In chapter 3 he teaches wives to be obedient, even to unbelieving husbands, and to adorn themselves with holiness. Likewise, husbands are to be patient with their wives and bear with them. And finally, all in general are to be humble and patient and kind to one another, as Christ was because of our sins.

In chapter 4 he teaches us to subdue the flesh with sobriety, watchfulness, temperance, prayer, and to find comfort and strength through the sufferings of Christ.[38] He instructs the spiritual rulers to inculcate the words and works of God alone, and each to serve the other with his gifts; and not to be surprised but to rejoice, if we have to suffer for the name of Christ.

In chapter 5 he exhorts the bishops and priests as to how they are to live and to tend the people. He warns us against the devil, who without ceasing pursues us everywhere.

Preface to the Second Epistle of St. Peter
1546 (1522)

This epistle is written against those who think that Christian faith can be without works. Therefore he exhorts them to test themselves by good works and become sure of their faith, just as one knows trees by their fruits [Matt. 7:20].

He begins accordingly by praising the gospel over against the doctrines of men. He says that people ought to hear the gospel alone and not the doctrines of men. For, as he says, "No prophecy ever came by the impulse of men" [II Pet. 1:21].

For this reason he warns in chapter 2 against the false teachers who are to come. They are preoccupied with works and thereby

---

[38] *Und mit Christus leiden trösten und stercken.* Editions prior to 1530 had read: *Und Christus leyden betrachtung etc.,* literally, "and contemplating the sufferings of Christ."

deny Christ. He threatens these men severely with three terrible illustrations and depicts them so clearly with their avarice, pride, wickedness, fornication, and hypocrisy that one must plainly see he means the clergy of today. For these have swallowed the whole world in their greed and are wickedly leading an irresponsible, fleshly, worldly life.

In chapter 3 he shows that the Last Day will come soon; and though in the sight of [fur] men it may seem a thousand years, yet in the sight of [fur] God it is as one day.[39] He describes what will happen at the Last Day, how everything shall be consumed by fire. [However, he also prophesies that at that time people will be scornful and, like the Epicureans,[40] will think nothing of faith.

In summary, chapter 1 shows what Christendom was to be like at the time of the pure gospel. Chapter 2 shows how it was to be in the time of the pope and the doctrines of men. Chapter 3 shows how, after this, people will despise both the gospel and all doctrine, and will believe nothing—and this is now in full swing—until Christ comes.][41]

---

[39] Editions prior to 1530 here added these unclear sentences, which Luther deleted from 1530 on: "Now all that die are in the sight of [fur] God, but what lives is in the sight of [fur] men. Hence, to each the Last Day comes quickly after his death." (WA, DB 7, 314, n. 19). Their meaning may perhaps be derived from his exposition of I Peter [3:8] in 1523-1524, where he says with respect to the reckoning of time alluded to in Ps. 90:4: "There are two ways of looking at it: one, in the sight of [fur] God; the other, in the sight of [fur] the world. . . . In the sight of God [fur Gottes angesicht] there is no reckoning of time. . . . A man dies; his body is buried and decays, lies in the earth and knows nothing. When the original man [der erst mensch] arises on the Last Day, however, he will think he has scarcely lain there an hour." WA 14, 70-71 .

[40] Tradition had long referred to the hedonistic ethics reflected in Luke 12:19 as Epicurean. While the Athenian philosopher Epicurus (342-270 B.C.) regarded pleasure as the absolute good, he did not thereby mean merely immediate bodily pleasures (sensual gratification) but also those derived from the intellectual and moral faculties. The Epicureans, of course, did not believe in any life to come (cf. Acts 17:18-32) since at death the disembodied soul dissolved into the primordial "indivisible" atoms from which it had been compounded in space. Cf. p. 267, n. 82.

[41] The concluding sentences, here set in brackets, did not occur in editions prior to 1530.

Preface to the Three Epistles of St. John

1546 (1522)

The first epistle of John is a genuine apostolic epistle and ought to follow right after his gospel. For as in the gospel he promulgates faith, so here he opposes those who boast of faith without works. He teaches in many different ways that works are not absent where faith is; and if they are absent, then faith is not genuine but is lies and darkness. He does this, however, not by harping on the law, as the epistle of James does, but by stimulating us to love even as God has loved us.

He also writes vigorously here against the Cerinthians,[42] against the spirit of Antichrist, which was beginning even then to deny that Christ has come in the flesh, and which is today for the first time really in full sway. For although people do not now publicly deny with their lips that Christ has come in the flesh, they do deny it with their hearts, by their teaching and life. For he who would be righteous and saved by his own works and deeds is as much as denying Christ, since Christ has come in the flesh for the very purpose of making us righteous and saving us without our works, by his blood alone.

Thus the epistle fights against both parties: against those who would live in faith without any works, and against those who would become righteous by their works. It keeps us in the true middle way, that we become righteous and free from sin through faith; and then, when we are righteous, that we practice good works and love for God's sake, freely and without seeking anything else.

The other two epistles are not doctrinal epistles but examples of love and of faith. They too have a true apostolic spirit.

---

[42] Cerinthus was a Gnostic-Ebionite heretic of Asia Minor about A.D. 100, who taught that the spiritual "Christ" came upon the earthly "Jesus" after his baptism and left him again prior to his crucifixion.

Preface to the Epistle to the Hebrews

1546 (1522)

Up to this point we have had [to do with] the true and certain chief books of the New Testament. The four which follow[43] have from ancient times had a different reputation.[44] In the first place, the fact that Hebrews is not an epistle of St. Paul, or of any other apostle, is proved by what it says in chapter 2[:3], that through those who had themselves heard it from the Lord this doctrine has come to us and remained among us. It is thereby made clear that he is speaking about the apostles, as a disciple to whom this doctrine has come from the apostles, perhaps long after them. For St. Paul, in Galatians 1[:1], testifies powerfully that he has his gospel from no man, neither through men, but from God himself.

Again, there is a hard knot in the fact that in chapters 6[:4-6] and 10[:26-27] it flatly denies and forbids to sinners any repentance after baptism; and in chapter 12[:17] it says that Esau sought repentance and did not find it. This [seems, as it stands, to be][45] contrary to all the gospels and to St. Paul's epistles; and although

---

[43] In terms of order, Hebrews, James, Jude, and Revelation come last in Luther's New Testament because of his negative estimate of their apostolicity. In a catalogue of "The Books of the New Testament" which followed immediately upon his Preface to the New Testament (see pp. 357-362) Luther regularly listed these four—without numbers—at the bottom of a list in which he named the other twenty-three books, in the order in which they still appear in English Bibles, and numbered them consecutively from 1-23 (*WA, DB* 6, 12-13), a procedure identical to that with which he also listed the books of the Apocrypha (see p. 337, n. 1). There was in practice considerable lack of unanimity on the extent of the New Testament canon even in the late Middle Ages. Erasmus' critical attitude toward these four books, known to Luther from his *Annotationes* to his 1516 Greek New Testament, was openly accepted by the Catholic Cajetan. Reu, *Luther's German Bible*, pp. 175-176.

[44] Contrary to Erasmus' ascription of authorship to Paul (following Jerome), Luther has in mind the statement from *Eusebius: The Ecclesiastical History*, III, iii, 5: "Some dispute the Epistle to the Hebrews, saying that it was rejected by the church of Rome as not being by Paul." Kirsopp Lake (trans.), *Eusebius: The Ecclesiastical History* (London: Heinemann, 1926), I, 193. Tertullian ascribed the epistle to Barnabas. *WA, DB* 7, 555 and 631, n. 344, 2.

[45] Beginning in 1530 the straightforward "is" of the earlier editions was replaced in the later editions by the milder words here given in brackets, probably in keeping with Luther's generally favorable judgment of the book as expressed in the next paragraph. *WA, DB* 7, 632, n. 344, 15/16.

one might venture an interpretation[46] of it, the words are so clear that I do not know whether that would be sufficient. My opinion is that this is an epistle put together of many pieces, which does not deal systematically with any one subject.

However that may be, it is still a marvelously fine epistle. It discusses Christ's priesthood masterfully and profoundly on the basis of the Scriptures and extensively interprets the Old Testament in a fine way. Thus it is plain that this is the work of an able and learned man; as a disciple of the apostles he had learned much from them and was greatly experienced in faith and practiced in the Scriptures. And although, as he himself testifies in chapter 6[:1], he does not lay the foundation of faith—that is the work of the apostles—nevertheless he does build well on it with gold, silver, precious stones, as St. Paul says in I Corinthians 3[:12]. Therefore we should not be deterred if wood, straw, or hay are perhaps mixed with them, but accept this fine teaching with all honor; though, to be sure, we cannot put it on the same level with the apostolic epistles.

Who wrote it is not known, and will probably not be known for a while; it makes no difference. We should be satisfied with the doctrine that he bases so constantly on the Scriptures. For he discloses a firm grasp of the reading of the Scriptures and of the proper way of dealing with them.

Preface to the Epistles of St. James and St. Jude
1546 (1522)

Though this epistle of St. James was rejected by the ancients,[47] I praise it and consider it a good book, because it sets up no doctrines of men but vigorously promulgates the law of God. However, to state my own opinion about it, though without prejudice to anyone,

---

[46] *Eine Glose*, literally "gloss," is an interpretation which explains away the apparent meaning. Emser, e.g., cited Jerome in making the "restore again" of Heb. 6:4 refer to baptism rather than penance, and he cited Cyprian in referring Heb. 10:26 only to those who wilfully persist in sin; on Heb. 12:17 he commented that "Esau was not sorrowful and contrite on account of his sin but on account of the loss involved in selling his justification to Jacob." WA, DB 7, 631, n. 344, 13.

[47] In the earliest general history of the church, *Eusebius: The Ecclesiastical History* (II, xxiii, 25), the author (died *ca.* 339) writes, "Such is the story of James, whose is said to be the first of the Epistles called Catholic. It is to be

I do not regard it as the writing of an apostle;[48] and my reasons follow.

In the first place it is flatly against St. Paul and all the rest of Scripture in ascribing justification to works [2:24]. It says that Abraham was justified by his works when he offered his son Isaac [2:21]; though in Romans 4[:2-22] St. Paul teaches to the contrary that Abraham was justified apart from works, by his faith alone, before he had offered his son, and proves it by Moses in Genesis 15[:6]. Now although this epistle might be helped and an interpretation[49] devised for this justification by works, it cannot be defended in its application to works [Jas. 2:23] of Moses' statement in Genesis 15[:6]. For Moses is speaking here only of Abraham's faith, and not of his works, as St. Paul demonstrates in Romans 4. This fault, therefore, proves that this epistle is not the work of any apostle.

In the second place its purpose is to teach Christians, but in all this long teaching it does not once mention the Passion, the resurrection, or the Spirit of Christ. He names Christ several times; however he teaches nothing about him, but only speaks of general faith in God. Now it is the office of a true apostle to preach of the Passion and resurrection and office of Christ, and to lay the foundation for faith in him, as Christ himself says in John 15[:27], "You shall bear witness to me." All the genuine sacred books agree in this, that all of them preach and inculcate [treiben] Christ. And that is the true test by which to judge all books, when we see whether or not they inculcate Christ. For all the Scriptures show us Christ, Romans 3[:21]; and St. Paul will know nothing but Christ, I Corinthians 2[:2]. Whatever does not teach Christ is not yet[50] apostolic, even though St. Peter or St. Paul does the teaching. Again, whatever preaches Christ would be apostolic, even if Judas, Annas, Pilate, and Herod were doing it.

But this James does nothing more than drive to the law and to

---

observed that its authenticity is denied, since few of the ancients quote it, as is also the case with the Epistle called Jude's." Lake, *op. cit.*, I, 179. Eusebius also includes both epistles in his list of "Disputed Books" (*History*, III, xxiv, 3). Lake, *op. cit.*, I, 257. Cf. the statement by Jerome (d. 420) in his *Liber de Viris Illustribus* (II) concerning the pseudonymity ascribed to the epistle of James and its rather gradual attainment of authoritative status. Migne 23, 609.

[48] Cf. p. 362, nn. 11, 12.
[49] See p. 395, n. 46.
[50] *Noch nicht* in editions prior to 1530 was simply *nicht*. WA, DB 7, 385, n. 29.

its works. Besides, he throws things together so chaotically that it seems to me he must have been some good, pious man, who took a few sayings from the disciples of the apostles and thus tossed them off on paper. Or it may perhaps have been written by someone on the basis of his preaching. He calls the law a "law of liberty" [1:25], though Paul calls it a law of slavery, of wrath, of death, and of sin.[51]

Moreover he cites the sayings of St. Peter [in 5:20]: "Love covers a multitude of sins" [I Pet. 4:8], and again [in 4:10], "Humble yourselves under the hand of God" [I Pet. 5:6]; also the saying of St. Paul in Galatians 5[:17], "The Spirit lusteth against envy."[52] And yet, in point of time, St. James was put to death by Herod [Acts 12:2] in Jerusalem, before St. Peter.[53] So it seems that [this author] came long after St. Peter and St. Paul.

In a word, he wanted to guard against those who relied on faith without works, but was unequal to the task.[54] He tries to accomplish by harping on the law what the apostles accomplish by stimulating people to love. Therefore[55] I cannot include him among the chief books, though I would not thereby prevent anyone from including or extolling him as he pleases, for there are otherwise many good sayings in him.

Concerning the epistle of St. Jude, no one can deny that it is an extract or copy of St. Peter's second epistle, so very like it are all the words. He also speaks of the apostles like a disciple who comes long

---

[51] Cf. Rom. 3:20; 4:15; 5:13, 20; 6:15-22; 7:5-13; 8:2; I Cor. 15:56; Gal. 3:23—5:1.

[52] This KJV rendering comes closest to Luther's German, which is a literal rendering of the Vulgate of Jas. 4:5. *Hass* is Luther's equivalent of the Latin *invidiae* again in Paul's catalogue of works of the flesh, where the RSV translates the word in Gal. 5:21 as "envy."

[53] Luther overlooks the fact that the James to whom the book is traditionally ascribed is not the brother of John [Matt. 4:21] martyred by Herod [Acts 12:2], but the brother of the Lord [Matt. 13:55] who became head of the apostolic church at Jerusalem [Acts 15:13; Gal. 1:19]. *BG* 7, 21, n. 2.

[54] Editions prior to 1530 here added, "in spirit, thought, and words. He mangles the Scriptures and thereby opposes Paul and all Scripture." *WA, DB* 7, 386, nn. 14, 15.

[55] Editions prior to 1530 read from this point, "Therefore, I will not have him in my Bible to be numbered among the true chief books, though I would not thereby prevent anyone from including or extolling him as he pleases, for there are otherwise many good sayings in him. *One* man is no man (cf. the proverbial expression: *Einer ist keiner.* Wander [ed.], *Sprichwörter-Lexikon,* I, 784, '*Einer,*' No. 44) in worldly things; how, then, should this single man alone avail against Paul and all the rest of Scripture?" *WA, DB* 7, 386, nn. 17-21.

after them [Jude 17] and cites sayings and incidents that are found nowhere else in the Scriptures [Jude 9, 14]. This moved the ancient fathers to exclude this epistle from the main body of the Scriptures.[56] Moreover the Apostle Jude did not go to Greek-speaking lands, but to Persia, as it is said, so that he did not write Greek. Therefore, although I value this book, it is an epistle that need not be counted among the chief books which are supposed to lay the foundations of faith.[57]

Preface to the Revelation of St. John [I][58]

1522

About this book of the Revelation of John, I leave everyone free to hold his own opinions. I would not have anyone bound to my opinion or judgment. I say what I feel. I miss more than one thing in this book, and it makes me consider it to be neither apostolic nor prophetic.

First and foremost, the apostles do not deal with visions, but prophesy in clear and plain words, as do Peter and Paul, and Christ in the gospel. For it befits the apostolic office to speak clearly of Christ and his deeds, without images and visions. Moreover there is no prophet in the Old Testament, to say nothing of the New, who deals so exclusively with visions and images. For myself, I think it approximates the Fourth Book of Esdras;[59] I can in no way detect that the Holy Spirit produced it.

Moreover he seems to me to be going much too far when he commends his own book so highly [Revelation 22]—indeed, more than any of the other sacred books do, though they are much more important—and threatens that if anyone takes away anything from it, God will take away from him, etc. Again, they are supposed to be blessed who keep what is written in this book; and yet no one knows

---

[56] Cf. p. 394, n. 44.

[57] Beginning in 1539 Luther placed this last paragraph prior to the epistle of Jude, rather than here, and titled it accordingly. WA, DB 7, 386, n. 22/30.

[58] This short preface appeared in the September Testament of 1522 and in other editions up to 1527. It was supplanted from 1530 on by the longer preface which follows. WA, DB 7, 404.

[59] II Esdras was numbered as IV Esdras in the Vulgate. Chapters 3-14 actually constitute a Jewish Apocalypse dating from about A.D. 90. Cf. pp. 349-350.

what that is, to say nothing of keeping it. This is just the same as if we did not have the book at all. And there are many far better books available for us to keep.

Many of the fathers also rejected this book a long time ago;[60] although St. Jerome, to be sure, refers to it in exalted terms and says that it is above all praise and that there are as many mysteries in it as words.[61] Still, Jerome cannot prove this at all, and his praise at numerous places is too generous.

Finally, let everyone think of it as his own spirit leads him. My spirit cannot accommodate itself to this book. For me this is reason enough not to think highly of it: Christ is neither taught nor known in it. But to teach Christ, this is the thing which an apostle is bound above all else to do; as Christ says in Acts 1[:8], "You shall be my witnesses." Therefore I stick to the books which present Christ to me clearly and purely.

Preface to the Revelation of St. John [II][62]

1546 (1530)

There are many different kinds of prophecy in Christendom. One is prophecy which interprets the writings of the prophets. Paul speaks of this in I Corinthians 12 and 14, and in other places as well. This is the most necessary kind and we must have it every day, because it teaches the Word of God, lays the foundation of Christen-

---

[60] The canonicity of Revelation was disputed by Marcion, Caius of Rome, Dionysius of Alexandria, Cyril of Jerusalem, and the Synod of Laodicea in A.D. 360, though it was accepted by others as Eusebius reports. Cf. p. 400, n. 63. Erasmus had noted in connection with chapter 4 that the Greeks regarded the book as apocryphal. WA, DB 7, 646, n. 22.

[61] Jerome accepted the apostolic authorship and canonicity of the Apocalypse. Cf. Johannes Kirchhofer, Quellensammlung zur Geschichte des Neutestamentlichen Canons bis auf Hieronymus (Zurich: Meyer und Zoller, 1844), pp. 327-328. In his epistle Ad Paulinum, De studia Scripturarum Jerome writes: Apocalypsis Joannis tot habet sacramenta, quot verba. Parum dixi pro merito voluminis. Laus omnis inferior est: in verbis singulis multiplices latent intelligentiae. Migne 22, 548-549.

[62] In his considerably revised and significantly new edition of the New Testament in 1530, Luther supplanted his earlier brief Preface to Revelation with a much more extensive one, which by his own admission was strong in its antipapistic orientation (cf. his February 25, 1530, letter to Nicholas Hausmann in Currie, The Letters of Martin Luther, p. 204; WA, Br 5, 242). This was the year

dom, and defends the faith. In a word, it rules, preserves, establishes, and performs the preaching ministry.

Another kind foretells things to come which are not previously contained in Scripture, and this prophecy is of three types. The first expresses itself simply in words, without images and figures—as Moses, David, and others of the prophets prophesy about Christ, and as Christ and the apostles prophesy about Antichrist, false teachers, etc. The second type does this with images, but alongside them it supplies their interpretation in specific words—as Joseph interprets dreams, and Daniel both dreams and images. The third type does it without either words or interpretations, exclusively with images and figures, like this book of Revelation and like the dreams, visions, and images that many holy people have had from the Holy Spirit—as Peter in Acts 2[:17] preaches from Joel [2:28], "Your sons and your daughters shall prophesy, and your young men shall see visions, and your old men shall dream dreams." So long as this kind of prophecy remains without explanation and gets no sure interpretation, it is a concealed and mute prophecy and has not yet come to the profit and fruit which it is to give to Christendom.

This is the way it has been with this book heretofore. Many have tried their hands at it, but until this very day they have attained no certainty. Some have even brewed it into many stupid things out of their own heads. Because its interpretation is uncertain and its meaning hidden, we have also let it alone until now, especially because some of the ancient fathers held that it was not the work of St. John, the Apostle—as is stated in *The Ecclesiastical History*, Book III, chapter 25.[63] For our part, we still share this doubt. By that, however, no one should be prevented from regarding this as the work of St. John the Apostle, or of whomever else he chooses. Since we would nonetheless like to be sure of its meaning or interpretation, we will give other and higher minds something to think about by stating our own views.

---

in which Luther explicitly noted in the Protestant confession presented at Augsburg, the absence of his dogma on the pope as Antichrist (*WA*, DB 7, 482). The new preface was retained in all subsequent editions of the New Testament and of the complete Bible and is here given as it appeared in the complete Bible of 1546, as translated from the text in *WA*, DB 7, 407-421.

[63] *Eusebius: History*, III, xxv, 2-4, "The arguments concerning [the Revelation of John] we will expound at the proper time . . . some reject it, but others count it among the Recognized Books." Lake, *op. cit.*, I, 257. Cf. p. 399, n. 60.

Since it is intended as a revelation of things that are to happen in the future, and especially of tribulations and disasters that were to come upon Christendom, we consider that the first and surest step toward finding its interpretation is to take from history the events and disasters that have come upon Christendom till now, and hold them up alongside of these images, and so compare them very carefully. If, then, the two perfectly coincided and squared with one another, we could build on that as a sure, or at least an unobjectionable, interpretation.

Accordingly we hold—as indeed the text says—that the first three chapters, which speak of the seven congregations in Asia and their angels, have no other purpose than simply to show how these congregations stood at the time, and how they are exhorted to be steadfast and to increase or reform. From these chapters we learn in addition that the word "angel" is to be understood later on, in other images or visions, to mean bishops and teachers in Christendom— some good, such as the holy fathers and bishops, some bad, such as the heretics and false bishops. And in this book there are more of the bad than of the good.

In chapters 4 and 5 there is prefigured the whole of Christendom that is to suffer these coming tribulations and plagues. There are twenty-four elders before God (that is, all the bishops and teachers in unity); they are crowned with faith, and praise Christ, the Lamb of God, with harps (that is, they preach); and they worship him with censers (that is, they exercise themselves in prayer). All this is for the comfort of Christians, that they may know that Christendom is to endure in spite of the plagues that are going to come.

In chapter 6 the future tribulations begin. First come the bodily tribulations, such as persecution by the temporal government, which is the rider with the bow upon the white horse. Then come war and bloodshed, which is the rider with the sword on the red horse. Then come scarcity and famine, the rider with the balance on the black horse. Then come pestilence and plague, the rider in the guise of death on the pale horse. For these four tribulations always surely follow the ungrateful and the despisers of the word of God, together with other [tribulations] such as the overthrow and the changing of governments, all the way down to the Last Day, as is shown at

401

the end of chapter 6. And the souls of the martyrs also speak of this in their crying aloud [6:10].

In chapters 7 and 8 begins the revelation of the spiritual tribulations, which are the many different heresies. Again this is preceded by a comforting image in which the angel seals the Christians and wards off the four evil angels in order that we may again be assured that, even under heretics, Christendom will have good angels and the pure Word—as the angel with the censer, that is, with the prayers, demonstrates. These good angels are the holy fathers, such as Spiridion,[64] Athanasius,[65] Hilary,[66] the Council of Nicaea,[67] etc.

The first evil angel is Tatian, with his Encratites,[68] who forbade marriage and wanted to become righteous by their works, like the Jews. For the doctrine of works-righteousness had to be the first doctrine in opposition to the gospel; and it also remains the last, except that it is always getting new teachers and new names, such as the Pelagians,[69] etc.

The second [evil angel] is Marcion,[70] with his Cataphrygians,[71] Manichaeans,[72] Montanists,[73] etc., who extol their own spirituality

---

[64] Spiridion of Cyprus according to tradition was one of the more prominent members of the Council of Nicaea. He was martyred under Diocletian, *ca.* 348.

[65] Athanasius (*ca.* 296-373), bishop of Alexandria after 328, was the most noteworthy defender of the Nicene Christology against the Arian heresy.

[66] Hilary (*ca.* 315-367), bishop of Poitiers after 353, was the most respected Latin theologian of his time, remembered as the "Athanasius of the West" because of his defense of orthodoxy against the Arians.

[67] The first ecumenical council of the church convened at Nicaea in 325 at the call of the emperor and Christian convert, Constantine; it established orthodox doctrine over against the Arian heresy.

[68] See p. 138, n. 14.

[69] The disciples of Pelagius and Coelestius taught a doctrine of salvation by works. Their teaching was vigorously opposed by Augustine and was condemned by the Council of Ephesus in 431.

[70] Marcion (d. *ca.* 160), a teacher of heresy at Rome, held that the Christian gospel is wholly a gospel of love to the absolute exclusion of law, that Paul alone had fully understood this contrast between law and spirit, and that Paul's ten epistles, plus an edited recension of Luke, were the only canonical Scriptures. Cf. *Eusebius, History*, IV, xi, 8-9. Lake, *op. cit.*, I, 331.

[71] Cataphrygians was the name given by a few early Christian writers to the Montanists; it emphasized their Phrygian origin. Cf. *Eusebius, History*, V, xvi, 1. Lake, *op. cit.*, I, 471.

[72] Manichaeans were not members of a Christian sect but followers of the Persian Manes (*ca.* 215-275) whose dualistic religion (conflict of light vs. darkness) involved a variety of heresies along with teachings of Buddha and Jesus, plus a severe asceticism. For nine years prior to his conversion Augustine had been a devotee of this movement.

[73] The Montanists were disciples of Montanus, a Phrygian "prophet" who began

above all the Scriptures, and who move—like this burning mountain [8:8]—between heaven and earth, as, for example, Münzer[74] and the fanatics in our day.

The third is Origen,[75] who embittered and corrupted the Scriptures with philosophy and reason, as the universities have hitherto done among us.

The fourth is Novatus,[76] with his Cathari,[77] who denied penance and claimed to be purer than others. Of this same sort were, later, the Donatists.[78] Our clergy, however, are all four [of these evil

---

to prophesy in Asia Minor about the year 172, according to Eusebius. Montanus proclaimed that the heavenly Jerusalem would soon descend near Pepuza in Phrygia. He claimed the immediate inspiration of the Holy Spirit for the prophets and prophetesses of his apocalyptic movement. Its rigorous asceticism won into membership *ca.* 206 the famous Tertullian, who characterized these sectarians as "Spirit-filled" (*pneumatici*) compared to the "animal men" (*psychici*) at lenient Rome.

[74] Thomas Münzer (*ca.* 1490-1525) believed that the church could be reformed only by the abolition of existing ecclesiastical institutions and the creation of new and pure ones. His ideal of society, shared by other Anabaptists, was a theocracy, a kingdom of God on earth, that would be ruled by God's Word, written in Scripture or revealed by his Spirit to chosen prophets. It was such notions that animated in large part the peasant rebellions, especially of 1524-1525, and against which Luther was forced eventually to take a strong stand in his *Letter to the Princes of Saxony Concerning the Rebellious Spirit*, 1524. LW 40, 47-59; and in *An Admonition to Peace, Against the Robbing and Murdering Hordes of Peasants,* and *An Open Letter Concerning the Hard Book against the Peasants,* all three written in 1525. PE 4, 205-281. See pp. 157-159.

[75] Origen, great Christian scholar of the third century, engaged in philosophical speculations which often issued in audacious theories: that creation is eternal, God finite, death indeterminate for the fate of the soul, and that all creatures—even the devil—will finally be saved. See p. 174, n. 17.

[76] Novatus was the name used by Eusebius and the Greeks generally for the Roman presbyter Novatian; it was perhaps coined by his enemy, Cyprian, to disparage the Roman as a follower of his own rebellious priest, Novatus at Carthage. Originally siding with Cyprian in relaxing the lifelong excommunication imposed on Christians who defected under the Decian persecution of 249-250, Novatian later joined and headed the rigorist party who deprecated such concessions.

[77] From a Greek term meaning "pure," Cathari was the name applied by Epiphanius and other Greek fathers to the Novatianists, who probably had no relation to the medieval European sect of the same name.

[78] The Donatists were a schismatic body in North Africa. It arose when the Numidian bishops refused to accept the consecration of Caecilian as bishop of Carthage in 311, on the ground that his consecrator had been a *traditor* during the Diocletian persecution, i.e., one who surrendered the Scriptures when their possession was forbidden. They consecrated as a rival Majorinus, who was soon succeeded by Donatus, from whom the schism is named. Augustine and other critics of these rigorists maintained that the unworthiness of the minister did not affect the validity of the sacraments.

angels] at once. The scholars who know history will be able to figure this out, for it would take too long to relate and prove everything [here].

In chapters 9 and 10 the real misery begins. For these earlier bodily and spiritual tribulations are almost a jest when compared with the plagues that are to come, as the angel himself also announces at the end of chapter 8[:13]. Three woes are to come, and these woes are to be inflicted by the other three [evil] angels—the fifth, sixth, and seventh. And with that the world is to end. Here both kinds of persecution, the bodily and the spiritual, converge. And there are to be three such persecutions: the first is to be great, the second greater, and the third is to be the greatest of all.

Now the first woe, the fifth [evil] angel, is the great heretic Arius[79] and his companions, who have plagued Christendom so terribly everywhere that the text here [9:6] says well: the righteous people would rather have died than to see such things; but they had to see them, and not die. Indeed, it says that the angel from hell, called the Destroyer,[80] is their king, as if to say that the devil himself rides them. For they persecuted the true Christians not only spiritually but also physically, with the sword. Read the history of the Arians, and then you will understand this figure and these words.

The second woe is the sixth [evil] angel, the shameful Mohammed[81] with his companions, the Saracens,[82] who inflicted great plagues on Christendom, with his doctrines and with the sword.

---

[79] Arius of Alexandria (ca. 250-336) was champion of a subordinationist teaching about the Person of Christ which was condemned at the Council of Nicaea. Cf. p. 402, nn. 65, 66, 67. Following Nicaea, however, the equivocal Emperor Constantine authorized the reinstatement of Arius and the exile of Athanasius. His successor in the East (337), Constantius, embraced Arianism, and after the death of the orthodox Constans in the West (350) actively persecuted the opponents of Arianism until his death in 361.

[80] In Rev. 9:11 the Hebrew *Abaddon* and its Greek equivalent *Apollyon* both mean "destruction."

[81] Mohammed (ca. 570-629) was founder of the syncretistic religion bearing his name, according to which Jesus was one of God's several prophets, not God's Son, and the crucifixion was only apparent, not real.

[82] Medieval writers applied the name Saracens to the Arabs generally, and later to the Mohammedan nations against whom the Crusaders fought. As early as 1518 Luther had used the *Fortalicium Fidei* of Alphonsus a Spina. Its fourth book was entitled: *de bello saracenorum*. WA 40[III], 670, n. 3.

Along with this angel, in order that this woe may be all the greater, comes the mighty angel with the rainbow [10:1] and the bitter scroll [10:9-10], that is the holy papacy, with its appearance of great spirituality. They measure and enclose the temple[83] with their laws, leave out the inner sanctuary,[84] and start a counterfeit church of external holiness.

In chapters 11 and 12, two comforting images are interspersed between these evil woes and plagues. One is that of the two preachers, the other that of the pregnant woman who bears a male child despite the dragon. They indicate that some pious teachers and Christians are nevertheless to remain, both under the first two woes, and under the third which is yet to come. And now these two last woes combine and make a final concerted attack upon Christendom. Thus, at last, all hell is loose.[85]

Then comes in chapter 13 (following the trumpets of the last of the seven angels, who blows at the beginning of chapter 12[86]) this seventh [evil] angel's work, the third woe, namely the papal empire and the imperial papacy. Here the papacy gets the temporal sword also into its power. It rules not only with the scroll of the second woe [10:8-10], but also with the sword of the third woe, for they boast that the pope has both the spiritual and the temporal sword in his power.[87]

---

[83] Rev. 11:1-2 were considered part of chapter 10 in editions of Luther's German Bible subsequent to 1530. *WA, DB* 7, 446, n. 11.

[84] *Chor*, literally "choir," is that part of the church immediately around the altar and separate from the nave. Luther used the same word when speaking of "the most holy place" in Solomon's temple (I Kings 6:5, 16). Luther's departure from the Vulgate, whereby in his 1529 rendition of Rev. 11:2 he changed *foris templum* (cf. the RSV, "outside the temple") to *intra templum* (*WA, DB* 5, 793)—German, *den innern chor des tempels* (*WA, DB* 7, 447)—is supported by Codex Sinaiticus among other Greek manuscripts of the New Testament.

[85] *Der Teufel . . . dem fass den boden ausstösset*, literally, "the devil knocks the bottom out of the barrel." The expression could mean "brings matters to a head" or "destroys utterly what he can no longer control." Cf. p. 195, n. 62.

[86] In Luther's Bible, and in his 1529 revision of the Vulgate, he made chapter 12 to begin with what was and is normally considered to be Rev. 11:15-19. *WA, DB* 7, 448; 5, 794.

[87] Pope Boniface VIII, in the bull *Unam Sanctam* of November 18, 1302, declared, "We are taught by evangelical words that in this power of his [Peter and his successors] are two swords, namely spiritual and temporal. . . . Therefore each is in the power of the church. . . . The former [must be exercised] (by the hand) of the priest, the latter by the hand of kings and soldiers, but at the will and sufferance of the priest. For it is necessary that . . . temporal authority be subject to spiritual power." Denzinger, *The Sources of Catholic Dogma*, No. 469.

Here, then, are the two beasts. The one is the empire. The other, with the two horns [13:11], is the papacy; it has now become also a temporal kingdom, yet with the appearance of [having] the name of Christ. For the pope has restored the fallen Roman Empire and conveyed it from the Greeks to the Germans,[88] though it is an image of the Roman Empire rather than the body of the empire itself as it once was. Nevertheless, he puts breath and life into this image [13:15], so that it has its estates, laws, members, and offices, and actually operates to some extent. This is the image that was wounded and healed again [13:3, 12].

The abominations, woes, and injuries which this imperial papacy has wrought cannot now be recounted. For, in the first place, by means of his scroll [10:8-10] the world has been filled with all kinds of idolatry—with monasteries, foundations, saints, pilgrimages, purgatory, indulgences, celibacy, and innumerable other articles of human doctrine and works, etc. In the second place who can recount how much bloodshed, slaughter, war, and misery the popes have wrought, both by themselves fighting and by stirring up the emperors, kings, and princes against one another?

Here, now, the devil's final wrath gets to work: there in the East is the second woe, Mohammed and the Saracens; here in the West are papacy and empire, with the third woe. To these is added for

---

[88] Charlemagne, king of the Franks and ruler of the vastest domain since the fall of the Roman Empire in the West to the invading barbarians in the fifth century, was also military protector of the papacy against its temporal enemies in Italy. In the year 800 he was crowned Roman emperor by Pope Leo III. Although a German, Charles henceforth regarded himself as successor to the line of emperors who had ruled at Rome. This fiction was fostered by the popes; and the German kings, after receiving the papal coronation, were called Roman emperors. From this came the name of the German empire during the Middle Ages, "The Holy Roman Empire of the German Nation." The popes of the later Middle Ages claimed that bestowal of the imperial dignity lay in the power of the pope; Pope Clement V (1313, at Avignon) even claimed that in the event of a vacancy, the pope was the possessor of the imperial power. Such a claim was supported by an eighth century document known as the "Donation of Constantine," whereby the first Christian emperor (306-337), from his new capital at Constantinople, was purported to have conveyed to the pope the title to the city of Rome, plus certain other lands in Italy and "the islands of the sea." In 1440 Lorenzo Valla, the Italian humanist and Renaissance scholar, proved the document a forgery. Ulrich von Hutten republished Valla's work in Germany in 1517 and thus it came to Luther's attention by about 1520. In 1537 Luther himself published an annotated translation of the text of the forged document. Cf. PE 2, 153 and 109.

good measure the Turk, Gog and Magog,[89] as will follow in chapter 20[:8]. Thus Christendom is plagued most terribly and miserably, everywhere and on all sides, with false doctrines and with wars, with scroll and with sword. That is the dregs, the final plague. After that come almost exclusively images of comfort, telling of the end of all these woes and abominations.

In chapter 14 Christ first begins to slay his Antichrist with "the breath of his mouth," as St. Paul says [II Thess. 2:8]. The angel with the gospel encounters the bitter scroll of the mighty angel [10:1, 8-10]. The saints and virgins[90] stand again about the Lamb and preach the truth. Upon the gospel follows the second angel's voice, saying that the city of Babylon shall fall [14:8], the spiritual papacy be destroyed.

Then follows further that the harvest shall come, and those who cling to the papacy against the gospel shall be cast outside the city of Christ, into the wine press of God's wrath. That is, by the gospel they are separated from Christendom and condemned to the wrath of God. There are many, and the wine press yields much blood. Or there may perhaps be some other punishment and judgment appropriate to our sins, which are beyond all measure and are over-ripe.

After this, in chapters 15 and 16, come the seven angels with the seven bowls. The gospel thereupon increases and attacks the papacy on all sides by means of many learned and devout preachers; and the throne of the beast—the pope's power—becomes dark and wretched and despised. But they grow angry and confidently defend themselves. For three frogs, three foul spirits, issue from the mouth of the beast and stir up kings and princes against the gospel. But this does not help; their battle takes place nonetheless at Armaged-

---

[89] Luther regards Gog as identical with Magog, the shorter undignified form being devised by the Holy Spirit in order to display his anger at this particular enemy. Derived from Ezekiel 38–39, the term is taken to refer to the Moslem Turks then threatening western Europe, indeed to all their Tartar forebears as far back as Genghis Khan, to whom the original name from Gen. 10:2 was applied. See Luther's own brief translation and preface from 1530, *Ezekiel 38 and 39: concerning Gog.* WA 30[II], (220) 223-236. Cf. Luther's view of the Turkish menace as a punishment of God in his *Defense and Explanation* (1520) of the thirty-fourth article condemned by the papal bull *Exsurge Domine. LW* 32, 89-90. See also p. 300, n. 152.

[90] Rev. 14:4 (KJV).

don. The frogs are the sophists, such as Faber,[91] Eck,[92] Emser,[93] etc. They croak much against the gospel, but accomplish nothing and remain frogs.

In chapter 17 the imperial papacy and papal empire is comprehended from beginning to end in a single image. As in a résumé, it is shown to be nothing (for the ancient Roman Empire is long since gone), and yet to be (for some of its lands indeed still exist, and the city of Rome besides). This image is presented here as one presents a malefactor publicly before a court—so that he may be condemned—that men may know that this beast too is shortly to be condemned and, as St. Paul says, "destroyed by the appearance and coming of our Lord" [II Thess. 2:8]. As he says in the text, the very patrons of the papacy begin this, those who are now its protectors, so that the clergy will sit utterly naked.

In chapter 18 this destruction begins. The glorious and great splendor falls to the ground, and the courtiers[94]—who rob endowments and steal livings—cease to be. For even Rome had to be plundered and stormed by its own protector[95] at the outset of the

---

[91] Johann Faber (1478-1541) as a lifelong friend of Erasmus had once been sympathetic toward efforts at reforming the church. When the underlying doctrinal cleavages became manifest he withdrew his support and became a zealous defender of Catholic orthodoxy, publishing his first attack against Luther in Rome, 1522. In 1530 he assisted in drafting the *Confutatio Pontifica* as the papal rebuttal to the Augsburg Confession.

[92] Johann Eck (Johann Maier aus Egg, 1486-1543), learned theologian and professor of theology in the university at Ingolstadt, Luther's opponent at the Leipzig Debate in 1519, was largely responsible for securing Luther's excommunication by Rome in 1520 and for drafting the *Confutatio Pontifica* at Augsburg in 1530.

[93] Jerome Emser (1478-1527), a former friend of Luther, had turned enemy after the Leipzig Debate in 1519. Cf. pp. 179-180.

[94] Cf. Luther's scorching attack on the Roman curia with its avarice and robbery in his list of matters to be discussed in councils, in *An Open Letter to the Christian Nobility* (1520). There Luther called these courtiers *des Papstes und der Cardinäle Gesinde*, i.e., members of the "family" or "household" —called *Dienstverwandte* in the Gravamina ("Grievances") of the German Diet at Worms in 1521—of the pope or of any of the cardinals. The term was broad; besides those actually residing in Rome it included all those to whom, by virtue of any special connection with the curia, the name "papal servant" could be made to apply. *PE* 2, 83-99, especially p. 88, n. 3.

[95] Luther's reference is to the sack of Rome by the armies of Emperor Charles V, in 1527. In this ironic situation the action of Charles revealed something of his inmost concern: he desired to be a defender of the papacy, yet papacy and empire were inextricably involved in the international tests of power that included the Turks in the East, and Francis I and the French in the West.

final destruction. Still they do not give up. They keep trying; they encourage, arm, and defend themselves. As he says here in chapter 19, when they can do nothing more with the Scriptures and scrolls, and when the frogs have croaked themselves out, then they take hold in earnest, try to win by the use of force, gathering kings and princes for the battle. But they stumble, for the one on the white horse, the one called the Word of God [19:13], wins; both beast and [false] prophet are captured and thrown into hell.

While all this is happening, there comes in chapter 20 the stirrup cup:[96] Satan, having been captured a thousand years before, is on the loose again after a thousand years and brings up Gog and Magog, the Turk, the red Jews.[97] But they shall soon go with him into the lake of fire. For it is our opinion that this image, which is separate from those which preceded, has been put in because of the Turks, and that the thousand years are to begin about the time this book was written, and that at that same time the devil was bound— although the reckoning need not be exactly to the minute. After the Turks, the Last Judgment follows quickly, at the end of this chapter, as Daniel 7[98] also shows.

At last, in chapter 21, the final comfort is depicted. The holy city, fully prepared, shall be led as a bride to the eternal marriage feast. Christ alone is Lord, and all the godless are condemned and go with the devil into hell.

With this kind of an interpretation we can profit by this book and make good use of it. First, for our comfort! We can rest assured that neither force nor lies, neither wisdom nor holiness, neither tribulation nor suffering shall suppress Christendom, but it will gain the victory and conquer at last.

Second, for our warning! [We can be on guard] against the great, perilous, and manifold offense that inflicts itself upon Christendom. Because these mighty and imposing powers are to fight against Christendom, and it is to be deprived of outward shape and con-

---

[96] *Letzetranck* is the final or parting draught of wine, this time in the cup of God's wrath.

[97] *Die roten Jüden* was Luther's name for the Tartars, forebears of the Turk. Cf. p. 407, n. 89 and WA 30^{II}, 224, l. 10.

[98] Cf. Luther's Preface to Daniel, in this volume, pp. 294-316.

cealed under so many tribulations and heresies and other faults, it is impossible for the natural reason to recognize Christendom. On the contrary, natural reason falls away and takes offense. It calls that "the Christian Church" which is really the worst enemy of the Christian Church. Similarly, it calls those persons damned heretics who are really the true Christian Church. This has happened before, under the papacy, under Mohammed, indeed with all the heretics. Thus they lose this article [of the Creed], "I believe in the holy Christian Church."

Some of the know-it-alls are even now doing that very thing. They see heresy and dissension and shortcomings of many kinds; they see that there are many false, many loose-living Christians. And so they decide offhand that there are no Christians anywhere. For they have heard that Christians are supposed to be a holy, peaceful, united, kindly, virtuous folk. Accordingly they think that there should be among them no offenses, no heresy, no shortcomings, but only peace and virtue.

They ought to read this book and learn to look upon Christendom with other eyes than those of reason. For this book, I think, shows plenty of gruesome and monstrous beasts, horrible and vindictive angels, wild and terrible plagues (not to speak of the other great faults and shortcomings that have always been in Christendom and among Christians) so that in the midst of such business natural reason necessarily had to lose [sight of] Christendom. Here we see clearly what ghastly offenses and shortcomings there have been prior to our times, when Christendom is thought to have been at its best. By comparison, ours is really a golden age. Do not think that the heathen did not also take offense at this and regard the Christians as self-willed, loose, contentious people.

This article, "I believe in the holy Christian Church," is as much an article of faith as the rest. This is why natural reason cannot recognize it, even if it puts on all its glasses. The devil can cover it over with offenses and divisions, so that you have to take offense at it. God too can conceal it behind faults and shortcomings of all kinds, so that you necessarily become a fool and pass false judgment on it. Christendom will not be known by sight, but by faith. And faith has to do with things not seen, Hebrews 11[:1]. Christendom joins with her Lord in the song, "Blessed is he who takes no offense at me"

[Matt. 11:6]. A Christian is even hidden from himself; he does not see his holiness and virtue, but sees in himself nothing but unholiness and vice. And you, stupid know-it-all, would behold Christendom with your blind reason and unclean eyes!

In a word, our holiness is in heaven, where Christ is;[99] and not in the world, before men's eyes, like goods in the market place. Therefore let there be offenses, divisions, heresies, and faults; let them do what they can! If only the word of the gospel remains pure among us, and we love and cherish it, we shall not doubt that Christ is with us, even when things are at their worst. As we see here in this book, that through and beyond all plagues, beasts, and evil angels Christ is nonetheless with his saints, and wins the final victory.

---

[99] Cf. Phil. 3:20; Col. 3:1.

INDEXES

INDEX OF NAMES AND SUBJECTS

414

Tabernacles, Feast of, 219 f.
Tabor, Mount, 162, 245
Talmud, Babylonian, 284 n. 112
Tartars, 271, 409 n. 97
Tatianists, 138 n. 14, 402 n. 68
Teachers, 148, 401
  false, 145, 201, 331, 385, 389, 391
Temple, 302, 305, 313 ff., 329 ff., 405
  n. 83
  depicts church, 293
  spiritual, 331
Temptation, 89, 200, 260
Ten Commandments, 159, 165, 173,
  243 f.
Tertullian, 280
Testament, 85, 90 f., 106, 246, 358
  beginning of new, 84, 280
  in Sacrament of the Altar, 85
  words of Christ, 86 ff., 246
Tetragrammaton, 248 n. 27
Thanksgiving, 95 n. 23, 98, 104, 136, 255
Thomas, St., Aquinas, 368 n. 18
Transfiguration, 162
Translating the Scriptures, xvii, 177-
  223, 249 (see also Bible, Luther)
Transubstantiation, 47, 59 n. 27, 77
Treasury, common, 69
Trent, Council of, 37 n. 10
Tribulations, 54, 402, 410
Trust, 65, 199, 339
  in God, 199, 345 (see also Faith)
Turks, 177, 266 f., 271, 296, 300 n. 152,
  409
Two kingdoms, 164 (see also King-
  dom)
Tyranny, 202, 287, 352
Tyrants, 151, 297, 303, 343

Unbelief, 243, 322, 371, 384 (see also
  Sin, against Holy Spirit)
  sin of, 14, 369
Unbeliever, 13, 370
Unchastity, 53, 372, 382 (see also Flesh)
Union with Christ, in sacrament, 50
Unity, in church, 67, 80, 201, 383

Vestments, 82
Virginity, 382
Vision(s), 285, 330, 398
Vow, 84, 138, 142
Vulgate, 32 n. 6, 231, 240, 340 n. 13 (see
  also Jerome)

Wartburg, 115 ff., 127, 206, 228
Widows, 388
Wilderness, The, 177, 202 n. 73
Wine, 86, 100, 106, 378
Wisdom, 215, 344, 380 ff.
  of God, 261, 344

meaning of, 261
  of Moses, 247
  spirit of, 344
Wise man, 259 ff.
Wiseacres, 277
Wittenberg Concord, xii
Wives, 388, 391
Woes, 404 ff.
Woman (women), 381, 388, 405
Word, xi, 217
  of Christ, 13, 82, 88 ff., 132, 134, 146
  of God, ix ff., 7, 12, 19, 52, 64, 82, 92,
    105, 107, 131 ff., 151 f., 158, 170 f.,
    200, 218, 262, 267, 333, 343 ff., 382,
    390, 399, 402, 409
Words of Institution, xiii, xiv, 55, 82 n.
  5, 88, 90, 92
Work, 63
  of law, 182
  of sacrament, 72
Work-righteousness, 375
Works, 6, 12, 57, 92, 111, 143, 149, 197
  f., 363, 368, 383
  of Christ, 360, 362
  external, 197, 270, 372
  of faith, 361, 371, 393
  of flesh, 196, 372
  of law, 195 f., 375, 384, 393
  of love, 368, 379, 384
  of true brotherhood, 69 (see also
    Good works)
World, 55, 151, 380, 389
  of Christians, 52
  end of, 281, 299
  open to gospel, 331
  spread of Christendom in, 285 ff.
Worms, Diet of, 227 f.
Worship, 132, 145, 239, 329, 351, 401
  external order of, 81
  false, 199, 269 ff.
  of saints, 199
  true, 272 f., 378
Worshipers, blindness of, 62
Worthiness, 12, 89 ff.
  of disciples, 55 ff.
  scholastics on, 368 n. 18
Wrath, 200, 210, 374
  of God, 106, 109, 252, 256, 281, 366,
    372 f., 407

Xerxes, 299, 306 n. 177

Yahweh, 248 n. 27
Youth, 258 f., 262, 339, 345

Zerubbabel, 303
Ziegler, Bernard, 206
Zion, 291, 321
Zurich, 227
Zwingli, Huldreich, x, xii

421

INDEX TO SCRIPTURE PASSAGES

422

Type used in this book
Body, 10 on 13 Caledonia
Display, Bulmer and Caledonia
Paper: Standard White Antique